'A wide-ranging and constantly engaging book, written under the pressure of real intellectual enthusiasm . . . Readers will learn a huge amount – both about why Lepanto changed so little, and about why it seemed to matter so much'
Noel Malcolm, *Sunday Telegraph*

'As a narrative of the battle, *Crescent and Cross* is unlikely to be surpassed. Hugh Bicheno brings to his subject not only deep knowledge, but also an enviable ability to convey both the glamour and the horror of sixteenth-century warfare'
John Adamson, *Literary Review*

'Bicheno's account of the battle, his detailed analysis of battle formations, vessels deployed, weapons used and the practical problems of operating on these vessels, is fascinating' Justin Cartwright, *Independent on Sunday*

'A multidisciplinary analysis that explores ship design, religious iconography and Ottoman political systems with equal historical passion. It's a book that will tread on the toes of specialists but should fascinate everyone else'
David Sutton, *Fortean Times*

'In *Crescent and Cross*, Bicheno roves enthusiastically on a wide-ranging tour across the 16th-century Mediterranean . . . The tone is cheerfully ideological, highly readable . . . In an age when the Muslim and Christian worlds continue to nurse misconceptions about each other, this is a timely book'
Justin Marozzi, *Financial Times*

Hugh Bicheno was born in Cuba of British parents, won a scholarship and took a First at Cambridge and has pursued careers as an academic, intelligence officer and freelance anti-terrorist consultant, mainly in South America but also in Italy. After many years abroad he now lives in Cambridge and devotes himself to writing about what happens when men confront each other in battle, and the culturally driven myths that commonly cloak the brutal realities. His previous books include *Gettysburg* and *Midway* in Cassell's 'Fields of Battle' series, and the recent *Rebels and Redcoats*, written in parallel to the BBC series on the American War of Independence presented by Richard Holmes.

CRESCENT AND CROSS

THE BATTLE OF LEPANTO 1571

HUGH BICHENO

PHOENIX

To *Erithacus rubecula*, with love

A PHOENIX PAPERBACK

First published in Great Britain in 2003
by Cassell
This paperback edition published in 2004
by Phoenix,
an imprint of Orion Books Ltd,
Orion House, 5 Upper St Martin's Lane,
London WC2H 9EA

A CIP catalogue record for this book
is available from the British Library.

ISBN 1 84212 753 5

Printed and bound in Great Britain by
Clays Ltd, St Ives plc

www.orionbooks.co.uk

CONTENTS

Maps and diagrams

ACKNOWLEDGEMENTS

The theme of this book was born of a conversation with Dr Peter Bayley, Drapers' Professor of French at Cambridge, to whom I owe many other insights into the mind of a period he knows so well, in which he alerted me to the striking paradox that the anniversary of the battle was the feast day of Our Lady of the Rosary.

Dr Jonathan Riley-Smith, Dixie Professor of Ecclesiastical History at Cambridge, kindly identified for me the themes about the theory and practice of crusading that I might most profitably pursue to illuminate the deep background.

I owe a great debt to Paul Rawlins, good friend and patient sounding board through this and earlier works, to Robin Jo Mina for her illuminating comments on Marianism and for tidying up my punctuation and syntax, and to my sons Scott Diego for identifying places where my argument cornered too hard, and Shaun Alaric for teaching me the basics of Adobe Illustrator.

Lastly, my thanks to my editor Keith Lowe for his support and guidance, and to Elaine Willis for coping stoically with my clamour for working copies of the illustrations in glorious technicolour, well in advance of schedule.

Even if written by someone more tactful, a multidisciplinary approach such as I have employed could not fail to attract potentially hostile scrutiny by a wide range of connoisseurs, specialists and cognoscenti – eclectic language ours, is it not? Having received expert advice on the location and density of the academic and cultural minefields through which I have chosen to tap-dance, if I am blown up the responsibility can only be mine.

CHRONOLOGY

Rulers 1500–1550

	1500	1505	1510	1515	1520	1525	1530	1535	1540	1545
Popes[1]	Julius II 1503–13			Leo X 1513–21		Clement VII 1523–34			Paul III 1534–49	
Austria	Maximilian I 1439–1519				Ferdinand I 1521–64					
Empire	Holy Roman Emperor 1508–19				Emperor Charles V (1519–58) divided Hapsburg inheritance with brother Ferdinand. Abdicated the Empire to him in 1558, and Italy, the Netherlands, Spain and Burgundy to his son Philip in 1555–56					
Castille Aragon	Isabella 1474–1504 / Ferdinand 1479–1516									
Portugal	Manoel I 1495–1521					John III 1521–57				
Florence	Republic 1494–1512			Medici 1512–27		Republic 1527–30	Alessandro 1530–37		Cosimo 1537–69	
France	Louis XII 1498–1515				François I 1515–47					
Ottoman	Bayezid II 1481–1512			Selim I 1512–20	Suleiman II 1520–66					
Persia	Ismail I 1501–24					Tahmasp I 1526–76				
Muscovy Russia	Ivan III 1462–1505	Vasily III 1505–33					Ivan IV 1533–84			
Hungary	Ladislas VI 1490–1516			Louis II 1516–26		John Zapolya 1526–40			[2]	
England	Henry VIII 1491–1547									[3]
Scotland	James IV 1488–1513		James V 1513–44						[4]	

[1] Alexander VI (1492–1503); Pius III (1503); Adrian VI (1522–23) – last non-Italian Pope for 450 years.

[2] Annexed by the Ottoman Empire in 1541, with Austria retaining a northern strip.

[3] Edward VI (1547–53).

[4] Regency for the child Mary Queen of Scots began in 1544.

Rulers 1550–1600

	1550	1555	1560	1565	1570	1575	1580	1585	1590	1595
Popes[1]	Julius III	Paul IV	Pius IV 1559–65	Pius V 1566–72		Gregory XIII 1572–85		Sixtus V	Clement VIII	
Austria	Ferdinand I 1521–64		Emperor from 1558		Maximilian II 1564–76			Rudolf II 1576–1612		
Empire Spain	Charles V					Philip II 1556–98				
Portugal[2]	John III 1521–57			Sebastian I 1557–78			To Spain from 1580			
Florence/ Tuscany	Cosimo made Grand Duke of Tuscany in 1569, died 1574					Francesco 1574–87			Ferdinand 1587–1609	
France[3]	Henri II 1547–59		Charles IX 1560–74			Henri III 1574–89			Henri IV 1594–1610	
Ottoman Sultans	Suleiman II 1520–66			Selim II 1566–74		Murad III 1574–95				
Persia[4]	Tahmasp 1526–76					Mahomad Mirza 1578–87			Abbas I 1587–1629	
Russia	Ivan IV 1533–84							Fedor I 1584–98		
England	Mary I 1553–58			Elizabeth I 1558–1603						
Scotland	Mary (deposed 1567, executed 1587)			James VI (I of England from 1603) 1567–1625						

[1] Julius III (1550–55); Marcellus II (1555); Paul IV (1555–59); Sixtus V (1585–90); Urban VII (1590); Gregory XIV (1590–91); Innocent IX (1591); Clement VIII (1592–1605).

[2] Interregnum 1578–80 ended by Spanish invasion.

[3] François II (1559–60); war of succession 1589–94.

[4] Civil war 1576–78.

Principal events of a long century

1492   Capitulation of Granada, last Islamic kingdom in Iberia
        Columbus, a Genoese employed by Castile, arrives in the New
        World.

1494   Charles VIII of France invades Italy, conquers Naples. Medici
        expelled from Florence.

1495–98 War of Holy League (Papacy, Empire, Spain, Venice and Milan)
        against France. French retreat from northern Italy punctuated by
        battle of Fornovo (1495). French in Naples ground down by
        Fernández de Córdoba (the 'Great Captain').

1496   Savonarola's 'burning of the vanities' in Florence.

1498   Burning of Savonarola in Florence. Vasco da Gama arrives in
        Calicut, India.

1499–1503 Venetian–Ottoman war. Venetian fleet defeated twice at Zonchio
        (Navarino), Patras and Lepanto lost. Spanish–Venetian force
        under Córdoba captures Cephalonia, war ends with surrender of
        most Venetian ports in Greece.

1500   Birth of future Emperor Charles V and Benvenuto Cellini.

1500–1505 Louis XII of France invades Italy, seizes Milan and Naples.
        Córdoba defeats French at Cerignola and Garigliano (both 1503),
        secures Naples for Spain. Pope Alexander VI confers title 'Their
        Catholic Majesties' on Spanish monarchs.

1503   Giuliano della Rovere elected Pope Julius II. Leonardo da Vinci's
        Mona Lisa.

1504   Michelangelo's *David* celebrates Florentine freedom from the
        Medici.

1504–16 Isabella of Castile dies, succeeded by her mad daughter Juana.
        Co-rule by Juana's father Ferdinand of Aragon with her
        husband Philip of Burgundy, and on his death with a Council of
        Regency until son Charles comes of age.

1506   Death of Columbus. Bramante begins rebuilding the basilica of
        Saint Peter.

1508–10 War of League of Cambrai (Papacy, Empire, France and Spain)
        against Venice.

1508–12 Michelangelo's Sistine ceiling, Raphael's *Stanze della Segnatura*
        frescoes.

1509	French destroy Venetian army at Agnadello. Spanish seize Venetian ports of Brindisi, Otranto and Taranto. Birth of Calvin. Erasmus's *In Praise of Folly*.
1509–10	Castilians take Oran, Mostaganem, Bougie, Tripoli and Algiers fort, fail at Djerba.
1510	Portuguese take Goa, held until 1965. Death of Botticelli and Giorgione.
1511	Djerba-based Uruj and Khair ed-Din 'Barbarosssa' attack Bougie and Tunis. Birth of Vasari. Copernicus establishes that planets circle the sun.
1511–16	War of Holy League (Papacy, Venice, Spain and England) against France.
1512	French defeat Holy League at Ravenna, Venice changes sides, Swiss and the Empire join the League, Sforzas restored in Milan, Medici in Florence. Selim 'the Grim' seizes power from his father Bayezid II.
1513	Swiss defeat French at Novara, Spanish defeat Venetians at La Motta. Giovanni dei Medici elected Pope Leo X. Machiavelli's *The Prince*.
1514	Fugger family (Augsburg financiers) authorized to sell indulgences. Selim suppresses Shi'ite rebellion in eastern Anatolia. Death of Bramante.
1515	Franco–Venetian army defeats Swiss at Marignano, drives them out of Italy. First Ottoman invasion of Persia. Barbarossa brothers seize Algiers.
1516	Death of Ferdinand. Charles becomes monarch of Castile, Aragon, Sicily, Naples, Burgundy and the Netherlands. Death of Bosch. Erasmus's Greek and Latin New Testaments. Sir Thomas More's *Utopia*.
1516–17	Ottoman conquest of the Mamluk Empire. Barbarossa brothers seize Bône and Constantine.
1517	Luther nails *Ninety-Five Theses* to door of Wittenberg cathedral.
1518	Uruj killed, Khair ed-Din becomes ruler of Algiers. Charles grants first licence for African slave trade. Birth of Tintoretto.
1519	Death of Maximilian. Charles inherits Austria, elected Emperor Charles V. Algiers admitted to the Ottoman Empire. Death of Leonardo da Vinci.
1519–22	Magellan circumnavigates the world. Cortés conquers Mexico.

1520	Death of Selim, succession of Suleiman II 'the Magnificent'. Death of Raphael, birth of Bruegel.
1521	Ottoman offensive in the Balkans, capture of Belgrade. Charles cedes Austria to brother Ferdinand. Pope confers title 'Defender of the Faith' on English monarchs after Henry VIII publishes an attack on Luther.
1521–23	Bourgeois (*Comuneros*) revolt in Castile.
1521–25	War of France and Venice against Hapsburgs.
1522	Suleiman expels Knights of Saint John from Rhodes. Knights' War against church principalities in Germany, suppressed by Charles V. Swiss hired by France shattered at Bicocca. Venice makes separate peace.
1523	Giulio dei Medici elected Pope Clement VII.
1524–25	Peasant revolts in Germany – condemned by Luther.
1525	François I defeated, captured at Pavia. Forced to sign humiliating peace treaty, begins secret negotiations with Istanbul for an alliance against the Hapsburgs. Grand Master of the Teutonic Order declares for Lutheranism. Birth of Palestrina. Tyndale's English-language New Testament.
1526	War of League of Cognac (Papacy, France, Venice, Milan and Florence) against Hapsburgs. Suleiman invades Hungary, King Louis and Hungarian nobility killed at Mohacs. Persia-sponsored Shi'ite revolts in Anatolia.
1527	Sack of Rome by Empire forces, Papacy and Venice make peace. Siege of Naples, Genoese defeat Spanish in naval battle of Capo d'Orso. Florence expels Medici. Birth of future Philip II of Spain.
1528	Andrea Doria revokes French alliance, becomes admiral of Spain.Birth of Luis de Requeséns and Veronese.
1529	Treaty of Cambrai. France makes peace, abandons Milan. Khair ed-Din expels Spanish from fort in Algiers harbour. Ottoman invasion of Austria, unsuccessful siege of Vienna.
1530	Milan makes peace, Florentine Republic crushed at Gavignara, Medici restored. Charles V grants Malta to the Knights, on condition they also hold Tripoli.
1531–33	Pizarro conquers Inca Empire.
1532	Second Ottoman invasion of Austria ends with siege of Güns. Andrea Doria installs Spanish garrisons at Coron and Patras in Morea. Rabelais's *Pantagruel*.
1533–55	Continuous, indecisive Ottoman war with Persia.

1533	1,500th anniversary of the Crucifixion. Khair ed-Din made kapudan, recaptures Coron and Patras. Unconverted Muslims expelled from Spain, ferried to North Africa by Algerines. Geneva independent. Birth of future Elizabeth I of England and Montaigne.
1534	Henry VIII makes final break with Rome. François I begins persecution of Protestants, Calvin flees to Geneva. Khair ed-Din takes Tunis. Alessandro Farnese elected Pope Clement VII. Loyola founds Jesuits.
1534–35	Anabaptist New Jerusalem in Münster exterminated.
1535	Charles V claims Milan following death of the last Sforza. With Doria conquers Tunis, installs a puppet ruler and leaves a Spanish garrison at the port of Goleta. Guicciardini's *Storia d'Italia*. Sir Thomas More executed.
1536	France occupies Savoy. Tyndale burnt at the stake in Flanders.
1536–41	Michelangelo's *Last Judgement*.
1536–38	Franco–Ottoman alliance. Third Valois–Hapsburg war, ends in stalemate. Austrian invasion of Ottoman Hungary shattered. Ottomans seize Morea ports of Nauplia and Monemvasia from Venice, raid Corfu and southern Italy.
1537	War of Holy League (Papacy, Venice, Spain, Empire) against Ottomans. Doria seizes Castelnuovo, installs Spanish garrison. Duke Alessandro dei Medici assassinated, cousin Cosimo crushes rebellion.
1538	Suleiman and Crimean Tatars suppress revolt in Moldavia. Khair ed-Din defeats Spanish–Venetian fleet led by Doria at Preveza.
1538–40	Venice sues for peace, surrenders claims in Morea, pays an indemnity. Castelnuovo garrison, abandoned by Venice, massacred by Ottomans.
1541	Crusade by Charles V and Doria against Algiers shattered by a storm. Ottoman Empire annexes Hungary. Birth of El Greco.
1542–44	Fourth Valois–Hapsburg war. Franco–Ottoman fleet under Khair ed-Din and Enghien winters in Toulon. Sack of Nice.
1544	Valois–Hapsburg peace after battle of Ceresole. War with Ottomans continues.
1545	Birth of Prince Carlos of Spain and Alessandro Farnese, future Duke of Parma.
1545–47	First Council of Trent session. First Index of Forbidden Books.

1546	Death of Khair ed-Din. Mehmet Sokolli appointed kapudan. Five-year Hapsburg–Ottoman truce in the Balkans. Death of Luther.
1547	First Schmalkaldic war, German Protestant nobles crushed by Alba at Mühlberg. Death of Henry VIII. Birth of Cervantes and Don Juan de Austria.
1547–56	War of Henri II of France and Maurice of Saxony against Hapsburgs.
1548	Five-year Ottoman–Hapsburg truce in the Mediterranean. Mary, child queen of Scots, betrothed to future François II and sent to France.
1550	Corsair leader Dragut seizes Mahdia, expelled by Andrea Doria. Vasari's *Lives of the Painters, Sculptors and Architects*.
1551	Second Schmalkaldic war. Ottoman fleet under Kapudan Sinan joins Dragut to recover Mahdia and seize Tripoli, raid Malta and ravage Gozo.
1551–53	Second Council of Trent session.
1551–62	Mehmet Sokolli, now Beylerbey of Rumelia, conquers Transylvania.
1552	Salih Reis appointed Beylerbey of Algiers.
1552–54	French invasion of Lombardy, defeat at Marciano.
1552–57	Ivan the Terrible annexes Kazan and Astrakhan.
1553	Maurice of Saxony killed at Sievershausen. French occupy Genoese Corsica.
1553–54	Accession of Mary I in England, marriage to future Philip II of Spain.
1554	Birth of Walter Raleigh.
1554–55	Salih Reis and Dragut take Bougie and Tlemcen. Piali appointed kapudan.
1555	Peace of Augsburg enshrines *cuius regio eius religio* principle in Germany. Gian'Pietro Carafa elected Pope Paul IV, provokes last Valois–Hapsburg war. French driven from Corsica by Genoa, from Siena by Spain and Florence.
1556	Charles V abdicates Spanish Empire to his son Philip II. Tripoli admitted to Ottoman Empire under Dragut. Salih Reis dies, Janissaries assassinate his appointed successor.

1557	Spanish army under Philip II defeats French at Saint Quentin. Valois and both branches of Hapsburg dynasties default on their debts. Hassan, son of Khair ed-Din, appointed Beylerbey of Algiers, restores order, defeats Moroccan attempt to take Tlemcen, counter-invades.
1558	Hassan defeats Spanish army near Oran. Piali raids Menorca and Naples. French capture Calais, defeated by Anglo–Spanish army at Gravelines. Charles V abdicates as emperor, dies. Maximilian of Austria elected. Accession of Elizabeth I of England.
1559	Treaty of Cateau-Cambrésis ends Valois–Hapsburg dynastic struggle. Gian'Angelo dei Medici elected Pope Pius IV. Calvinist academy in Geneva.
1559–61	Henri II of France killed jousting, son François II dies within the year, Mary returned to Scotland. Catherine dei Medici becomes regent for child Charles IX.
1560	Hapsburg expedition routed at Djerba.
1561–62	Ottoman–corsair fleets raid across the western Mediterranean.
1562–63	Maximilian recognizes Ottoman Transylvania, resumes payment of tribute. First French War of Religion, battle of Dreux. Last session of Council of Trent.
1563–70	War among Denmark, Sweden and Poland. Union of Lithuania and Poland.
1564	Spanish recover Peñón de Vélez, held ever since. Birth of Shakespeare, Marlowe and Galileo. Death of Michelangelo and Calvin.
1564–68	French-supported Sampiero Corso leads Corsican rebellion against Genoa.
1565	Unsuccessful Ottoman siege of Malta. Mehmet Sokolli appointed grand vizier. Philip agrees with Alba to concentrate resources in the Netherlands.
1566	Austria invades Hungary, Suleiman counter-invades, dies at Szigetvar. Succession of Selim II. Election of Pope Pius V, future saint.
1567–68	Alba crushes uprising in the Netherlands, defeats Louis of Nassau at Jemmingen.
1567–70	Second and Third Wars of Religion in France, battles of Saint Denis, Jarnac and Moncontour. Ends with Pacification of Saint-Germain.

1568	Treaty of Adrianople/Edirne between the Holy Roman and Ottoman empires. Uluch Ali appointed Beylerbey of Algiers. Hawkins and Drake ambushed at San Juan de Ulúa, near Vera Cruz, English corsairs seize Spanish bullion shipments to the Netherlands. Mary Queen of Scots seeks asylum in England.
1568–71	Revolt of nominally converted Muslims (Moriscos) in Granada.
1569	Explosion in Venice Arsenal, great fire of Istanbul. Pius V makes Cosimo dei Medici Grand Duke of Tuscany (investiture 1570).
1569–70	Failure of Ottoman attempt to excavate a canal between Don and Volga rivers.
1570	Pius V excommunicates Elizabeth of England, declares her deposed. Ottoman invasion of Cyprus.
1570–71	*See Chronologies introducing Chapters Seven to Nine.*
1571	Battle of Lepanto. Death of Cellini.
1572	Netherlands revolt revived by Dutch corsairs. Election of Pope Gregory XIII. Massacre of French Huguenots on Saint Bartholomew's Day.
1572–73	Fourth War of Religion in France. Brutal pacification of the Netherlands by Alba.
1573	Don Juan captures Tunis. Alba replaced by Requeséns. Birth of Caravaggio.
1574	Uluch Ali and Cicalazâde Sinan Pasha recapture Tunis (held until 1881), take Goleta. Death of Selim, succession of Murad III. Death of Vasari.
1575	Second Spanish Hapsburg default on debts.
1575–80	Fifth, Sixth and Seventh Wars of Religion, Catholics form Holy League with Spain.
1576	Ottoman-supported Saadi pretender seizes Fez, capital of Morocco. Sack of Antwerp by mutinous Spanish soldiers. Death of Titian.
1577	Death of Luis de Requeséns, succeeded by Don Juan in the Netherlands. England allies with Netherlands rebels.
1577–80	Francis Drake circumnavigates the world, raiding Spanish settlements and ships.
1577–90	War between Ottoman and Persian empires.
1578	Death of Juan de Austria. Alessandro Farnese remains in military command. Moroccan crusade of King Sebastian of Portugal destroyed at Alcázarquivir.

1579	Grand Vizier Mehmet Sokolli assassinated.
1580	After Alba victory at Alcántara, Philip becomes King of Portugal. Truce between Spanish and Ottoman Empires.
1582	Gregorian replaces Julian calendar in Roman Catholic countries.
1582–83	Santa Cruz twice defeats Franco–Portuguese fleets in the Azores.
1584	William of Orange assassinated, son Maurice succeeds.
1585	Gregory XIII declares crusade against England, dies. Sixtus V elected.
1585–89	Eighth War of Religion, battle of Coutras.
1586	Drake raids Florida. Santa Cruz prepares England invassion fleet (Armada).
1587	Mary Queen of Scots executed. Ottoman–Spanish truce extended.
1588	Death of Santa Cruz. Failure of Armada under Medina Sidonia. Death of Veronese.
1589–94	War of French Succession, battles of Arques and Ivry.
1592	Muslim year 1000. Deaths of Farnese (Parma) and Montaigne.
1593	Start of 'Long War' between Holy Roman and Ottoman empires.
1594	Henri IV decides Paris is worth a Mass. Death of Tintoretto.
1595	Death of Murad, succession of Mohammed III.
1596	Second Armada against England fails. Third Spanish default on debts. Austrian army destroyed by Cicalazâde Sinan Pasha at Kerestes.
1597	Third Armada against England fails.
1598	Huguenots granted religious freedom, Franco–Spanish peace. Death of Philip II.
1599	English East India Company founded. Birth of Velázquez.
1600	Henri IV marries Marie dei Medici. Shakespeare's *Hamlet*.

FOREWORD

'**M**archer Lord of the Horizon' and 'Rock That Bestrides the Continents' were among the titles you had to use if you were addressing the Ottoman Sultan in his days of glory. In the sixteenth century the Ottomans ruled the centre of the world; they had conquered the lands of the eastern Roman Empire – not just its heartland, Constantinople, which they had captured in 1453 – but outlying areas in North Africa, Egypt and Arabia that had only been part of the Byzantine empire at the very height of its territorial extension under Justinian, almost a thousand years before. Queen Elizabeth I, anxious to promote English trade with The Grand Turk, was careful to use the grandiloquent titles he bestowed upon himself. In Protestant Europe, in any case, he counted as a useful ally against militant counter-reformation Roman Catholicism. *'Liever Turk dan Paus'* ('Better Turk than Pope') cried the rebellious Dutch during the siege of Leyden, when to allow ships to come to the relief of the town they opened the dykes, flooded the land, and wrecked their own agricultural livelihood for years to come. The later sixteenth century was an era when religious wars gripped Europe. That of Catholicism against Islam (in the shape of the Turks) is the subject of Hugh Bicheno's multi-dimensional and extremely readable work.

We are used to reading about the wars of the Hapsburg and Valois dynasties in early modern times. France was gripped in a vice between the Hapsburgs who ruled Germany and the Hapsburgs who ruled Spain and the Netherlands. But the Hapsburgs, in turn, had to face the Turks, who threatened the German branch of the dynasty through the Balkans and the Spanish through the Mediterranean. The first theatre produced two pieces of grand drama, the sieges of Vienna in 1529 and 1683. The second produced several, but the battle of Lepanto in 1571 was a high point. The Roman Catholic powers constituted a Holy League, led by Spain but essentially empowered, in naval and financial matters, by Venice. The Ottoman Empire was still, at the time, expanding – even, thanks to a base offered them by the king of France at Toulon, threatening Spain herself as well as Malta. The Turks had undertaken the conquest of all the outposts left by the Crusaders as they retreated – Rhodes and then, after an epic struggle (which Mr Bicheno describes exceedingly well and, given the clash of rival Greek and Turkish versions of what happened, fairly), Cyprus. The Holy League was too late to relieve Cyprus in 1570, but not to confront a Turkish invasion of the Adriatic the following year. The two enormous fleets encountered each other at Lepanto, the then (Italian) name for the gulf that almost separates the Morea from the Greek mainland and Athens. Lord Byron, in a subsequent Greek war, died of disease on land not far from where the naval battle was fought. Most of the warships were narrow galleys with guns only in the bows, but the Venetians had built other, larger galleys, hybrids strong enough to accommodate broadside gunnery. On one side, prominently displayed, the green banner of Allah, thick with Koranic inscriptions at the masthead of one flagship; on the other, a great Cross was hoisted above the war galley of young Don Juan of Austria. In the end superior seamanship gave the victory to the Christians, and Lepanto has since been regarded as one of the decisive battles of history. Oddly enough, a thousand miles away and two decades before, Ivan the Terrible took Kazan, the capital of the Turks' Tatar cousins – also, for Russians, a decisive battle.

Mr Bicheno is a very good teller of naval tales and when, in the last section of the book, he deals with the battle itself, the story is easy to follow. Be it said that I started reading the manuscript with an hour or two to spare in the waiting room of Ankara station and finished it, after a six-hour journey, as the bus pulled into Kadiköy, the old Chalcedon, on the Asiatic side of the Bosphorus. But this book is not just about the battle. It also deals with the culture of both sides, the religion, the painting (the battle figures strongly in Christian mythology and iconography) and the concepts of chivalry that were involved on both sides (considerable). Mr Bicheno understands that the Ottoman Empire of the period was not at all the half-savage and half-luxurious enterprise that the non-conformist Liberal mind of the later nineteenth century imagined (by then, paradoxically, the Protestants were on the whole the anti-Turks, whereas Catholics had more understanding). It was very much a going concern and the formerly Byzantine Greeks, far from being oppressed, were essentially partners in the making of the empire in its great days. There is an exceedingly good Greek historian, Dimitri Kitzikis, whose *L'empire ottoman* has been translated into Turkish as 'A Turkish-Greek Condominium.' At Lepanto, it is a fair bet, many if not most of the Ottoman galleys would have been commanded in Greek. In the sixteenth century the Greek Orthodox were just as hostile to Roman Catholicism as the Protestants were, and when Cyprus fell to the Turks it was in large part because the Venetian defenders could not rely upon the locals. Another world, and if you wish to have a very readable and knowledgeable account of the many sides to it, Hugh Bicheno's book is the right start.

Norman Stone

ANKARA

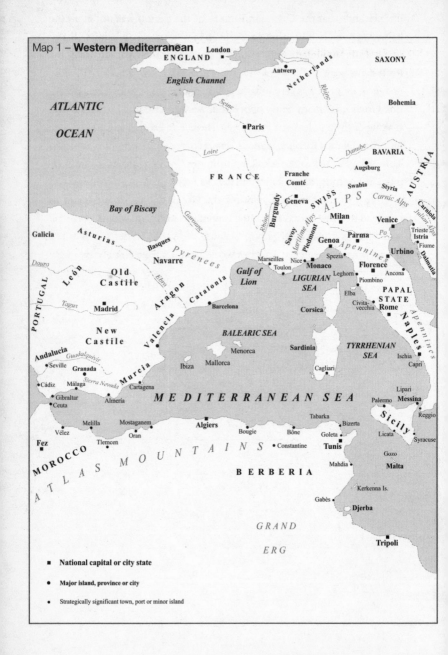

Map 1 – **Western Mediterranean**

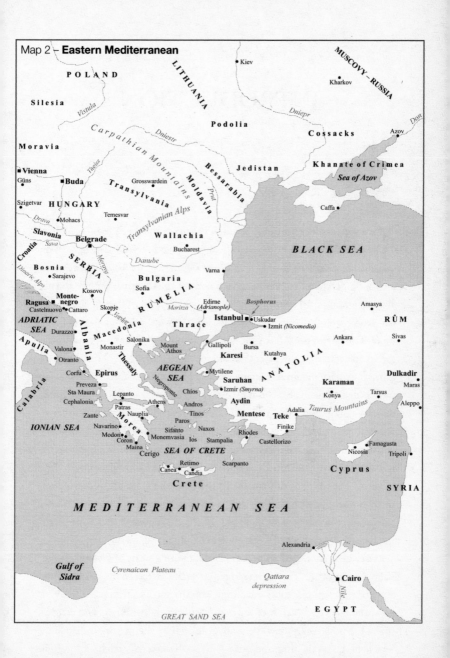

Map 2 – **Eastern Mediterranean**

POLAND

Silesia

Vistula

LITHUANIA

• Kiev

MUSCOVY – RUSSIA

• Kharkov

Dniepr

Don

Podolia

Cossacks

Azov •

Moravia

Dniestr

Carpathian Mountains

Bessarabia

Jedistan

Khanate of Crimea

Sea of Azov

■ Vienna

Güns

■ Buda

Transylvania

Grosswardein

Moldavia

Prut

Caffa •

Tisza

Szigetvar

HUNGARY

Temesvar

Transylvanian Alps

BLACK SEA

Drava • Mohacs

Slavonia

■ Belgrade

Wallachia

Bucharest •

Sava

Croatia

Dinaric Alps

Bosnia

• Sarajevo

SERBIA

Morava

Danube

Varna •

Kosovo

Bulgaria

Sofia •

Monte-negro

Ragusa ■

Castelnuovo • Cattaro

Skopje •

RUMELIA

Vardar

Edirne
(Adrianople) •

Maritza

Bosphorus

Amasya •

ADRIATIC
SEA

Durazzo •

Albania

Macedonia

Thrace

Istanbul ■ Uskudar

Izmit (Nicomedia)

Ankara •

RÛM

Sivas •

Apulia

Valona •

Thessaly

Salonika •

Mount
Athos

Gallipoli •

Bursa •

ANATOLIA

Otranto •

Monastir •

AEGEAN
SEA

Karesi

Kutahya •

Corfu • Epirus

Preveza •

Sta Maura •

Lepanto

Cephalonia •

Zante •

Patras •

Nauplia •

Athens •

Negroponte

• Mytilene

Chios •

Saruhan

• Izmir (Smyrna)

Aydin

Karaman

Konya •

Tarsus •

Dulkadir

Maras •

Taurus Mountains

Aleppo •

Navarino •

Morea

Modon •

Coron •

Maina

Cerigo

Andros •

Tinos •

Paros

Sifanto • Naxos

Monemvasia • Ios

Stampalia

Mentese

Teke

Adalia •

Finike •

Rhodes •

Castellorizo •

IONIAN SEA

SEA OF CRETE

Scarpanto

Famagusta •

Nicosia •

Tripoli •

Retimo •

Canea •

Candia •

Crete

Cyprus

SYRIA

MEDITERRANEAN SEA

Alexandria •

Gulf of
Sidra

Cyrenaican Plateau

*Qattara
depression*

■ Cairo

Nile

EGYPT

GREAT SAND SEA

5

INTRODUCTION

In a sixteenth century crowded with events the passage of time has revealed to be extremely significant, one has received disproportionate attention. The sustained artistic celebration of the battle of Lepanto, fought on 7 October 1571 between the fleets of the Ottoman Empire and an alliance among the Papacy, Spain and Venice, fully merits use of the adjective 'iconic' even in the strictest definition of the word, referring to venerated images of sacred persons or events. In addition, were the importance of events measured by the places named for them or by the volume of literature they have inspired, Lepanto would have to be counted among the most outstanding in all of human history. To understand this fully we must do more than review the rich and diverse cast of men (and at least one woman) who fought there and the weapons and tactics they employed – it is also necessary to explain its apotheosis into a symbolic battle between good and evil second only to Armageddon, which will bring about the end of history, military or otherwise. To that end, the most intriguing aspect of the Lepanto cult is that the anniversary of this episode of mass homicide is still celebrated by the Roman Catholic church as the feast day of Our Lady of the Rosary, icon of life-giving love and compassion.

An historical event has at least four identities, none necessarily more valid than another. The closest to reality is the scattered mosaic of participants' perceptions, soon subsumed into the second, which is a body of accepted facts to which memories retrospectively conform. The third is the value-added canonical version, coloured by the propaganda use to which it is put at the time and later. The fourth seeks to reach back through the intervening stages to rediscover the first, but cannot be other than a construct shaped by language and society, and by the intellectual climate of the time in which it is written. Accounts in English have tended to accept the myth, created by more involved or less sceptical cultures, of a 'decisive' clash between the Islamic and Christian faiths at Lepanto, even while admitting that in practical terms it decided almost nothing. This makes it a uniquely suitable portal through which to explore the concept of multiple realities, by sketching in the broad contemporary context (*Chronology*), then in Part I identifying what made Lepanto an iconic battle while examining the socio-geographical (The Stage), technological (Props), political (The Players), and ideological (The Plot) currents that came together to make it the subject of effusive artistic expression (Billboard). In Part II the battle itself is re-examined in more strictly military terms as one of several significant clashes among competing empires, shaped by the training and morale of the participants, their preferred style of combat, and the operational and tactical calculations of the rival commanders.

Active memory of the 11 September 2001 terrorist assault on the United States will have faded by the time this book reaches the shelves, but will have burrowed deep to revive ancestral memories and fuel atavistic fears. As I write, Muslim warriors in love with death (*Ghazis*) are once again the dreaded 'other' in a way they have not been for centuries. The more worldly-wise among them may have smiled into their beards to hear western commentators proclaim the essential peacefulness of Islam – for although the term *dar al-Islam* does indeed encompass the concept of an abode of peace, they are fighting against what they regard as *dar al-harb*, the house of war where unbelievers ceaselessly struggle amongst themselves. As though to confirm their opinion, following an uneasy period of declining credibility since the Soviet Union – the last eastern bogeyman – was revealed to be a hollow shell, the knee-jerk instinct of several *dar al-harb* governments was to exploit the terrorist spectacular to increase their power at the expense of civil liberties. The domestic political utility of an external threat is an historical constant, and never was this more evident than in the sixteenth century, when the nation state Moloch first began to take its modern form.

Ominously, Saint John the Divine predicted Armageddon would take place at Har (now Tel) Megiddo in Palestine, where the first battle history records was fought in 1468 BC and many have been since. The mouth of the Gulf of Corinth–Patras, where the battle of Lepanto was fought, is another military neural point, and one particularly laden with cultural associations: it is almost within sight of Odysseus' Ithaca and of Messolonghi, where Lord Byron died romantically in 1824; the Athenian Admiral Phormio defeated the combined Peloponnesian fleets off Lepanto in 429 BC; and in 31 BC at nearby Actium/Preveza the forces of Anthony and Cleopatra suffered decisive defeat at the hands of Octavian, later the first Roman Emperor–God Augustus. Some who fought there in 1571 would have known that Venice lost the gulf after naval defeats in 1499 and 1500 at Zonchio, not far to the south off Navarino, and that at Preveza in 1538 the Ottoman Admiral Khair ed-Din 'Barbarossa' had humiliated a larger Holy League fleet under the no less renowned Hapsburg Captain General of the Sea Andrea D'Oria (hereafter *Doria*).[1]

This overburden of historical associations and symbolic significance outweighs the actual geopolitical results of the 1571 battle, which were slight. The Ottomans had already completed their invasion of Cyprus (the proximate cause of the war), they quickly rebuilt their fleet, and within two years military stalemate and financial imperatives persuaded Venice to drop out of the alliance, accept the loss of Cyprus and pay a humiliating indemnity for having tried to retain it. Not much later Spanish and Portuguese attempts to extend their North African holdings were defeated, establishing a western Mediterranean status quo that lasted until the nineteenth century. Nor was Lepanto by any stretch of the cliché the 'turning point' in the struggle between Islam and Christianity, for the Ottomans seized Crete from Venice in 1645–70 and besieged Vienna for the last time in 1683. Despite this the battle always features in lists of 'decisive' battles, reminding one of the dialogue between Old Kaspar and his grandson in Robert Southey's 'The Battle of Blenheim':

> 'But what good came of it at last?'
> Quoth little Peterkin.
> 'Why that I cannot tell,' said he,
> 'But 'twas a famous victory.'

If he could have made it rhyme Old Kaspar might have gone on to say that battles by themselves normally decide nothing other than which side was stronger and/or more skilled on the day, except insofar as they reflect the underlying social, economic and technological dynamism of the combatants. In *The Face of Battle* John Keegan concluded 'battles belong to finite moments in history, to the societies which raise the armies which fight them, to the economies and technologies which those societies sustain'. Indeed, but what are we to make of battles that transcend their temporal co-ordinates to become part of the folk memory that defines our culture? The paradigms are the doomed stand by the mixed force of Greeks commanded by the Spartan King Leonidas at Thermopylae in 480 BC, and of Travis, Bowie, Crockett and their men at The Alamo in 1836, which belong to all time in a very different way than they did to their own. For contemporaries they prompted panicked flight from Attica and eastern Texas, ahead of King Xerxes' Persian host and General Santa Anna's Mexican army. Subsequent victories for the Greeks at Plataea and for the Texans at San Jacinto were far more celebrated at the time, and rightly so. Those put in imminent danger cannot be expected to draw solace from the triumphs of the human spirit that hindsight may excavate from the rubble of defeats.

Once the danger is past, however, myth formation can be extremely rapid and may create a lasting cultural legacy. The defenders of The Alamo drew strength from the example set by Leonidas' men 2,316 years earlier, and to fast-forward a further 104 years Britons had the parallel very much in mind after the fall of France in 1940, the moral effect of which was cushioned by the subsequent miracle of Dunkirk and largely reversed by the aerial Battle of Britain, however insubstantial in numerical terms both may have been in the cataclysmic final balance of the Second World War. We know, now, that Hitler and his General Staff regarded Britain as a minor threat once deprived of her French ally, and that the preparations they made for an invasion were desultory. But on the other side of the English Channel only someone sanguine to the point of coma could have failed to share the general view that invasion was imminent, and contemporary opinion is no less an historical fact than the nuts and bolts of a particular episode as revealed by subsequent research. It is peculiarly pointless to belittle an event because it was not 'really' as important as people believed at the time, more useful to identify why they believed it was, and how that belief influenced events.

Battles get on the 'greatest' lists because they are invested early with symbolic status, to which later chroniclers add by repetition. However, although some may gain, some can lose status in the telling, or by historical accident. The battle of Maldon in 991, one of many English defeats by the Vikings in the tenth century, achieved cultural immortality because the loyalty unto death of ealdorman Byrhtnoth's bodyguard was celebrated in an Old English epic poem transcribed in the eighteenth century. No such literary legacy celebrates the battle of Stamford Bridge, where the last great Viking invasion was annihilated by King Harold II of England, nor the grim stand by Harold's house carls around his body at the battle of Hastings, fought three weeks later against the Normans. In terms of their long-term consequences the two battles and the fact they were fought so close together were of infinitely greater significance than Maldon, but the songs they surely inspired have not survived, and Old England lacks a fitting requiem.

This is mainly because the stories societies wish to hear about their own past are supportive of their collective self-image, and the events chosen for particular attention will be 'iconic' in the modern usage of the word to signify emblematic, which may make purists wince but thriftily encompasses several themes I wish to touch upon. Lepanto was invested with a miraculous aura at the time and so became a lastingly powerful cultural artefact, in part because it featured many themes of universal appeal but also because it is still a source of intense pride to the descendants of the victors, for whom the centuries since have not provided many other moments of unequivocal greatness to celebrate. It was arguably the high-water mark of what was indisputably 'the Spanish century', and a last appearance near the centre of the geopolitical stage for the Papal and other Italian mini-states.

Less easily explicable is why the name recognition of Lepanto in France, the ally of the Ottoman Empire at the time and a nation that still had centuries of *gloire* to come, should be higher than for many other more recent battles of strictly national significance. French scholars have paid particular attention to the period, notably Fernand Braudel whose two-volume *The Mediterranean and the Mediterranean World in the Age of Philip II*, first published in 1949, retains the power to inflict an acute sense of inferiority on any honest scholar who reads it. However, in seeking to correct overemphasis on politics and personalities it moved the goalposts rather too far, for Braudel's Mediterranean is a vast amphitheatre in which individuals are little more than the puppets of impersonal forces. Ironically his influence on a generation of historians itself contradicts this, promoting him into the category of one who may not have changed our world, but has altered our perception of it, which amounts to nearly the same thing.[2]

For our purposes it is no less significant that despite Braudel's emphasis on the 'structural' elements of the history of human endeavour, including the macro-parameters set by geography, geology, climatology and oceanography, some of his own school subsequently paid close attention to the highly 'circumstantial' subject of Lepanto. In part this was because western historians only began to mine the Ottoman archives systematically after Braudel revived interest in the area and the period. Bless them, for I do not read modern let alone classical Turkish and without their research much that took place on the other side of the hill would have remained concealed from me. But I also found it intriguing that Braudel's French disciples should have pursued the subject when he considered it of mainly psychological importance, despite a Francocentric tradition that makes the Anglo variety look meek by comparison. The outline of my thesis came from pondering why the academic members of a state apparatus famed for the single-minded pursuit of its own interest should have concerned themselves with an event that affected France only indirectly, which in turn involved confronting what Braudel considered 'the great problem, in truth without a satisfactory solution, [which is] to locate a moment in time within the long lines of history, that is to research the antecedents, the vast context that enveloped it, and the consequences that can be traced to it'.[3]

I concluded that the longest line that ran through Lepanto to the present day was the great investment made in it by the Roman Catholic church, illuminating a seldom-discussed aspect of an enterprise to which the French bureaucracy is fully committed. If the European Community can be said to possess an ideological dimension (admittedly a largish if), it is probably corporativism (aka Third Way), the Roman Catholic blueprint for social and political stability as the precondition for the recovery of Christian unity, shattered during the turbulent sixteenth century. The whole project harks back to the creation of a unified western Christendom by Charlemagne, and beyond him to the Roman Empire. From the Roman

Catholic point of view, bearing in mind that the word 'catholic' means 'universal', if the genie of nationalism can be returned to the bottle then the schismatic churches created to serve the interests of nation states will wither away, and the painstaking task of winning over a continent that has largely reverted to paganism can begin again. In the absence of any compelling vision of the future one drawing on an idealized past may acquire uncommon power. It has happened before, and it is no coincidence that the founding treaty of the European Union was signed in Rome.

There is, of course, nothing like a palpably common threat to encourage unity, and although other Holy Leagues were decidedly secular alliances made by the popes among and against Spain, Venice, France and the thrice misnamed Holy Roman Empire, the one that fought Lepanto was directed at a highly successful rival of Christianity, and was the last time the Papacy was able to play that card before the wars of religion deepened the divisions and exacerbated the barbarism of an already savagely fractious continent. There were to be other formal Crusades, most notably the failed invasion launched against England in 1588, but none that served to enhance Rome's moral authority or lent credibility to the forgiveness (indulgence) of the Crusaders' sins. Although today remembered as the final straw that led Martin Luther to nail his *Ninety-Five Theses* to the door of Wittenberg cathedral in 1517, generally considered the start of the Protestant Reformation, indulgences were originally granted to those joining a Crusade and became corrupted after Pope Innocent III introduced cash payment as an alternative to active service, to reduce the mass of untrained sinners who flocked to the Crusader banners and cost more to keep than they could repay in battle.

Every historical work explores themes that in isolation may seem to have little bearing on the present day, but which taken together are the warp and woof of modern perception. The sole non-trivial political issue today confronting England, among the first kingdoms to declare religious independence from Rome, is whether or not to surrender sovereignty on the altar of European integration, with the attendant dismemberment of the multinational concept of Great Britain historically defined in terms of that emancipation. The issue that cannot be evaded is whether the tapestries on either side of the English Channel are sufficiently alike, or less poetically whether there is sufficient cultural common ground for minimum operative levels of trust. There does not appear to be, and as an historian I cannot see how it could be otherwise.

If, patient reader, you are wondering what this has to do with a 432-year-old battle, the link is that very few of the many books about Lepanto have been written in English. Thanks to their protective wet ditches the English-speaking peoples are not easily interested by quarrels in far-off places among people about whom they know nothing, as Neville Chamberlain once put it. But as he discovered to his sorrow in 1939, and as both the British and Americans have rediscovered time and again since, they cannot be ignored with impunity and it is therefore prudent to have a fair grasp of what makes those quarrelsome far-off people tick. If it is not the mainspring, folk memory is certainly the governor of collective atti-tudes, or to mix metaphors the default setting of the mental processes by which information is perceived, evaluated and filed, and many foreign policy debacles have been the product of governments sending 'signals' interpreted by the other side according to a very different code book. At the root of this incomprehension lies the fact that peoples draw their own unique emotional truth from a folk memory independent of the verifiable facts and many times more persuasive, not least when a large psychic invest-ment is required to sustain it in the teeth of evidence to the contrary. All belief systems, religious or secular, depend on the phenomenon for their vitality – faith cannot be acquired, still less refuted, by the exercise of reason.

We have recently emerged from a century that had more in common with the sixteenth than with any other either before or between them, both marked by a mental predisposition in the West that can only be described as apocalyptic. Let us hope, and let those whose religious beliefs are not contaminated by hatred pray, that the Gadarene ideological madness and attendant genocide of the twentieth century does not spill over into the twenty-first as it did so foully from the sixteenth into the seventeenth. The 1,500th anniversary of the crucifixion of Christ fell in 1533, and although it produced a surge of desperate behaviour in some places, notably the Anabaptist New Jerusalem of Münster, it cannot be the reason why the millenarian mentality persisted for another hundred years. In the Muslim world the year 1,000 AH came and went in the Christian AD 1592 without causing similarly generalized unease, and the syndrome does seem to be more associated with western culture than with any biological imperative inherent to humankind. As briefly discussed in Chapter Four, the apotheosis of Lepanto owed much to a widespread perception in the Christian world that the whole of human existence was in crisis, and a consequent desire to believe that the battle had exorcised one of the more tangible threats.

The geographical place, now Návpaktos, is just a short flight away, but the event remains far off in time and even more so in the distance between modern perceptions of it by different cultures. For some the clash of socio-religious tectonic plates continues, as underlined by the ease with which ancient enmities were revived and became genocidal during the 1990s in the Balkans. Folk memory of the threat once posed by Islam and the Ottoman Empire may also simmer near the surface of the resistance by Mediterranean members of the European Community to the accession of secular Turkey, although equity and rational self-interest argue for her inclusion as soon as possible at a time when outraged Muslim sensibilities have tangibly become the most serious threat to western interests. Should a rebuffed Turkey turn instead to the cultivation of her neighbours and of the Turkic republics newly independent of Russian tutelage, future historians may see it as the moment when Middle Eastern, Mediterranean and Asiatic geopolitical divides not unlike those prevailing in 1571 began to re-emerge. Europeans are not alone in idealizing a past before feckless complacency and brutal folly destroyed their claim to be in the forefront of civilization.

Thanks to the psychological compensation of a language-based 'special relationship' with the United States, the British generally lack the sense of cultural urgency that motivates the French to dream of a future in which they will be the intellectual leaders of a new Roman Empire. But a more profound divide comes from the Protestant belief in the personal responsibility of man, the keystone for a concept of freedom unique to the English speaking peoples. Transmuted into the high Victorian cult of progress, it continues to dominate mainstream Anglo-American thought even after the twentieth century convincingly demonstrated the fragility of even the most basic human decency. By contrast the collectivist Roman Catholic interpretation of original sin, although obviously serving useful institutional purposes, reflects a more realistic perception that the natural state of humankind tends to barbarism.

Thus the deep background – but the main differences between the English-speaking and mainland European historiographic traditions can be attributed more demonstrably to sharply different national experiences than to religious inheritance, and this is most noticeable in their divergent views on war. Oversimplifying heavily, English-speakers have tended to portray the emergence of centralized nation states and the growing ability of governments to impose the costs of their decisions on future genera-tions as the by-product of war, whereas the mainland tradition leans more to the view that rulers indulged in foreign wars precisely in order to increase their domestic powers. I find the latter a more convincing argument. Not only does it create a coherent framework for the study of the post-Renaissance period, it also offers an explanation why, in countries the French categorize as Anglo-Saxon, liberties fiercely upheld in earlier times against foreign and domestic tyrants have been tamely surrendered in our own during the prosecution of otherwise singularly unsuccessful 'wars' on crime and poverty.[4]

These differences in the default interpretation of events may help to explain why military history still tends to be presented in unnatural isolation from domestic politics in English, but the main reason for its ever-growing popularity seems to be nostalgia for a time when power relationships were more clear-cut and less insidious. This owes something to the roseate vision of a simpler past that grew up alongside the myth of progress, more to a low-level but pervasive revulsion at the loss of a sense of the sublime in an era of militant mediocrity. By any measure of comfort and physical well-being even the poorest western Europeans today enjoy standards beyond the hopes of their grandparents or the imagina-tion of Renaissance princes, and if a cause and effect could be shown, the loss of the creative highs of the past would be considered a fair price to pay for the elimination of the squalid lows of endemic disease and violence. But it cannot, and therein lies the attraction of reading about a far less humane but more effervescent time, when some at least of the tax burden that rulers imposed on their subjects went to decorate the world with works of lasting beauty.

Lepanto's artistic apotheosis owed much to being fought when the Mannerist attenuation of the High Renaissance was giving way to the Baroque, a designation applied to the style prevailing in art, music and life in general between the decline of the Renaissance and the start of the amusingly named Age of Enlightenment. A clash among hundreds of beautifully shaped, painted and decorated warships, caparisoned with standards, banners and pennants, and packed with warriors dressed in as much finery as they could afford, was a subject perfectly matched to the artistic sensibilities of the age. Chapter Five develops the thought that since the early Baroque was in many respects an expression of the 'hearts and minds' component of Rome's counter-attack against austere Protestantism, the artistic exaltation of Lepanto deserves consideration as one of the catalysts of an immensely influential stylistic transition.

It was also among the first of what a later age would call banner headline events to take place after printing presses had become common, with the result that many accounts survive. In this field also Lepanto drove like a piton into one of the most significant fracture lines in the rock face of European culture, for it was a time when the oral tradition was very much alive and stories were still propagated by means of poems and songs, ephemera previously lost to the world but now written down and published in anthologies. The first of these to deal with Lepanto was a collection of verse, bound together with an eyewitness account by Count Nestor Martinengo of the 1570–71 siege of Famagusta in Cyprus, which suggests that the transition from historical event to cultural artefact took place almost immediately, possibly because people did not then think in terms of such hard and fast categories.[5]

There is an echo of this perception in perhaps the most scrupulously even-handed short account of Lepanto, Guido Quarti's factual preamble to his collection of contemporary popular songs. For Quarti, the remarkable thing about Lepanto was not the battle itself but the broad social range of people who celebrated it, many of the songs being in obscure local dialects. Thence to José López de Toro's encyclopedic 1950 collection of works devoted to Lepanto by over 200 poets, in Italian, Latin, Spanish, Catalan, French, German and English, and it is evident that the subject has been a phenomenon of extraordinary and far-reaching cultural vitality. López himself waxed lyrical:

> The victory at Lepanto was a magical key that threw open the
> doors to historians; a glowing ember that set the language of preachers

on fire; a touchstone against which critics might compare similar events; a higher light to illuminate enigmas for philosophers and, finally, the lyre from whose strings poets plucked the most varied and moving tunes … it seemed that all tongues had been impatiently awaiting the news before giving jubilant voice to hymns of thanks to the Lord of all armies, to the hero Don Juan de Austria and his court of generals, and to all the components of the valiant forces of the Holy League.

López published his work at a time when Spain was still recovering from a civil war that began with churches, monasteries and nunneries being sacked and their occupants hunted down like rats, so he naturally emphasized the religious dimension to the exclusion of all else. As a result, although he ended with a translation of the poem 'Lepanto' written in the epic style by Gilbert Keith Chesterton in 1911, it did not occur to him to question why the subject had reached across the gulfs of time, language and culture to arouse such enthusiasm in an Englishman who had not at that time embraced the Roman Catholic church.

The answer lies in the poem itself – Chesterton was indeed a devout Anglo-Catholic well before his conversion to Rome, but he was also a great storyteller and found the high drama of Lepanto irresistible. Heroic individual leadership survived longer in sea battles than on land, but this was the last occasion when it was celebrated in the traditional form of long, narrative epic poetry. It featured at the end of the interminable *La Austriada* written by Juan Rufo, who was present at the battle, while Alonso de Ercilla did not let the fact that he was writing about the conquest of Chile prevent him from inserting a graphic 'vision' of Lepanto in his own *La Araucana*. James VI of Scotland, founder of the in-and-out-of-the-Roman-Catholic-closet Stuart dynasty of Great Britain, also wrote a lost poem in Latin, which López believed was echoed in a poem dedicated to James by Thomas Moravius. Shakespeare might have done the subject justice, but with reason to be circumspect about his religious leanings, he barely tiptoed around the subject in the enigmatic *Othello*.

There can be no doubt about the centrality of Lepanto in the life of Shakespeare's great Spanish contemporary, and the largest individual contribution to the battle's secular legacy was that a soldier called Miguel de Cervantes was wounded and lost the use of his left hand there. Later captured and held to ransom, he emerged to write a work that gently mocked heroism and mourned the passing of chivalry. *Don Quixote* is the Everest of Spanish letters and one of the highest peaks of world literature, and the man who wrote it was known in his day as 'El Manco de Lepanto'. The nickname may have been intended as a sneer, for *manco* means both 'one-handed' and 'defective' or, more snide yet, 'oarless', but to Cervantes, here speaking of himself in the third person, it was a badge of honour:

> He was a soldier for many years and a prisoner for five and a half, during which time he learned to have patience in adversity. He lost his left hand to a shot from an arquebus at the battle of Lepanto [and] although this wound may seem ugly, he considers it handsome because it was earned on the most memorable occasion that past and present centuries ever witnessed, or that future centuries may hope to see.

Apart from Cervantes, the one actor familiar to English speakers is the young man in nominal command of the Holy League fleet, the illegitimate son of Emperor Charles V whom others have dubbed 'Don John' to avoid the name association with Don Juan Tenorio, literature's most famous fornicator. In fact the association is quite appropriate, as Don Juan de Austria had the sultry good looks associated with love children (*Colour Plate 1*) and a libido the equal of his fictional namesake, and, as various panting biographies attest, the centuries have not dimmed his lustre in the eyes of those who like their heroes to look the part. One of the Lepanto fables is that his half-brother, Philip II of Spain, was jealous of him, spitefully denied him the title of 'Royal Highness', held him back from greater glory and, according to Chesterton and others, may later have had him poisoned. Why this suspicion should have gained currency when the king could have consigned his half-brother to obscurity with a flick of the pen is not easy to deduce. This said, had Juan lived to read *Don Quixote* he might well have recognized something of himself in the old man pathetically seeking to transcend in glory the limitations of the station into which he was born.

His supporting cast included two men, Alvaro de Bazán, Marquess of Santa Cruz, and Alessandro Farnese, future Duke of Parma, who were touched with military genius, and many of the names that make Renaissance Italy such a rewardingly intricate field of study. Lepanto was also the last major battle where the military monastic orders played a significant role, the oldest being the aristocratic corsairs of the Order of Saint John, wearing the laurels of their epic defence of Malta in 1565, while the youngest, likewise devoted to pious piracy, was the Order of Santo Stefano formed by the newly created Grand Duke of Tuscany, Cosimo dei Medici. Also present were members of Spanish crusading orders originally created during the long Reconquest of the Iberian Peninsula, and of the Burgundian companion Order of the Golden Fleece, whose pendant lamb was the sole decoration worn by Philip II in several of his portraits.

One can seldom find out much about those defeated in battle at this time, especially if they were killed, but an epic requires a worthy opponent and the void has been filled by western stereotypes. Thus the deaths of Ali Pasha, the Ottoman admiral, and of Mehmet Scirocco, Governor of Alexandria and commander of the Right Wing, are normally portrayed in a suitably heroic light, and the escapes of the Croatian Pertev Pasha, the Ottoman land general, and of the Calabrian Uluch Ali, the Governor of Algiers and commander of their Left Wing, condemned by some as opportunistic or cowardly. We may safely discount this, as both preserved the esteem of a sultan and a grand vizier not noted for charitable judgement of those who failed them, and Uluch Ali went on to command the new Ottoman fleet. Propaganda aside, what remains is the assessment of those who defeated them and this, bridging the gulf of racial and religious enmity, often shows more genuine respect for the Ottoman enemy than for other members of the Christian coalition.

When I began my research it was a jolt to input 'Lepanto' on my Internet browser, that invaluable aid to lateral thinking, only to find several thousand entries. Many hours of trawling produced a wide range of items that underline how very living history can be. Thus the latest of countless Lepanto monuments is the statue of its hero erected at Návpaktos in the year 2000 by the Cervantes Society of the USA, on the anniversary of the battle. Deep in the Protestant Bible Belt of the United States can be found the town of Lepanto, Arkansas, birthplace of Jimmy (not Jimi) Hendrix, who won the Congressional Medal of Honor for repeated acts of heroism while fighting the Nazis on the day after Christmas, 1944. The LePanto restaurant at the Radisson SAS Saint Helen's Hotel in Dublin is so named because Lord Gough, a previous owner of Saint Helen's House, reputedly fought in the battle. A very old stained glass window in the Duomo in Florence depicts some technically intriguing hybrid warships of the time, while the battle is also depicted in a modern stained glass window by Guido Nichen in the church of Notre Dame du Rosaire in Villeray, Montréal.

More poignantly, every year in Zacatecas, México, there is a colourful street pageant commemorating victory over the Turks, in which the participants carry arquebuses and wear helmets, turbans and body armour. This by the descendants of a people with little reason to celebrate the triumph of Spanish arms over anyone, anywhere. Lepanto also inspired a painting by the great Filipino artist Juan Luna, a reminder that the ever-rebellious Islamic Dayaks of the southern Philippines are still known as Moros (Moors), the name bestowed on them by the Spanish conquistadors, who were astounded to meet the enemy they had driven out of the Iberian peninsula on the other side of the globe. Moro warriors used to tourniquet their limbs with wire and keep coming, panga in hand, even when shot, and this led to the adoption of the .45 calibre automatic pistol by the US Army in its own fruitless attempt to 'pacify' them after taking the archipelago from the Spanish in 1898.

In sum, to explore all the cultural ramifications of this one event would be a life's work. Having other plans, I have chosen instead to treat it both as an historical event subject to the rules of evidence, and as an independently valid work of theatrical propaganda. The chapter headings in Part I (Stage, Props, etc.) underline this duality, emphasized in the 'Plot' chapter by comparing the situation of the Renaissance church to the *trace italienne* system of fortification that developed at that time, while the 'Billboard' chapter seeks to explain the heavy symbolic importance attached to Lepanto. In the second half of the book I have employed a reductionist approach to arrive at a construct of my own, based on a systematic estimate of the probable numbers and armament employed by the two sides, which should lay to rest the idea that the Holy League fleet was a David to the Ottoman Goliath. The object is not to demystify but rather to emphasize that myth and reality cannot be easily disentangled. No galley battle on this scale had been fought since antiquity and it was never to be repeated, so to interpret it we must depend on inherent military probability, and the safe assumption that it rapidly degenerated into a brawl in which the senior commanders could direct only a small number of galleys by personal example. Precisely who did what, to whom and when was shrouded in the dense smoke that limited the perception of the participants to their own immediate surroundings, and much that they reported as fact was merely speculation informed by prejudice and post-battle gossip.

Just as the strategic dimension requires us to examine the context of a Mediterranean world that no longer exists, so a fuller understanding of the operational and tactical levels demands a detailed look at the fighting galley, a weapons system that dominated war in the Mediterranean for millennia only to vanish so completely that today we can only make educated guesses about some of its key characteristics. In Chapter Two I have summarized the current state of scholarly opinion on the subject of Renaissance armament, but the galley remains tantalizingly elusive. Ergonomic analysis has shed light on its performance under oars, but to resolve the contradiction between a large lateen sail that is most effective into the wind and a hull lacking the keel and freeboard to take advantage of it may require a working replica to be built, upon which to rediscover lost skills.[6] With regard to individual weapons, the effectiveness of battleaxe, mace, pike, halberd, single and double-handed sword, arrows and bolts against steel or fabric protection is not self-evident, and we cannot know how far and how accurately a good composite bowman could fire, for the physiognomy shaped by a lifetime of practice is no more. Gunpowder weapons hold fewer mysteries, but their combat effectiveness also remains largely speculative in the absence of reliable casualty figures broken down by cause.

The men behind the weapons were smaller than we are today, but much tougher and with markedly more robust immune systems, who could endure and survive hardship and wounds that today, without anti-biotics and prompt hospitalization, would kill even élite soldiers. On the Christian side vermin crawled on filthy skin even under the finest clothing, although there were eccentrics like Queen Elizabeth of England who famously took a bath every month whether she needed to or not. Galleys were cesspits, deliberately submerged from time to time to reduce the stench and to drown infestations of lice, fleas and rats. The 'quality' were more flowery in speech, but the words they committed to paper show an attention to nuance we may safely assume was also a characteristic of conversation at a time when all were armed, alert to even a hint of insult and quick to avenge it. What we now term poor impulse control policed upper class notions of honour, and was the margin between life and death among swaggering soldiers and bullying bravos of all descriptions.

All this before even confronting the formal enemy, in this case the infinitely more hygienic Muslims, who were far ahead of their opponents in medical understanding, more prosperous and cultured, and who produced much of the finery under which upper-class western European lice led stress-free lives. Ironically, the gilt embroidery that trims the Virgin Mary's satin cowl in some Renaissance paintings is Arabic script and reads 'There is no God but God and Muhammad is his prophet'. If they could bridge the cultural chasm, modern Europeans might more easily identify with refined Ottoman sensuality than with their own comparatively crude ancestors. But at the time western propaganda portrayed them as the befoulers of sacred places and, when not buggering each other – Shakespeare wittily dubbed them 'Ottomites' – serial defilers of Christian maidens, their galleys powered by slaves from the lands their locust-like swarms allegedly left barren in their wake.

This was mainly a projection of the darker side of western culture, soon to make itself manifest in the wholesale breakdown of civilized restraint known as the Thirty Years War. Although merciless towards paganism, Islam has always been more tolerant than Christianity of other monotheisms, and the see of the Greek Orthodox Patriarch was still Constantinople, also known as Istanbul following its conquest by the Ottomans in 1453. Jews fleeing Christian persecution prospered and reached positions of authority in the Ottoman regime, which offered a career open to talent regardless of ethnic origin and did not subject the sincerity of religious conversion to forensic scrutiny. On the other side of the religious divide we have Pope Paul IV's description of the Spanish, the most rigorous religious and ethnic cleansers in Europe, as 'those heretics, schismatics, cursed of God, a race of Jews and Moors, the dregs of the world'.

We shall return to these themes in greater detail – here let it suffice to say that anyone who wishes to portray Lepanto as a battle between good and evil on any other than the most abstract metaphysical plane has an uphill task. By modern standards King Philip II of Spain, the Venetian oligarchs and Saint Pius V, the last but one pope to be canonized and the architect of the Holy League, were genocidal bigots, and we would need to paint the Ottomans very dark indeed to make the enemies of their faith shine by comparison. Rather than affirm or rebut the canonical account, I have treated it as a phenomenon with a cultural validity of its own. Reality and myth impinge upon each other in the field of motivation, and this was of fundamental importance in a battle where two armed hosts convinced of the righteousness of their cause shot, hacked and stabbed each other until one was utterly overthrown. Lepanto was one of those rare occasions where, even among those worth taking prisoner for the ransom they might command, most only surrendered when too wounded to continue fighting.

The Duke of Wellington declared it no more possible to write an accurate account of a battle than of a ball, but if one attempts it nonetheless, the essential first step is to check the names of those known to have attended against the invitation list, to establish who was there, in what strength and occupying what space. It is surprising how many anomalies this exercise alone detects. The Orders of Battle in *Appendix C* produce lower totals than those usually given because I have purged them of minor vessels (fustas, brigantinas and fragatas) and of the duplications and uncertain identifications in contemporary lists.[7] Lastly many of the Ottoman names are my best guess at what emerged from prisoner interrogations, transcribed according to Spanish and Venetian rules of spelling and pronunciation. The battle maps are also the first in which every galley has been depicted and in which a unifying explanation of the depictions by contemporary illustrators is offered. In conjunction with the Appendices, the maps submit the working documents upon which I based my interpretation for the reader's scrutiny. Feedback is welcome and I will incorporate, and gratefully acknowledge, any illuminating technical correction or convincing alternative interpretation in future editions.

Although this book skates briskly over controversies dear to the hearts of academic historians, it leans heavily on the growing body of monographs generated by their polemics. The selection of the data upon which even the best informed opinion is based cannot be other than subjective, and there are some important questions to which there may never be fact-based answers. Rather than hedge the narrative about with qualifiers I refer those who wish to explore certain issues in greater depth to the *Endnotes* and the *Bibliography*. As well as sourcing quotations, these refer to works that fail the penguin test, a term drawn from the anecdote about a child who asks a librarian for a book on penguins and is given a handsome, richly illustrated volume, which she returns because it contains more than she wishes to know about penguins. What they also contain are fuller notes, references and discussions of particular issues than would be appropriate in a book that seeks to give an overview of them all.

I have translated technical terms where there is an accurate equivalent in English, and refrained from doing so in the interest of brevity or where there is a unique connotation. Thus 'one man per oar' and 'three [or more] men per oar' rather than *alla sensile* and *al scaloccio* for the two methods of rowing used in the galleys at Lepanto, but *mosquete* rather than 'musket' for the Renaissance equivalent of an anti-tank rifle, *pedrero* rather than 'cannon designed to fire a stone ball', *sipahis* instead of 'non-hereditary feudal service Ottoman cavalry' and the anglicized 'conquistadors' rather than 'Spanish explorer/conquerors'. I have extended this principle to place names as well, choosing whichever of several alternatives seem to me most appropriate. With the exception of Shi'a and its adjective, I have not employed diacritical marks and render Arabic or Turkish words in conventional English forms, fully aware that these seldom reflect proper pronunciation – but for that matter Quixote is pronounced *key-hoh-tay* in Spanish, Florence is Firenze, Leghorn is properly Livorno, and so on. I share Mark Twain's view that 'a man who writes a book for the general public is not justified in disfiguring his pages with untranslated foreign expressions', and have employed previously translated texts where possible. Otherwise, the translations are my own, side by side with the originals in the verse extracts where precise meaning has sometimes been sacrificed to scansion or rhyme.

PART I

ICONIC BATTLE

CHAPTER ONE

THE STAGE

The 'where' of battle is dictated by topography on land and by geography at sea, the proximity of land objectives almost invariably dictating where naval battles take place. This is particularly true of the Mediterranean whose history, as Braudel pleasingly put it, 'can no more be separated from the lands surrounding it than the clay can be separated from the hands of the potter who shapes it'. The peninsulas and islands of its convoluted coastline both define and are defined by it, as a geographical entity and as a socio-cultural influence whose waves rippled out across the surface of the world, occasionally meeting and cancelling each other out but more often breaking on the furthest shores to deposit the seeds of globalization. During the sixteenth century the foundations were laid for the Tokugawa shogunate that was to impose unified authority in Japan until the latter half of the nineteenth century, the Mogul Empire consolidated and expanded its hold on north and central India and the Hindu kingdom of Vijayanagar reached its apogee in the south. These were of greater significance to the majority of the world's population than contemporary events in Europe, but all were influenced by contact with the probing Europeans without much affecting them in return. This worldwide cultural diffusion was similar in kind to the effect of the early Roman Empire within its more limited sphere, and marked it as something uniquely definitive in the history of humankind.

Because the voyages of exploration and conquest were centrifugal, without a balancing reflux, the Mediterranean momentarily became the cultural hub for the whole world, while the common frontier of the Egyptian, Minoan, Greek, Punic, Roman, Byzantine, Latin, Arabic, French, Hispanic and Ottoman civilizations remained the most dynamic social and economic marketplace in the world. Those who fought at Lepanto, therefore, had every reason to believe the outcome would define the mainstream of human history. But not long afterwards there was a paradigm shift and the struggle for supremacy in the Mediterranean faded, to be replaced by the lower intensity operations of those known either as corsairs or pirates, depending on one's point of view. The main players turned their backs on the inland sea not only because there were more attractive prospects or pressing problems elsewhere, but also because it had proved an intractable strategic problem area, where the certain costs of campaigning outweighed even the most optimistic estimate of possible benefits.

America – or at least that part named the United States thereof – later achieved what Europe spectacularly failed to do, namely to marry North European and Mediterranean influences more or less harmoniously, in part because human beings are a pioneer species and when there are not new lands to occupy they turn against each other. The latter process underlay the broad sociological changes in Europe during the sixteenth century, at first beneficial as populations recovered from the Black Death pandemic and reclaimed lands that had fallen into disuse, then malignant as numbers surged and urban concentration increased. Simultaneously, the adoption of financial mechanisms such as letters of credit permitted money to beget money on a scale never before seen, reducing the value of the peasant farmer both as a producer and as a potential soldier. With the exception of Rome, which drew her revenues principally from land rents and contributions from the faithful worldwide, the cities at the epicentre of the Italian Renaissance became rich through finance and trade. The wealth generated by commerce paid for elaborate fortifications as well as cathedrals, and hired professional soldiers as well as sculptors and painters, while the standard of living of the common man deteriorated not merely relative to the powerful but in absolute terms.

There were other contributory factors in what, taking an optimistic view of underlying human nature, we might call the beginning of the Age of Inhumanity, but as it affects our story the post-pandemic population surge is the most important, providing an explanation for the fact that so many of the wretched rowers propelling the galleys at Lepanto were technically volunteers, because life ashore was even worse. Across the centuries, a letter by the Genoese military and financial entrepreneur Gian'Andrea Doria to Don Juan in 1572 retains the power to jolt: 'the poor find it difficult to survive, especially in winter when the need for clothing is added to the lack of bread and there is no possibility of work. . . . So next spring it will be possible to collect voluntary prisoners at Genoa for the manning of ten galleys'. As we shall see, those who came to depend on this spiritless and unskilled jetsam developed a new form of galley warfare, one in which rowers were no longer expected to pull individual oars or to double as combatants, but this in turn reflected a chronic dearth of appropriately skilled men.

The Mediterranean has never been a bountiful resource, having little of the continental shelving where marine life abounds, while most of the coasts around it are only marginally productive. Its shores never sustained a seagoing population comparable to that of the northern coasts of Europe, nor were its woods able to regenerate themselves fast enough to keep pace with the shipbuilding requirements of competing empires. By the end of the century the western Mediterranean powers increasingly looked to the north for both timber and sailors, only to be invaded by more than they wanted of both under English and Dutch flags. Timber was not a problem for the Ottomans, who could draw upon the vast resources of the Black Sea forests, but the shortage of skilled crews was a very real constraint and probably definitive in curtailing their maritime ambitions. The Venetians were aware of this and implored their Holy League allies to forgo ransom and put to death the Ottoman sailors captured at Lepanto, even though many of them were Orthodox Christian Greeks.

The rivers flowing into the Mediterranean do not replace the water lost through evaporation, so there is constant replenishment from the Atlantic through the Gibraltar bottleneck and through the Bosphorus from the Black Sea, into which massive river systems drain. The combined effect is an overall system of counterclockwise currents, with a clockwise spin-off in the Gulf of Sidra. *Map 3* shows the pattern of currents and summer winds above a summary of major naval or amphibious events, which together persuasively suggest that geophysical considerations were at least as important as geographical proximity in the division of the

Mediterranean into eastern and western spheres of influence. From the east, any advance along an African coast with few sources of drinking water was precluded by the combination of adverse currents and the winds prevailing during the summer campaigning season. Ottoman armies perforce were shipped from Greece, but this exposed their lines of communication to predation by the Knights of Saint John in Malta, a thorn in their side they attempted to remove without success in the famous siege of 1565. The Ottoman presence in the western Mediterranean was chiefly maintained by semi-autonomous corsairs who favoured the galliot, better under sail and more seaworthy than the larger galley, because they regularly undertook longer stages at sea than anybody else.[1]

From the west, galleys from Spain had the benefit of a following current along the North African coast, but secure harbours were few and expensive to maintain while wind conditions could be treacherous, so for longer forays the usual approach was past France, down the coast of Italy and across from Sicily. Although usually balanced by favourable winds, this route also faced adverse currents, particularly where the slight tidal difference between the Tyrrhenian Sea and the Mediterranean was exaggerated by the narrow straits of Messina. A different technical practice evolved in response to this and to the frequency of harbours along the way, and although Spanish, French and Italian corsairs also favoured less labour-intensive vessels, the western galley (*ponentina*) was generally a heavier, shorter-ranged and more powerful warship than the lighter eastern type (*levantina*) preferred by the Venetians and Ottomans.

Another meteorological determinant for the division of the Mediterranean into two spheres of influence was that the campaigning season of tolerably predictable, moderate weather began earlier in the eastern Mediterranean, giving Ottoman seaborne operations a head start on those of their rivals. This usually worked to their advantage but did not at Lepanto, where half the Ottoman fleet was under strength and sluggish after trying to do too much in one year. Although the ponderous assembly of the galleys of the Holy League may have ensured their crews were fresher, it also meant that head winds nearly prevented them reaching the Gulf of Patras at all, and there was no time left to follow through on their crushing victory. The penalty for operating outside the normal campaigning season could be severe: when Emperor Charles V, galled by insolent

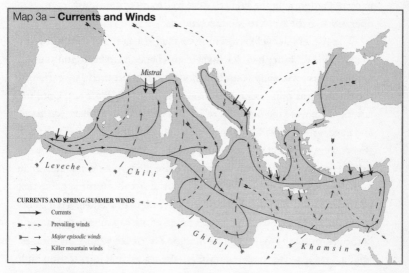

Map 3a – **Currents and Winds**

Mistral

Leveche　　*Chili*

Ghibli　　*Khamsin*

CURRENTS AND SPRING/SUMMER WINDS

→ Currents

⊷ → Prevailing winds

⊶ → *Major episodic winds*

→ Killer mountain winds

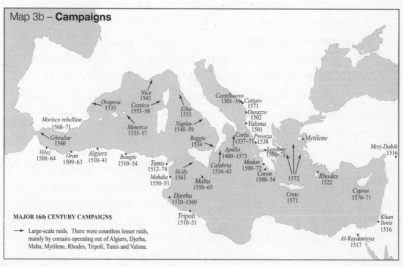

Map 3b – **Campaigns**

Oropesa 1535

Nice 1543

Corsica 1553–58

Elba 1553

Castelnuovo 1501–39

Cattaro 1571

Durazzo 1502

Valona 1501

Morisco rebellion 1568–71

Gibraltar 1540

Menorca 1535–57

Naples 1548–59

Reggio 1534

Corfu 1537–71

Preveza 1538

Mytilene

Merj-Dabik 1516

Vélez 1508–64

Oran 1509–63

Algiers 1510–41

Bougie 1510–54

Tunis 1512–74

Apulia 1480–1573

Lepanto 1500–71

Sicily 1561

Mahdia 1550–51

Calabria 1536–43

Modon 1500–72

Coron 1500–34

1572

Rhodes 1522

Cyprus 1570–71

Malta 1550–65

Djerba 1510–1560

Crete 1571

Khan Yunis 1516

MAJOR 16th CENTURY CAMPAIGNS

→ Large-scale raids. There were countless lesser raids, mainly by corsairs operating out of Algiers, Djerba, Malta, Mytilene, Rhodes, Tripoli, Tunis and Valona.

Tripoli 1510–51

Al-Raydaniyya 1517

31

corsair raids, ignored expert advice and assaulted Algiers in late October 1541, his fleet was shattered by a storm, his army stranded and forced to capitulate. For several years thereafter the Ottoman and allied corsair fleets, in combination with the French, were free to mount seriously damaging operations in the western Mediterranean.

The Algiers debacle is a reminder that just as those inhabiting the Mediterranean shores had to win their sustenance from both land and sea, neither on its own being bountiful enough to support them, so warfare in the theatre was quintessentially amphibious (*B&W Plate 6a*). Until the advent of railways the transport of heavy items such as artillery was faster and cheaper – and over broken terrain only practicable – by sea or river. Rivers were a predictable medium, but the movement of armies by sea risked encountering a storm that might erase them more completely than even the most comprehensive defeat in battle. Yet this was the game that had to be played, because the open sea was a no-man's-land and the coasts could only be secured within visual range of a small number of natural harbours, or places that could be modified to create secure anchorages. Inland, artillery had rendered obsolete the traditional fortification built on a naturally dominant feature (hence *rocca*, the Italian word for fortress), but the typical Adriatic, Aegean and Ionian fortified port was built into an escarpment and presented a would-be besieger with a fiendishly complicated tactical equation. From the landward side, terrain offered even old-fashioned, high fortress walls the protection from direct fire that the low profile ramparts of the bastioned *trace italienne* system of fortification (*Diagram 2*) sought to recreate on the plains, while even the largest galley was outgunned and fatally vulnerable to plunging fire from land artillery.

For as long as a fortified port remained open to receive supplies and reinforcements it could hold out indefinitely against any except the most sustained assault, and prolonged blockade was not an option for galleys unless they had a safe anchorage nearby – hence the priority given by the Ottoman commanders to taking the fort of St Elmo on the headland between the Grand Harbour and the parallel bay of Marsamuscetto during the siege of Malta in 1565 (*Map 6*). A prudent besieger also offered the defenders hope for decent treatment if they capitulated, against the certainty of sadistic slaughter if they did not, underlining that all warfare is ultimately psychological. Where the enemy chose to give battle in the open, an outright decision such as the Ottoman conquest of Syria and Egypt in 1516–17 could be achieved relatively quickly. But seemingly insignificant fortified places, especially if built on solid rock like St Elmo and difficult to attack by mining, could blunt the teeth even of an army well equipped with siege artillery. A coastal stronghold with an arid hinterland, manned by a garrison that did not care what happened to the local civilian population, posed a conundrum unamenable to strictly military solutions. The cheapest and sometimes the only solution was to bribe the defenders and offer them safe passage to somewhere other than the territory of whoever had hired them.

When drawing *Map 1* of the western and *Map 2* of the eastern Mediterranean in the sixteenth century, I abandoned the convention of marking land frontiers because they give the impression that the political units of the time exerted something akin to the territorial control a modern reader will associate with national boundaries. They did not, and an accurate graphical presentation of the bewildering variety of spheres of authority prevailing during the sixteenth century would be virtually indecipherable. Thus Ceuta in Morocco and Messina in Sicily remained republics – and a source of annoyance to Iberian viceroys – throughout this period, and the Aegean islands of Paros, Ios and Stampalia (Astipálaia), lost to the Ottomans in 1540, were not the possessions of Venice as a polity but the property of the Pisani, Quirini and Venier families respectively. Local accommodations permitted the Lomellini of Genoa to continue to lease the coral-producing islet of Tabarka from the Spanish crown until 1786, despite its being within sight of the northern coast of Tunisia, but in 1566–67 the Ottomans took Chios from the Genoese Giustiniani, Naxos from the Crispi, Andros from the Sommaripa and Sifanto (Sífnos) from the Gozzadini. These were the price paid by the Genoese for their otherwise extremely profitable alliance with Spain, although the last two were regained by the Holy League in 1572, Naxos only briefly but Sifanto until 1617.

What I have done instead is to mark the places I shall be mentioning, and ask the reader to imagine a patchwork quilt of micro-terrains with their own unique history, determined to uphold their own customary rights against the authority of their nominal overlords. We shall discuss the major players and their interaction in a later chapter, but some of the supporting cast have been so resistant to external influences as to merit consideration as part of the geographic features that shaped them. The paradigms are the Afghans, and following the September 2001 assault on the United States most of my readers now know that for centuries they have kept their fighting skills honed by endless tribal warfare, uniting only to savage any outsider rash enough to invade their desolate land. Thus also the highland Albanians, Berbers, Calabrians, Corsicans, Druse, Karamanids, Kurds, Montenegrins and Sards, fierce tribes scattered around the Mediterranean perimeter, whom Thomas Hobbes might have had in mind when he wrote, 'no arts; no letters; no society; and which is worst of all, continual fear and danger of violent death; and the life of man, solitary, poor, nasty, brutish, and short'. But throughout history, when shown a new weapon or combat technique the mountain tribesmen have swiftly made it their own, and with the exception of a few conquerors of the 'kill 'em all, let God sort 'em out' persuasion such as the truly dread Timur (Tamerlane), they have been a thorn in the side of every national or supranational entity that has ever tried to control them.

With every economically viable niche in the mountains and high plateaus filled, surplus men perforce made their way to the lowlands and coasts where, being both fearless and trained for war since childhood, they made much-sought-after mercenaries. The best known were the merciless Swiss, invincible through much of the fifteenth and well into the sixteenth century but lacking the political organization to make lasting conquests in their own right, unlike the Ottoman Turks who emerged from obscurity as mercenaries and eventually absorbed their erstwhile employers. All the tribes mentioned above were present at Lepanto, some fighting for both sides. Uluch Ali, an Algerian corsair of Calabrian origin, commanded the Ottoman Left Wing, while many other Calabrians and the strong contingent of Corsicans serving on Venetian galleys would have preferred to fight against their Spanish and Genoese overlords. The Ottoman fleet included a squadron of Albanian corsairs from Valona, now Vlore/Vlora and still a city associated with organized crime, while the entourage of the Venetian grandee Niccolò Suriano included descendants of the Albanian national hero George Castriotis, an Ottoman governor (Iskander Bey, hence 'Skanderberg') who led a successful rebellion in the mid fifteenth century.

If not quite in the same class as the quasi-geological mountain tribesmen, the long ribbon of Italianate Slav civilization between the Julian and Dinaric Alps and the north-eastern Adriatic owed no less to a topography that permitted a degree of autonomy, despite being caught between the rock of Ottoman expansion and the hard place of Venetian and Austrian resistance to it. The star tightrope walker was the city state of Ragusa (Dubrovnik), an oligarchical republic with appetizing shipbuilding and trade resources, which preserved her independence at the price of nominal tribute despite being surrounded by the annexationist Ottoman Empire, hated by her commercial rival Venice, cut off from direct support by either branch of the Hapsburg Empire, and even her devotion to the Roman church arousing the acute suspicion with which that august institution has always regarded enthusiasm.

Further north, the inhabitants of Dalmatia and the Istrian peninsula were somewhat less menaced by the Ottomans than by the mutual hostility of their Christian neighbours. Cut off from the Venetian mainland by the Austro-Hungarian province of Carniola, which reached out to the Adriatic at Trieste and Fiume (Rijeka), and permanently at war with the nest of low-rent Croatian pirates (*Uskoks*) at Senj (*Map 4*), they were the only non-metropolitan people to profess something akin to loyalty towards Venice and were her most dependable source of fighting rowers, if at a price grudgingly paid by their tight-fisted employers. When Shakespeare made the villain of *The Merchant of Venice* an anti-Jewish stereotype, he was clearly unaware that the vengeful avarice he attributed to Shylock was regarded as typically Venetian by the many enemies of the Most Serene Republic.

Geography has long defined the political destiny of this much-disputed corner of the Mediterranean. The Ottomans merely seized the crown of the Byzantine Empire when they took Constantinople in 1453, having long before assumed most of its territorial mantle. Of all the ways in which western historians have understated the Ottomans' achievements, the discounting of their justified claim to be considered the true successors of the Roman Empire has been the most marked. For example Vienna, the prize that was forever to remain beyond their grasp, had been a major Roman fleet base and was regarded as part of their historical inheritance. Other Asiatic hordes were assimilated by the civilizations they overran, but the Ottomans learned from those they conquered without losing their

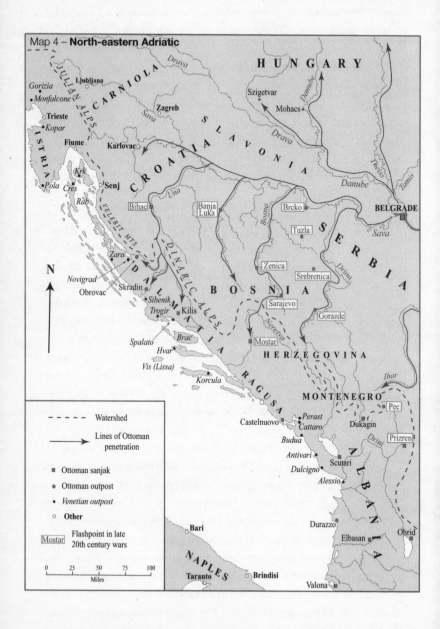

Map 4 – **North-eastern Adriatic**

HUNGARY

Gorizia
Monfalcone
Trieste
Kopar
Pola
Cres
Rab

Ljubljana

JULIAN ALPS

CARNIOLA

Drava

Szigetvar

Mohacs

Danube

Zagreb

Sava

S L A V O N I A

Drava

Fiume

Karlovac

Krk

Senj

C R O A T I A

Una

Bihac

Banja Luka

Brcko

BELGRADE

Theiss

Danube

Tamis

VELEBIT MTS

Zara

Novigrad

Obrovac
Skradin

D A L M A T I A

DINARIC ALPS

B O S N I A

Tuzla

Zenica

Srebrenica

Sarajevo

Drina

S E R B I A

Sava

Bosna

Sibenik
Trogir

Kilis

Spalato

Brač
Hvar

Vis (Lissa)

Korcula

Nereva

Mostar

Gorazde

H E R Z E G O V I N A

R A G U S A

Ibar

M O N T E N E G R O

Pec

N

Castelnuovo

Perast
Cattaro

Dukagin

Prizren

Budua

Antivari

Scutari

Drin

Dulcigno

Alessio

A L B A N I A

Drin

Bari

Durazzo

Elbasan

Ohrid

N A P L E S

Taranto

Brindisi

Valona

Legend:

- - - - Watershed

———▶ Lines of Ottoman penetration

■ Ottoman sanjak

● Ottoman outpost

• Venetian outpost

○ Other

Mostar Flashpoint in late 20th century wars

0   25   50   75   100
Miles

36

own identity. As a people defined by war, among the first things they copied were the means to defeat their opponents, and perhaps their most significant borrowing was the practice of waterborne campaigning learned from the Byzantines, with particular emphasis on the use of rivers to extend their dominions. As it affects our story and, as *Map 4* suggests, events even 500 years later, the Ottoman advance along the Sava and its tributaries is the most significant. But it was the Morava–Ibar system, which joins the Danube below Belgrade, and the avenues provided by the Maritza and Vardar rivers from the Aegean that doomed the Balkan principalities (*Map 2*). The process was well advanced before the fall of Constantinople, but afterwards all of Serbia was occupied by 1459, Bosnia by 1463 and Herzegovina by 1483, while even Montenegro accepted vassal status in 1499.

It was not so much the physical barrier of mountains that defined the extent of the Ottoman Empire, rather the navigable length of logistically indispensable rivers.[2] The Ottoman way of war can be compared to a tidal bore originating in Istanbul (Constantinople) and Edirne (Adrianople), gathering power as it advanced through the settlements along the great Balkan rivers until it encountered an obstacle or the stream beds could no longer contain it. The wave might destroy the obstacle or swirl damagingly around it, but unless it could win land to award to its soldiers and create a new source of energy to extend the trajectory of a subsequent surge, the end of the campaigning season would see it dispersed again along the length of its advance. The areas of flow and ebb between Buda and Vienna, and in northern Croatia and Slavonia, became wastelands dotted with fortified outposts and inhabited by irregulars whose endless raids and counter-raids became the stuff of legend. Although, as we shall see, the Ottomans tried to follow the same procedure in their seaborne campaigns, they could not recreate the cumulative striking power of their riverine operations and the usual rules of relative distance from supply bases came into play. This shaped the political map of the north-eastern Adriatic, where Ottoman outposts in Dalmatia depended on tenuous lines of supply across the watershed and could not be dependably reinforced by sea while the opposite and northern coasts were in enemy hands. Relatively safe from overland attack but exposed to the seaborne hostility of their deadly commercial rivals at the head of the Adriatic, the Ragusans accepted the status of an Ottoman tributary state, while the inhabitants of Dalmatia and Istria had little choice but to throw in their lot with Venice.

Across the Adriatic, most northern Italians still regard southern Italy as part of Africa and the dividing line they draw lies either north or just south of Rome, depending on the degree of snobbery involved. But both sides of this horizontal division are in turn bisected diagonally by the formidable barrier of the Apennines and Braudel argues that this was the true dividing line, with the two sides facing east and west culturally as well as geographically. In the sixteenth century the word 'Italy' was simply a geographical description, despite a common written language not in any important way more difficult to read than modern Italian. Historians of the period immediately before this use the term 'Latin' (from Latium, the area around Rome) instead, to suggest a notional continuity from the Western Empire through the Roman Catholic church, in contrast to the Greek civilization of the Eastern/Byzantine Empire and its instrument the Orthodox church.

From the time they first became lagoon dwellers the Venetians exploited this divide, first swearing fealty to the Eastern Emperor in defiance of a Rome under the domination of the Franks, later organizing the sack of Constantinople by the Franks of the Fourth Crusade, until at last in 1508 they briefly unified Christendom – against themselves. Their reputation for being the most unprincipled and opportunistic of the Italian states was hard won in a very competitive field and it is as well to remember that the overused adjective 'Machiavellian' was born of this place and time. Not to stray any further from the theme of this chapter, suffice it to underline that despite their close cultural affinities, the subdivisions of Italy more often made common cause with foreign powers – including the alien Ottomans – than with each other, and poor land communications within the peninsula certainly contributed to their chronic fragmentation.

Geography was destiny in North Africa also, where the folds of the mighty Atlas mountains progressively squeeze the area of rewarding human habitation on a diagonal from ancient Mauretania, now Morocco, through western and eastern Numidia, now Algeria and Tunisia. Once the fertile heartland of the Carthaginian Empire, later along with Libya the breadbasket of Rome, climate change and the ecological degradation wrought by the highly destructive goat had greatly reduced the area of land under cultivation by the time we are considering. But it was an area where energies had been channelled into maritime activities long before the Phoenicians arrived from today's Lebanon to found Carthage; just how long is illustrated by the fact that the original inhabitants of the Canary Islands, the first overseas conquests of the Kingdom of Castile, spoke a Berbero-Libyan language that seems not to have included the words of Carthaginian and Latin derivation acquired by other branches of the linguistic group on the African mainland. Spain's overseas holdings today are limited to the Canaries, which include the island of La Gomera; the North African outposts of Ceuta, Melilla and Alhucemas; the Chafarinas Islands – and an uninhabited rock where once stood a fortress that dominated the port of Vélez de La Gomera. The area around Vélez bears the name of the Gomara or Ghomerah, a Berber tribe that has inhabited the central Mediterranean coast of Morocco since ancient times.[3]

When the Vandals under Gaiseric crossed into North Africa from Spain in the mid fifth century, exploiting the death throes of the western Roman Empire, they rapidly developed into a corsair kingdom stretching from Mauretania to Libya, and roamed the Mediterranean at will for a century until destroyed by the great Byzantine commander Belisarius in 533. But the tradition lived on through and beyond the great Islamic expansion of 632–732, under successive Arab dynasties until the Touareg Almoravid dynasty thrust the Saharan Berbers into the mainstream of North African affairs in the eleventh century. The Berber mountain tribes, whose alliance with the Arabs had hugely facilitated the original Muslim conquest of the area, overthrew the Touaregs in turn to found their own Almohad dynasty, after which the much-disputed coast acquired the generic name of Berberia, whence the 'Barbary Coast' of bodice-ripping novel and film. By comparison with the longevity of corsair culture in North Africa, not finally suppressed until the nineteenth century, the Viking era in northern Europe was brief to the point of insignificance, although their descendants the Normans added their contribution to the Mediterranean pot in the eleventh century, conquering Sicily and southern Italy and briefly establishing a colony in Tunisia until thrown out by the Almohads.[4]

Thus the foundations upon which the Barbarossa brothers and Turghud Reis (Dragut) were to build the corsair principalities in the first half of the sixteenth century. At the same time there was a fundamental change in world view, with the concept of a continental 'Europe' replacing a vision of

Christendom that extended to the old frontiers of the Roman Empire and embraced North Africa more closely than northern Europe – Saint Augustine, whose influence on Christian theology is second only to that of Saint Paul, was a native of Numidia and as Bishop of Hippo (Bône) died besieged by Gaiseric in 430. This transition in mental geography certainly began when the Muslim expansion swept across North Africa and into Spain, Gibraltar (originally Jebel al-Tarik) taking the name of the leading invader Tarik ibn Ziyad, but the straits he crossed were not recognized as a natural or permanent geopolitical and cultural divide until quite recently. It is deeply misleading to pre-date a nationalist consciousness by labelling those born Christians who became servants of the Ottoman Empire as 'renegades', for they did not see the world in those terms and neither should we. Seafarers throughout the Mediterranean supplemented their income from fishing or trade with smuggling or piracy from time to time, but the specialist corsair states developed because of the unique niche created by geography and accentuated by climate change along the coast of North Africa.

If oceanography, climatology, geology and geography provided the stage, the backdrop featured a common deadly enemy that could defeat the largest fleet or mightiest army. Whenever the players massed for war, particularly if further crowded into vermin-infested ships, they created the optimum conditions for devastating outbreaks of pestilence. In the sixteenth century there were frequent if now less virulent outbreaks of bubonic, pneumonic and septicaemic plague, the key components of the episode of mass extinction known as the Black Death, for which the primary vector was the flea of the black (ship's) rat, as well as of water-borne typhus (tellingly known as 'camp fever') and cholera. There was also a new and improved strain of mosquito-borne malaria imported from the New World, in exchange for a cocktail of pathogens against which the Amerindians had no immunity and which enabled a handful of men to conquer a continent.

It is not clear where syphilis came from, but as well as disabling the French army in Italy in the late fifteenth century (whence the appellation 'French disease'), the sterility it caused extinguished the Valois dynasty of France and contributed to the sordid procreative history of Henry VIII of England. The personal hygiene inculcated by Islam made Ottoman armies less prone to epidemics than the Christian, and, calling into question their allegedly indiscriminate proclivities, they also appear to have suffered less from sexually transmitted diseases, although the explanation more probably lies in a higher degree of acquired immunity, pointing to Asiatic origins for syphilis and possibly gonorrhoea as well. It was not until the discovery of antibiotics in the mid twentieth century that the proportion of soldiers killed by enemy action first exceeded those felled by disease, a factor at least as significant as the uncertainties of the weather in making the Mediterranean powers hesitant to embark upon major seaborne operations, even over comparatively short distances.[5]

All of the above considerations worked powerfully to produce a *normal* condition of strategic stalemate in the Mediterranean. It required an heroic effort to attempt to tip the balance, and the war precipitated by the Ottoman invasion of Cyprus in 1570 was the last time the western powers chose to make it. In Cyprus, as in the conquest of Crete in 1645–46, the native inhabitants were inclined to regard the Ottomans as liberators from their hated Venetian overlords, incidentally underlining that siege warfare was labour-intensive and even the Ottomans could not ship enough men by sea to compensate for lack of support among the local population. For all the skill and heroism of the Knights of Saint John, the fact that the native Maltese regarded them as the lesser of two evils decided the outcome of the great siege of 1565. Unlike the fortresses on Cyprus, which fell relatively quickly (Nicosia embarrassingly so), the Venetian stronghold of Candia held out on Crete until 1669, but only because it became an all-Venetian garrison enclave. Despite near-total domination of the waters around it until 1657, the Venetians could not reverse the verdict of their erstwhile subjects on the rest of the island.

Braudel, whose great work was first published before the French 'civilizing mission' in North Africa had come bloodily unstuck, believed an historic opportunity was missed when the Spanish chose not to build upon ancient Christian foundations after their first wave of conquests along the North African coast in the first decade of the sixteenth century. But the remaining Christians felt no need of liberation, and were anyway outnumbered by embittered Jews and Muslims expelled from Spain, while the Spanish were wealth extractors, not colonists or tradesmen, wherever they went. The effective frontiers of their overseas empire mark where they met with tenacious resistance, for without the possibility of a native population that could be reduced to docility, land alone was of no great interest to men who on many occasions proved they would rather die than work with their hands. From this arose the policy of building forts manned by soldiers from Spain itself (*presidios*), not so much to control the surrounding territory as to deny strategic locations to their enemies. They did not even serve as customs houses or as foci for settlement. There were always alternative ports, with the result that the communities in which they were placed invariably stagnated, and this made the presidios net drains on the exchequer as well as being truly miserable places to be posted.

Thus while it is tempting to regard the presidio system as the residue of an abandoned grand imperial design, they were far from being mere wood shavings on our admittedly rough-hewn Mediterranean stage. The 1559 Treaty of Cateau-Cambrésis, signed the year following the death of Charles V, gave his son Philip II a freer hand in the western Mediterranean than the emperor had ever enjoyed. This Philip exercised to confirm Spanish tenure of four mainland presidio territories including Piombino, long a cause of disagreement, and another on Elba, all covering the coast of supposedly friendly Tuscany. In addition it restored the Duke of Savoy and put him and the Grimaldis of Monaco on notice that Spanish shipping would henceforth cross their tiny stretches of territorial waters without paying for the privilege. In keeping with the spirit of the times they ignored the warning with impunity once Spain became embroiled in the struggle for the Netherlands, while in Tuscany Grand Duke Cosimo dei Medici developed Leghorn as an alternative to Piombino and as a base for his own fleet of corsairs. But Cateau-Cambrésis confirmed a Spanish commitment to the presidio system *in preference* to the maintenance of a fleet to police their lines of communications, a reasonable choice given the strategic and operational factors we have reviewed in this chapter, made compelling by the fragility and cost of the alternative we shall examine next.

CHAPTER TWO

PROPS

The 'how' of battle hinges on weapons and the habits they require of the men who use them. One of the casualties of our time is the venerable didactic device of provocation to stimulate fruitful discussion, replaced by inflexible orthodoxies in which passionate conviction precludes rational discussion. There is no need to give examples of the latter, but the fecundity of the debate sparked by the 'Military Revolution' hypothesis, first proposed by Michael Roberts in 1955 and revitalized by Geoffrey Parker in 1976, marks it as a fine example of the former. The core argument is that gunpowder weapons and attendant military innovations during the sixteenth and seventeenth centuries led to sharply rising costs, which in turn were instrumental in the evolution of the centralized, bureaucratic nation-state. Any lively polemic is likely to have a chicken-and-egg component, but the debate has tended to overlook a greater truth, which is that the significance of technology in warfare is secondary to the varying intensity of the desire to dominate – or the disposition to sacrifice all rather than be dominated – of different social groups over time. Where there's a will, there's a weapon.

The idea that the history of warfare was abruptly transformed by the mobile artillery accompanying the French invasion of Italy in 1494 was first mooted in *Storia d'Italia*, written at the end of his life by the Florentine Francesco Guicciardini (1483–1540), seeking to make sense of the disasters that had befallen Italy in his lifetime. It has had a long shelf-life, although siege artillery had already featured prominently in the expulsion of the English from France in 1453, marking the end of the Hundred

Years War, in the fall of Constantinople the same year, and in the final decade of the centuries-long Reconquest of Iberia ending with the fall of Granada in 1492. Had cannon permitted the weaker party to prevail in any of these wars we might more confidently judge them to have been decisive, but instead concentration, in both senses of the word, was as usual the definitive factor. The issue is of particular relevance to Lepanto, where the basic technology of the principal weapons platform – the oared galley – was thousands of years old, but where the concept of a gunpowder revolution has heavily influenced the historiography of the battle. This owes much to Venetian accounts that emphasize the role of artillery, in which they were strong, to finesse the embarrassing fact that the best infantry on board their galleys came from Spain and her dominions in Italy. Any credit that could not be attributed to the guns perforce accrued to the infantry, and the Venetians were not alone in believing Spanish triumphalism posed a more present danger once the Ottoman threat was blunted.

The design continuities in galley construction from ancient times were not solely the result of working with organic materials within the parameters set by natural forces. There seems always to have been a referential element, a carry-over from previous designs even when new materials did not demand it, as in the exaggerated curvature (sheer) of the hull from bow to stern and the inward-pointing extremities that were a functional necessity in the bundled reed craft in which Palaeolithic man first put to sea. Reeds are like straws and tying them off at bow and stern with the same rope to lift them out of the water serendipitously countered hogging, the stress caused when a wave lifts only the centre of the vessel, while the sheer countered the opposite problem of sagging in the trough. Narrow vessels of wooden construction such as the classical Greek triremes still required some sheer and a tensioned cable attached to strong points in the bow and stern, but their ornate, inward-curving bow and stern posts served no functional purpose – and had not for millennia. Two thousand years later still, it was reflected in the exaggerated upward sweep of the stern on the galleys at Lepanto, while the richly decorated spur in the bows was a vestigial reminder of the ram it had been in classical times.[1]

In practical terms the bowpost had to be flattened in order to accommodate fixed forward-firing cannon and the stern made heavier to balance them, but the embellishments expressed the tendency of men to identify with the spirit of weapons, historically most pronounced in sailors who depend on their ships to prevail over the elements as well as the enemy. Even the eminently practical Cristoforo da Canal, the Venetian commander in the Adriatic until his death in action against corsairs in 1562, wrote that 'the perfect galley should capture precisely the attributes of a graceful young woman, whose every aspect should manifest swiftness, vivacity and extreme agility'. Form and ritual are of immense and abiding importance not only in preparation for battle but as a sustaining force in combat itself. A cannon with a lion's head at the muzzle was not intrinsically more accurate and reliable than one without, but the decoration made the gun crew feel more proud of it and more inclined to handle it carefully. Decorations picked out in gold leaf did not convey any practical advantage to a warship, but they sent a message to the men on board that it was a valued artefact, one worth fighting for. This without counting the magical element, for if good luck charms, amulets, talismans and individual weapons can be seen as minor gods, each with a single devotee, then crew-served weapons are totems, group cult objects to be propitiated with carefully performed ceremonies so that they may protect those who serve them. To adapt the adage about the scarcity of atheists in foxholes, there may be very few strict monotheists on the eve of battle, or as Richard Holmes puts it:

> Military ritual is more than the delight of martinets, the bane of
> perpetually scruffy soldiers and the abiding interest of a whole sub-
> species of military historians. It is a comprehensive framework of
> behaviour designed to serve . . . as a precaution against disorder and a
> [psychological] defence against the randomness of battle.[2]

An unwillingness to adopt new weapons and tactics might reflect social conservatism or reluctance to write off investments of time and money made in older types and skills, but the comfort of the tried and true when confronting the harrowing uncertainty of battle should not be underestimated. Warfare is not a rational pursuit for those at the cutting edge and has never been characterized by the single-minded pursuit of strictly military effectiveness. It would be extraordinary if changes in the means and methods employed in it were ever more than incremental within a given culture, and for most of history the military ecology of the Mediterranean was self-contained. At sea the process of change was one of extremely slow evolution, because the optimum was arrived at early and improved thereafter only at the margin.

The fighting galley was *not* superseded by the square-rigged carrack or the later galleon (both hereafter 'ship'), and did not disappear completely from the Mediterranean or that other inland sea, the Baltic, until steam replaced muscle power in the nineteenth century. Some paintings depict ships shattering galleys with broadsides (*B&W Plate 8*), but this happened seldom, and if a galley were successfully trapped neither party had any interest in fighting to a finish, the galley because the outcome was certain and the ship because the enemy crew were the most valuable item on board. An invoice of 16 November 1573 records Juan de Austria's purchase of a captured Turkish galley and lists the following priced in escudos, a Sicilian gold coin worth 352 Spanish maravedis, coins containing a little under a gramme of silver:[3]

Woodwork (hull, oars, masts, spars, ship's boat, etc.)	1,800 (28%)
Cables, sails, rigging and supporting ironwork	330 (5%)
One bronze centreline cannon (2,532 lbs)	610
Two bronze sakers (1,115 lbs)	270
Two bronze falconets (496 lbs)	120
71 iron cannon balls	40
Total artillery	1,040 (16%)
32 slaves (plus 100 escudos for chains and bars)	3,300 (51%)

If we further calculate that the seller would have retained those captives who had given proof of being worth a ransom greater than 100 escudos, the hardware value of a galley was clearly several times less than that of the human software. A large Ottoman galley such as the one priced here carried a minimum of 150–170 rowers, 50–75 soldiers, a sailing crew of about 30 and a command element of about 15. The slaves captured at Lepanto changed hands at a severely discounted 30 escudos per head, but even at that price the lowest value of the above example, if its entire human complement had been enslaveable and exclusive of ransoms, would have been 8,000–9,000 escudos, the equivalent of around three tonnes of silver and enough to give pause to the most bloodthirsty religious fanatic.

The fighting galley reigned supreme in the Mediterranean throughout the sixteenth century, during which it had to satisfy the demands of endemic warfare as well as coping with the elements. Given that fiercely competing cultures all adopted much the same solutions these were, evidently, the best that could be achieved with the materials and technology available *to accomplish the purpose for which the galley was intended*. This was to act as an instrument of amphibious warfare, and it was the galley's ability to run ashore and off again routinely that explains why the ship could not replace it. The requirement dictated a vessel with a shallow draught powered by oars, which in turn demanded a narrow hull to reduce drag, with the rowers sitting as low as possible not only to achieve the most mechanically efficient stroke, but also because of the inherent instability of the design. The result was a vessel with a waterline length of at least eight times and a draught of one third the beam, a low freeboard and lethally poor seakeeping qualities. Galleys could not compete with the high freeboard ships in rough conditions, but inshore and in light airs they could manoeuvre around them to attack from bow and stern, avoiding the broadside-firing guns and quickly closing to board (*B&W Plate 4*).

Another seldom stressed advantage of the galley over the ship was that it could be built comparatively cheaply and much more rapidly, making it possible for combatants to launch substantial fleets on demand. Faced with unwanted war in 1570, the Venetians added about eighty oared fighting vessels to their permanent fleet within a few months, about half of them entirely new, and provided the Pope with another twelve refurbished hulls, while after the disaster at Lepanto the Ottomans built 150 new galleys in time for the next campaigning season. If the huge Arsenale shipyard (from *darsena*: dockyard in both Italian and Spanish, in turn from the Arabic *dar as sinaa*: house of industry) at Venice was the eighth wonder of the world, as the Venetians have always proclaimed, then the even bigger one at Istanbul was indisputably the ninth. The advantages of this 'surge' capability were many, the foremost being that it was a great deal cheaper to build a fleet when needed than to maintain one in being, such that even Venice, whose much-beset shipping lanes carried her lifeblood, had an active Adriatic fleet of only twenty-four galleys before Lepanto, with a small additional squadron based in Crete.

Unlike ships, even active galleys spent over half their working lives out of the water, not merely to economize on personnel costs but because the Mediterranean provides a rich culture for marine infestation, in particular the teredos worm which is to wooden ships what the death-watch beetle is to timbered houses. Weed and barnacles also rapidly increased drag and galleys had to be brought ashore monthly to scrape the hull and to apply a liberal coat of expensive tallow. An active galley had a short life expectancy, but one laid up ashore could last almost indefinitely – one of the galleys given to the Pope in 1570 was originally built as a quinquereme *bastarda* (see below) by the master shipwright Vettor Fausto in 1529.[4] In contrast large ships spent most of their lives in the water, cost more to maintain while laid up and, even after the discovery that copper sheathing discouraged marine infestation, had to be rolled to a dangerous angle for scraping. Given the daunting level of attrition that unpredictable weather and inexact navigation imposed on both types, the cheaper and more easily 'stored' galleys provided a more appropriate response to the demands of warfare in the Mediterranean.

Optimized for oar propulsion and with a high centre of gravity, galleys were very far from ideal sailing vessels, but a large lateen sail rigged on two long yards bound together along about a quarter of their length (*antenna*), set diagonally on a low mast mounted one third of the length from the bow, resolved two problems in one. Even a moderate headwind could render forward progress under oars impossibly demanding, but the lateen was most effective into the wind and although the galley hull lacked the bite in the water to take full advantage of this, it could still sail a course five compass points from the wind. A further point could be gained and leeward drift corrected by the employment of half the oars – front or back, working in shifts and with the unused oars feathered and held flat by a rope loop that permitted them to be brought back into action quickly. This was the normal mode for cruising and was known as 'quarter rowing'. Variations in the height of the mast seem to have been a function of the physical weight of the sails and antennae employed. Canal complained that the single sail made of heavy canvas on a short mast preferred by the Venetians put them at a disadvantage under sail even by comparison with the heavier western Mediterranean types, which could choose from three sails of different sizes and lighter material, while Ottoman sails were the lightest of all.

The ever-present danger of dipping the leeward side under water appears to have been handled by using the unemployed oarsmen as moveable ballast, although how this can have been accomplished with chained rowers is not apparent. In addition the large single oars, which with their counterweighted butts weighed about 130kg each, could be pushed under the midships gangway to the other side of the galley, permitting trim to be fine-tuned with the shift of over 3 tonnes in an ordinary galley. With a following wind the antenna would be 'goose-winged', swung across the hull and nearly horizontal to the mast, while all the oars might be lifted clear of the water and lashed. Although the evidence for these techniques comes from eighteenth-century writings by French sailing masters, the western Mediterranean galley did not evolve much after Lepanto and most if not all of them were common practice by the late sixteenth century.

Like the early galleons, large galleys were pigs to steer under sail in light air and initially employed a square sail on a second, shorter and forward-leaning mast at the bow to help bring them around. In the ship this developed into the bowsprit, but the forward-firing armament of the galley precluded this and instead it developed into a foremast and sail almost as large as the main. The Venetian galleasses, the converted merchant galleys (*galere grosse*) that played an important but equivocal role at Lepanto, had three masts – one near-contemporary engraving shows a fourth acting as a proto-bowsprit – while twin side-steering oars as well as a rudder bear witness to how unhandy they were. Yet they managed to keep up with the fleet when the square-rigged troop and supply ships fell behind, and this cannot have been thanks to the twenty-seven five-man oars they mounted per side, set higher and therefore at a less efficient angle than on the fighting galleys, proof of which is that at Lepanto they had to be towed out in front of the line and were unable to rejoin the battle after the Ottoman fleet had passed around them. The answer may be that they coped well with the strong headwinds that almost kept the Christian fleet from reaching the Gulf of Patras, less well with light breezes on the day of battle.

A further absolute constraint on galley design was the law of diminishing returns with regard to the poor power–weight ratio of human beings, such that beyond a certain number the additional mass of extra rowers plus the added drag of a hull made larger to accommodate them cancelled out their efforts. By about 1540 the norm was twenty-four to twenty-six three-man rowing benches per side, with the space of one bench per side taken up by platforms for the ship's boat and the baker's oven, which would be cleared to become the place where boarding parties assembled before battle. Thirty years later normal western Mediterranean galleys were powered by three or four men pulling one oar (*a scaloccio*) while flagship (lantern) galleys of twenty-seven to thirty benches used five or more. The perhaps apt name *bastarda* or *bastardella* designated galleys with more than three individual oars per bench (*alla sensile*), on which the inner rowers could ship their oars and act as pikemen in battle without serious loss of propulsion, whereas the innermost man on the large single oars was not only the most mechanically efficient but also set the pace. The best-equipped galleys also carried a 'quarter' of about one spare rower per bench, and these may have doubled as pikemen in battle. Paintings of Lepanto show mainly the (much easier to depict) single oar system, but some Ottoman and Venetian galleys – and all the smaller craft – employed individual oars or a combination of the two types.

Diagram 1 gives an overhead view of a typical Venetian line galley. Infantry command posts were the forecastle, the stern, the midships ramp between them, the ship's boat and oven platforms, and the two lateral parapet (*arrumbada*) commands per side divided by them, all of which had to balance each other fore and aft as well as laterally. This was complicated by the rectangular rowing frame, which extended beyond a shallow hull that flared outwards at about 30 degrees and provided outriggers for the oars. However, it also multiplied the weight of the soldiers standing at the sides behind heavy wooden shields (*empavesada*) or mattresses, leverage more pronounced towards the bow and stern where the hull narrowed and the flare increased to about 45 degrees. Until two galleys locked together, any rush to the point of impact would lower a galley's defences precisely when and where they were most needed.

For three-man benches the single oar was less efficient than individual oars; however, the latter required affordable free men – especially as they were expected to fight as well – who were in declining supply everywhere, particularly in the western Mediterranean. In between these and the chained slaves and criminals was the intermediate category of rowers,

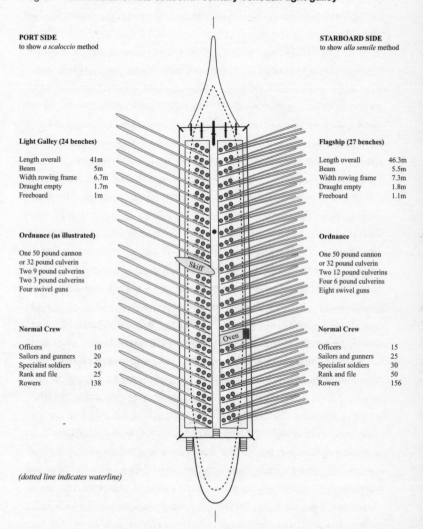

Diagram 1 **Schematic of late sixteenth century Venetian light galley**

PORT SIDE
to show *a scaloccio* method

STARBOARD SIDE
to show *alla sensile* method

Light Galley (24 benches)

Length overall	41m
Beam	5m
Width rowing frame	6.7m
Draught empty	1.7m
Freeboard	1m

Flagship (27 benches)

Length overall	46.3m
Beam	5.5m
Width rowing frame	7.3m
Draught empty	1.8m
Freeboard	1.1m

Ordnance (as illustrated)

One 50 pound cannon
or 32 pound culverin
Two 9 pound culverins
Two 3 pound culverins
Four swivel guns

Ordnance

One 50 pound cannon
or 32 pound culverin
Two 12 pound culverins
Four 6 pound culverins
Eight swivel guns

Normal Crew

Officers	10
Sailors and gunners	20
Specialist soldiers	20
Rank and file	25
Rowers	138

Normal Crew

Officers	15
Sailors and gunners	25
Specialist soldiers	30
Rank and file	50
Rowers	156

(dotted line indicates waterline)

51

usually Greeks, conscripted by what the Royal Navy was later to call press gangs, who were adequately skilled but could be depended upon to turn on their masters if the battle went against them. Christians or criminals condemned to the galleys might have their chains symbolically removed before battle, but a prudent rowing master might at the same time shackle his pressed rowers.

The only detailed analysis we have of the workings of any of the fleets involved was written by Canal, who complained that even in the permanent Venetian fleet each galley operated largely according to the whim of its commander. He identified the factors that led to the universal adoption of the heavy single oar pulled by unfree rowers after Lepanto, noting greater breakage among the lighter oars and the tendency of free rowers to cause trouble ashore, or to desert in order to obtain signing-on bonuses from other galleys. The most important reason for the abandonment of the one man per oar system was probably the need to reduce the allotment of personal trade goods carried by the galleys, of greater significance than wages in the recruitment of volunteers, in order to mount more artillery. This was just one of many trade-offs a galley commander had to make in a system so finely balanced that fighting power in pitched battle could only be bought at the expense of the speed and range that made for greater success in normal, lower intensity operations.[5]

The full-scale replica of Don Juan's flagship in the Museu Marítim, Barcelona, weighs 237 tonnes empty, required 290 rowers (about 17 tonnes), carried over 300 sailors, soldiers and gentlemen adventurers (maybe 21 tonnes including arms and armour), who consumed a minimum of 2 tonnes of food and (mainly) water a day, considerably more in hot weather or when working hard, which steadily reduced the ballast of an intrinsically top-heavy vessel. By comparison the mass of guns in the bow may seem inconsiderable, but *La Real* was a 'pure' battleship and her weight distribution is not a useful guide to the problems the captain of a 150 tonne Venetian 'line' galley had to resolve, not the least of which was that every extra man or gun on board decreased cruising range and ate into a limited cargo capacity that together were more certainly profitable than the occasional capture of prizes.

Ottoman practice was significantly different, reflecting both their land tactics of overwhelming an enemy with numbers and the fact that the bulk of their troops were archers, accustomed to fighting from the moving platform of a horse but not to close-order drill. Although their galley hulls were wider and the rowing frames correspondingly less prominent, they did not parapet the sides and fought mainly from the midships ramp and the bow, where their preference for fewer cannon and the lighter guns firing stone balls (*pedreros*) allowed them to mass larger boarding parties than the Christian norm. Jacobo Ragazzoni, the Venetian Senate Secretary sent to Istanbul in April 1570 in a last-ditch effort to avoid war, reported that Ottoman galleys carried more extensive rigging than the Venetian norm (presumably because their masts and antennae were lighter), but lacked the crews to make proper use of it because they had no sea militia. In fact they had, and it performed rather better than the Venetian system at times of general mobilization.[6]

> The Turkish galleys are higher than ours; nearly all of them have a single oar per bench, usually rowed by three men, and their oars are much lighter than ours. It is said they use this system in order to tire the rowers less. They cannot carry more than three cannon per galley, and many have only one.[7]

The word 'cannot' is misleading, because the broader Ottoman galley was an intrinsically better heavy weapons platform than the Venetian. What Ragazzoni accurately described but failed to interpret correctly was that the Ottoman design reflected a deliberate choice of seaworthiness and long range troop delivery over the guns in which the Venetians had invested so heavily, and this in turn was a function of the resources on which the two fleets could draw. The Ottoman Empire encompassed a larger population (18–30 million during the century) than Iberia (5–9 million) and Italy (8–13 million) combined, and the strategic conundrum for the Sultan and his advisers, by land or sea, was how to turn that numerical advantage into military effectiveness. Speed was of the essence if anything significant were to be achieved at the frontiers of the empire within one campaigning season, and whatever their virtues in battle and their indispensability in siege warfare, heavy guns slowed land operations to a crawl and reduced the number of soldiers a galley could carry. Their solution on land, convincingly demonstrated at the 1453 siege of Constantinople, was to cast huge bombards on the spot, while at sea their preference for men over guns was unarguably a sensible trade-off in a fleet optimized for amphibious operations.

Tactically, a large western galley (*ponentina*) could pack more ordnance in the bow without fatally compromising trim, but it required more men per oar and had proportionally less space aboard for their food and water, the gain in fighting power paid for in diminished combat radius. But once inertia had been overcome, its greater momentum tended to even out the effects of drag between oar strokes, permitting a higher top speed under oars that enabled it to run down a lighter eastern galley (*levantina*). Although a levantina could, in theory, dodge a ponentina's bow armament and counter-attack from the sides or astern, galleys seldom cruised alone and could cover each other's flanks while reducing the enemy's room for manoeuvre by pursuing in line abreast. In any engagement involving equal numbers – properly handled – the lighter craft were doomed unless they could stay out of range until the rowers in the heavier galleys tired.

Thus the calculation for normal galley warfare, involving modest squadrons and revolving around commerce raiding and small-scale amphibious operations to raid coastal settlements. Open sea encounters were extremely rare and large fleet actions even more so, the typical engagement between fighting galleys being an ambush carried out within sight of the coasts they all hugged. Those caught at a tactical disadvantage, be it positional or numerical, ran away if they could, ashore if they could not, or surrendered after generally token resistance. Both Dragut, the founder of the Tripoli corsair principality, and his great opponent Jean de la Valette, Grand Commander of the Knights of Saint John during the siege of Malta in which Dragut was killed, spent time chained to rowing benches in enemy galleys, with no one thinking less of them. Some suggest that Muslim commanders carried their treasure with them because of fear that it might be appropriated by the Sultan, to whom in principle everything in the Ottoman Empire belonged, but the custom was also common among Christian commanders. While rich clothing, jewellery and inlaid armour worn off the battlefield can be seen in the same light as a peacock's extravagant mating display, in combat it announced that the life of the wearer was worth a great deal of money to those who spared it.

Entrepreneurial warfare has logical limits and can never be as annihilating as struggles over abstract ideals. Combat as a justification for social dominance has even more inherent restraints and, like the longbow and crossbow before them, gunpowder weapons were denounced by the quality not so much because they devalued traditional close-quarters fighting skills and could perforate body armour, but because they were indiscriminate and voided the battlefield contract whereby a wealthy man might be spared for ransom and a poor man might become rich. This trans-actional calculation is implicit in the gently ironic last line of the passage from *Don Quixote* in which the errant knight denounces firearms:

> . . . a devilish invention . . . which allows a base and cowardly hand
> to take the life of a brave knight such that, without his knowing how
> or why, when his valiant heart is full of furious courage, there comes
> some random shot – discharged perhaps by one who fled in terror from
> the explosion the damned machine made in firing – and extinguishes
> one who deserved to enjoy life for many a long year.

There is reason to doubt that any individual missile weapon before the advent of the rifle could penetrate the hardened armour of a well-made helmet or breastplate. The best pieces of armour bore the dimple of a 'proving' shot fired at close range and, as late as 1815, British infantry recorded the rattle of musket balls bouncing off the cuirasses of the French heavy cavalry at Waterloo. Bernardino de Cárdenas, Marquess of Beteta, was killed at Lepanto despite wearing the finest armour money could buy, when a ball from a Turkish swivel gun crushed his chest, deforming but not penetrating his breastplate. However, armour of that quality was the preserve of few, there were always areas that could only be protected by chain mail, and septicaemia may have been a more certain killer of gentlemen than of humbler soldiers, who would have acquired greater resistance from the cuts and abrasions of a less sheltered existence.

A review of the weapons employed at Lepanto calls into question whether the victory of the outnumbered Holy League can be attributed to a compensating imbalance in the number of gunpowder weapons on each side. The figures in *Appendix B* probably overestimate the number of guns in the Holy League fleet and underestimate the Ottoman total, yet once the galleasses are subtracted from the equation, which they were after the first skirmish, the Holy League advantage in heavy ordnance was slight. Although the shock effect and the casualties inflicted by its superiority in medium guns in the moments before the two fleets came together should not be underestimated, thereafter the bow ordnance would only have been fired again by those galleys that were able to disengage from their first opponents to attack others. As to handgunners, the Venetians still employed as many crossbowmen, and the proportion of pole arms (mainly pikes) to handguns (arquebuses and some mosquetes) in a Hapsburg Tercio at this time was about 3:1, which produces a figure of approximately 5,300 hand-gunners for the Holy League, opposed to about 4,000 Janissaries, whose arquebuses were slower to reload but longer and consequently more accurate (*B&W Plate 2c*). The Ottomans also made greater use of swivel and hook guns, so the number of individual firearms in both fleets was probably about the same, and since the majority of the Ottoman soldiers were armed with the lethal composite bow, they had a staggering overall superiority in missile arms.

The windlass-drawn steel crossbow (*B&W Plate 2b*) probably had the best combination of accuracy and penetrating power of all the individual missile weapons in use at Lepanto. In the hands of those who, like the 75-year-old Venetian Admiral Sebastiano Venier, had attendants on hand to keep them supplied with drawn and loaded weapons, its rate of fire was not inferior to the Ottoman recurved composite bow, and of course it required considerably less physical strength and exertion even of those who had to load their own, arguing for greater consistent accuracy through-out the battle. The difference in draw weight was impressive – as much as 200kg for the crossbow against less than half that for the composite bow, although the laminated construction of the latter doubled this by harnessing both elasticity and compression. The shorter crossbow bolt generated less kinetic energy than the long arrow, but at close range both could pierce low quality plate armour and few Ottoman troops even wore chain mail. Bolts and arrows fired at close quarters might go straight through an unarmoured man, whereas the arquebus ball flattened to inflict a more savage wound.[8]

Bows, long or composite, disappeared from the battlefield because they depended on a vanishing peasant culture in which the necessary physique and skill was developed over a lifetime of constant practice. But some other explanation is necessary for the eclipse of the user-friendly crossbows, which were no slower to load, less prone to failure and more accurately lethal than smooth-bore handguns. The answer almost certainly lies in shock, a generally underestimated factor in the military revolution debate. Battles are won by breaking the opponent's spirit and broken armies suffer most of their losses during the subsequent pursuit, with the victorious army often taking higher casualties on the battlefield itself. Visual impact is an important component of shock but noise is more so, and from the paean of the Greek hoplites to the enraged screams encouraged by twentieth-century bayonet-fighting instructors, menacing noise has not only advertised the wrath to come but has intimidated in its own right. Archery, for all its deadliness, was a silent killer with minimal visual impact, whereas guns roared and belched flame and smoke like dragons – not for nothing were bombards also known as basilisks.

Artillery did not become standardized until the later eighteenth century, and at the time of Lepanto there was a bewildering number of lesser dragons, with great variety even within generally recognized categories. The following are only broad approximations and individual weapons in museums may fall well outside them. The rock to cling to is calibre, today synonymous with bore diameter but then a measurement of interior barrel length as a multiple of bore. In 1537 the Italian mathematician Niccolò Tartaglia set out the ratio of calibre to mass of shot in his *La Nova Scientia* and both the Emperor Charles V in 1549 and Henri II of France in 1550 issued edicts about the standardization of calibres for their armies, without noticeable result. Guns were expensive and a 'waste not, want not' attitude prevailed, particularly on Ottoman galleys where antiques lacking trunnions – the pivots at mid-barrel that permitted them to be elevated and depressed – nestled side by side with the latest models.[9]

Bombards and basilisks were very large bore, 8–10 calibre wrought iron or cast bronze muzzle-loading siege guns that might fire iron or stone shot. Cast iron was one third the cost of bronze by weight, but had to be cast thicker and heavier for the same bore, making it a poor choice for larger guns. The cheapest were the wrought iron guns made by binding sheaves of iron together with heated hoops, like a cooper constructing a wooden barrel, hence the name given to the gun tube. These were lighter than bronze guns and those designed to fire lower density stone shot were lighter still, permitting some very large pedreros to be mounted on the centreline of the Ottoman galleys. A wrought iron bombard weighing

1,500 pounds fired a 20 pound stone ball, whereas a bronze culverin type of the same weight fired only a 9 pound iron shot.

Cannon (Italian *canna* – tube) were the most standardized, presaging their adoption as general-purpose artillery on land and sea, and becoming the generic name for industrial ordnance. They were 16–24 calibre cast bronze or cast iron guns ranging from the 12-pounder quarto cannon weighing 2,000–2,500 pounds, through demi-cannon, bastard cannon, cannon serpentine and full cannon to the massive 60-pounder double or royal cannon weighing 10,000–12,000 pounds. 'Bastard' designated a long cannon or a short culverin.

Culverins (Spanish *culebrinas* – snake guns) were longer bronze guns of smaller bore than cannon of the same weight, ranging in calibre from the unflatteringly named *passavolante* (flying past), a 36 calibre 6-pounder weighing around 3,000 pounds, to the bastard culverin, a 22 calibre 12-pounder of about the same weight, although the variations could be enormous. Thus the guns identified as falconets (1- to 2-pounders) and sakers (6- to 9-pounders) on the galley bought by Don Juan in 1573 weighed 250 pounds and 550 pounds respectively, yet museum examples of the former run to 500 pounds and of the latter to 1,500 pounds. Culverins ranged from the falconet through those mentioned plus the falcon, demi-saker, demi-culverin and culverin proper to the 32-pounder (or more) double/royal culverin weighing over 7,000 pounds. Fired horizontally, the distance before the ball first touched the surface ran from 200ft (60m) for the falconet to 650ft (200m) for the royal culverin, 25–30 per cent further than cannon of comparable bore. Extreme distances with the barrel elevated to 45 degrees was ten to fifteen times as great, but accuracy degraded beyond usefulness at these ranges.[10]

The ability of the galley to point itself at a target permitted the bow guns to be fixed in wooden blocks, such that the barrels could be elevated but not traversed. This posed no obstacle to reloading when the guns were breech-loaders, with removable powder chambers held in place by wooden wedges to make a somewhat unsatisfactory seal, but the powerful muzzle-loaders on the centreline were mounted on sliding frames within the blocks, secured by ropes like the carriage guns on ships. These could be drawn back along the central gangway for reloading, but the limited depth of the firing platform would seem to have been a compelling reason to have flanked them with shorter cannon. Nonetheless, the long culverins, which sacrificed weight of shot for range and presumably had to be reloaded from the bow spur, were the preferred armament on Venetian galleys. They had no shortage of ordnance, however, and re-equipped their fleet with the larger-bore cannon for war.[11]

The preference for culverins is explained by the peculiarity of smooth-bore ballistics. Spherical shot rattles along the barrel and, depending on the spin imparted by the last contact before emerging from the muzzle, may hook or slice alarmingly. But it may also acquire topspin, with the effect that many a gratified golfer has observed when a sinfully topped ball bounds straight and true along the fairway, or ricochets to dry land off the surface of a water trap. Short-range smashing power was obviously to be preferred in battle, but in normal police operations the premium was on being able to shatter the rudder or the oars of a fleeing corsair. A high calibre gun like the passavolante gave the pursuer more throws of the random ballistic dice, increasing the chance of skipping a disabling shot into the target.[12]

The Venetians melted down most of the Ottoman guns they were awarded from the spoils of Lepanto because they judged them grossly inferior to their own, and in this area at least their overweening conceit had some basis in fact. A Spanish contemporary judged Venetian guns almost as good as German and Flemish, recognized to be the best:

> . . . the Germans are phlegmatic people and do things more accurately and patiently than the Spanish or the Italians who are choleric people, especially the Spanish who are the most choleric of all; . . . after the castings of Germany, the castings of Venice, where the German style and rules are strictly followed, are considered very good.[13]

In addition to their shared choleric humour, another reason why the Ottomans as well as the Spanish fell behind in the production of ordnance was their chronic shortage of skilled workers, a product of social organizations that can fairly be described as anti-industrial. Technology transfer being a phenomenon as old as trade, they had no difficulty in obtaining superior ordnance for as long as they could pay for it, not a problem for either at the time of Lepanto. The Ottomans also captured a large number of modern guns with Nicosia in 1570, but they still preferred large wrought iron pedreros on the centreline for the operational reasons explained above.

Swivel guns were for close-range work and could be mounted on even the smallest oared and sailing vessels – flagships were accompanied by swift barges (*fragatas*) with twelve or more one-man benches per side, used mainly to transmit orders but also to carry boarding parties to attack the unengaged side of an enemy vessel, in which role they would mount two swivels in the bow. Swivel gun trunnions were held in an iron yoke set into a stanchion, the assembly permitting full elevation and traverse. The longer swivel guns, usually breech-loaders, included the lighter falconets, half-pounder serpentines, and sub half-pounders like the Spanish *esmeril*, Venetian *moschetto* and Turkish *prangi*. The Spanish *morterete*, Venetian *bombardello* and Turkish *darbezen* were short, wider bore swivels that functioned as massive shotguns at point-blank range, making them the weapons of choice to discourage small-boat pirates intent on swarming up the sides of merchant ships. The forecastle guns were decked over on the big ponentinas, protecting the heavy gun crews and creating valuable extra fighting deck space for additional swivel and handgunners.

Spanning the gap between artillery and small arms was the barely portable muzzle-loading *mosquete*, the most user-punishing weapon ever devised. A complete semantic circle was closed in the middle of the seventeenth century, when the term 'musket' replaced 'arquebus' to describe the standard infantry matchlock firearm, for the latter in turn had taken the name of (and was a miniaturized version of) the large German *Hackenbüchse* (hook gun), first employed to defend city walls in the early fifteenth century. The hook held on to the rampart and absorbed the recoil, but when reinvented by the Spanish in the 1520s the mosquete used the more violent 'corned' gunpowder (which had permitted the arquebus to be reduced in size in the 1470s) and was fired from a forked rest, giving it a brutal kick. In the Introduction I called it the Renaissance equivalent of the anti-tank rifle and that was precisely its function, the 'tanks' in question being the French heavy cavalry (*gens d'armes*), who were largely impervious to normal arquebus fire. The arquebus weighed 10 pounds and fired a sub half-ounce projectile; the mosquete 20 pounds and a ball of over 2 ounces, and only large, robust men could handle it. They were accordingly paid extra, and the honorific 'musketeer' survived to distinguish the infantry élite even after the name no longer referred to a distinctive weapon.

It seems probable that the Ottomans developed their own version sooner than the Spanish. Following appalling losses suffered while storming field fortifications defended by hook guns at the second battle of Kosovo in 1448, the élite infantry Janissaries, already equipped with arquebuses, adopted the heavy guns as well. Given that they were regularly pitted against armoured knights in the Balkans for much of the following century, it would be remarkable if they had not retained them. The Spanish Tercio only evolved in the sixteenth century and settled on a 3:1 proportion of mosquetes to arquebuses (*B&W Plate 6a*). If this was the battle-proven optimum, it is reasonable to believe the proportions would have been no different in the Janissary corps, which had been dealing very successfully with the problem the mosquete was reinvented to solve, for very much longer. The hook gun itself was ideal for use at sea and was part of the standard equipment of all the galleys at Lepanto (*B&W Plate 2a*). As the example of the unfortunate Bernardino de Cárdenas testifies, if you hit the container hard enough the contents will not prosper, even if the blow does not penetrate.

Thus the lasting usefulness of percussion weapons (axes and clubs, with or without spikes), which are the oldest weapons wielded by man. In an age when maces are carried by elderly worthies on state occasions, it is easy to forget that its size was once both a practical and symbolic indicator of the strength and virility of the user. For this reason the drooping spiked ball on a chain was perhaps less common than film-makers would have us believe. War clubs were most popular in eastern military cultures and, not coincidentally, the tall turbans gave better protection than the armoured helmet against a blow to the head. Although some sipahis wore body armour and pointed, conical helmets with cheek, nose and neck guards (*B&W Plate 3d*), Ottoman soldiers generally depended on their shields. Like the handgunners in the Christian armies the Janissaries did not even wear steel helmets, but their heavy tunics offered more protection than is usually supposed, witness to which is that Antonio da Canal, a senior Venetian commander at Lepanto, wore a quilted garment of his own devising and was unharmed despite being hit by several arrows. Weight and convenience alone cannot explain why even the mounted soldiers of warlike societies that produced the best horses and steel in the world should have preferred layered cloth to armour, and this faith may have reflected their long monopoly of silk and cotton textiles. Towards the end of the sixteenth century the English were to find the canvas 'buff coat' offered adequate protection against sword and pike, while in the seventeenth a layered garment known as 'silk armour' was alleged to be pistol-proof.

Eastern edged weapons were usually of better quality. The scimitar (*B&W Plate 2d*) was an Ottoman innovation, greatly superior to the straight sword in the slashing mode without sacrificing thrusting effectiveness. Neither could penetrate plate armour, but most helmets (*B&W Plates 3* – but see Don Juan's armoured collar in *Colour Plate 1*) left the neck vulnerable and while Achilles' heel may have lacked magical protection, for everyone else the most common disabling wounds were to the groin and hamstrings. Niccolò Machiavelli, like many an intellectual since, got carried away by theory and in his *Art of War* (1520) declared that men armed with swords and bucklers would move 'nimbly' among the pikemen and hack them down. The remaining lifespan of anyone attempting this against a contemporary pike-wall would not have been measurable with the time-pieces then available. At Lepanto Alessandro Farnese boarded an Ottoman flagship armed with a sword in either hand, but he was an exceptionally skilled and fully armoured knight wearing a closed helmet (*B&W Plate 3c*), and we may be sure there were no pikemen opposite, for he would have sunk without a struggle if parried in mid-jump.[14]

Once an enemy galley was boarded the battle would have been fought over decks and benches slippery with blood, entrails and bodily wastes voided in terror and agony, and when the contestants slipped or dragged each other to the ground the dagger was king. Farnese could easily have been stabbed through the eye-slit once brought down, and armour would have been a disadvantage in body-to-body combat. When two men are struggling together on the floor pure strength will usually prevail and, then as now, wrestling was the favourite competitive sport of the Anatolian peasant. It is unusual to read descriptions of tooth-and-claw fighting, but accounts of Lepanto tell of men who leaped into the water together in order to drown each other, something a man wearing armour would only do in a frenzy of rage, and probably more often the result of clinging to the unencumbered Anatolian who was trying to throw him in.

The culmination of this review of the weapons employed at Lepanto brings us to pole arms. By 1571 the halberd, with its axe-head, hook and spike, had become a staff of office for Hapsburg sergeants, while the Ottoman sipahis carried a light lance as well as their composite bows, and some later illustrations show their gun crews with spears. But these were playthings compared to the long two-handed pike, which was a collective arm – by which I mean that its superiority lay not so much in its length as in the manner of its employment. Every other non-gunpowder weapon so far mentioned was a skill or strength multiplier, and in combination with armour offered the balance of offensive and defensive qualities necessary for individual combat. The power of the pike lay in its use by tightly massed formations, for if their squares broke up pikemen could look only to their swords, or more commonly their feet, for salvation.

Pikes were a constant in western galley warfare – an illustration of a Genoese flagship at the beginning of the sixteenth century clearly shows stands of pike stored along either side of the midships gangway, while Furttenbach's much-reproduced drawing of the Knights of Malta flagship early in the seventeenth century shows five musicians, ten hand-gunners and twenty-five pikemen posed on the bow.[15] The pike was almost certainly the true 'technological advantage' of the Holy League fleet at Lepanto, for it was the weapon around which the 'Great Captain' Gonzalo Fernández de Córdoba built the mobile squares of the Spanish Tercio, which dominated land warfare for 140 years. Lepanto falls almost exactly between Cerignola (1503), where Córdoba defeated the vaunted Swiss in French service, and Rocroi (1643), where Enghien extinguished the Old Tercios' aura of invincibility, and in 1571 the most effective infantry force since the Roman legion was at its most dominant. Light cavalry screened for it, artillery and handgunners supplemented it, but the power of the Tercio lay in its mass of disciplined pikemen. Untrained individuals might use pikes to turn their own galley into a daunting hedgehog, but the pikemen of the Tercios are better compared to the shooting quills of an aggressive porcupine. Working as a team with their handgunners, they would board an enemy galley and scour the length of it, giving those in their path a stark choice between being skewered or swimming for their lives.[16]

In *I Napoletani a Lepanto*, writing about the role of his own compatriots only twenty-five years after Naples had at last been liberated from the ruinous Bourbon heirs of the Hapsburg dynasty, Luigi Conforti still had to admit that 'without the Spanish soldiers and Don Juan de Austria there would have been no victory at Lepanto'. Over two centuries later at Trafalgar, where Nelson's flagship mounted more heavy ordnance than the whole Hapsburg fleet at Lepanto, prizes could only be taken and victory assured by boarding parties armed with pistols, cutlasses, dirks – and pikes. History is usually told around the doings of captains and princes, but the star of our play is the anonymous Spanish infantryman who upheld the honour of his king and his church at push of pike, probably the most psychologically demanding of all the hellish methods devised by men to impose their will on one another.

CHAPTER THREE

THE PLAYERS

A proper appreciation of the 'who' at Lepanto requires us to reject entrenched ethnic stereotypes. In his pioneering *The Ottoman Impact on Europe*, Coles observed that in most general histories of Europe the Ottomans provide 'ominous noises off . . . ushered directly on the stage for the purpose of being "decisively" defeated at Lepanto'. This is as true today as it was when he wrote it in 1968, and Coles's own title provides the clue – we remain indifferent to far-off people except in so far as they have affected us. In addition there is mainstream reluctance to accept how very profoundly the Ottomans affected early modern Europe, even in the political sphere where their contribution was arguably greater than any other single influence. To mention only the most significant, they provided the means for France to frustrate the hegemonic ambitions of Charles V, without them German Protestantism might have been smothered in the cradle, and they were instrumental in the transformation of the principality of Muscovy into the Russian Empire. They are, therefore, the leading actors in a drama that from their point of view was a tragedy akin to the defeat of Varus' legions in the Teutoburg Forest in AD 9, which caused the Emperor Augustus to abandon plans for the conquest and civilization of Germany.[1]

I use the term 'Ottomans' rather than the ethnic designation 'Turks' because the former used the latter term to describe the Anatolian tribesmen whom they systematically excluded from positions of imperial authority. The clan of Othman did not even constitute a majority in Karesi, their first conquest, and until Selim the Grim conquered Syria, Egypt, northern Iraq, and became the protector of the holy cities of the Hejaz in 1516–20, the majority of the population of the empire was not even Islamic. This was to be expected, for from the beginning the justification for Ottoman rule was the *Ghaza* (holy war) on behalf of Islam, such that their excuse for conquering the other Muslim principalities in Anatolia was that they obstructed the task of dismembering the Byzantine Empire, the rock upon which the first great wave of Islamic expansion had broken during the seventh Christian century. They had largely accomplished this for the first time by 1400, when their mandate encompassed most of Anatolia and as far as Wallachia in the Balkans (known to them as Rumelia), when the empire was broken up after the fierce Bayezid I chose to provoke the even fiercer Turco-Mongol Timur, who routed him at Ankara on 28 July 1402 and displayed him to his erstwhile subjects in a cage until he beat his own brains out against the bars.

What happened afterwards confirmed that the Ottomans were much more than just another nomadic horde, with no identity beyond a common loyalty to their warlord. Timur restored the autonomy of the Anatolian princes, while the emperor of Byzantium and the Christian princes of Rumelia, vassals since the 1370s, took the opportunity to reassert their own. Timur also divided the Ottoman heartlands among Bayezid's four sons, but somehow, even as they disputed the succession to the death, by 1415 the Ottomans had once again become the dominant force on either side of the Dardanelles straits, although a damaging naval intervention by Venice preserved the division between Anatolia and Rumelia until 1422. Military prowess alone cannot explain this recovery, for most of their unique infantry corps as well as their aura of invincibility had been destroyed by Timur. But he could not take away a moral authority that none of their Anatolian rivals could aspire to, won by waging the Ghaza more successfully than anyone since the followers of the Prophet first erupted out of Arabia to bear his word across half the world, and a diplomatic finesse that cannot be dismissed as mere cunning.

More tangibly, the Ottomans developed a comprehensive but light-handed system of civil administration combined with an effective method of mobilizing resources for war that was far superior to any alternative, Muslim or Christian. It is misleading to equate it with hereditary Christian feudalism, nor was it tribal or clan-based save in its distant origins. To think of it as a 'system' at all may be conducive to error, for like all great empire-builders the Ottomans depended less on military might and territorial control than on a widely held belief that they not only were but *should be* dominant. Among Muslims this derived from their monopoly of the mystique of the Ghazi, defined by Ahmedi, a fourteenth-century Turkish poet whose saga is the earliest written Ottoman historical source, as 'God's sweeper who cleanses the earth from the filth of polytheism'. They also claimed legitimacy arising from Greek mythology and the historical legacy of Alexander the Great. Finally, there was clear evidence of divine providence in the earthquake that destroyed the walls of besieged Gallipoli and other Byzantine fortresses on the northern side of the Dardanelles in 1354, facilitating the historic acquisition of the Ottoman foothold in the Balkans that remains Turkish territory to this day. Like the favour shown to Joshua the Israelite at the siege of Jericho, the event created an abiding aura of manifest destiny.

Nonetheless, and with added impetus after Timur identified the weakness of their previous, more haphazard methods of control, the Ottomans did adopt a uniform method of imperial government. In the expansion phase it consisted of establishing suzerainty over a neighbouring state by extracting tribute, either following military defeat or more often by the threat of same. If the tributary state showed proper submission – if, in practice, it either served or at least did not obstruct Ottoman purposes – this relationship might continue indefinitely, as it did with Montenegro and Ragusa in the west and the Khanate of Crimea in the north. The next stage was to supplant the native dynasties and impose direct control, a process that might be accelerated or delayed by the imperatives of further expansion. Following the fall of Constantinople all the submission in the world could not save the Byzantine remnant of Trebizond, or Caffa and the other Genoese colonies around the Black Sea, but the highland Albanians and the Karamanids with their strongholds in the Taurus mountains demonstrated the other side of the coin and preserved or fought to recover their autonomy throughout the fifteenth century, despite being enveloped early by the Ottoman tide.[2]

The principle of submission also governed the protection afforded Christians and Jews within the empire, who paid a tribute additional to the taxes levied on the rest of the civilian flock who were known as the *reaya*. Conversion to Islam was not a prerequisite for serving in the Ottoman armies and throughout the era of expansion large contingents of Balkan Christians with their own chaplains fought for the Sultan and formed part of the tax-exempt *Askeri* (military plus Ottoman officials). The Greek Orthodox church was given preferential treatment over the Roman Catholic and the authority of the Patriarch in Constantinople reinforced, shrewdly co-opting an institution that had survived centuries of Latin oppression and was to prove no less resistant to Islamic assimilation. Driven out of the Iberian and Italian peninsulas by Roman Catholic persecution, Mediterranean (Sephardic) Jews provided invaluable commercial and administrative skills to the Ottomans and prospered accordingly, although nominal conversion to Islam was required in order to become a member of the imperial bureaucracy.

The consolidation phase began with a census and a survey of all taxable resources and the terms under which they were held, conducted by a commissioner and a scribe appointed by the Sultan. On this was based the *timar* system, a validation or award of non-hereditary land tenure to reconcile local customs and classes with the institutions of the Ottoman ruling class, contingent on further military service and revocable at any time. Timar holders, themselves *sipahis* (cavalrymen), supplied mounted and foot soldiers in accordance with the extent of their land grants. The sipahis of a given district were under the command of a governor (*bey*), whose symbol of office was the horsetail standard (*sanjak*) made infamous to Christians by the Mongols, and who in turn answered to a provincial governor-general (*beylerbey*), who had a two-horsetail standard. These were not quite the equivalent of western governors and governors general, for there was a strict separation of powers and Ottoman civil–religious magistrates (*Khadi*) actively policed their treatment of the flock. Abuses against the flock might lead to the revocation of a timar even in peacetime, while on campaign sipahis might be executed for minor offences such as permitting their men to graze their horses on peasant lands, the men *and horses* in question sharing their fate. The contrast with the normal behaviour of Christian lords and their armies was stark, and the good order and discipline of the Askeri in war and peace was long a defining characteristic of the Ottoman Empire.

The natural decline in the Ghazi ethos as warriors grew older and wished to enjoy the fruits of their campaigning was well matched to the task of consolidation, but the front line demanded restless spirits and when the period of rapid and extensive conquest came to an end, frontier beys adopted either a live-and-let-live policy or conducted plundering raids that hardened attitudes against them in the territories beyond. *Map 5* and its accompanying chart show how beylerbeyiks created during the period of most rapid expansion (1512–65) were aggressive frontier concentrations intended as springboards for further invasions more often than they were settlements to affirm a conquest. Not all of them were accompanied by land redistribution, and integration within the empire was more superficial where it did not take place. Thus the Mamluks of Egypt were imperfectly subsumed rather than supplanted, and the last western beylerbeyik was Sarajevo, created in a belated attempt to inject some dynamism into a long-stagnant border province where the pre-conquest native nobility retained title to their hereditary possessions until the twentieth century.

During the reigns of Selim and Suleiman the principality of Georgia was absorbed, but Circassia preserved a totally submissive relative autonomy, remaining the premier source of high-quality slaves. Poland–Lithuania (for peace on their southern frontiers), Venice (for her Aegean and Ionian islands), Austria (for the sliver of Hungary the Hapsburgs retained) and France (following the defeat and capture of François I by the Hapsburgs at Pavia in 1525) all became tribute-paying states, in Ottoman eyes therefore no less obliged to show submission than the conquered Christian frontier provinces of Moldavia, Wallachia, Hungary and Transylvania. The Ghazi frontier now extended the length of the southern Mediterranean coast, such that Algeria, Tripoli and Tunisia enjoyed the exceptional status of semi-independent Muslim frontier provinces, later Regencies, where the Janissary garrisons were, uniquely, given land grants in lieu of uncertain payment from Istanbul, thus becoming more identified with their locality than with the Porte (see below). By the end of the sixteenth century the Regencies and the Kingdom of Morocco can best be regarded as allies rather than subjects of the Porte.

The 'Barbary pirates' have received cursory and deliberately misleading treatment at the hands of western historians, for reasons acutely dissected by Sir Godfrey Fisher in his landmark *Barbary Legend*. The epithet was originally a corruption of Berberia, which I use instead as a reminder that names matter, and in lieu of couching my lance at the propaganda windmill comprehensively demolished by Fisher. As he observes, while there is abundant evidence of indiscriminate piracy connived at when not actively promoted by Christian princes, there is none to prove that Muslim raiders were anything other than properly regulated corsairs, who unlike their opposite numbers did not prey on their own kind:

> Moreover their judicial methods apparently offered a remarkably favourable contrast to the procrastination, corruption and expense so notoriously characteristic of English and most other Christian courts of Admiralty. While we seldom have the advantage of being able to examine the Turkish point of view, the mutual recriminations or glaring discrepancies in English, French, and Venetian reports and histories afford a student much food for thought and often considerable enlightenment.[3]

OTTOMAN BEYLERBEYIKS
(* garrison establishments)

Capital	Date established	Province	Date annexed
Edirne (later Sofia and Monastir)	1365	Rumelia	1361–85
Ankara/Kutahya	1393	Anatolia	1354–91
Amasya/Sivas	1413	Rûm	1392–97
Konya	1512	Karaman	See Endnote 2
Diyarbekir	1515	Upper Tigris	1515
Aleppo	1516	Northern Syria	1516
Damascus	1520	Southern Syria	1517
Cairo*	1520	Egypt	1517
Maras	1522	Dukaldir	1515
Algiers*	1533	Algeria	1516
Kapudan Pasha (Admiral)	1533	Gallipoli/Aegean Is./Alexandria	1354–1517
Erzurûm	1533	Armenia	1514
Mosul	1535	Mid Tigris	1516
Baghdad*	1535	Iraq (lower Tigris)	1534
Sana*	1540	Yemen	1538
Buda	1541	Hungary	1541
Basra*	1546	Persian Gulf	1546
Van	1548	Kurdistan	1533
Temesvar	1552	Transylvania	1552
al-Khatif*	1555	Luristan	1550
Tripoli*	1556	Libya	1551
Jidda*	1557	Red Sea (Abyssinian expedition)	1520
Caffa*	1568	Crimea (Volga–Don expedition)	1475
Tripoli*	1570	Lebanon (Cyprus expedition)	1516
Nicosia	1570	Cyprus and southern Anatolia	1570
Tunis*	1574	Tunisia	1574
Trabzon	1578	Trebizond (Caucasus campaigns)	1461
Childir	1578	Georgia (Caucasus campaigns)	1578
Kars	1580	Karabagh (Caucasus campaigns)	1534
Sarajevo	1580	Bosnia	1463

Adapted from the chart in Inalcik (1)

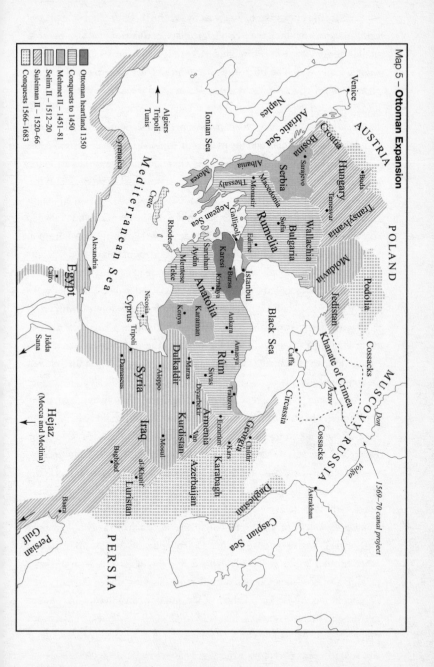

Map 5 – **Ottoman Expansion**

Ottoman heartland 1350
Conquests to 1450
Mehmet II – 1451–81
Selim II – 1512–20
Suleiman II – 1520–66
Conquests 1566–1683

Algiers
Tripoli
Tunis

Venice

AUSTRIA

POLAND

MUSCOVY RUSSIA

Naples

Adriatic Sea

Croatia

Bosnia

Hungary

Buda

Transylvania

Moldavia

Podolia

Cossacks

Don

Sarajevo

Serbia

Wallachia

Temesvar

Ionian Sea

Albania

Morea

Thessaly

Macedonia

Sofia

Bulgaria

Rumelia

Monastir

Jedistan

Khanate of Crimea

Volga

1569–70 canal project

Crete

Aegean Sea

Gallipoli

Edirne

Istanbul

Black Sea

Azov

Cossacks

Astrakhan

Rhodes

Karesi

Kastagra

Bursa

Sarukhan

Ankara

Amasya

Caffa

Cyprus

Nicosia

Aydin

Mentec

Teke

Anatolia

Konya

Karaman

Rum

Sivas

Trabzon

Circassia

Caspian Sea

Alexandria

Cairo

Egypt

Mediterranean Sea

Cyrenaica

Tripoli

Damascus

Aleppo

Maras

Dulkaldir

Diyarbekir

Armenia

Van

Erzurum

Kars

Chaldiri

Georgia

Karabagh

Azerbaijan

Daghestan

Syria

Kurdistan

Mosul

Iraq

Baghdad

al-Khabur

Luristan

PERSIA

Basra

Persian Gulf

Hejaz
(Mecca and Medina)

Jidda
Sana

The traffic in human beings was by far the most profitable aspect of raiding, and the fact that co-religionists could not usually be sold made the activity seem more guided by religious motives, on both sides, than it really was. The liberality with which slaves were treated and the cleanliness of their Algiers quarters contrasted sharply with the cruelty and negligence that characterized similar establishments in northern Mediterranean ports, the worst commonly held to be those run by Papal officials in Civitavecchia and the market in Toulon in the realm of His Most Christian Majesty, the King of France, where on at least one occasion the prohibition against selling Christians was shamelessly ignored. This followed the most celebrated atrocity attributed to Khair ed-Din 'Barbarossa', at that time conducting combined operations with the French, who is alleged to have ordered the sacking of Nice against the terms of capitulation in 1543. Some very purple prose has been written about this episode, particularly in French, yet it was they who did the deed against the wishes of Barbarossa, who sailed away before they carried it out. Muslims were widely renowned for keeping their word – and for explosions of murderous rage when they were the victims of bad faith. Since Christians did not regard any agreement with them as binding, the wonder is not that from time to time the Ottomans indulged in savage reprisals, but that they did not do so more often.

Any attempt to correct a gross imbalance in the way history has traditionally been told risks overcompensating and nobody involved in Mediterranean raiding had clean hands, but adventurers from all over the world came to be based in Berberia not because it was lawless, but because it was precisely the opposite. A ship's captain, of any faith, could walk the streets of these alleged nests of pirates more safely than in any Christian port (with the sole exception of Venice), and above all he was less likely to have his vessel or any legitimate prize seized arbitrarily by the port authorities. Those who operate at the margins of the law are happiest when those margins are clearly defined, and this helps to explain the large numbers of so-called Christian 'renegades' serving under the Ottoman flag. Shakespeare's fictional Othello aside, not one Muslim captain – indeed no Muslim of note – ever converted to Christianity, because, without prejudice to the possibility that Islam may be an intrinsically more attractive religion, there were no advantages and many perils in doing so.

Servitude under the Ottomans was a well-regulated condition in which the essential humanity of the slave was not denied. Gratuitous cruelty was not merely offensive on moral grounds, it was also commercially unsound – why damage the merchandise? Mistreatment of slaves was more common in blame-obsessed Christian societies where a shaky moral basis for the institution was constructed on the alleged soullessness of Africans and the divine damnation of the Muslims. But as we shall see, the three galleys of the Knights of Malta at Lepanto fought alone because no Venetian captain would serve alongside them, still less go to their rescue, and suffered greatly because of the particular hatred they aroused among the Ottomans. Although entry to the order was limited to junior noblemen who could prove that their family had never indulged in 'vile' commercial activity, they were indiscriminate plunderers as well as notoriously cruel slavers, the common enemies of all Mediterranean seafarers regardless of their faith.[4]

To return to the process of Ottoman expansion, we have no difficulty in relating it to comparable historical themes in our own culture, such as the Domesday Book in Norman England or the process whereby the authority of the East India Company was extended throughout the subcontinent, but the Ottoman slave system and the harem were institutions that remain alien to our instinctive understanding and tend to be misrepresented. The mothers of the many royal sons could not fail to become key players in a monarchy where there could only be one survivor in the struggle for the throne upon the death of the father. The clearest example of this was the success of Roxelana, Suleiman the Magnificent's favourite wife, in eliminating the rivals to the succession of her allegedly unworthy son Selim (*Colour Plate 2*), which some western commentators have identified as marking the end of Ottoman dynamism. This despite abundant evidence that Suleiman's conquests were a classic example of imperial overreach and that his successor, whoever he was, would have suffered the adverse consequences of economic and social problems with which the Ottoman system was ill-designed to cope.

Women with exceptional sexual skills have dominated some of the most powerful men in history – Napoleon waxed explicit about this when explaining why he was so reluctant to divorce the errant Josephine – and despite an embarrassment of choice the Ottoman sultans were no exception. Roxelana is a case in point; sultans sometimes married the daughters of minor foreign potentates for political reasons, but she was only a Ukrainian slave-girl and her marriage to Suleiman was a love match. She then caused the harem to be moved from the old to the new palace, at first to monopolize his favours and later to choose his consorts and ensure that none should receive undue attention, thus institutionalizing an influence over him so powerful that in 1556 she persuaded him to kill the popular Mustafa, previously his favourite son by another woman. The following letter, presaging the demise of Grand Vizier Ibrahim in 1536, illustrates a seldom-discussed constant across the barriers of time and culture:

> My Lord, your absence has kindled in me a fire that does not abate. Take pity on this suffering soul and speed your letter, so that I may find in it at least a little consolation. My Lord, when you read my words, you will wish that you had written more to express your longing. When I read your letter, your son Mehmed and your daughter Mihrimah were by my side, and tears streamed from their eyes. Their tears drove me from my mind . . . You ask why I am angry with Ibrahim Pasha. When – God willing – we are together again, I shall explain, and you will learn the cause.

Ottoman succession was a free-for-all from which the winning candidate emerged as destiny's elect to extinguish the bloodlines of his brothers, and Roxelana's son may well have been the best genetic choice. Primogeniture in the western monarchies merely avoided civil war at the time of succession and did nothing to curtail the influence of ambitious mothers and of both female and male favourites, as well as permitting certifiable imbeciles to become monarchs and saddling the exchequer with parasitic royal families of limited utility even when loyal, while the history of Europe is littered with the rebellions of legitimate and illegitimate pretenders. Furthermore the governance of an established empire requires different skills to those involved in the winning of it, chief among them the ability to attract support at the time of succession and to choose competent and loyal subordinates thereafter. Selim did this without the help of his mother, and the fact that westerners have dubbed him 'the Sot' is simply the reverse side of the sycophantic title 'the Magnificent' bestowed on his father. Had his navy won at Lepanto, no doubt he would be known to us as Selim the Splendid, regardless of his appetites, and his love poems would be held to show his cultivated nature instead of mocked as a sign of weakness.

If lubricity prevents honest appreciation of an institution that functioned more as a lifelong welfare agency for deserving women than as the gigantic brothel of fevered western imagination, our efforts to understand the *gulam* system trip over the semantic difficulty that the word translates as 'male child slave', in our culture a term redolent of degradation, whereas at the height of the empire almost the entire Ottoman élite, military and civil, was drawn from the gulam pool. The process began with the fifth of all war booty to which the Ottoman rulers were entitled, including captives who, they had the wit to realize, could be turned into a force to balance the politically undependable Anatolian Turks who made up the bulk of their army. The infantry Janissary (new troops) corps, originally formed from prisoners of war captured at the fall of Adrianople in 1361, guarded the Porte (from 'gateway to happiness', as the imperial palace was known) and also filled the operational gap between the mounted sipahis and the peasants who fought on foot. From this developed the first modern regular army, consisting of a core of Janissary infantry armed with handguns and the household cavalry known as the sipahis of the Porte, with its own engineering and artillery corps and known collectively as the *kapi-kulu* (slave of the Porte) army, to differentiate it from the timariot sipahis.[5]

The kapi-kulu army was the military wing of a non-hereditary ruling class based on a periodic collection of likely Christian peasant lads from the Balkans called the *devshirme*. Poor city dwellers, Christian and Muslim alike, were known to send their children to the country in an effort to get around their exclusion from what was seen as a golden opportunity for social advancement, and peasant parents were known to bribe the collectors to take their surplus offspring, of which there were many in the sixteenth century. Bosnian Muslims demanded that their children be included, but these went straight to the palace along with the brightest of the general intake for intensive 'inner service' training, to become imperial officials. The rest were sent to Turkish peasant families who were responsible for their spiritual training as Muslims and their physical development as men fit for military service. Officials also acquired gulams of their own by purchase or capture and, following similar training, these pursued their own careers owing nothing except gratitude to their 'masters'.

Far from locking people into a menial status, therefore, the gulam system redeemed young infidels from ignorance and was the first attempt in world history to create a sustainable meritocracy, 'the single institution which made the Ottoman Empire so fantastically strange, the ceaseless production, elevation and disappearance of the highest in the state, the very Ottomans themselves'.[6] For so long as the non-hereditary principle was strictly adhered to and the wealth and influence accumulated in life was recycled upon the death of an official, it was spectacularly dynamic. Everyone writing about the Ottoman Empire at its zenith quotes from the clear-eyed letters of Ogier Ghiselin de Busbeq, the polymath Flemish gentleman who introduced the tulip and lilac to Europe, written when he was the ambassador of the Holy Roman Empire to the Porte in 1554–62, and so shall I:

> Thus it is that Nation, Dignities, Honours, Offices, etc., are the Rewards of Virtue and Merit; as on the other side, Dishonesty, Sloth and Idleness, are among them the most despicable things in the whole world. And by this means they flourish, bear sway and enlarge the Bounds of their Empire every day more and more. But we, *Christians*, to our shame be it spoken, live at another manner of rate; Virtue is little esteemed among us, but Nobleness of Birth (forsooth) carries away all the Honour and Preferment.[7]

Busbeq had an axe to grind, but there is no reason to question his judgement that intrigue and corruption were no more endemic at the Porte than at his own imperial court, while producing better results. He was deeply impressed by the high level of public order within the empire, but in common with other western observers did not appreciate the genius of the Ottoman system, which was that in effect it created a vast police force that fought wars, rather than a parasitic army providing no useful function in peacetime. Although the kapi-kulu army was a salaried garrison force, it was also responsible for maintaining order in urban areas, while the rural timariot sipahis both acted as tax collectors for the Porte and, as shepherds to the flock, were responsible for the suppression of banditry. Finally there were the *azaps*, originally a salaried corps conscripted from and maintained by the Anatolian peasantry for use as marines in the fleet, but by the mid sixteenth century also the main source of garrison troops for border fortresses.

Behind this executive arm of the state was the judicial authority of the separate Khadi service with its own chief in Istanbul and two senior subordinates in Anatolia and Rumelia. These made judgements based on religious law as defined by a supreme court of learned theologians known as the *Ulema*, and on civil law as laid down by imperial statute, the convenient fiction being that there could be no incompatibility between them. The Ulema and the *muftis*, provincial officials appointed to interpret religious law, also issued opinions (*fetwas*) that were markedly more tolerant of the wild holy men who punctuate the history of Islam (known as dervishes, or fakirs if Arab) than western ecclesiastical authorities were of theirs. This extended even to the Shi'ite sect, which denied legitimacy to every civil and religious authority produced by the Muslim world since the Christian year 874 and developed a class of Mullahs who acted as intermediaries between God and man, unlike the Ulema of the Sunni majority whose members were honoured only as learned individuals. But despite the intrinsically subversive nature of Shi'a, made patent when the Persian Safavid dynasty adopted it as a means of destabilizing Ottoman authority, the sort of sectarian religious persecution that became commonplace in Christendom never took root in Islam.

However, the Ulema did not bless the war with Persia, on the grounds that it was distracting the Ottomans from the Ghaza. The Safavids, surrounded by other Muslim states, were unable to fight the infidels and so were unable to aspire to the prestige and power of convocation that holy war bestowed on the Ottomans. But the latter in turn had to renew their claim to religious leadership by striking north-west against the infidels and south-east against Persia alternately. One may see this also as a prudent refusal to engage in war on two widely separated fronts, but the Ulema spoke with the authority of the words and deeds of the Prophet, and for all their power the sultans listened respectfully. Despite this, the spirit of the Ghaza wound down during the sixteenth century, symbolized by the decline in military effectiveness of the Anatolian *akincis*, light cavalry settlers who disputed the no-man's-land at the frontier with the infidels. They embodied the Ghazi ethos and their abolition in 1595 and replacement by mercenary Crimean Tatars marked the end of a 300-year-old tradition. The turn of the century also saw Persia resurgent under Shah Abbas, with a modern army modelled on the kapi-kulu, which forced the Ottomans to make peace with the infidels. Busbeq foretold this forty years earlier:

> . . . on their side, there is a mighty, strong and wealthy Empire, great Armies, Experience in War, a veteran Soldiery, a long series of Victories, Patience in Toil, Concord, Order, Discipline, Frugality and Vigilance. On our side there is public Want, private Luxury, strength weakened, Minds Discouraged, and unaccustomedness to Labour or Arms, Soldiers refractory, commanders covetous, a Contempt of Discipline, Licentiousness, Rashness, Drunkenness, Gluttony; and, what is worst of all, they used to conquer and we to be conquered. Can any Man doubt, in this case, what the Event will be? 'Tis only the *Persian* stands between us and Ruin.[8]

The threat posed by Shi'a and the Persians provoked Selim the Grim to push aside his temporizing father in 1512 and to conquer northern Iraq, Syria and Egypt in lightning campaigns a few years later. We can only speculate what course history might have taken if instead he had driven north to Vienna or east to Astrakhan, as his successors tried to do after the windows of easy opportunity, open on all sides in Selim's time, had closed. The conquest of the rich, well populated new provinces more than doubled imperial revenues and made native Muslims the majority population for the first time, so that along with vastly increased assets came new responsibilities that fundamentally altered the character of the empire. Also, as the defenders of the holy cities of the Hejaz and of the maritime trade with India and the Orient that had made the Mamluk Empire so prosperous, the Ottomans were now compelled to combat the marauding Portuguese in the Red Sea and, later, the Persian Gulf. The western predators not only disrupted trade in the Indian Ocean but also supplied the Persians with modern weapons and expertise, and although Selim's conquests hugely increased the population and wealth under Ottoman control, they no less greatly exacerbated the problem of geopolitical dispersion, always the Achilles' heel of an empire with no natural frontiers.

The more profound change, however, was that Ottoman ambitions now became schizophrenic, at once claiming legitimacy as the successors of the eastern Roman Empire, while also seeking to assume the mantle

1. Beautiful weapons systems – the Lepanto flagships of Ali Pasha and Don Juan (ABOVE *National Library of Turkey*; BELOW *Museu Marítim*, Barcelona)

4. Bruegel's depiction of galleys attacking galleons (*Scala*)

5a

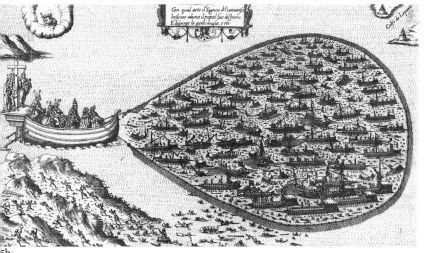

5b

5a. Papal galley – Protestant view (*Herzog August Bibliothek Wolfenbüttel*)

5b. Papal galley – Roman Catholic view (*Museo Storico Navale*, Venice)

6a

6b

7

6a. Amphibious operations (*Scala*)

6b. The siege of Nicosia (*Museo Storico Navale*, Venice)

7. Venice putting one over on Spain – Titian's modified allegory
(*Bridgeman Art Library/Prado*, Madrid)

8. The technological superiority thesis – Vroom's galleon destroying a galley (*National Maritime Museum*, Greenwich)

of the historic Muslim caliphate. Under Selim's son Suleiman the Magnificent – known as 'the Law-Giver' to his own people – the empire became more theocratic, thereby undermining the tolerant relationship with the Greek Orthodox that had facilitated the consolidation of conquests around the Aegean, while further enraging the irreconcilable Shi'ites. Although I am confident Muslim scholarship has addressed this issue in depth, if anything illuminating has been translated into English I am unaware of it. To adapt Coles's sentiment expressed at the start of this chapter, in the history of the Ottoman Empire the Shi'ite Persians provide the ominous noises off, to be ushered on stage for the purpose of suffering 'decisive' defeats that only temporarily contained the threat they posed.

More directly affecting our theme, Selim's conquests made it inevitable that his son would expel the Knights of Saint John from Rhodes in 1522, for which he received the effusive congratulations of the Venetians, and that his grandson would invade Cyprus in 1570, to their fury. Both operations were necessary, in the case of Cyprus really overdue, to eliminate bases for Christian corsair activity that were no longer on the fringes but at the heart of a greatly expanded empire, and preying on exponentially growing Ottoman seaborne trade. Braudel estimated that by the late sixteenth century the Ottoman merchant fleet had reached 80,000 tonnes, with 20,000 tonnes flying the flag of the Ottoman tributary city state of Ragusa, against 60,000 Spanish (considerably more was devoted to Atlantic trade) and 40,000 Venetian. This marked a departure from the custom of the middle eastern Islamic states to enjoy the benefits of maritime trade without the risks by leaving it in the hands of the infidel Pisans, Genoese and Venetians. As the great Kurdish warlord Saladin wrote in 1174 to the Caliph in Baghdad, even in the midst of the Crusades and on pain of excommunication by the outraged Popes, 'there is not one of them but brings to our lands his weapons of war and battle and bestows upon us the choicest of what he makes and inherits'.[9]

The Pisans and Genoese found compensation in the western Mediterranean, but geography denied this recourse to Venice and as Ottoman maritime power grew, so she found herself obliged to fight for her bases in the Aegean through much of the fifteenth century, for the Ionian in the 1530s and finally in 1571 for her hold on the Adriatic, the sea with which she was symbolically married every year in a ceremony that defined her very existence. There was no objective reason why Venice should not have been the prosperous ally of the Ottoman Empire, but most wars are fought for dominance, not profit, and despite paying tribute for Cyprus, their remaining Aegean islands and Zante, the Venetians refused to show proper submission. They would not grovel and faced with an Ottoman demand for the cession of sovereignty over Cyprus in 1570, similar in spirit to their own extortion of it from the widow of the last Lusignan king in 1489, they rejected it out of hand.

While other Christian states were impoverishing themselves by expelling Jews, the Venetians created the first ghetto in order to retain their expertise while limiting their contact with a populace that believed them to be maiden-ravishers and baby-killers on a par with the dreaded Turk. Protestants were not so fortunate and were unceremoniously drowned in the lagoon. In a triumph of image over substance, a state run by and for the benefit of a hermetically closed group of families (no new names were admitted from 1381 to 1646, a unique exclusivity) grown rich at the expense of their souls was mourned by Wordsworth when Napoleon abolished the decrepit republic in 1802:

> Once did She hold the gorgeous East in fee;
> And was the safeguard of the West: the worth
> Of Venice did not fall below her birth,
> Venice, the eldest Child of Liberty.
> She was a maiden City, bright and free;
> No guile seduced, nor force could violate;
> And, when she took unto herself a Mate,
> She must espouse the everlasting Sea.

Art historians forgive them for the sake of their patronage of architects like Sansovino (1486–1570) and Palladio (1508–80), but above all because they nurtured the Venetian school of painters, upon whom more later. The military historian also cannot withhold admiration for the personal courage of such as the nonagenarian Duce Enrico Dandolo, who led the successful assault on the sea wall of Constantinople in 1203, and of Duce Pietro Loredano at Gallipoli in 1416, measured against whom Sebastiano Venier, the fierce Venetian commander at Lepanto and future Duce, was a woolly lamb. But eldest children of liberty they were not and, barring the quirk of refusing to bend the knee to any human agency, they would do anything for money. Some believe this made their society innately stronger than Islamic cultures, in which wealth accumulation for its own sake was discouraged, but it was also frowned upon in contemporary Christian societies. While it is tempting to see the lavish outlay on religious works by the Venetian oligarchs as an effort to offset their avarice and to buy their way into heaven, it seems to have been a manifestation of a sincere belief that they were God's chosen.

In 1499 Marshal Trivulzio wrote the epigraph for the coming century in a letter to his employer, Louis XII of France: 'To carry out war three things are necessary – money, money and yet more money'. To provide this necessity, Louis made Cardinal George d'Amboise the first of the great French finance ministers who were to make possible the wars of the next three centuries. Although we now regard the French system that emerged from this as the most omnipresent example, the Venetian precedent is a better candidate for the prototype of today's bureaucratic oligarchies, one of its innovations being the creation in 1542 of quartermasters (*provveditori*) in response to the rising cost of war, particularly fortifications. These were the ancestors of the Austrian and Prussian office of the quartermaster general (QMG), around which the entire concept of a general staff grew up. But in its original Venetian form the office was part of the first ever effort, seldom emulated since, to apply cost–benefit analysis to state spending, at this time overwhelmingly devoted to military outlays. In this it was markedly successful, for the Venetian oligarchy not only punched well above its geopolitical weight but also continued to prosper, despite being surrounded by enemies, throughout a century during which greater empires bankrupted themselves.[10]

Chief among these was the greater of two empires created when the Emperor Charles V divided his vast inheritance with his younger brother Ferdinand in 1522, granting him the ancestral Hapsburg lands that for convenience are referred to as Austrian, although they included many peoples who would have fiercely resented the designation. But to call the dominions kept by Charles 'Spanish' is even more misleading, for his affections lay more with his Burgundian inheritance from his father Philip the Fair, and with the kingdoms of Aragon, Naples and Sicily inherited from his grandfather Ferdinand, than with the Castilian fighting frontier with Islam of which he was technically only co-ruler with his mentally unbalanced mother Juana. Philip II revered his father's memory, but he could not have governed in a more different manner and he made his capital in the heart of Castile, known as the very plural 'these our kingdoms'. (Old) Castile itself only became a kingdom in 1034, to which were added the Christian principalities of León, Galicia and Asturias. Toledo (New Castile), Murcia, Extremadura, Andalucia and Granada were 'reconquered' from Islamic rulers and eventually completely assimilated, but Navarre was disputed with France well into the sixteenth century and retained considerable autonomy. Castilian overseas conquests began early in the fifteenth century in the Canary Islands, from which Cristoforo Colombo/ Cristóbal Colón departed to claim the Americas for Castile in 1492 and, following the conquest of Granada in the same year, Castile was responsible for a series of assaults upon the somnolent Islamic principalities of North Africa during the first decade of the sixteenth century.

This was detrimental to the interests of greater Spain in every respect, for it released the genie of Ottoman–corsair collaboration in the form of the Barbarossa brothers, sons of a Turkish father and a Greek mother origi-nally from Mytilene. Uruj, the eldest, at that time had received only two galleys and a robe of office from the Sultan, but this and the common threat sufficed to make him a leader of what had been only a loose association of sea-rovers who probably made more money from legal trade than from piracy. However, the Castilian attacks also revealed how feeble the North African dynasties had become, and the Barbarossas and their emulators were to replace them in Algiers, Tripoli and Tunisia over the next decades. As a result the Catalans, Genoese and Venetians were not only shut out of the profitable North African markets but also assaulted by flotillas of corsairs in what had hitherto been the more peaceful western half of the Mediterranean. The beneficiaries of this excess of Castilian zeal were the Dutch and English commercially, the French politically, and the Ottomans territorially.

There were, therefore, very distinct strands in the development of Iber-ian policy in the Mediterranean, a traditional Aragonese dynastic interest that encompassed the Balearic Islands, Sardinia, Sicily and southern Italy, and a Ghazi-like Christian empire emanating from Castile. There was a no less important third strand represented by Portugal, but it influenced our area of interest mainly by its incursions into the Indian Ocean, with the consequences we have already noted. All shared a sense of belonging to the 'Hispania' of the Roman and Visigothic empires but, as in Italy, localized loyalties and customs were predominant. España is no less an imperial concept than Great Britain, and if the fissiparous nature of the former has been more in evidence over time, this is mainly because the imperial role was thrust upon it before the heartland was properly consolidated.

When Charles V abdicated his many crowns and titles he did so in stages. The duchy of Milan and the kingdom of Naples were passed to Philip in 1546 and 1554 without ceremony or even pretence of consultation. The transmission of seventeen separate titles constituting the Netherlands was approved by a general assembly of those estates at Brussels in October 1555. On 16 January 1556 he abdicated (as Carlos I) 'these our kingdoms' and the lands of the orders of Santiago, Alcántara and Calatrava in a document in the vernacular. On the same day, by documents written in Latin and prior formal consent by their estates, Philip also inherited the kingdom of Sicily, and by separate deed the county of Barcelona and the kingdoms of Aragon and Sardinia. Charles abdicated the Free County of Burgundy (Franche-Comté) and Charolais to Philip in April 1556 but did not relinquish his title of Holy Roman Emperor until February 1558, giving time for his brother Ferdinand to ensure that he would be elected in his place, an arrangement prefigured when Charles arranged Ferdinand's election as king of the Romans in 1531.[11]

In 1559 Venetian ambassador Michele Suriano estimated that Philip II drew about 1.5 million ducats (gold coins worth 375 maravedis/grammes of silver) in annual revenues from Castile and the same amount from the Netherlands, compared with 400,000 from the Indies, 260,000 from Aragon, 200,000 from the lands of the erstwhile crusading orders and a mere 40,000 from Navarre. Naples produced revenues of about 1 million ducats, but her running costs exceeded this by 50 per cent because of a crushing burden of interest on loans raised to pay for the constant wars of the preceding sixty years, while her main sources of income had been sold or mortgaged. 'You cannot imagine a method of extracting money from subjects which has not been used in this kingdom', the ambassador wrote, 'many of them take to the streets because they have no other way of making a living. This situation breeds more thieves and outlaws than there are in all the rest of Italy'.

He might have written much the same about Milan, even more fought-over than Naples and only lately acquired. Sicily, an undisputed Aragonese kingdom since 1284, was largely self-governing and self-financing but confronted rising direct and indirect costs from her front-line status in the struggle for North Africa as the sixteenth century progressed. Suriano also failed to note that imperial financial and political credit was at a low ebb in the Netherlands, after forty years during which the territories had acted as the true 'treasure chambers of the Spanish kings, the mines, the Indies, which so long sustained the emperor in his wars in France, Italy and Germany, and saved his kingdom, honour and prestige'.[12]

It was the change from a Burgundian emperor to a Spanish king that was to undo this relationship. The Netherlands were soon to revolt more against their role of cash cow to an empire increasingly seen as Spanish than for the religious reasons later adduced to unify opposition in the northern provinces, even though half the valuable Spanish wool trade passed through the Netherlands while one third of their exports went back to Spain. Franche-Comté is usually seen as an indispensable stage in the France-circumventing 'Spanish Road' to the Netherlands but to some extent it was the other way around, with the Netherlands being retained by Charles and their political links with the Holy Roman Empire severed as an extension of his desire to bequeath his beloved Burgundy to his own son. As a man whose first language was French and who caroused like one of them, as a leader who rode with his armies and as a monarch who was often among them, Charles commanded deep personal loyalty from the earthy Netherlanders, which he reinforced by honouring their princes with membership of the Burgundian Order of the Golden Fleece and by showing respect for their customary rights. His son lacked his cosmopolitanism and charisma, with fateful consequences for his authority.[13]

In contrast to our map of the Ottoman Empire, the development of the ramshackle Hapsburg domains can only be illustrated by a description of the incestuous rats' nest of dynastic combinations by which it was put together. The marriage of second cousins Isabella of Castile and Ferdinand of Aragon in 1469 was the second attempt to unite the two crowns, Isabella having usurped the line of her father's first marriage to his first cousin Maria of Aragon. Holy Roman Emperor Maximilian I acquired Burgundy by marriage and his line became conjoined with the Spanish by the marriages of his daughter Margaret to Juan, Isabella and Ferdinand's heir apparent, who took to her with such enthusiasm that he is alleged to have died as a result, and of his own heir Philip the Fair to Juana the Highly Strung, which produced the aforementioned brothers Charles and Ferdinand, and three daughters. One of the latter married Emmanuel the Fortunate of Portugal, who had previously married two of Isabella and Ferdinand's daughters (the third married Henry VIII of England), another married Emmanuel's son by one of those earlier marriages, and the third married Louis II of Hungary and Bohemia. Ferdinand I of Austria outbred with Anne of Hungary, becoming the brother-in-law twice over of Louis, and was elected to succeed him after he was killed at Mohacs in 1526. But Ferdinand's heir Maximilian II reverted to the Hapsburg norm and married the daughter of his uncle the Emperor Charles V and Isabella of Portugal, herself the daughter of Emmanuel's union with one of Charles's aunts.

The other daughter of Charles and Isabella married back into the Portuguese line, which also provided Philip II's first wife, product of which union was the psychopathic Crown Prince Carlos (b. 1545), who had to be locked up for the good of the realm and died of dietary excess in 1568. His second marriage to Mary of England, the daughter of his great-aunt, was barren, his third to Elizabeth of Valois was productive but only two daughters survived to marry into the houses of Savoy and … Austria. His fourth marriage was to the daughter of his sister Maria and his first cousin Maximilian II, which produced a new heir, Ferdinand, in December 1571 (*Colour Plate 4*). Ferdinand died in 1579 when his full brother, the future Philip III, was one year old. Philip II's sickly line contrasted sadly with the robust by-blows of Charles V's non-marital dalliances. These were Margaret (b. 1522) and Juan (b. 1547), both acknowledged and given the nebulous title 'de Austria'. Margaret was married briefly to Duke Alessandro dei Medici, assassinated in 1537, then to Ottavio Farnese who in 1547 inherited the duchy of Parma, created by Pope Paul III for his own illegitimate son in 1534. Alessandro Farnese, who fought with such distinction at Lepanto under the command of his younger uncle Juan, was the survivor of twins born to this marriage in 1545.

The Burgundian inheritance was entitled to a regent of royal blood, and the weakness of the legitimate line meant that Margaret, Juan and

Alessandro were all to be broken by involvement in the Netherlands labyrinth, ultimately the graveyard of Spanish aspirations. Much is made of the self-indulgent habits of the post-classical era Ottoman sultans, but for genuine, compound degeneracy we need look no further than the pharaonic consanguinity of the Hapsburg marriages – all enjoying Papal dispensation in defiance of scripture as well as natural law. Defiance of those ordinances resulted in the genetic exhaustion that led to the extinction of the senior line in Austria in 1619 and, after two further intermarriages with the Austrian house, to the pathetic final product of the Spanish line, the drooling, impotent Carlos II (d. 1700).

Philip II possessed neither the self-confidence nor the breadth of vision that drove Charles V, and at Cateau-Cambrésis he trimmed the imperial robes he inherited but could not, for the reverence he bore his father's memory, entirely cut them to suit his limited ability to wear them. His contemporary Selim II also laboured in the shadow of an immensely charismatic father, but his was a mature empire with institutions peculiarly well adapted to its multinational nature. Philip's disparate inheritance was barely one generation old, and only the personal magnetism he lacked could have held it together. Symptomatically, he preferred the stab in the back to confrontation, literally in the case of rival princes and scheming subordinates, metaphorically in dealing with those who served him with unrequited loyalty. Animated by formulaic religiosity he built the brow-beating palace and monastery of San Lorenzo del Escorial on a pattern of the grill used to roast the saint on whose feast day an army nominally under his command (although actually led by Emanuele Filiberto of Savoy) defeated the French at Saint Quentin in 1557, the only military achievement to which he could credibly lay claim.

Even less than for the Ottoman Empire is it appropriate to speak of a 'system' when referring to imperial Spanish governance. It consisted of layer upon layer of feudal rights largely detached from obligations, a grotesquely swollen class of tax-exempt gentlemen (*hidalgos*), many of them as indigent as Don Quixote, crowned by a small cluster of immensely wealthy grandees whose most jealously defended right was to wear hats in the presence of the king. Unlike the Ottoman Askeri, the hidalgos contributed nothing to the general welfare in peacetime and were of ambivalent value in war, each being convinced that he was a born leader of men without necessarily possessing the requisite skills. Fiercely loyal to the crown in the abstract, their attitude to its practical authority was captured by the phrase 'I obey but do not comply'. On the other hand they and the lower orders that aspired to be like them were, as individuals, arguably the most stubbornly fearless fighting men in history. This combination of strong personalities and weak institutions won, in little more than a single generation, the first truly global empire for Spain and for the militant, persecuting Roman Catholicism with which her destiny has been so inextricably intertwined.

What would otherwise have been a lethally individualistic mass was converted into a disciplined force in stages. The first and most crucial step was the manner of recruitment, for the volunteers produced by a community felt bound to their duty by a web of personal loyalties and were therefore less likely to desert than rootless mercenaries. In principle, a company of raw recruits under a crown-commissioned captain was sent first to the Italian presidios for basic training and then on to join a column (*coronelía*) of 1,000 men in the field, three of which made up a Tercio. In practice it was never that tidy and numbers varied considerably, but as a rule the higher the proportion of Castilians, the more dependable the Tercio. This had its limits, and the downside of collective individualism became apparent when soldierly honour was offended beyond endurance by delayed payment of wages, a frequent occurrence. Responses ranged from strikes, such as the refusal of German troops at Taranto to board galleys sent for them in 1571, through the looting of the towns and villages they were supposed to be guarding, until that hard-to-predict moment when discipline snapped across whole armies and beastly breakdowns of order occurred, the sack of Rome in 1527 and of Antwerp in 1576 being the most notorious examples.

The Ottoman imperial guard learned to exploit succession struggles to extort extra payment, and in time this became an entitlement on which a new sultan or beylerbey skimped to his peril. If the Janissaries were not paid or did not receive supplies promptly they did not waste time with indirect protests but made their grievance patent in the person of the man in charge, which may explain why standards set by Ottoman paymasters and commissaries were not equalled in the west for centuries. But because the vast majority of their armies came from the ranks of the timariot sipahis, akincis and azaps who were maintained by remittances from their own lands or communities, cash payments were a much smaller problem for the sultans than for their western counterparts, being limited during our period to a kapi-kulu of about 16,000 Janissaries, 12,000 sipahis of the Porte and a few thousand other arms. These received a lump sum payment at the start of a campaign and a substantial bonus upon their return and, coupled with severe punishment for the slightest infraction, the effect was that mutinies in the field were virtually unknown. The result was a paradoxical contrast between an army of slaves who were not servile, paid in advance without fear that they might desert, and another composed of free men who generally fawned upon those above them in a social order defined solely by birth, who in return feared and distrusted but nonetheless cheated them whenever possible.

While it is no longer fashionable to write of national character, not long ago it was a commonplace to note the association of virility with paying subordinates as little as possible in Hispanic culture. This may have been something that became ingrained through emulation of the manner in which Spanish monarchs used money to reinforce their authority. Because so much of the wealth of their realms was in the tax-exempt hands of the nobility and the church, it could only be tapped by recourse to various forms of extortion. We will consider later how the church was milked, but the despoliation of the nobility was easier because grandees could not refuse appointment to political and military offices where the always tardy and usually niggardly remittances from Spain obliged them to spend their own money, or suffer the ignominy of seeing their administration fail. Thus one of the richest, the Duke of Alba, was ruined by his time in the Netherlands and after a lifetime of loyal service his heirs inherited interest on debts greater than the revenues from his lands. The very able Alessandro Farnese and his successor Ambrogio Spinola, either of whom might have salvaged the Spanish position in the Netherlands if properly supported, fell into disfavour not only because of the lethal mixture of envy and distrust that mediocre people always feel towards the talented, but also because there was no more money to be squeezed out of them.

If the flesh of the Hapsburg Empire in Europe was put on by dynastic marriages, the award of cross-landholdings provided the skeletal framework. Thus the northern Italian Medici, Pallavicini, Farnese and Gonzaga, and the Roman Orsini, Piccolomini and Colonna families, to name only those who feature in our story, had large estates in Naples. The backbone of the Hapsburg fleet was provided by the Genoese Doria, Lomellino, Grimaldi, Centurione, Sauli and Mare clans, which all had important holdings in Sicily, while the Dorias, Spinolas and Pallavicini also had lands in Lombardy and Spain itself. All of these could be forfeit if they refused to do the king's bidding, but in addition they were all obliged to become the creditors of the monarchy so that, to extend the body politic analogy, the central nervous system of the empire was an extensive network of financial extortion and counter-extortion where a mutiny in the unpaid army of the Netherlands and a simultaneous outbreak of civil unrest in Genoa might well be no more than the related symptoms of a dispute over the terms of a forced debt renegotiation between the crown and its bankers.[14]

Empires usually offer subject peoples some psychological compensation for their loss of autonomy, but the *pax hispanica* imposed on Italy after 1559 generated only resentment, even among the classes that most benefited from it, as summarized in a 1570 dispatch from the governor of Milan to Philip II:

> … in Italy there is no state, no power, no prince, nor man who owns a castle … nor one who does not, who desires the maintenance and increase of Your Majesty's states; and all are past masters in giving good words and pretending the contrary … I do not know whether there is any one in the whole world who is subject to the Spanish nation and empire and who is devoted to them, but does not rather abhor their name … And this is much more the case in Italy than in any other part of the world.[15]

On the back an unknown hand wrote '… these Italians, although they are not Indians, have to be treated as such'. Philip II himself would not have put it so crassly, but it is noteworthy that some member of his Castilian secretariat felt free to express the sentiment on a document addressed to him. The inevitability factor we observed with reference to the Ottoman Empire does not seem to have worked for the Spanish, who were generally regarded as uncouth barbarians by their European subjects. This may have led them, through the process of overcompensation associated with the socially and culturally insecure throughout the ages, to adopt the manner remarked by the Venetian ambassador in 1581: 'The only noteworthy thing about them is a certain loftiness and dignity which in Italy we call "Spanish composure" and which makes all foreigners hate them. They let it be known that not only is there no other people which bears comparison with them, but that everyone should be grateful to be ruled by them'.[16]

Not the least of the foci of resentment towards the hegemony of His Catholic Majesty was to be found in Rome. This review of the principal actors in the Lepanto drama has skirted the role of the Roman church because although it only played a small part on stage, it was the co-ordinator without whom the battle would not have taken place and, equitably enough, it was the only participant unequivocally to benefit from it. The modern ecumenical Papacy dates from the accession in 1958 of the subsequently beatified Angelo Roncali, who took the name John XXIII last used by the anti-Pope Baldassare Cossa in 1400–1415. Although it is too early to tell whether it was a real watershed, few would dispute that Roncali opened the windows of an inward-looking, sectarian cabal run mainly by an Italian oligarchy dominated by a small number of Roman families. Many of those families were represented at Lepanto, giving them a personal interest in burnishing its iconic status.

The dual significance of the battle arose from the fact that it was the product of a contest among three empires, not two, for as Hobbes observed eighty years later, 'The Papacy is not other than the Ghost of the deceased Roman Empire, sitting crowned upon the grave thereof.'[17] There are good reasons why Vasari's Lepanto murals dominate the Sala Regia in the Vatican, where popes give audience to secular rulers, for it was the moment when one of the more dynamic successors to Saint Peter took the tattered shreds of spiritual authority his office still enjoyed, as well as the revenues from his secular patrimony that were rarely spent on furthering the general interest of Christendom, gambled them on the result of a highly uncertain military adventure – and won.

CHAPTER FOUR

THE PLOT

The 'why' of Lepanto also requires us to review treasured preconceptions about western cultural pre-eminence. Lord Acton – of personally grateful memory for the fine collection of books on this period he bequeathed to the Cambridge University Library – declared that modern European history began under the stress of Ottoman conquest. Less felicitously Braudel mooted the idea that Ottoman expansion was driven in part by a desire to reach out to western culture, without specifying what they might have found even subconsciously attractive in a culture they believed was defined by savage internecine warfare, and governed by dirty and treacherous idolaters who copulated with their own children. To the contrary, with few exceptions said dirty and treacherous idolaters beat a path to the Sublime Porte with petitions for financial and military assistance against each other. We have seen how the 'Barbary pirates' were a projection onto the alien other of qualities more certainly associable with, say, the Knights of Malta, whose outstanding fighting ability should not obscure the fact that they routinely committed sickening crimes and licensed the scum of the earth to sail under their banners. Likewise the sack of defenceless Tunis by Charles V in 1535 equalled any atrocity ever imputed to the Ottomans, and included the wanton destruction of art and literature, the systematic desecration of mosques and the murder or enslavement of thousands of men, women and children. Far from being ashamed of it, Charles commissioned twelve tapestries to celebrate his Crusade.[1]

Such were the cultural values of the greatest Christian prince since

Charlemagne, one who was known to find Papal intransigence irksome and, if only for reasons of state, inclined towards less dogmatic, more inclusive Humanism, which if adopted might have kept the Roman church genuinely catholic. So also a cultural blind spot that still afflicts many historians, thus:

> Now Islam was a religion of a very different stamp from Christianity. Doctrinally it represented a far more intransigent form of their shared Judaic monotheism; and politically it spread as a result not of missionaries but of conquerors. The result was a faith a good deal less disposed to accommodate and perpetuate the cultures it encountered than was Christianity.[2]

This is an indefensibly partisan statement, and the idea that Christianity has been more tolerant and possessed of greater intrinsic power of persuasion is laughable. The suggestion of a common ancestry is also questionable – scholars with high cross-cultural reputations argue, persuasively, that the Judaeo-Christian elements in the Koran have been overstated.[3] However, my aim is not to compare one with another, rather to treat Islam and Christianity alike as historical phenomena, neither of them susceptible to rational analysis and both subject to exploitation by individuals and institutions more concerned with advancing their own interests than with the actual teachings of the holy men in whose names they profess to act. Edward Gibbon, the finest prose stylist ever to address himself to a historical theme in the English language, put it succinctly:

> If the Christian apostles, St. Peter or St. Paul, could return to the Vatican, they might possibly enquire the name of the Deity who is worshipped with such mysterious rites in that magnificent temple. At Oxford or Geneva they would experience less surprise, but it might still be incumbent on them to peruse the catechism of the church and to study the orthodox commentators on their own writings and the words of their Master. But the Mohammedans have uniformly withstood the temptation of reducing the object of their faith and devotion to a level with the senses and imagination of man.[4]

More recently there has been a regrettably triumphalist tone in what amounts to a new tradition of western historicism, notably the jocularly blasphemous 'end of history' thesis, which purports to show how safely neutered capitalism and democracy represent the fulfilment of a process of historical inevitability and have resolved every important question. A recent extension of this to the military sphere asserts that following Lepanto, 'the future of military dynamism was no longer with horsemen, nomads or corsairs, but returned to the old paradigm of classical antiquity: superior technology, capital-creating economies, and civic militias'.[5]

There is no disputing the role of technology and economic dynamism in military power, although to claim them as the decisive factors in western world dominance prior to the nineteenth century is to equip hindsight with a radio telescope. However, the suggestion that Lepanto represented the belated restoration of a Greco-Roman cultural continuum goes to the heart of this chapter. With regard only to the military details, the closest thing to an effective civic militia at Lepanto was Ottoman, and the only (alleged) technological novelty was the galleass, a marginally useful Venetian expedient akin to the large oared artillery platforms built by the Ottomans since the beginning of the century. That in due course Christian societies became more intellectually open, innovative, prosperous and militarily dominant is undeniable, but it requires a leap of wilfully blind faith to believe that this was prefigured by Lepanto. At that time the Ottomans better represented the pluralism and tolerance upon which the West congratulates itself today, while one may fairly question how 'progressive' the outcome was in the light of the social stagnation, economic backwardness and conspiratorial, sanguinary politics in all countries where the Roman Catholic church remained dominant.

Let us not, therefore, impose any backdated significance, still less a forward-looking purposefulness on any episode in a chaotic post-Renaissance period when only the blissfully ill-informed could possibly have believed they really knew what was going on. The revolutionary nature of much that occurred at that time is difficult to systematize even today, although we can pick and choose among events to fasten on those we judge most important in the light of later developments. Princes generally clung to traditional ways because it is a fact of political life that reforms made under pressure fan the discontents they seek to assuage, and there was no moment during the century when the pressure on existing institutions was other than intense. Lacking even the necessary mental framework to make sense of the economic and social processes rocking the ground under their feet, most of them chose to act pre-emptively in order to impose some predictability on a cascade of otherwise uncontrollable events.

The great exception was Philip II, who was averse to meeting trouble halfway. We may judge him harshly as a king and still feel pity for him as a man who endured a string of appalling personal tragedies, and who towards the end of his life had to believe the face of God had turned away from him, as one after another his enterprises failed. Yet he still did his lonely duty with dignity and to the best of his limited ability until his body failed him. So also the much-derided popes, usually old men in whom a very human desire to leave their 'nephews' and other family members well provided for took precedence over answers to the challenges faced by their church that are much easier to identify in retrospect than they were at the time. Most of us are only too aware how little control we exercise over our own lives, yet we tend to project grand designs into the minds of those long dead. But they were no more prescient than we, and no less prone to believe fervently that what made them think well of themselves was also advantageous for the rest of humankind. Therein, rather than in the broad sweep of tidy structural themes and alleged inevitabilities, lies the true fascination of history.

The events of our period have also suffered from a distortion inherent in the modern creation of a large and growing mass of people who make a living by words detached from deeds. Historical events are subjectively perceived and subconsciously edited according to the cultural formation and economic interest of the observer, and the class under reference is inextricably associated with governments that depend as much on mental control as on coercion for the economic surplus they appropriate for their own purposes, among them the maintenance of a perception of legitimacy through state-funded education. Consequently there has been a bias, akin to a gentle cross-current on a long voyage, that over time has created a marked divergence in the perception of the state by those who, directly or indirectly, depend on it for their livelihood and self-esteem, and those who generate the surplus. Thus a predisposition among many intellectuals, regardless of their fields of expertise, to see the growth of highly centralized big government not only as inevitable but as a 'good thing', and a tendency to judge historical developments in terms of whether or not they were on course towards what most see as a self-evidently desirable outcome.

Yet government, reduced to its essentials, is indistinguishable from the protection rackets of Mafia-like criminal fraternities, many of which can trace their ancestry back to popular, proto-nationalist resistance movements against foreign overlords. The tightly centralized empires known as nation states began to develop during our period as 'good things' only as a few sharks are preferable to the shoals of piranha with which the previous multitude of smaller political associations is commonly equated. To push the analogy a little further, the sharks were governed by the prudent predator principle, whereby a potential prey item might be left alone because it performed some function they found useful, or because its value was lower than the cost of acquiring it. That cost was often prohibitive at the contested margins of empires, for although ideology and prestige often outweighs cost–benefit analysis in the imperial mentality, disaster always looms over operations against minor objectives pursued with resources corresponding to their prospective utility, rather than commensurate to the strategic exposure they involve.

It is, however, in the nature of protection rackets that they must constantly test each other's boundaries, thus the gang wars of the underworld, the damaging 'rides' (*chevauchées*) through enemy territory of the late Middle Ages, and the raids and counter-raids of our period, all seeking not so much to take assets away from an opponent as to demonstrate his weakness. During such expeditions the physical symbols of an opponent's power would be destroyed and the population massacred or carried off to servitude, leaving a residue of dispossessed individuals to bear witness to their ruler's failure to protect them. Conquest, in principle, required a different approach and as we have noted, the success of the Ottoman system of territorial expansion lay in the control exercised over troops who looked to a stable personal reward at the end of a campaign, and were therefore inclined by self-interest to preserve the physical assets and the goodwill of populations they absorbed. Conquest by contemporary western soldiers, who had no personal stake in the prosperity and governability of the territories they occupied, and for whom loot provided compensation for their lack of assured remuneration, differed in no important detail from the brutal modalities of merely punitive raids.

A full-scale invasion might not have conquest as its ultimate end, but could instead seek to provoke a trial of strength, as eloquently expressed in the reply given by Suleiman to emissaries from Ferdinand of Austria during the massive Ottoman expedition of 1532:

> Know that my purpose is not against you, but has been against the king of Spain [the Emperor Charles V] from the very first time I took the kingdom of Hungary with my sword. When we shall have reached his German frontier, it will not be fitting for him to abandon his provinces and kingdoms to us and take flight, for the provinces of kings are as their very wives. And if they are left by fleeing husbands to fall prey to outsiders it is an extraordinary indecency. The king of Spain has long been proclaiming that he wants to take action against us, but it is I who by the grace of God am advancing with my army against him. If he is a man of courage, let him await me in the field, and the issue will be whatever God wills. If, however, he chooses not to await my coming, let him send tribute to my imperial Majesty.[6]

Which explains why this particular elephant gave birth only to the insignificant mouse of the siege of Güns (Köszeg) in western Hungary. The invasion was simply a provocation, emphasized by denying Charles's claim to the title of Roman emperor, which Suleiman considered belonged to his house by right of conquest. But it also underlined the signature Ottoman failure to appreciate that their enemies might not react as they would to a given set of circumstances. Charles did not feel his honour or his interest was invested in a mere border fort, so Suleiman's army had to retrace its steps with nothing to show for a year's campaigning.

Peace is not a natural condition but one brought into being by increasing the benefits of non-violence while simultaneously raising the risks of war. What we call 'appeasement' is a failure to maintain a balance between carrot and stick, rewarding the threat of violence without making the prospect of resorting to it correspondingly unattractive. The term is often used to describe Venetian policy during our period, but this underestimates the deterrent value of her fleet and the diplomatic skill with which it successfully appealed for Papal authority to be used on her behalf when threatened by the Ottomans. The Venetians used the word *antemurale* to describe the status of Cyprus and their other island holdings, and in the terminology of the *trace-italienne* system of fortification this was not a bastion but rather an

Diagram 2 *Trace Italienne* system of fortification

Overhead view

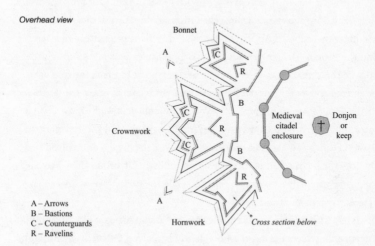

A – Arrows
B – Bastions
C – Counterguards
R – Ravelins

Cross section

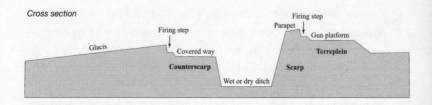

Principle of the bastioned trace
(fire from the recessed flank of Bastion A rakes the angled face of Bastion B and vice versa)

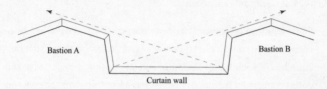

outwork built to keep the enemy at a distance from the bastioned trace, such as the bonnet, horn and crown works portrayed in *Diagram 2*. As such it was entitled to the unqualified support of the fortified place without falling within its walls, a neat encapsulation of the Venetian point of view.[7]

But what was the fortified place in question? Certainly not the Spanish Empire, whose *antemurale* against the Ottoman threat lay across the central Mediterranean, with Apulia, Calabria and Sicily representing one flank and the North African presidios the other. Malta was not so much the apex of this outwork as an arrow exposed beyond it to break the first wave of an enemy assault. Nor did the Venetian islands contribute to the defence of the Holy Roman Empire, and Venice herself was sheltered – if on a mutually begrudged basis – by Austrian Carniola and the remnant of Austro-Hungarian Slavonia and Croatia. Given the distances involved and the logistical constraints, there was no realistic Ottoman threat to the territorial integrity of western Europe while the twin crownworks of the Hapsburg dynasty stood firm.

Latin Christendom was another matter, involving as it did a complex interplay between a distant, ambivalently perceived Ottoman threat and rending internal dissension that posed dangers much nearer home. To extend further the analogy with the fortifications in *Diagram 2*, Rome was the ancient donjon and the Papal State the citadel bounded by militarily obsolete but symbolically significant towers, linked by a tall but dilapidated wall. The rest of Italy was the more modern bastioned trace and greater Christendom provided the outworks, all of which were manned by mercenaries paid in part – at times almost entirely – from revenues provided by the local churches. The Papal State itself incurred heavy military costs only during the war Paul IV fomented against the Hapsburgs in 1556–58, and during Saint Pius V's Holy League against the Ottomans in 1570–73. As Braudel commented:

> Their religious policies and indeed their policies in general in Christendom, were pursued less at their own expense than at that of the national churches. The churches of France and Spain were abandoned to the covetousness and financial needs of His Most Christian Majesty and His Catholic Majesty respectively.[8]

The concentric lines of Christendom began to break down during the sixteenth century, as commanders of the outermost works such as Henry VIII of England decided their interests were better served by seizing all the church revenues within, to become independent fortresses. But the far greater danger was that those manning nearer and more powerful works might turn covetous eyes upon the citadel or even the donjon itself. It was therefore in the vital interest of the popes to keep the attention of the out-work commanders fixed over the glacis towards the external threat, or jealously upon each other. None went further than the Neapolitan Gian' Pietro Carafa (Pope Paul IV), who entered into treasonous communication with the Ottomans in an attempt to organize a combined assault with the French upon the empire of Charles V. The emperor was fortunate that Paul IV's short papacy coincided with the first of a succession of weak kings in France and did not occur during the lifetime of his great rival François I, who made no secret of the reason for the Ottoman alliance he pursued from the time of his defeat and capture at Pavia in 1525, finally formalized in 1536:

> I cannot deny that I am most anxious to see the Turk remain very powerful and ready for war, not on his own account – for he is an infidel, and the rest of us are Christians – but to weaken the emperor's power, force him to heavy expenditures, and reassure all other governments against so great an enemy.

There were, however, limits to how far along that path the Papacy might walk, and Paul IV wildly exceeded them. Following the death of his uncle in 1559, Cardinal Carlo Carafa was made the scapegoat and condemned by his peers. It would have been appropriate to import an Ottoman executioner and his bowstring, but instead the strangulation was a botched ordeal in which the cord broke twice, and Carafa was finally throttled with a bed sheet.

Upon the abdication in stages of Charles V in 1556–58, the Hapsburg Empire became divided into two parts with most of its exposure to the Ottoman threat concentrated in the Austrian branch. Surrounded by the territories of the Spanish branch and with the divide and rule option discredited by the partisan folly of Paul IV, successor popes prudently desisted from stirring trouble between France and Spain and emphasized the Ottoman threat instead. In truth it needed little emphasis, for during Suleiman's reign the powerful detached redoubt of Rhodes and the hornwork of

Hungary–Transylvania had fallen, while the counterguards of Croatia and Slavonia had become half-occupied ruins. But when Leo X and Clement VII preached the Crusade on behalf of the struggle in Hungary they generated scant enthusiasm, and when Paul III declared Charles V's expedition against Tunis to be a Crusade he was merely providing an excuse for a diplomatically prudent contribution from national church revenues to an initiative embarked upon by the emperor to enhance his own prestige.

The practical problem faced by the Papacy was that, unlike the Muslim Ulema, it was a sovereign secular power as well as a source of spiritual leadership, and every ruling made in the latter capacity was devalued by usually well-founded suspicions that its real purpose was to increase its own territory and revenues. The Papacy had long since exhausted its power of convocation, as Pius II lamented in 1462:

> If we send envoys to ask aid of sovereigns, they are laughed at. If we
> impose tithes on the clergy, they appeal to a future council. If we issue
> indulgences and encourage the contribution of money by spiritual
> gifts, we are accused of avarice. People think our sole object is to amass
> gold. No one believes what we say. Like insolvent tradesmen we are
> without credit. Everything we do is interpreted in the worst way, and
> since all princes are very avaricious and all prelates of the Church are
> slaves to money, they measure our disposition by their own.

Pius IV preached the Crusade and issued indulgences for the Djerba campaign in 1560 and for the relief of Malta in 1565, but again in a supporting role. The popes had better success as the organizers of Holy Leagues in which the national interests of the participants converged, although the term was used to dignify coalitions put together by Alexander VI and Julius II against France in 1495 and 1511, and against Venice in 1508. Paul III successfully brokered the anti-Ottoman coalition that broke up in acrimony after the setback at Preveza in 1538, but it was the decisive financial contribution made by the Papacy to the Holy League of Lepanto that allowed it to reap the greater reward. To amplify the teaser at the end of the last chapter, the only clear winner was the Roman church, not so much in its contest with Islam but rather in helping it to recover the moral authority necessary to combat the Protestant Reformation. This was fair, for without the single-minded efforts of Saint Pius V (*Colour Plate 3*), the ex-Inquisitor General and devotee of Saint Thomas Aquinas (*c.* 1225–74), both members of the order known as the 'hounds of God' (*Domini canes*), the battle would not have taken place.

The reputation of the Dominican order is indelibly stained by its central role in the Inquisition, but it was born of an attempt to revive devotion within the Roman Catholic church. Secular readers may not know why Roman Catholics click beads at prayer, so an explanatory aside is in order. The beads are prayer counters specific to the cult of the Virgin Mary, in a religious exercise known as the Rosary, of Eastern Christian origin but in its present form associated with the Castilian Dominico Guzmán (*c.* 1170–1221), who founded the (Black) Friars Preachers and was canonized in 1234. Saint Dominic has been unfairly linked to the genocidal 1208–26 Crusade against the Cathars (Albigensians) of southern France. This was the work of Innocent III (1198–1216), that most imperial of popes, and in 1215 the Fourth Lateran Council rubber-stamped his view that a Crusade could be declared against any secular lord who failed to suppress heresy in his lands when required to do so by Rome. Saint Dominic in fact modelled the order he founded on the austerity and systematic devotion of the unlovely Cathars, whose inhuman fanaticism was, fatally for them, compounded by strident demonization of Papal corruption, although they were daubed with the accusations of devil-worship and sexual licentiousness that secular as well as spiritual authorities commonly employ to justify their extermination of those who defy them.

The mystery of the Rosary was revealed to Saint Dominic by the Virgin Mary, who made him promises that were to be amplified on a return visitation in the fifteenth century to Alain de la Roche, a French Dominican monk. We must examine these promises closely because the iconography of Lepanto and even the anniversary of the victory of the Holy League was to be associated so closely with the cult of the Rosary. Any attempt to summarize the promises would be open to suspicion of malicious bowdlerization, so it is best to let them speak for themselves:

1 Whoever shall faithfully serve me by recitation of the Rosary shall receive signal graces.

2 I promise my special protection and the greatest graces to those who shall recite the Rosary.

3 The Rosary shall be a powerful armour against hell, destroying vice, decreasing sin and defeating heresies.

4 It will cause virtue and good works to flourish; it will obtain for souls the abundant mercy of God; it will withdraw the heart of men from the love of the world and its vanities, and will lift them to the desire of eternal things. Oh, that souls would sanctify themselves by this means.

5 The soul which recommends itself to me by the recitation of the Rosary shall not perish.

6 Whoever shall recite the Rosary devoutly, applying himself to the consideration of its mysteries, shall never be conquered by misfortune. God will not chastise him in His justice, he shall not die an unprovided death; if he be just he shall remain in the grace of God, and become worthy of eternal life.

7 Whoever shall have a true devotion for the Rosary shall not die without the sacraments of the Church.

8 Those who are faithful to recite the Rosary shall have during their life and at their death the light of God and the plenitude of His graces; at the moment of their death they shall participate in the merits of the saints in paradise.

9 I shall deliver from purgatory those who have been devoted to the Rosary.

10 The faithful children of the Rosary shall merit a high degree of glory in heaven.

11 You shall obtain all you ask of me by the recitation of the Rosary.

12 All those who propagate the holy Rosary shall be aided by me in their necessities.

13 I have obtained from my Divine Son that all the advocates of the Rosary shall have for intercessors the entire celestial court during their life and at the hour of death.

14 All who recite the Rosary are my sons, and brothers of my only son Jesus Christ.

15 The devotion of my Rosary is a great sign of predestination.

To the secular mind, the greatest mystery of the Rosary is how a ritual borrowed from the schismatic Eastern church and tainted by association with a sect exterminated for heresy came to be a central pillar of the Counter-Reformation. The mystery deepens when we consider that a difference of opinion with the Medici and the church hierarchy over the matter of earthly vanities led to the judicial murder of the Dominican Girolamo Savonarola (1452–98) in Florence, yet in 1520 it was the Medici pope Leo X who gave the cult of the Rosary official approval. Part of the explanation lies in the fact that, in the same year, Leo X excommunicated the rebellious Augustinian monk Martin Luther, whose brimming cup of outrage overflowed when the sale of indulgences was subcontracted to secular bankers. This can also be traced back to the papacy of Innocent III, who was the first to issue them for cash and the first to declare a Crusade in order to extend the boundaries of the Papal State. There is a clear line from him to the warrior pope Julius II (1503–13), and from the Fourth to the Fifth Lateran Council of 1512-17, both of which smothered demands for reform and sanctioned the issue of indulgences.

The connection between the corruption of the crusading ideal and the Protestant Reformation is disputed, but there was no doubt in the mind of the great Humanist philosopher Erasmus, who sent his friend Sir Thomas More, without comment, a copy of the decree issued by Leo X at the close of the Fifth Lateran Council together with a copy of the *Ninety-Five Theses* nailed by Luther to the door of Wittenberg cathedral in the same year. He was less reticent in a letter to another correspondent: 'The Pope and the emperor have a new game afoot: they now use the war against the Turk as an excuse, though they have something very different in mind. We have reached the limits of despotism and effrontery.' They had indeed: the defining characteristic of the Crusade, born of a desire to affirm the unity of Christendom, had become the catalyst for its fragmentation.[9]

The battle of Lepanto took place when the cult of Our Lady of Victory, icon of the Hispanic Reconquest, was merging with that of Our Lady of the Rosary, proof of which is that in fulfilment of a pre-battle promise Don Juan de Austria donated the banner of the former, one of many flown over his flagship, to the first monastery to adopt the latter, at Monte-Síon in Spain. Saint Pius V declared the anniversary of Lepanto to be the feast day of Our Lady of Victory (*B&W Plate 5b*), and two years later the worldly

Vatican insider Gregory XIII changed this to Our Lady of the Rosary, in whose name it is celebrated to this day. The sociology of the cult of the Virgin Mary as the queen of battles and persecution would repay close examination. It is tempting to equate it with Hispanic machismo via the aggrieved mother mechanism identified by Oscar Lewis in *The Children of Sanchez*, but that is a subject I must leave to others.[10]

Rather than drown in the deep theological waters over which, unknown to most of the participants, the fleet of the Holy League rowed in 1571, let us paddle instead in the less mysterious shallows of the merely human interests at play. The last non-Italian to become pope before the present Polish incumbent was the Flemish Adrian Dedel, formerly tutor to the future Emperor Charles V, then Grand Inquisitor and Regent of Castile, who took the name Adrian VI (1522–23). Guicciardini, whose abiding influence on the military history of our period we have already noted, dismissed the learned and devout Adrian as the last 'barbarian pontiff', which tells us all we need to know about his world view and that of the institution under reference. While it is seldom enlightening to discuss religion without reference to faith, those of a secular persuasion may still find some common ground with thoughtful believers in a view of the Latin church as a privately held Italian multinational corporation devoted, above all, to maintaining its circumstantially won / divinely awarded monopoly of the central keep, and thus the potent brand name of the Roman Empire.

In its defence, the Latin church did much to moderate the cultural legacy of imperial Rome. If the Greeks gave us the tradition of battle as a ritualized, head-on clash to distil the horror into one concentrated encounter, the Romans gave us total war, systematic campaigns of extermination or subjugation without any marked preference for one over the other. The unique quality of the Roman machine was summed up in the words Tacitus put in the mouth of the Caledonian chief Galgacus, haranguing his woadies prior to battle with Tacitus' father-in-law Gnaeus Julius Agricola in AD 84:

> There is now no nation beyond us, nothing save the waves and the
> rocks and the Romans, still more savage, whose tyranny you will in
> vain appease by submission and concession. Alone of all men they

covet with equal rapacity the rich and the needy. Plunder, murder and robbery, under false pretences, they call Empire, and when they make a wasteland they call it Peace.

In words that opponents of today's European Community might echo, Galgacus continued, 'our possessions and properties they consume in taxes, our crops in subsidies', to conclude, 'do not believe [their] value on the battlefield is proportionate to their insolence in peace'. Alas for Galgacus, it was. Calculated, cold-blooded ruthlessness in war and the pursuit of long-term dominance rather than immediate sensual gratification has been the ideal of military professionalism ever since. Alongside it, often ignored but never silent, has been heard the awkward voice of Christianity insisting that those involved in war should not enjoy it, and imposing on military historians the convention that they must wring their hands over the savage events they chronicle.

Long before the elaboration of Just War theory by Saint Pius V's revered Saint Thomas Aquinas, the Koran laid down demands for justification, restraint and proportionality in war that differ only in their succinctness from Aquinas's *jus ad bellum* and *jus in bello*.[11] However, once the hurdle of 'Thou shalt not kill' had been successfully negotiated Christian theologians found it easier than their Islamic peers to justify merciless wars against heresy, and this cannot be divorced from the calculation of imperial authority that had once made the Christians themselves the object of persecution by some of the Roman emperors. Likewise echoing its secular heritage, the Roman church was more tolerant than Islam of polytheists, consistent with its flexible adaptation of pagan celebrations and symbols to Christian purposes.[12]

The period 1520–1648 was a time of passionate belief, more alike in intensity to the mood that produced the ideological holocausts of the twentieth century than to any time in between, and why this should have been so is the greatest unanswered question in the wider study of humanity. It is as though from time to time the fear of death, which all religions seek to assuage, becomes so intolerable that whole societies prefer to seek it collectively rather than wait for it to come to each member individually. The earlier period is analysed in *The Four Horsemen of the Apocalypse* (Cambridge 2000) by Andrew Cunningham and Ole Peter Grell, two scholars specializing in the history of medicine, an intriguing linkage speaking to the manner in which medical science now enjoys the prestige once reserved for religion. I will not attempt to precis the book, and recommend it to anyone seeking to get into the mind of a period far closer to our own in spirit than in time.

War, famine, pestilence and religion/ideology are indeed the basic ingredients, but precisely what it is that cooks them together to produce an apocalyptic vision is impossible to say. Although not invariably, it seems to accompany fundamental changes in our perception of the universe, specifically during the period when understanding is struggling to catch up with discovery. This is the only obvious link between the popular religious hysterias of Reformation Europe and the 'population bomb' and other pseudo-scientific scare stories of the late twentieth century, but it does not explain why strident affirmation in response to uncertainty, a constant in history, attracts a sufficient following to become repressive orthodoxy at some times and not others. That it can be a profitable wave to surf is self-evident, but since every philosophical or theological work ever written has masticated one aspect or other of the phenomenon without producing a definitive answer, the reader must excuse me if I limit myself to stating that the period we are examining was one such for western Europe, and leave it at that.

It should however be self-evident that when people believe that the sins of humankind have reached critical mass and the collective end is nigh, they will either attempt to extract the maximum enjoyment from the time remaining or else seek to make themselves spiritually worthy of more favourable consideration in the life to come. Conversely they will be less concerned with the maintenance and reform of earthly institutions, leading to polarization between those whose hopes for present comfort and future salvation are vested in them, and those who see them simply as expressions of earthly avarice and tyranny, when not also as palpable evidence of a satanic conspiracy (*B&W Plate 5a*). In the West we lack a comparable body of scholarship on Muslim holy warriors, but the informed current view of the Christian Crusader state of mind is that spiritual considerations were paramount, and that the activity involved individual hardship and expense unconditioned by calculation of earthly reward.[13]

There is always a minority that resists the temptation to leap off the cliff *du jour* and regards the rest with sometimes sardonic detachment, as expressed by Michelangelo in the *Last Judgement*, when he put the face of a senior Vatican bureaucrat on the body of a lascivious demon rampantly welcoming falling souls. Probably those genuinely in no doubt whatever that the end of the world as we know it is imminent have always been an even smaller minority, but they invariably generate vastly more heat than light and the majority will always be swayed by suspicion that if there is a great deal of smoke then hell's portals must indeed be gaping and/or catastrophic global warming looms. The mechanism whereby this may be turned to the benefit of the doomsayers is to offer the rich and powerful an opportunity to lubricate the biblical eye of the needle, along the lines of 'leave the praying/thinking to us and give us your money', or as Abbot Guibert de Nogent put it more elegantly when defining the Crusades in 1115:

> God has instituted in our time holy wars, so that the order of knights
> and the crowd running in its wake . . . might find a new way of gaining
> salvation. And so they are not forced to abandon secular affairs
> completely by choosing the monastic life or any religious profession,
> as used to be the custom, but can attain in some measure God's grace
> while pursuing their own careers, with the liberty and in the dress to
> which they are accustomed.

In practice it is difficult to decide which was the tail and which the dog in the ensuing militarization of Latin Christendom. At one level it permitted the Papacy to see off the challenge posed by the Hohenstaufen dynasty, which failed – where the Hapsburgs later succeeded – in turning the Holy Roman Empire into an hereditary office. It also increased church revenues and, by strengthening the element of service in the code of chivalry, helped to moderate the behaviour of the armoured class. On the other it legitimized xenophobia, which at the popular level rapidly escaped clerical control and gave rise to mob pogroms against the Jews. There was no natural resting place for this impulse short of nationalism, which in time led to the expropriation of church wealth and, finally, to the shrinking of the Papal State to a small enclave around Saint Peter's, all that remains today of the grant made by Charlemagne's father Pepin in AD 756.

Another element working to reduce Papal authority was that once vernacular translations of the Scriptures were made widely available thanks to the invention of the printing press, the extent to which the Roman church had abused its long monopoly of literacy became apparent. As Setton observes, 'the universal language and the universal church were going down together'. This has never happened in Islam, in which the sacred language of the Koran remains the lingua franca of all believers worldwide. Understandably loath to surrender that advantage, the Roman church clung to Latin as it did to the anti-scriptural practices that most offended the Protestants, for to do otherwise would have been to admit centuries of compound error, and to embrace the vernacular would have exposed to forensic examination the sumptuous shroud of scholastic obscurantism with which it had long clothed the body of Christ.

Possibly the greatest abuse of literacy by the Papacy was directly linked to its temporal authority by the *Constitutum domni Constantini imperatoris*, the most infamous forgery in history. It is, needless to say, a can of exceptionally vigorous worms about which little historical consensus exists beyond the evident falsity of the document in question. The second part (*Donatio*) purported to be a deed by which the Emperor Constantine conferred primacy upon Pope Saint Sylvester I (314–335) over the patriarchates of Antioch, Alexandria, Constantinople and Jerusalem, as well as directly over all bishops, denying delegation of power to the patriarchates. Roman cardinals were granted the same honours as imperial senators and the church a parallel imperial household. The Pope was to enjoy the same vestments and visible honours as the emperor, and in joint ceremonies the emperor, on foot, would lead the Pope's horse. The forger went on to gold-plate the fabrication by having Constantine make Saint Sylvester and his successors the gift of sovereignty not merely over Rome and Italy, but over all the western empire, specifying that since Constantine had established a new capital bearing his name in the East, it was improper to retain secular power where God had established the residence of His earthly representative.

The first part (*Confessio*) related how Constantine was instructed, baptized and thereby cured of leprosy by Saint Sylvester, and expounded views on the Holy Trinity, the fall of man and the incarnation of Christ that the church had not, at the purported time of writing, declared to be doctrine. An echo of the decrees against the veneration of images made by the Synod of Constantinople in 754 argues for a date of fabrication sometime after that date, and before its earliest direct quotation by Frankish authors *c.* 850. Intriguingly, they used it to establish an historical antecedent for the transfer of the imperial title to the Franks at the coronation of Charlemagne in 800, and the first reference to the document in Roman sources was at the end of the tenth century. The first executive use of the document was by Pope Leo IX in the polemic with the Eastern Patriarch Michael Caerularius that ended in their mutual excommunication and the Great Schism of 1054, unhealed to this day.

Subsequently Urban II, the father of the Crusades, and other popes including the limitlessly ambitious Innocent III used the document to substantiate territorial claims and to justify a temporal supremacy to match their spiritual authority. Their opponents were reduced to quibbling about the legal interpretations placed upon a document whose validity they did not question, and even the Greek clergy used it to claim equal status and privileges from the Byzantine emperors. Following the fall of Constantinople, the desire of the Ottoman sultans to pose as the heirs of Constantine actually increased the importance of the *Constitutum* in the eyes of the Orthodox church. But at about the same time several prelates in the West, working independently, concluded that it was an evident forgery, although Lorenzo Valla's conclusive demonstration of the unpalatable truth, arrived at in 1440, was not published until 1518.

Like all successful deception operations, the *Constitutum* told people what they wanted to hear and it lived on thanks to the human propensity to continue believing in something they feel should be true, even after it is proved to be false. In addition there was by then an accretion of precedents that made it a fact in law, and the truth about it was not a weapon that any of the heirs of the Franks could use against the Roman church without also damaging their own claim to legitimacy. Protestant churchmen were similarly inhibited, once the socially revolutionary aspects of their creed were suppressed attendant upon their alliance with conservative aristocratic protest in the 1550s, with the result that canon law and civil jurists continued to cite the document, knowing it to be false, throughout the sixteenth century. Thus Charles V, no doubt fully aware that it was a charade, nonetheless led Clement VII's horse at his coronation as Holy

Roman Emperor at Bologna in 1530. However, the next time a secular emperor included the Pope in the ceremony was at Paris in 1804 when Napoleon, the godfather of nationalism, not only omitted to lead Pius VII's horse but also crowned himself.

Libraries of books have been written about the origins and development of what is known as the 'Caesareo-Papal' issue, most of them in German because although Italy was no less held back from unity and a sense of nationhood by secular Papal pretensions, it was not also torn by the rancorous ideological divisions that scarred the history of Germany. It may be argued that the coincidence of the unifications of Italy and Germany with the disappearance of the Papal State in 1871 was circumstantial, but it is striking nonetheless. Amid cries of 'It's not that simple!' from all sides, let me hasten to qualify the above by admitting that there were sub-plots aplenty, not the least of them provided by the Wittelsbach dynasty in Bavaria, which was the most persistent German foe of Hapsburg imperialism but also provided 'the prototype of the Counter-Reformation State – a country stifled beneath the heavy hand of a vast clerical establishment and an absolutist prince'. At the other extreme was no less repressive Scotland, where the representative estates overthrew the erratic Mary and instituted their own Protestant intolerance, and England where they imposed a more radical religious settlement than Elizabeth wanted, but to which she had the wit to accede. Despite this, nostalgia for a united Christian community persisted and Elizabeth ordered celebration of the Roman Catholic victory at Lepanto even though Saint Pius V had excommunicated her and declared her overthrown a year earlier.[14]

In modern Europe we may live in a secular age, as the cliché has it, but the principal novelty is a tendency to label as 'extremists' those who believe their sacred texts are indeed divine revelations. Yet the epithet is seldom applied to the Roman church, as though its claims to exclusive truth have passed into the collective subconscious, giving it a special dispensation even among those who believe themselves to be freethinkers. For example, the instrumental role of the Roman Catholic clergy on both sides of the Atlantic in keeping the terrorist pot bubbling in Northern Ireland has long been grossly underreported, even as Protestant sectarianism has been ceaselessly denounced. For Rome, the separation of church and state means only that the state shall not interfere with the church, not vice versa, and it is easy to trace this back to our period and beyond. Even among those who deny that its policies have ever been justified by considerations of spiritual welfare and life everlasting, it merits grudging admiration as the longest-lasting and most successful political ideology in history, compared to which all the 'isms' of the nineteenth and twentieth centuries were little more than the wind passed by societies surfeited with envy and fear.

To drag this back to Lepanto, in at least one Roman Catholic country the connection has been patent. Admiral Luis Carrero Blanco (1903–73) was appointed the first president of the governing council of Spain when Generalissimo Francisco Franco Bahamonde (1892–1975) began to relinquish the iron hold on power he had exercised since the end of the Spanish Civil War of 1936–39. Six months later, in December 1973, the admiral died with almost unbearably apt symbolism when a culvert bomb placed by the Basque nationalist ETA blew his armoured limousine into the courtyard of a Madrid nunnery. Twenty-five years earlier Carrero had published a book titled *The Victory of the Christ of Lepanto*. Those educated by the Jesuits do not use sacred words carelessly, so let us explore why he did not call it simply 'The Victory of Christ at Lepanto'. Published in the aftermath of the bloodiest assault on the political influence of the Roman Catholic church in Spanish history, the book could not be other than referential, so when we ask in what way the Christ of Lepanto differed from the one who died on a cross at Golgotha, the answer is clear. Like his mother – Our Lady of Victory – Carrero's Christ was Spanish, he was a Crusader, and he was a defiantly anti-Protestant, tangible icon of Roman power, embodying not so much the apostolic succession as its imperial remit.

There was, however, a parallel movement for Roman Catholic regeneration that historians no longer regard as part of an omnibus 'Counter-Reformation' but rather as a separate response, as though the Roman church simultaneously amputated infected extremities while producing antibodies to suppress its own tumours. This dichotomy was apparent in the work of the Nineteenth Ecumenical Council, which met intermittently between 1545 and 1563 at Trento in north-eastern Italy. Very summarily, the Papacy at first rejected appeals from German princes and clergy alike to summon a free Christian council to address the issue of church corruption, and to resolve the doctrinal differences that had divided Christendom since 1064 and now threatened to tear Germany apart. Charles V urged the Pope to summon a general council, proposing Trento as the venue, but François I of France was intensely hostile to any initiative that might reduce his rival's problems. When the strongly conciliar Cardinal Alessandro Farnese became Pope Paul III (1534–59) he issued convocations to all patriarchs, bishops and abbots, but the initiatives failed in the face of Protestant and French hostility. It was not until Charles and François concluded the Peace of Crespy in 1544 that the way was clear to convoke what was by then a purely Roman Catholic council at Trento towards the end of 1545.

Charles wanted the council to concentrate on reform, but among its first decrees in 1546 was the affirmation of the doctrine of original sin and the pronunciation of anathema against opposing doctrines. In 1547 the scandal of absentee holders of ecclesiastical benefices was addressed, no small matter for an institution dominated by prelates who regarded even the seemingly minor reform of requiring bishops to reside in their sees as a dangerous novelty. Against this, the council abandoned all pretence of ecumenicism and issued an intemperately broad condemnation of heresy. Nothing further of substance emerged until Pope Julius III (1550–55) reopened negotiations with Charles. Henri II of France continued to sabotage the project but the Protestant princes sent ambassadors and some effort was made to open the door to them, until Maurice of Saxony slammed it shut again by attacking the emperor. As we have seen, reconciliation was the last thing on the mind of Paul IV, and it was not until he was succeeded by Pius IV (1559–65), and Charles by his brother Ferdinand in Germany and by his son Philip in Spain, that the final session of the Council began in 1562.

The new emperor proposed a plan for church reform to preserve the formula that had brought peace to Germany (that the religion of a territory should be that of its ruler), but it was rejected. A small and soon rescinded concession was made in permitting the laity a greater participation in the Mass, but overall the council was devoted more to sharpening the Protestant–Roman Catholic divide and to strengthening Italian predominance than to reform. However, everyone wanted to bring the Council to a conclusion, and in 1563 the thorny issues of indulgences and clerical immorality were finally addressed, balanced by an expanded Index of Forbidden Books that included the works of Erasmus, and by a resounding affirmation of the veneration and invocation of saints. These and previous decrees were confirmed by Pius IV in January 1564 and broadly accepted in Roman Catholic countries. The entry in *The Catholic Encyclopedia* (1912, online 1999) concludes: 'Although unfortunately the Council, through no fault of the fathers assembled, was not able to heal the religious differences of western Europe, yet the infallible Divine Truth was clearly proclaimed in opposition to the false doctrines of the day, and in this way a firm foundation was laid for the overthrow of heresy and the carrying out of genuine internal reform in the Church.' Need one say more?

Institutions only reform themselves when the interests of those running them are threatened, and the Italian clergy were not so much moved by Protestant agitation that did not affect them directly, as by a wave of stern monasticism emerging from hegemonial Spain. Mystics like Saints Juan de la Cruz (1542–91) and Teresa de Avila (1515–82) had been co-opted in the past, but the Jesuits were a potentially double-edged sword. Although now only the shadow of its former self, the Society of Jesus can pride itself on having done more than any other to make the Roman church intellectually respectable. It was founded by Saint Ignacio de Loyola (1491–1556), a Basque knight crippled for life in 1521. During his convalescence he determined to adopt a paramilitary approach to spiritual life and after a year at prayer he made a penitential pilgrimage to Jerusalem. Later he studied at Paris and graduated in philosophy, having gathered six followers including Saints Peter Canisius and Francisco Xavier. By now all ordained priests, they went to Rome and proposed a new religious order, stripped of ornaments such as the choral mass, to serve the Pope according to the principle 'we must always be ready to believe that white is black, if the hierarchical church so disposes', as propounded by Saint Ignacio in *Spiritual Exercises*, the Field Service Manual of the Counter-Reformation.

The Jesuits are highly relevant to our story because they supplied the chaplains on the Hapsburg galleys in the Holy League fleet at Lepanto, as well as two of its most distinguished historians.[15] They gained Papal approval in 1540 and became the magnet for precisely the type of knightly vocation described by Guibert de Nogent in 1115, as such representing a new solution to the concept of penitential war that gave birth to the Crusades, which Jonathan Riley-Smith argues was 'one of the most radical expressions of European thought, . . . too uncomfortable to secure for itself a permanent place in the theology and practice of Christian violence'. The older tradition lived on in orders such as the Knights of Saint John on Malta, but the Jesuits represented a development of the parallel ideology pronounced by learned prelates as early as 1100, which held that the heavenly Jerusalem was just as important as the terrestrial city and the Holy Sepulchre, and could be won by fighting the enemies of the church in the West.[16]

The Roman church regarded proselytism with extreme caution because of experience with the likes of Savonarola, but it was not equipped to defend itself in the realm of ideas and came to depend on the Society of Jesus for lack of any other resource. It is seldom advantageous to have princes beholden to you, and the later history of relations between the Jesuits and the Papacy reflects the ambivalence that men who are conservative by inheritance feel towards those in their own camp whom they consider 'too clever by half'. During our period, however, the missionary efforts of the Jesuits, coupled with the enlightened educational methods they pioneered, salvaged Roman authority in central Europe, particularly in Poland where they laid the foundations for the revival of Roman Catholic fortunes in the latter half of the twentieth century, when Poland almost alone countered a worldwide slump in vocation. An early tribute to their intellectual power came when the Protestant churches banned the writings of Saints Peter Canisius and Roberto Bellarmino (1542–1621), who refuted Luther's catechism and defended Roman teachings using the terminology of Protestant theology against itself.

At the time of Lepanto the order was under the command of its 'second founder', Saint Francisco de Borja (1510–72). The great-grandson of Pope Alexander VI and of King Ferdinand the Catholic, he was made viceroy of Catalonia by Charles V in 1529 and became a Jesuit after the wife by whom he had eight children died in 1546. Ordained in 1554 and made Commissary of Spain and Portugal by Loyola, he became general of the order in 1565, was entrusted with founding what was to become the Gregorian University by Pius IV, and launched the missionary work in the Americas that in time produced the fascinating anomaly of Paraguay. There the Society organized and led the Guaraní in armed resistance to Hispanic encroachment, as captured by Robert de Niro's brilliant portrayal of a warrior Jesuit in the film *The Mission*. Their English reputation as the shock troops of the Counter-Reformation arose from their role in subverting the Protestant settlement, and there are ten Jesuits among the forty English and Welsh martyrs (selected from 200 previously beatified candidates) canonized by Paul VI in 1970 to remind the ecumenically minded Anglican church of its very own original sin.

To leaven what has so far been a somewhat cavalier treatment of the Italian clergy, mention must also be made of one who should be the patron saint of the 'Mandarin' bureaucratic tendency, the nobleman Carlo Borromeo (1538–84). Born to great wealth and to the hereditary abbacy of Arona, he had ecclesiastical posts heaped on him by his maternal uncle Pius IV (of a minor Medici line), such that he was already the archbishop of Milan, a cardinal and Vatican Secretary of State before being ordained a priest and made a bishop in 1564. He was the most energetic proponent of reopening the Trento council for its final session in 1563, one of whose central purposes was to abolish the abuses of which he had been such a prominent beneficiary, and the principal author of the catechism that survived 300 years, as well as almost maniacally detailed instructions on the exact performance of all clerical duties. In 1565 Saint Pius V released him to reside in Milan, the first archbishop to do so in a century, where he set a unique example of pastoral care and devotion. When Luis de Requeséns y Zúñiga was appointed Spanish viceroy of Milan following his stewardship of Don Juan at Lepanto, Borromeo did not let their friendship stand in the way of his assertion of ecclesiastical independence, culminating in a precedent-setting excommunication of the astounded Requeséns and his departure to what must, by that time, have seemed more straightforward duties in the rebellious Netherlands.

The remaining element in the recovery of the Roman church was to give substance to what had become formulaic calls for Christian unity against the Ottoman–Islamic threat. In the convocation by Paul III to the Trento council in November 1544, the terms were (my italics), 'in order more securely and freely to bring to the desired conclusion those matters . . . which relate to the removal of religious discord, the reform of Christian morals, *and the launching of an expedition under the most sacred sign of the cross against the infidel*'. When we consider that a desire to embark upon a Crusade was the given reason for the French invasion of Italy in 1494, which toppled the dominoes whose fall Guicciardini was to lament so influentially half a century later, the Papacy's desire to recover the banner of the cross can be seen as inseparable from its simultaneous struggle to reform under intense pressure while preserving its autonomy.

To return to *Diagram 2*, the Council of Trent erected a bastioned trace around the citadel of the Roman church, a project vigorously brought to fruition by Borromeo. Meanwhile the Dominicans rooted out all those within whose loyalty was in any way suspect, with the Rosary akin to the oaths of allegiance with which secular imperial ideologies have sought to affirm their legitimacy in more recent times. Lastly Loyola directed a corps of daring and imaginative warriors to conduct raids upon rebellious outworks, keeping them on the defensive while giving those still loyal pause for thought about what might be the consequences were they also to stray from the fold. Like a fortress threatened by two mutually hostile armies, the Roman Catholic church then sallied to do battle first with the less pressing Ottoman foe, to break a long sequence of retreats and defeats and to infuse its own troops with renewed confidence in its leadership, before engaging the more dangerous threat from its own schismatics and heretics. As to the medieval donjon of Rome itself, the holders of the dubious title deed had progressed as far as embracing the Renaissance principle that ostentation was power, but saw no reason for further change. In the following chapter we shall review that principle, which came to assume ever greater importance once the church realized that it could no longer control hearts and minds by way of a firm grip on other parts of the anatomy of Christendom.

CHAPTER FIVE

BILLBOARD

The manner in which Lepanto was 'sold' to contemporaries and to posterity provides the key to understanding its cultural significance. As a schoolboy I recall feeling aggrieved that the Council of Trent had not taken place along the river of that name in central England, as I had guessed in an exam, and outraged that the adjectival form was 'Tridentine', which had led me to further speculation about the relationship between the Trinity and Neptune's sceptre. I still think it deserved some credit for chutzpah, but alas, my imaginative effort received an 'F'. The shadow of another fell upon me as it dawned that I had reasoned myself into writing a chapter on the artistic counterpoint to the social and political developments addressed by the Tridentine decrees. Unfortunately it is a subject about which little consensus exists among art historians, who are prone to bickering over categories. It is no less misleading to slice artistic trends into named segments than it is to employ the 'Age of . . .' convention in more general historical works, but the following terminology has become too well established to be ignored.[1]

'Mannerism' refers to an overemphasis on style over content associated with Giorgio Vasari (1511–74), whose written work is to the history of art what Guicciardini is to military historians, and whose work with the brush is represented here (*Colour Plate 6a*) by one of the two paintings of Lepanto in the Sala Regia of the Vatican commissioned by Pope Gregory XIII. The other is the more familiar one of the opposing fleets lined up almost spur to spur in what is little more than a pedantic exercise in perspective. Mannerism is said to have marked a plateau between the

High Renaissance represented by Michelangelo (1475–1564) and the return to observed nature by Caravaggio (1573–1610) and to Classicism by Annibale Carracci (1560–1609) in the Baroque, which became the dominant style across Europe during the seventeenth century. This division breaks down when we consider the enormously influential Venetian school, in which Titian (1487–1576) anticipated the use of light and the didacticism of the early Baroque, while Tintoretto (1518–94) is considered to have short-circuited straight from the High Renaissance to the Baroque.[2] Not particularly illustrative of this is Tintoretto's portrait of the Venetian Admiral Sebastiano Venier (*Colour Plate 5*), for unfortunately his rendition of the battle in the Palazzo Ducale was lost to fire in 1577. The busy canvas (*Colour Plate 6b*) that replaced it is by Andrea Vicentino (*c.* 1539–1617), who had assisted with the original and presumably got the commission because the master himself was fully taken up with the cycle commissioned by the Fraternity of the Rosary for their chapel in the church of Saints Giovanni and Paolo. The cycle showed the Holy League commanders led by Saint Dominic but, alas, it too was lost to fire, in 1867.

There was certainly nothing Mannerist about the work of Veronese (1528–88), whose *Battle of Lepanto* (*Colour Plate 7*) is a Baroque apotheosis. The supplicants around the Virgin Mary are Saints Peter, Mark and James, for Rome, Venice and Spain, with Venice herself in a white bridal veil next to Saint Justina. The latter was a minor saint who already had a church dedicated to her in Venice, on whose feast day the battle was fought and who thus became the patron saint of the Venetian navy.[3] A dog-like lion of Venice gazes down on a battle scene below, where shafts of brilliant light bless the Holy League fleet while darkness envelops the Ottoman, upon which flaming arrows rain. Veronese's *Thanksgiving for Lepanto* (not reproduced here) over the throne in the Collegio Hall of the Palazzo Ducale is less inspired. Like the Vicentino painting, it was commissioned by Sebastiano Venier during his brief term as *duce* in 1577–78 and shows Venier in his ducal robes with Saints Mark and Justina next to him, Faith with a chalice crouched on the other side, all with a hand extended towards another unconvincing lion. Beyond Venier stands Agostino Barbarigo in the full armour that failed to save his life at Lepanto. Saint Justina looks down towards the throne, the rest are gazing up at Christ on a cloud with a riotous assembly of angels behind him. Whatever style we may ascribe to them, these are self-evident works of political propaganda and conveyed the same message to those entering the halls of state of the Palazzo Ducale as Vasari's paintings were intended to impress upon those granted an audience in the Sala Regia of the Vatican.

The passionate vision of El Greco (1541–1614), who moved from Rome to Toledo in 1577 and spent the rest of his life in Spain, is also impossible to cram into the Mannerist straitjacket. He did apotheosis better than anyone but unfortunately Philip II did not like his work, and the six mediocre paintings of Lepanto in the Escorial (not reproduced here) were executed by the Genoese Luca Cambiaso (1527–88) towards the end of his life in the style of Michelangelo, perforce making them representative examples of the Mannerist style. These are purely descriptive works, little more than exercises in cartography devoid of emotion. While it is not surprising that the Venetians did not exalt the role of Don Juan, the other work Philip II commissioned to celebrate Lepanto also ignored his half-brother. This was Titian's portrait of him holding up his newborn son to receive a palm frond from an angel (*Colour Plate 4*). There is an element here of Philip as Abraham, offering up his son in thanksgiving for the outcome of the battle portrayed in the background, symbolized by the slave crouched at his feet, but it is really a review of God's blessings upon His Catholic Majesty, the son in whom He is well pleased.

The Mannerist/Baroque divide is harder still to sustain if we look to northern Europe, and seems to have a useful application only if we limit our focus to Rome. The Papal court devoted a far greater part of its enormous revenues to the arts than any other could afford to do, and artists respond to money as heliotropes to the sun. A tentative redefinition of the origins of the Baroque might be the exuberant response of the artistic community once Roman patronage came back on line in the latter sixteenth century. The Venetian anomaly may have reflected that there was no break in local funding from oligarchs who, despite their shattering defeat at Agnadello in 1509, maintained a corporate self-confidence that the Papacy took longer to recover following the sack of Rome in 1527. The highly developed commercial astuteness of the Venetian school is here captured by *B&W Plate 7*, a journeyman classical allegory that Titian adapted by painting a turban on Neptune and putting a spear in the hand of Minerva, renaming it *Spain Coming to the Aid of Religion* and selling the unconvincing composition to Philip II. It still hangs proudly in the Prado museum, although a better title would be *Venice putting one over on Spain*, and as such a fair symbolic representation of the economic advantages the Venetians hoped to derive from their alliance with the Papacy and Spain in the Holy League of Lepanto.[4]

We should not forget that Rome then was the Disney World of the day and that, government functions aside, the pilgrim–tourist trade has always been its principal economic activity. But during most of the sixteenth century it was a slum punctuated with ruins, infested with foot-pads and aggressive prostitutes, and regularly wracked by cholera epidemics resulting from using the Tiber as both sewer and source of drinking water. Seen in that light, the urban renewal begun by Sixtus V (1585–90) was shamefully long overdue on economic as well as humanitarian grounds. The Magic Kingdom element of Baroque splendour that has balanced the decline in the numbers of pilgrims with millions of secular tourists owes much to Camillo Borghese, who took the name Paul V (1605–21) and who modestly had his full name and title inscribed across the facade of the basilica of Saint Peter. Indeed, one can scarcely turn a corner in Rome without encountering the eagle over a dragon of the Borghese coat of arms. But the architecture was merely advertising, and it was the pictorial arts that had to make the sale. Here faith – mysterious, unreasoning and at times orgasmic – was exalted. The most important leap it had to make was across the chasm of the seemingly adamant prohibition contained in the three-part Second Commandment, which bears quoting in full:

> Thou shalt not make unto thee any graven image, or any likeness of any thing that is in heaven above, or that is in the earth beneath, or that is in the water under the earth:
>
> Thou shalt not bow down to them, nor serve them: for I the Lord thy God am a jealous God, visiting the iniquity of the fathers upon the children unto the third and fourth generation of them that hate me; And showing mercy unto thousands of them that love me, and keep my commandments. (Exodus 20:4–6)

Canon lawyers may deal with matters spiritual, but they are lawyers nonetheless and the last phrase provided a technicality that opened the door to the sumptuary idolatry apparently slammed and bolted by parts one and two, justifying it as a means of focusing men's minds on the object of their devotion. Along with a greater allowance for human sensuality, in particular among its own servants, the collective consciousness of the Roman church also knew that the Protestants had foolishly devalued the institutional advantages of what Dostoevsky's Grand Inquisitor, after rebuking the returned Christ for the doctrinal mess he had left for the church to clear up after his last visit, identified as mankind's yearning for miracle, mystery and authority. This was a psychological advantage Rome had no intention of surrendering. However, the jolt administered by furious Protestant iconoclasm was the catalyst for the Tridentine require-ment that the High Renaissance celebration of the human body should be harnessed to didactic needs, and the manner of presentation made secondary to the emotional appeal of the subject matter.

The figure of Cardinal Alessandro Farnese (1520–89), grandson of his namesake Pope Pius III, stands alongside Borromeo as one of the pillars of the less reactionary, more positive part of the Roman Catholic Reformation.[5] Elliott argues that he not only gave the Jesuits the Baroque prototype church of the Gesù in Rome, but was also the inspiration for their signature cultural eclecticism and commitment to scholarship, accord-ing to the Baroque elements of dynamism and unity which Mannerism had conspicuously lacked.[6] My own view, product of my great fondness for them, is that Farnese is a better example than Borromeo of the genius of the Italian people, who have a more profound acquaintanceship than most with bad laws and with irredeemably corrupt and fatuously incom-petent rulers, and who prosper by largely ignoring both. Tridentine Roman Catholicism rejected the ecumenical coherence of Humanism along with the harsh visions of Zwingli, Calvin and Luther, but it indirectly affirmed a quintessentially Italian love of family, of earthly delights, of being comfortable within one's own skin, and of looking good for no higher purpose than because it is a pleasing thing to do.

What other people could have given us Pope Urban VIII (1623–44), who commissioned Gian'Lorenzo Bernini (1598–1680) to erect that totem of the High Baroque, the bronze canopy (*baldacchino*) over the altar in Saint Peter's, itself over the tomb of the Apostle, and to encrust it with the emblems of his family? This is not some austere statement of ethereal devotion but accessible human vanity, emphasized by the sequence of bas-relief variations of the Barberini coat of arms on the marble pedestals, which show a woman in labour and a child emerging from the womb, proudly celebrating the birth of the Holy Father's grandchild. In time this led to the ornamental excesses of the Rococo, here represented by the obscure Sebastian de Caster's battle scene (*Colour Plate 8a*), in which the galleys have become absurdly stylized and the event reduced to a flamboyant spectacle.

To return to our period, Lepanto provided a rare opportunity for Italian artists to celebrate a significant contemporary victory. In the most achingly lost opportunity in the history of art, competing frescoes by Leonardo and Michelangelo were to have graced the walls of the Great Hall in the Palazzo Vecchio in Florence, but never progressed beyond the sketching stage. They were to have celebrated Cascina (Michelangelo) and Anghiari (Leonardo), minor battles if parochially important victories over Pisa in 1364 and Milan in 1440 respectively.[7] The battles other than Lepanto celebrated on Venetian walls and ceilings were of similar vintage, and it seems likely that the slide of Italy into military irrelevance helped to keep alive a tradition of heroic representation, while to the north harsh reality produced some of the most gut-wrenching depictions of war ever painted.

The Martyrdom of the Ten Thousand, painted by Nuremberg's Albrecht Dürer (1471–1528) for Frederick of Saxony in 1501, pointed the way to a darker sensibility with its gruesomely realistic depiction of Turks inventively massacring Christians. But it was the Flemish Pieter Bruegel (*c.* 1520–69), walking in the proto-surrealist footsteps of Hieronymus Bosch (*c.* 1450–1516), who took it to an unbearably intense level with *The Triumph of Death*, whose many revolting details include a starving dog gnawing on a baby next to its dead mother, a choir of skeletons in surplices under a crucifix, desperate men being driven into a glittering box decorated with the cross of Saint John, and a slain king surrounded by skeletons looting his barrels of money. It would be as well to ponder – at length – on the fact that Philip II purchased this appalling and deeply subversive allegory, not to destroy it but to hang it in his private apartments. One conclusion we may draw is that the man who provided the muscle for the Papally-inspired Crusades against the Ottomans in 1570–73 and against the English in 1588–97 was no Crusader, and did not share his half-brother Juan's

Italianate view of war as an arena for chivalric posturing, blessed by the Virgin Mary and attendant saints.

There is no equivalent in Islamic culture of the pornography of violence that has been such a profitable genre for western artists ever since the Renaissance. Sado-eroticism infuses many depictions of martyrdom while rape is a hardy perennial, liberally adorned with bulging buttocks and thrusting breasts. Sometimes the sadism is not even disguised by a religious or classical theme, as in the painting of the Saint Bartholomew's Day massacre in Paris reproduced on pages 196–197 of Thomas Arnold's *The Renaissance at War*. This shows a naked woman being dragged by her hair; another ripped open and her baby torn out; children dragging the body of another child; men, women and children being clubbed and stabbed to death; defenestration, decapitation, disembowelment; drowning and hanging. This was not propaganda but in effect a snapshot of an event that took place in the largest city in Christendom, and of ordinary people calmly doing extraordinarily disgusting things. The point is not that western society was more violent and cruel than others – there is too much competition for that claim to stand, and most would agree that the blue ribbon for diabolical ingenuity goes to the infamous 'death of a thousand cuts' devised by the exquisitely cultured Mandarins of Manchu China. What is extremely remarkable is that sixteenth-century battle art is relatively antiseptic, with little of the mutilation and agony that features so heavily in religious pictures.

Our colour plates illustrate that in art Lepanto became a prettified Italian artefact and as such entered the collective consciousness of the West. Thus the Howard Baker play *Scenes from an Execution* concerns the rebellion of the painter Galactica against sexism, etc., who expresses it in a vast canvas of Lepanto that depicts the butchery and rejects the glorification of war. We shall examine next the military reality of a geopolitical showdown between the Spanish and Ottoman empires, in which the Italians were no less the willing mercenaries of the Spanish than were the Greeks of the Ottomans. The artistic heritage of Greece and Rome, like European affairs in general, could no longer be contained within the limited amphitheatre of the inland sea. Braudel questioned the (once) orthodox view that the Baroque was a symptom of the decadence of Mediterranean culture, 'unless decadence and the disintegration it implies can be credited with a powerful capacity for diffusing a dying civilization'. But just as hanged men ejaculate, should we not suppose that civilizations also make one last supreme effort to escape genetic extinction?

Juan de Austria's galley *La Real* occupies a place somewhere between pictorial art and literature and provides a further fascinating glimpse into the complex mind of Philip II. After he appointed his half-brother to the post of Captain General of the Sea in January 1568, Philip ordered the construction of the massive galley at the Ataranzas of Barcelona where her replica, the most evocative of all Lepanto artefacts, sits proudly today (*B&W Plate 1b*). The vessel was not merely intended to be larger and more imposing than any other, but also to have moral authority, and to that end was rowed to Seville for embellishment. The Flemish influence that worked upon Charles V was merely attenuated, not lost, in his Spanish son, and Philip entrusted the moral design of *La Real* to Juan de Mal-Lara (*c.* 1524–1571), a notable Humanist who had spent three weeks as a guest of the Inquisition in 1561 under suspicion of having written heretical verse. Contradicting his rigidly orthodox image, in 1566 Philip commissioned Mal-Lara to produce four Latin verses and an octave in Spanish for each of six paintings in his collection, to underline their didactic or symbolic significance.

Two years later Mal-Lara's instructions were to create an environment 'of great benefit and delight' for the young Juan de Austria, and he turned the poop of *La Real* into an elaborate Humanist classroom of more than a hundred works of sculpture, bas-relief, marquetry, embroidery and painting, each with its own Latin epigram. Even the benches where Juan and his officers dined had place settings inlaid with allegorical dishes identifying princely virtues. Thus the olives are subtitled *Vivitur Exiguo Melius* (live better with less), and the translated epigram reads, 'Take sparingly of the pleasurable: delectation exhausts the young and weakens adult men'. The great majority of the illustrations and epigrams were pre-Christian, featuring Roman gods and astrological signs, while on the canopy that shaded the poop were six ancient commanders (Minos, Jason, Themistocles, Julius, Pompey and Augustus) and six modern counterparts (Roger of Sicily, Roger de Lauria, Jaime I and Alfonso V of Aragon, Andrea Doria and Charles V). Hovering over the ensemble might have been the words 'Big Brother Is Watching You, Rather Anxiously'. The only specifically religious

Diagram 3 *La Real* lantern

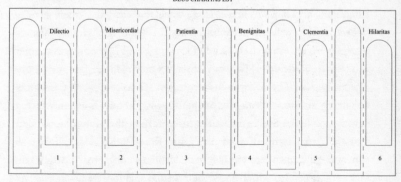

DEUS CHARITAS EST

Dilectio   Misericordia   Patientia   Benignitas   Clementia   Hilaritas

1   2   3   4   5   6

GOD IS LOVE (I John, 4.16)

1. **Dilectio** Qui diliget fratrem suum in lumine manet
   Esteem He that loveth his brother abideth in the light (I John, 2.10)

2. **Misericordia** Beati misericordes
   Compassion Blessed are the merciful (Matthew, 5.7)

3. **Patientia** Beati qui persecutionem patiuntur
   Forbearance Blessed are they that have been persecuted (Matthew, 5.10)

4. **Benignitas** Beatus est dare quam accipere
   Generosity It is more blessed to give than to receive (Acts, 20.35)

5. **Clementia** Beati mites
   Mercy Blessed are the meek (Matthew, 5.5)

6. **Hilaritas** Hilarem datorem diligit Deus
   Cheerfulness God loveth a cheerful giver (II Corinthians, 9.7)

motif was on the three towering lanterns mounted high astern. These were twelve-sided, with six full-length glass panels and six smaller ones, the latter with a Christian virtue inscribed above and an apposite biblical phrase below. *Diagram 3* shows the central and largest lantern, unfolded.[8]

Pausing to observe that 'it is more blessed to give than to receive' was a singularly appropriate epigram for a vessel that carried as many guns as *La Real*, let us leave her to track the impact of Lepanto on literature. Spanish letters were entering their Golden Century, and Lepanto was tagged and copyrighted as the Spanish victory it was. From various seemingly autobiographical episodes in his writings it seems that when Cervantes was newly enlisted (having fled Spain following a street brawl in which a man was killed), news came of the formation of the Holy League, and that the 'natural brother of our good King Philip' was coming to command it. He enlisted in Diego de Urbina's company of Miguel de Moncada's Tercio, which joined Don Juan's squadron at Genoa. At Lepanto he fought on board *La Marchesa*, one of Gian'Andrea Doria's galleys commanded by Francesco Sancto Pietro, and wrote, '… on that day, so fortunate for Christianity because it disabused the world and all the nations of the error they were in, believing the Turks were invincible by sea, on that day when Ottoman pride and arrogance was shattered'. In *Letter to Mateo Vázquez* he wrote:

A esta dulce sazón, yo triste estaba	At this sweet time a sad case was I,
con una espada de mani asida	with a sword brandished in one hand
y sangre de la otra derramaba.	and blood pouring from the other.
El pecho mío de profunda herida	I felt the deep wound that my breast
sentía llegado, y la siniestra mano	had suffered, and that my left hand
estaba por mil partes ya rompida.	was shattered in a thousand pieces.
Pero el contento fué tan soberano	But the happiness that lifted my soul,
que a mi alma llegó, viendo vencido	upon seeing the coarse infidel nation
el crudo pueblo infiel por el cristiano,	overthrown by victorious Christendom
que no echaba de ver si estaba herido.	made me not even look to my wounds.

One of the plays written by Cervantes's staggeringly prolific contemporary Félix Lope de Vega y Carpio (1562–1635) was entitled *The Holy League*, a work with the message that the victory was a sign from God. But Lope de Vega's Crusade was the Vincible Armada of 1588, from which he may well have returned with unprintable thoughts about divine providence. Luis Vélez de Guevara (c. 1579–1644) did the subject greater honour in his *The Eagle of the Water*, written towards the end of his life, although he put by far the most stirring words in the mouth of the Calabrian–Algerine corsair Uluch Ali:[9]

Genizaros valientes	Brave Janissaries, you warlike
de Marte belicosos descendientes	sons of Mars, proud whip in Allah's
de Ala, azote arrogante,	hand, lightning bolts over Europe
rayos de Europa, soles de Levante,	and to the Levant radiant suns,
que de las turcas lunas	you who have borne the Turkic moons
habeis adelantado las fortunas,	to glory, whose crescent swords
cuyos corbos alfanjes	like comets have lit the Danube
fueron cometas del Danubio al Ganges,	and the Ganges, now take you to
hoy bajais siendo dueños	the sea in warships numerous
de tantas alabanzas como leños,	as the high praises you have earned,
del mar con el tridente	to puncture the western fleet
a castigar la armada del poniente	with the trident and to punish
y su pretesto loco con Luchali Baja,	its mad folly and presumption,
Piali y Siroco,	with your Generals Uluch Ali,
vuestros tres generales del sol	Scirocco and Piali, the sun's
antorchas y de Ala fanales.	torch bearers and lanterns to Allah.[10]

Shakespeare, treading on the thin ice of his own religious convictions in violently anti-Spanish and anti-Roman Catholic England, made only fleeting reference to the conflict in *Othello*, the following section containing three neologisms that failed to catch on:

Duke of Venice: The Turk with most mighty preparation makes for Cyprus: – Othello, the fortitude of the place is best known to you: and although we have there a substitute of most allowèd sufficiency, yet opinion, a sovereign mistress of effects, throws a more safer voice on you: you must therefore be content to slubber the gloss of your new fortunes with this most stubborn and boisterous expedition.

Othello: The tyrant custom, most grave senators, Hath made the flinty and steel couch of war

> My thrice-driven bed of down: I do agnize
> A natural and prompt alacrity,
> I find in hardness; and do undertake
> These present wars against the Ottomites.

James VI of Scotland, with even more reason to be wary of the ravening Protestants who held sway in his kingdom, nonetheless wrote a lost poem in Latin to celebrate Lepanto, a flavour of which may perhaps be reflected in another dedicated to him as 'King of Britain, France and Scotland' by Thomas Moravius. The following excerpt has an expressionist value that does not require it, and a period charm that would be lost in translation:

> *Turcarum impatiens, horrendum infrenduit ore*
> *Omnipotens, pallore ingens stupefactus Olympus*
> *contremuit, tellus penitis agitata latebris*
> *horruit, attonitus fundo mugivit ab imo*
> *Oceanus, summo trepidarunt vertice montes*
> *horridaque obscuris Plutonia regna cavernis.*

It is believed by those inclined to do so that Lepanto was foretold by Michel de Nostredame aka Nostradamus (1503–66), the Jewish convert, alchemist, apothecary and physician to Charles IX of France, in Quatrain 94 of his first 'Century', completed in 1555:

> *Au port Selin le tyrant mis a mort,*   In port Selin the tyrant put to death,
> *La liberté non pourtant recouvrée:*   Liberty not yet recovered:
> *Le nouveau mare par vindicte et remort*   The new spoiled by spite and remorse
> *Dame par force de frayeur honorée.*   Lady honoured by force of fear.

Century Two, Quatrain 79 refers to a 'great Chyren' with a curly beard, dyed black, who will subjugate a cruel and proud people and liberate all the captives under the banner of 'Seline', but in later Centuries we find that Selin and the great Chyren are one and the same, the conqueror of Italy and Christian king of all the world, who clears the sea of pirates, blocks out the sun, and joyously does harm to the proud glory of Venice. Gibberish, but not without historical interest as an insight into the subconscious of a man who moved in rarefied circles. The great Chyren Selin is obviously Charles V, who loomed over France during Nostredame's life-time, and 'the new spoiled by spite and remorse' is the Protestant Refor-mation. Therefore the 'lady honoured by force of fear' is probably a veiled reference to the cult of Our Lady.

The era of the epic narrative poem closed with a flourish in the cele-bration of Lepanto. We might speculate that it also marked the end of an 'Age of Heroism', as long-range weapons reduced the role of individual prowess in battle, although the fact that Achilles was killed by an arrow before the walls of Troy should make us wary of placing too much empha-sis on a techno-cultural explanation. Epic poems continued to be written, the latest of which I am aware being *The Alamo: An Epic*, published by Michael Lind in 1997, but they have been as light poetic cruisers next to the Dreadnoughts of old.[11]

In the latter style, the degenerate gambler Juan Rufo (1547–1620) wrote *La Austriada*, a twenty-four canto poem dedicated to the Empress of Bohemia and Hungary (Juan de Austria's older half-sister) in 1582. Rufo claimed to have been with Don Juan in the Granada campaign, although at the time he was in Madrid, immersed in a scandalous love affair. Later, in flight from his creditors – an activity that punctuated his life – he signed on as a common soldier in the company of the Duke of Sessa and fought at Lepanto. *La Austriada* grinds through a prolonged exercise in sycophantic name-dropping, but Rufo knew his market and it was a commercial success that rehabilitated him – he is one of the mourners in El Greco's 1586 *Burial of Count Orgaz*. Rufo frequently makes use of words specific to the bullfight, and much the same imagery is employed in the florid ode 'For the Victory of Lepanto' by 'the divine' Fernando de Herrera (1534–97), who also wrote one of the more useful contemporary accounts of the battle.

Alonso de Ercilla y Zúñiga (1533–94), a much better poet than Rufo, published the three volumes of *La Araucana* in 1569, 1570 and 1578. Although it concerns the conquest of Chile, from which he returned in 1562, he inserted a dream of Lepanto in Book III (Canto XXIII) in which he also name-drops, if not so shamelessly as Rufo. Although he had once been a page to Philip, and despite his relationship by birth and by marriage with the highest in the land, he died in poverty, not knowing that his work would come to be seen as one of the jewels of Spain's literary Golden

Century. Following a ponderous roll call of the vast variety of peoples in the Ottoman host he neatly changed styles to contrast it with a balladic description:

> *Vi allí también de la nativa España*   From my native Spain I see
> *la flor de juventud y gallardía,*   the flower of youth and gallantry,
> • *la nobleza de Italia y de Alemaña,*   Italian and German nobility,
> *una audaz y bizarra compañía:*   a bold and valorous company:
> *todos ornados de riqueza extraña,*   all wond'rously dressed in rich array,
> *con animosa muestra y lozanía,*   with resolute and brave display,
> *y en las popas, carceses y trinquetes,*   and from sternposts, masts and stays,
> *flámulas, banderolas, gallardetes.*   standards, pennants and streamers play.

His descriptions of combat and its consequences, though gleaned from others, are generally more vivid than those of Rufo, who was there, and dwell on the common fate of men upon whom the fortunes of war have turned their back. Both can be considered primary sources, and I shall intersperse my account of the battle with other excerpts.

After a two-century hiatus, the poetic celebration of Lepanto made a last appearance in a most unexpected place. The Romantic movement produced a vision of Don Juan as the knight in shining armour captured in the painting (*Colour Plate 8b*) by the Filipino revolutionary hero and uxoricide Juan Luna y Novicio (1857–99). But it was in Britain that a revival of interest in highly glamorized chivalry and the Crusades merged with the Roman Catholic revivalism associated with Cardinal Newman, one product of which was the two-volume *Don John of Austria* published in 1883 by Sir William Stirling-Maxwell. The epigramist Hilaire Belloc (1870–1953) often wrote of 'Mary's victory at Lepanto', and his dear friend Gilbert Keith Chesterton (1874–1936) composed the rollicking poem 'Lepanto' in 1911. The following illustrates the romantic vision of Roman Catholicism that eventually led Chesterton to follow Newman and submit to Rome, and a very twentieth-century demonization of the alien other that contrasts unpleasantly with the Humanism of *La Araucana*:

> White founts falling in the Courts of the sun,
> And the Soldan of Byzantium is smiling as they run;
> There is laughter like the fountains in that face of all men feared,

It stirs the forest darkness, the darkness of his beard;
It curls the blood-red crescent, the crescent of his lips;
For the inmost sea of all the earth is shaken with his ships.
They have dared the white republics up the capes of Italy,
They have dashed the Adriatic round the Lion of the Sea,
And the Pope has cast his arms abroad for agony and loss,
And called the kings of Christendom for swords about the Cross.
The cold queen of England is looking in the glass;
The shadow of the Valois is yawning at the Mass;
From evening isles fantastical rings faint the Spanish gun,
And the Lord upon the Golden Horn is laughing in the sun.

• • •

He moves a mighty turban on the timeless houri's knees,
His turban that is woven of the sunsets and the seas.
He shakes the peacock gardens as he rises from his ease,
And he strides among the tree-tops and is taller than the trees;
And his voice through all the garden is a thunder sent to bring
Black Azrael and Ariel and Ammon on the wing.

Giants and the Genii,

Multiplex of wing and eye,

Whose strong obedience broke the sky

When Solomon was king.

• • •

King Philip's in his closet with the Fleece about his neck
(Don John of Austria is armed upon the deck.)
The walls are hung with velvet that is black and soft as sin,
And little dwarfs creep out of it and little dwarfs creep in.[12]
He holds a crystal phial that has colours like the moon,
He touches, and it tingles, and he trembles very soon,
And his face is as a fungus of a leprous white and grey
Like plants in the high houses that are shuttered from the day,
And death is in the phial and the end of noble work,[13]
But Don John of Austria has fired upon the Turk.

As I write, honours are cascading upon the wonderful films of the first two parts of J.R.R. Tolkien's trilogy *The Lord of the Rings*, a work wreathed in magical smoke for many of my generation. Written during the Second World War, it was curiously unaffected by that titanic struggle and looked further back for inspiration, echoing Chesterton's vision. Thus, to cite only one of many examples, Tolkien's black riders, the *Nazgûl*, and Chesterton's 'Black Azrael and Ariel and Ammon on the wing'. Tolkien wrote that applicability does not an allegory make and declared a cordial dislike for the latter, but methinks he did protest too much. The trilogy tells of swarthy Southrons and black Orcs speaking an uncouth lingua franca who issue forth from Asia Minor-shaped Mordor to besiege Minas Tirith (Vienna 1683), and are hurled back by the fair-skinned horsemen from the steppes of Rohan (Jan Sobieski's Poles). Furthermore, one of the arch-villains is called Saruman (Suleiman), also known as *Sharkû*, ('elder' in Orc, as is *Sheik* in Arabic). The only question is whether the author was deliberately tapping into an archetype, or whether his subconscious led him along a comfortably familiar path. Tolkien was a devout Roman Catholic, and I do not believe in coincidences.

PART II

MILITARY BATTLE

CHAPTER SIX

SCENE SETTERS

For all the cultural overlays and the lack of those consequences that Braudel believed alone entitled an *événement* to be considered significant, Lepanto was the grandest military event in a century studded with them. Equally unarguably, it was a no less grand folly for the combatants to have risked so much against so little prospect of reward, but therein lies another way in which the battle is emblematic. From time to time men are overcome by an impulse to do spectacularly reckless things simply because they are men, representative of which was to spend hours forming up in handsome opposing lines with banners waving and bands playing, prior to smashing together and reducing a breathtakingly beautiful work of structured art to random conceptual dross. Even the sober Spanish grandees with whom Philip II had ring-fenced Juan de Austria got carried away by the moment, and only Gian'Andrea Doria the Genoese and Uluch Ali the Calabrian–Algerine, the most experienced naval commanders on their respective sides, seem to have kept their heads. The rest had scores to settle, and doubts to resolve as warriors and as representatives of dominant military cultures, regardless of the consequences.

It bears repeating that no naval battle on the scale of Lepanto had been fought since antiquity. Large Ottoman and Venetian fleets had clashed at Zonchio in 1499 and 1500, but although the fate of the Gulf of Patras, Morea and Aetolia hung in the balance, very few vessels actually closed to combat, and losses were minor. The same can be said of the 1538 skirmish in which Barbarossa attacked the Holy League fleet under the command of Prince Andrea Doria, Gian'Andrea's great-uncle, as it withdrew from an attempt to blockade him in Preveza Bay. The root of the defeat lay in the failure of the Holy League land force under the Papal commander Marco Grimani to establish an artillery fort at Actium (*Map 9*), but the Venetians found it convenient to demonize Doria, ruler of their ancestral rival Genoa, in order to justify a decision to cut their losses. They negotiated a truce later in 1538 and formally abandoned the alliance in 1540. One bitterly resented consequence of this defection was the loss of Castelnuovo, a fort controlling the mouth of Cattaro Bay taken from the Ottomans earlier in the campaign (*Map 4*), where the Spanish garrison was put to the sword while the Venetians at Cattaro and Perast sat on their hands.[1] More specific scene-setters for Lepanto came at five-yearly intervals over the preceding decade, with the abject disaster for Hapsburg arms at Djerba in 1560 and the humiliating loss of Cyprus by the Venetians in 1570, which contrasted embarrassingly with the heroism of the Knights of Malta during the epic siege of Malta in 1565.

One of Djerba's earlier entries in the western historical record was in 1284, when the Aragonese Admiral Roger de Lauria (whose image opposite Jason looked down upon Juan de Austria's dinner table on *La Real*) led a punitive expedition against it, in between the battles off Messina and Naples that doomed Angevin power in Sicily. In 1501 King Ferdinand the Catholic ordered his 'Great Captain' Gonzalo Fernández de Córdoba to repeat at Djerba his exploit in capturing Cephalonia the year before, but the expedition was stillborn when war with France for control of Naples broke out again. Djerba continued as before until the projection of Castilian ambition into the Mediterranean a decade later, financed by Cardinal Jiménez de Cisneros and led by Pedro Navarro, himself a sometime corsair and Córdoba's chief siege engineer. These expeditions won Oran, Mostaganem, Bougie, Tripoli, and a fort commanding Algiers harbour with little difficulty, forcing the local Muslim rulers to pay tribute to Castile. But, as noted earlier, they also let the genie of an Ottoman-backed corsair renaissance out of the bottle.

Some thought Djerba to be the island of Aiaia, where Circe turned Odysseus' men into swine, and it certainly seems to have had that effect on the Spanish.[2] In August 1510, while Navarro was seizing Tripoli, a second invasion force of 16,000 soldiers invaded Djerba under the command of García de Toledo, whose son and namesake was to become the Spanish Captain General of the Sea after the death of Andrea Doria. The landing party was ambushed by some light cavalry and dissolved in flight, Toledo dying pike in hand while unsuccessfully trying to rally his men. So great was the panic that four ships also surrendered to the Muslim horsemen, while others that ran to the Kerkenna Islands were so demoralized that they were taken by canoe-borne raiders. Ten years later another Hapsburg expedition against Djerba led by Hugo de Moncada, viceroy of Sicily, was more successful. Although part of it was later defeated by the corsairs in an open sea engagement, Moncada's fleet successfully landed 14,000–15,000 men. The local sheik made submission and promised good behaviour in future – an undertaking of limited utility given that he had no control whatever over the corsairs who used the island – and Moncada sailed away, leaving the status quo unchanged.[3]

The next chapter in the Djerba saga came after the great corsair Turghud Reis (Dragut), a Karamanid whose early military training had come in the service of the Mamluks, settled there and raided Italy seemingly at will, in 1548 even taking Pozuoli and Castellamare in the Bay of Naples. In 1550 he seized Mahdia on the African mainland, ousting its native ruler, only to be expelled in turn by a Hapsburg expedition led by Andrea Doria, who also tried to blockade him at Djerba. Once again a fleeting Christian success only served to strengthen the corsair–Ottoman nexus, as Suleiman took this as a declaration of war and sent a large fleet under Kapudan Sinan Pasha to avenge the insult in 1551. The combined fleets of Dragut and Sinan recovered Mahdia, raided Malta and Gozo, and then captured Tripoli from the Knights of Saint John, who had been entrusted with it by Charles V in 1530 as the price for permitting them to establish themselves in Malta. Tripoli became the second corsair principality formally admitted to the empire in 1556, although Djerba retained a considerable degree of autonomy.

Following declarations of bankruptcy by the Valois and both branches of the Hapsburg dynasty in 1557, the Treaty of Cateau-Cambrésis in 1559 marked a durable lull in their long rivalry. With his back covered, Philip II was prevailed upon by the Grand Master of the Knights and by Duke Juan de la Cerda of Medinaceli, viceroy of Sicily, to attempt the recovery of Tripoli. Pius IV in turn was prevailed upon to declare it a Crusade, to which he contributed three galleys (all lost) under Flaminio Orsino (killed) as well as the 'graces' from ecclesiastical revenues that funded the whole expedition. From the start it was bedevilled by divided command and gross indiscipline, including mass desertion and two violent mutinies, while one overloaded transport rolled over in Genoa harbour with great loss of life. Not least, Juan de Mendoza took the twelve royal galleys under his command back to Spain rather than serve under the 20-year-old Gian'Andrea Doria who was deputizing for his great-uncle, the 93-year-old Prince Andrea.

The invasion was supposed to take place at the end of the 1559 campaigning season, to gain the winter months to take Tripoli before the Ottoman response could arrive, but adverse weather delayed it and in the meantime the city was reinforced and the fortifications improved. The expedition diverted to Djerba and arrived on 14 February, unaware that a quick reaction force of seventy to eighty galleys with 100 Janissaries each was standing by in Istanbul under the command of Piali Pasha.[4] Dragut himself was trapped, but the expedition leaders almost came to blows over loot and while they were thus occupied he was able to escape by dragging his galleys overland to the open sea. Meanwhile two galliots under Uluch Ali raced to advise Piali, and on 10 May a fast barge arrived to advise the still bickering Hapsburg commanders that a large Ottoman fleet had been sighted off Gozo on the 6th. The Christian fleet was in the midst of a panicky re-embarkation when the enemy was sighted on the 11th, and before Piali had made any aggressive move it dissolved into devil-take-the-hindmost flight led by Gian'Andrea's galleys, which were packed with the prized olive oil of Djerba.

Viceroy Medinaceli and Gian'Andrea later escaped in small craft, but the entire land force under Alvaro de Sande was captured, along with Medinaceli's son and principal lieutenants. Despite the speed with which the Genoese galleys decamped, Gian'Andrea lost five of his twelve galleys, Antonio Doria one of his four, Bendinelli Sauli and Stefano di Mare each one of two, while the Grimaldi lost both of theirs. Of the Sicilian contingent only two belonging to Count Cicala escaped. All four under Berenguer de Requeséns (captured along with son-in-law Juan de Cardona) were lost, as were two galleys belonging to the Marquess of Terranova. All five of the Neapolitan contingent under Sancho de Leyva (captured) were lost, as were two of four sent by Duke Cosimo dei Medici of Florence. Cosimo lost the others to Algerine galliots off Elba in 1561, prompting him to devolve corsair activity to the Knights of Santo Stefano in order to shield his own fleet and commerce from Ottoman retaliation. The parallel with the status enjoyed by the corsairs of Djerba seems to be exact, and it is interesting to note how both sides respected the view that holy warriors were legitimately a law unto themselves.[5]

From Istanbul, Busbeq reported that before setting out for Djerba there had been great apprehension in the Ottoman fleet, because 'the *Turks*, for a long time, have had a great Opinion of the *Spaniards*, as knowing that they have waged great Wars, and come off with good Success'.[6] They returned jubilant, towing their prizes backwards with their standards dragging in the water, and paraded thousands of captives through the streets of Istanbul. Cardona was spared this humiliation, being put ashore at Chios by Piali in order to manage a discreet (for which read not shared with the Porte) ransom for his father-in-law, but the rest were dependent on the good offices of Busbeq for their maintenance while in captivity, and for their eventual liberation in 1562–63 as part of the truce negotiations between Vienna and Istanbul.

Although it was a decade when silver from Potosí (in today's Bolivia) began to flow into Seville almost as fast as Philip II could spend it, he could ill afford losses on the scale of Djerba, where twenty-seven of forty-five galleys and fourteen of thirty ships were lost, along with 18,000 men and some of the highest in the land. Djerba was a greater reverse even than the Armada of 1588, for although the ships lost in the latter expedition were more expensive to build and carried more guns, the human cost was only 10,000 men and the English only took two or three prizes. At Djerba there was a wholesale *transfer* of galleys and ships and, including galley slaves, about 22,000 valuable men went from one side of the strategic balance sheet to the other. The damage was compounded on 19 October 1562, when some twenty-five of twenty-eight galleys under Juan de Mendoza (nine Spanish, six from Naples and the rest from the Genoese entrepreneurs Antonio Doria, Sauli and Mare), were lost in a storm off Málaga, with Mendoza and 2,500 sailors and soldiers drowned, plus at least the same number of rowers.

Nor did the failure of the Armada lead to loss of control over the waters around Spain or of the Atlantic artery, whereas after Djerba the Ottomans and their corsair allies roamed at will in the western Mediterranean, threatening the Hapsburg lifeline to Italy and undermining royal authority by raids along the coasts of Italy and even of Spain itself. Naval losses continued to mount over the following year, notably the remaining Sicilian squadron of seven galleys captured off the Lipari Islands by Dragut, by now Ottoman Beylerbey of Tripoli. This was followed by the loss of Viscount Cicala, a relative of Andrea Doria, with three of his galleys to a fleet of galliots commanded by Dragut's deputy, Uluch Ali. When his father was not ransomed, Cicala's 16-year-old son Scipione became a Muslim and entered Ottoman service, eventually becoming the Cicalazâde Sinan Pasha who retook Tunisia in 1574 and, as grand vizier, smashed the army of the Holy Roman Empire at Kerestes in 1596.[7]

Despite Gian'Andrea's role in the original debacle, the standing of his house with Philip II rested on the firm foundation of its emerging role as his principal banker, a function in which the supply of fighting galleys was only part of an intricate and mutually binding financial relationship. There is however another strand in the confidence that Philip continued to place in the military abilities of Gian'Andrea. The prudent king could not fail to note that at Djerba the young Genoese had shown a commendable concern for the bottom line while the Spanish commanders found proud but expensive defeat. Nor could he fail to contrast the seamanship of Gian'Andrea with the crippling disaster that overtook the royal fleet under Juan de Mendoza off Málaga two years later, an event that also underlined the loss-limiting virtues of leasing galleys rather than owning them. In 1556 it had cost the king nothing when the teenager Gian'Andrea had the importance of maintaining weather room in a storm burned into his soul during his first seagoing command, when of sixteen galleys only his flagship escaped being wrecked on the coast of Corsica.

Mendoza's refusal to serve under Gian'Andrea in the Djerba expedition may well have been, as he stated, under instructions from Philip to preserve the royal fleet at all costs, but the insult rankled. In 1563, when Oran was besieged by Dragut and Barbarossa's son Hassan, now Beylerbey of Algiers, Philip summoned the Genoese to join a relief force at Barcelona under the command of Francisco de Mendoza, Juan's brother, and rather than accept a subordination that was not specified in his contract Gian'Andrea put his brother Pagano in command and stayed on board as a 'volunteer'. Mendoza relieved Oran in mid June, when it was mere days away from capitulation, and his reward was to be sharply criticized by the king, working from notes thoughtfully provided by Gian'Andrea, for failing to trap Dragut's fleet. Thereafter royal contracts with Doria included additional payment for his expertise.

Command of the fleet passed to Sancho de Leyva, now back from captivity, who fell into temporary disgrace when he led an expedition in 1563 that failed to recapture Vélez de la Gomera, a corsair base opposite Málaga that had changed hands several times. The issue was resolved permanently when a massive expedition in 1564 under García de Toledo secured the fortified rocky island (*peñón*) that controlled the entrance to Vélez harbour. The *Peñón de Vélez* remains a Spanish enclave in Moroccan territory to this day, along with Ceuta and Melilla, captured in the fifteenth century and now garrisoned by the Foreign Legion Tercios 'Great Captain' and 'Duke of Alba'. These do not, of course, bear any comparison with the British possession of the *Peñón de Gibraltar*. As far as Toledo and other royal commanders were concerned, the writing on the wall was that Philip, scalded by Djerba, would not approve any military undertaking that did not enjoy overwhelming numerical superiority, and that however undependable they thought him to be, Gian'Andrea Doria had the ear of the king.

The foregoing provides the subtext for the 1565 siege of Malta, usually portrayed as a victory won by the *chevaliers sans peur et sans reproche* of Saint John amid the indifference of Christendom in general and of His Catholic Majesty in particular. Fearless they usually were, for the Knights of Malta were the volunteer cream of European chivalry, their genealogy checked back for at least four generations to ensure that no taint of anything other than the profession of arms stained their escutcheons. We may, however, fairly question whether an association dedicated to indiscriminate commerce raiding, whose members committed a sufficient number of serious transgressions to keep the gibbets on the headland of the Grand Harbour tenanted with aristocratic corpses, can accurately be described as beyond reproach.

The *casus belli* for the Ottoman assault was the seizure in the waters between Zante and Cephalonia of a great merchant ship belonging to Kustir Agha, the chief eunuch, by three Maltese galleys under the command of the legendary Mathurin d'Aux de Lescout Romegas. The cargo of this ship was valued at 80,000 ducats and represented the little all of many ladies of the harem, not the least of them Mihrmah, Suleiman the Magnificent's favourite daughter by the late and sorely missed Roxelana. They added their voices to the long-standing request of the North African corsairs to excise the Maltese carbuncle, supported by the Imam of the

Great Mosque who appealed to Suleiman to liberate believers enslaved by the Knights:

> Only thy invincible sword can shatter the chains of these unfortunates, whose cries are rising to heaven and afflicting the very ears of The Prophet. The son demands his father, the wife her husband and her children. All, therefore, wait upon thee, upon thy justice and thy power, for vengeance upon their – and your – implacable enemies.

It was a formidable undertaking. As we have seen, shortly before the Knights of Saint John were expelled from Tripoli, their Maltese stronghold received a damaging visit from Dragut, who landed in Marsamuscetto Bay and marched around Mount Sciberras (where Valetta stands today). Rebuffed at Marsa Creek, he sailed on to depopulate the island of Gozo. Over the following fourteen years, particularly after the election of Grand Master Jean Parisot de la Valette in 1557, the Knights drew upon the large revenues from their chapters throughout Europe to build imposing fortifications. Marsamuscetto was denied to the enemy by a detached hornwork at St Elmo, the Mount Sciberras headland, while the old medieval citadel of St Angelo was thoroughly modernized, the settlement of Senglea was fortified on the side facing the Corradino Heights across French Creek, Birgu was fully enclosed, and both were sealed off from the mainland by massive bastioned traces. *Map 6* shows how Senglea was left open on the Birgu side, and Birgu to St Angelo, from which it was separated by a ditch in which three galleys sheltered during the siege (two more were submerged in the dockyard), while Kustir Agha's great ship remained in plain sight. Although contemporary prints show it much as I have drawn it, the Saint Michael bastion defending Senglea seems to defy the rules of *trace italienne* fortification, and was presumably adapted to a topography subsequently altered beyond recognition.

If in addition we consider that Malta was an arid, rocky island whose meagre crops were scarcely sufficient to feed its small native population, to which the timber and even the soil for the earthworks built outside the Knights' masonry walls had to be brought from Sicily, the whole was a place that no Christian power would have contemplated attacking. Although the Ottoman assault failed, in part because Valette ordered the Maltese and their animals into his fortified places, burned their crops and poisoned the wells, it was still an awesome demonstration of a unique

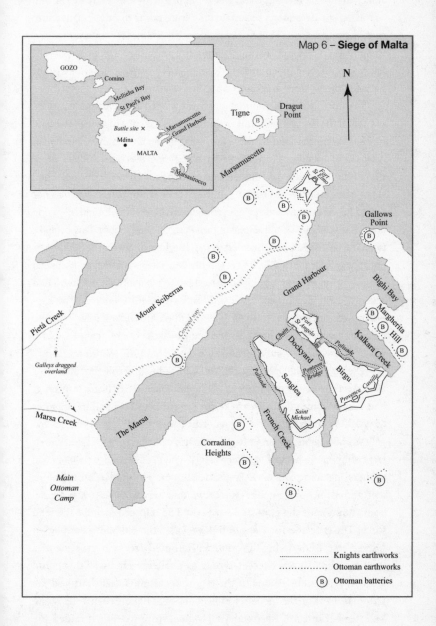

Map 6 – **Siege of Malta**

N

GOZO

Comino

Mellieha Bay

St Paul's Bay

Battle site ×

Marsamuscetto
Grand Harbour

Mdina

MALTA

Marsasirocco

Tigne

Dragut
Point

Marsamuscetto

Fort
St Elmo

Gallows
Point

Bighi Bay

Grand Harbour

Margherita
Hill

Kalkara Creek

Mount Sciberras

Covered way

Pietà Creek

*Galleys dragged
overland*

Chain

Fort
St Angelo

Dockyard

Birgu

Palisade

Pontoon
Bridge

Provence Cavillie

Senglea

Palisade

Saint
Michael

Marsa Creek

The Marsa

French Creek

Corradino
Heights

*Main
Ottoman
Camp*

.... Knights earthworks

.... Ottoman earthworks

(B) Ottoman batteries

143

ability to move a very large and well-equipped army efficiently by sea, and of the logistical resources to sustain it far from home throughout an entire campaigning season. These were military capabilities far superior to anything Spain could command, negating the advantage that possession of Sicily should have given her in the struggle to control the choke-point between the western and eastern Mediterranean.

Suleiman was a land animal and by now aged and gout-ridden, so he entrusted the expedition to his most battle-tested subordinates. The land force was commanded by that rare being in the Ottoman hierarchy, an Anatolian Turk named Mustafa Pasha, who first came to the Sultan's attention at the 1522 siege of Rhodes, and rose in rank through distinguished service in Hungary and Persia. Although now white-haired, age had not dulled his fanaticism and savagery. Suleiman divided command by giving equal status to 35-year-old Kapudan Piali Pasha, a Serbian foundling brought up in the palace who was married to the daughter of Selim, the heir apparent. The Sultan abjured Piali to reverence Mustafa as a father, and Mustafa to look upon Piali as a beloved son, strange advice from one who had recently strangled his own beloved son Bayezid for rebellion. The supporting cast included Hassan of Algiers, Uluch Ali, and a similarly named corsair captain (*reis*) who had once been a Black (Dominican) Friar and whose likewise black galley was feared throughout the Mediterranean.

The 80-year-old Dragut was given a co-ordinating role, but fatally for the enterprise he did not arrive at Malta until Mustafa, at Piali's insistence, had already committed his army to the reduction of Fort St Elmo in order to win Marsamuscetto for the fleet. This consisted of approximately 160 galleys and galliots, six larger oared warships described as galleasses, eleven large ships and a host of smaller vessels. The fleet carried 30,000–40,000 soldiers, including over 6,000 Janissaries, but until it could be brought into a protected anchorage neither the crews (another 20,000–25,000 potential combatants) nor the guns on board could be released to assist the land force. The crucial error was not to have taken the old Maltese capital of Mdina first. Built on high ground with limited access in the style of a medieval *rocca*, it was protected only by a tall, turreted wall that could scarcely have endured one of the countless assaults that shattered the Ottoman army on the modern fortifications of St Elmo, Senglea and Birgu. Valette sent most of his cavalry to Mdina, from whence it raided the Ottoman line of supply from their first anchorage at Marsasirocco, in the far south of the island. Finally, on 7 August, it sacked the main Ottoman encampment and slaughtered those left behind when all able-bodied men were committed to attacks on Birgu and Senglea. Fearing that a relief force had landed to their rear, the Ottoman commanders broke off the assault when the fall of Senglea seemed likely.

Acting on false intelligence supplied by a brave captured knight (who paid for it with an agonizing death), on 22 May Mustafa had launched a preliminary assault against the Castile bastion, the strongest point in the defences. Watching this, defiantly exposed atop the adjacent Provence bastion, Valette discovered how greatly the long Janissary arquebuses outranged his own when several men fell around him. Later he was presented with evidence from the body of an Ottoman officer that the Ulema had declared the campaign a holy war, and that those who fell were guaranteed a place in paradise. If not before, at this point he knew the struggle was to the death, a fact he communicated to his brothers in ringing tones. Valette's style emanates from the cutting reply he sent on 9 June, when the knights holding St Elmo suggested the time might have come to evacuate, after they had beaten off countless assaults against incredible odds and their work was reduced to rubble:

> This evening, as soon as the relieving force has landed, you may take the boats back. Return, my Brethren, to the Convent and to Birgu, where you will be in more security. For my part, I shall feel more confident when I know the fort – upon which the safety of the island so greatly depends – is held by men whom I can trust implicitly.

Needless to say, the knights thus addressed remained and died at their posts. Fierce fire from St Angelo forced Mustafa to approach St Elmo along the northern side of the Sciberras peninsula and enabled the garrison to blunt the first attacks relatively easily, only to lose the ravelin in front of the work to an opportunistic dawn attack after Janissary engineers found its defenders asleep. Upon arrival Dragut ordered the construction of a battery on the Tigne headland, still known as Dragut Point, and of a covered way along the southern flank of Mount Sciberras to bring counter-fire to bear on St Angelo, to cut St Elmo off from reinforcement, and to bring the hornwork itself under converging fire. This doomed the fort, where the last of 1,500 men died fighting on 23 June, having inflicted 8,000 casualties – including a high proportion of the Janissaries – over the preceding two months. Dragut did not live to see it, as he was killed by a rock fragment kicked up by a culverin ball from St Angelo while supervising the emplacement of a counter-battery on 18 June. When the brilliantly dressed party of Ottoman officers felt it undignified to disperse, another shot killed the Agha of the Janissaries. Mustafa still refused to take cover and stood in full view while every gun that could be brought to bear fired at him across the Grand Harbour.

Contempt for danger was not limited to the Christians, nor ruthless cruelty to the Muslims. After Mustafa set the heads of the knights killed at St Elmo on pikes and sent their crucified bodies floating across the harbour, Valette ordered the massacre of hundreds of captives held in the underground cells of Birgu, and fired their heads across to the Ottoman lines. Mustafa got the message. Looking across the water at St Angelo he commented, 'If so small a son has cost us so dear, what price shall we have to pay for so great a father?' But with St Elmo in his hands and a new battery installed on Gallows Point, and with Piali and the fleet now installed in Marsamuscetto, the Grand Harbour was at last effectively closed.

Ringed by Ottoman batteries and with the zigzag of assault trenches closing inexorably on the landward side, the defenders could only gaze in astonishment, as the defenders of Constantinople had in 1453, to see a flotilla of galleys dragged overland from the Pietà inlet to the Marsa, pre-saging an amphibious assault on the incomplete fortifications on the French Creek flank of Senglea. For the next two months Mustafa, now joined by the sizeable force under the command of Piali, deployed every technique of the besieger's art, and it seems fair to conclude that, given the limits of contemporary military technology, it was not possible to take the place within one campaigning season, even if the original sin of ignoring Mdina had not been committed. This underlines the strategic equilibrium we discussed in Chapter One, and suggests the miserable Christian showing at Djerba and elsewhere in the following years had led the Ottoman high command to hold their opponents in contempt. Suleiman and Mustafa should have remembered how the Knights of Saint John on Rhodes, almost within sight of Asia Minor, held out against them for six months in 1522.

But no fortress, however strong and valiantly defended, could hold out indefinitely when cut off from outside support. The Knights had made no friends by their contempt for the new men and money that were transforming European society, and were widely believed to be as miserly as they were avaricious. As in 1522, in 1565 there was a general feeling that they should pay for any relief sent to them, for Valette had prudently invested in bricks and mortar rather than in the quicksand of princely goodwill. The attack on Malta also came after the Duke of Alba had persuaded Philip II to concentrate military power in the north, to exploit France's weakened state following the first of her civil wars of religion and to put a lid on popular unrest in the Netherlands. Even if Philip had not already decided that the geopolitical fulcrum of his empire had moved away from the Mediterranean, Charles V had given Malta to the Knights, along with the obligation to hold Tripoli, because both cost more to defend than they produced in revenues, and his son had little to gain and possibly another fleet to lose by going to their aid.

These developments left Alba's kinsman García de Toledo, viceroy of Sicily, holding a very weak hand indeed, and further constrained by orders from his sovereign to avoid battle even if the result of doing so were the fall of Malta. Intense lobbying by the Knights' representatives in Rome loosened the Papal purse strings, or rather obtained the usual 'graces' conceded to Philip from the revenues of the Spanish church, and the Crusade was wearily proclaimed and preached by Pius IV, now at the end of his life. There were further delays because the Genoese entrepreneurs were distracted by a French-inspired revolt on Corsica led by Sampiero Corso, and were no more anxious than Philip to risk a repeat of Djerba. Far from it being the case that Toledo deliberately delayed sending a relief force, it is a tribute to his diplomatic skill and persuasive leadership that it sailed at all, and to his operational genius that it arrived at the precise moment when its relatively small weight could decisively tip the balance.

Toledo assembled fifty-eight galleys and five ships carrying a land force of about 8,000 soldiers under Alvaro de Sande, another of the erstwhile Djerba captives. This small force was built around the Tercio of Sardinia, plus contingents from the Tercios of Naples and Lombardy, and 1,500 gentlemen adventurers provided by Cosimo dei Medici on behalf of Pius IV. In return for this and subsequent favours Cosimo was to be elevated to the rank of Grand Duke of Tuscany in 1569 by Pius V, to the outrage of both branches of the Hapsburg dynasty, no less hostile than the Hohenstaufen had been to Papal exercise of secular power. Also present for the Pope were Ascanio della Corgna and Pompeo Colonna, the latter repaying Pius IV's 1559 revocation of his predecessor Paul IV's excommunication of Marc'Antonio Colonna, Duke of Paliano and Tagliacozzo, and the restoration of family lands within the Papal State.

The fleet vanguard was commanded by Sancho de Leyva, veteran of defeats at Vélez de la Gomera as well as Djerba, who led nineteen galleys in one of the royal flagships, flanked by the flagships of the Genoese entrepreneurs Stefano di Mare and Giorgio Grimaldi, seven of the rest from Naples, four from Cosimo dei Medici, three from the Genoese Piero Battista Lomellino, and two provided by Alvaro de Bazán, later Marquess of Santa Cruz. Toledo commanded the centre (the 'Battle') of twenty galleys, eight of which were royal, three more each the property of Bazán and Medici, two each from Savoy and Genoa, and two Knights of Saint John galleys that had been away from Malta before the Ottoman assault. Juan de Cardona commanded the rearguard of seventeen galleys, seven from Sicily, seven provided by Gian'Andrea Doria, and three by the Genoese Marco Centurione. Barring the pointedly absent Venetians this was a roll-call of the Holy League contingents at Lepanto, and a dress rehearsal of the mixed order in which they were deployed to ensure that none should think they could hold back unnoticed.

On Malta, Mustafa and Piali had been looking over their shoulders with increasing nervousness as the siege wore on. From reports by scouts sent to observe Toledo's laborious assembly at nearby Syracuse they knew the relief fleet was relatively small, but Piali had divided his command and stripped his galleys of men and artillery to assist the land campaign, while their hulls were foul with marine growth after more than four months without maintenance. Suleiman, who had himself failed before Vienna, might withhold punishment for abandoning the siege, but Piali knew the bowstring was the best he could look forward to if the fleet were caught unprepared. Thus when Toledo's force sailed past the Grand Harbour firing signal guns on its way to Mellieha Bay in the far north of the island, Piali immediately disengaged from the siege and ordered the vessels left at Marsasirocco to rejoin the rest at Marsamuscetto. Mustafa could only comply, and abandoned even the hard-won prize of St Elmo. On 8 September the Knights recovered the ruins, to look down with relieved astonishment on the retreating Ottoman host.

After he discovered the modest size of the land relief force, Mustafa disembarked about 9,000 men, while the fleet hastily departed Marsamuscetto and rowed north to St Paul's Bay, separated by a headland from Toledo's own swiftly abandoned anchorage. Mustafa marched his demoralized troops to do battle with the Christian army but had the worst of it, and only the indiscipline of the Christian cavalry under Corgna, which charged far ahead of Sande's infantry and suffered a severe check, permitted Mustafa to re-embark most of his men. Before that, Valette had registered alarm for the first time at the prospect that Mustafa might annihilate the unrepeatable relief effort, snatching a last-minute victory that would have negated the advantage so dearly won by his knights and by the anonymous but no less heroic Maltese who fought alongside them throughout the siege.

The importance of the siege of Malta looms rather larger in hindsight than it did at the time, and it is seldom appreciated that it confronted Philip II with a strategic dilemma, because any check he might inflict on the Ottomans risked driving them into a deeper alliance with France. Although it was to bedevil him no less than it had his father, Protestant agitation also worked to Philip's advantage in one respect, as the treaty of Cateau-Cambrésis might have marked just another truce in the Hapsburg –Valois dynastic rivalry had not France subsequently been so weakened by her civil wars of religion. This was a double bonus, for after Charles V's brutal Tunisian Crusade of 1535 cemented a new relationship with the Papacy at the expense of French influence, François I entered into a formal alliance with the Porte in 1536. Although primarily directed against Hapsburg hegemony, it also had serious repercussions for Venice:

> all Europeans who wished to do business in the Levant . . . were eventually obliged to accept the protection of the French crown. Venice ceased to dominate those markets, the commercial entente of 1536 and the [further commercial treaty] of 1569 being almost as serious a blow to the economic life of the Republic as the shifting of the major trade routes from the Mediterranean to the Atlantic.[9]

The treaty of 1569 was the work of the French ambassador to the Porte, Bishop François de Noailles of Dax, who was to exploit the shock of defeat at Lepanto to obtain a further Ottoman agreement in principle to a military alliance against Spain. Noailles was en route to Paris from

Istanbul with a draft treaty in which Selim undertook to provide a 200-galley fleet every year to assist the French in an assault on Spain and the Spanish holdings in Italy, all territories that might be gained to remain French, when the massacre of Saint Bartholomew's Day (24 August 1572) undid his fine work. Although the Ottomans knew little and cared less about the domestic politics of the Christian states, they tolerated Protestants in their own dominions and subsidized their rebellions in Germany and the Netherlands, as much because of their common hatred of idolatry as for the trouble they caused the Hapsburgs. Thus when Catherine dei Medici, regent for Charles IX, unleashed the massacre, she not only rejected the alternative policy of unifying Huguenots and Roman Catholics in a war against Spain, but also called into question the status of France in the black and white Ottoman world view. A relieved Philip II wrote that the Saint Bartholomew's Day massacre 'was indeed of such value and prudence and of such service, glory and honour to God and universal benefit to all Christendom that to hear of it was for me the best and most cheerful news which at present could come to me'.[10]

The period 1564–70 saw a wholesale changing of the guard in European cultural, religious and political affairs. The domino effect of the 1566 outbreak of violent iconoclasm across the Netherlands has received more than adequate attention from Anglophone historians, not least because when the Spanish shut the English out of the bullion market of Antwerp, Queen Elizabeth released English corsairs not only to compete with the Dutch 'Sea Beggars' for the rich pickings to be had from seaborne trade between Spain and the Netherlands, but also to raid across the Atlantic. It was almost as definitive a moment in the formation of the English national identity as it was for the Dutch, and another example of a counterproductive Spanish attempt to put out a corsair brushfire.

The accession of Saint Pius V, the Counter-Reformation pope par excellence, was arguably more important in the greater scheme of things. Matching bas-reliefs on the saint's monument in the basilica of Santa Maria Maggiore remind us that he claimed credit for the victory of the French Roman Catholics over the Huguenots at Moncontour in 1569 as well as for Lepanto. He was only too willing to alienate ecclesiastical revenues in order to extirpate Protestantism and combat Islam, and Roman Catholic princes were placed in the uncomfortable position of having all their usual excuses swept away by this unprecedented Papal largesse. He was regarded as an *energúmeno* (a demanding and uncontrollable spirit) in Madrid, while in 1567 a Viennese imperial councillor expressed a trenchant opinion of the Pope's condemnation both of the compromise religious settlement in Germany, and of ongoing negotiations for the 1568 Treaty of Adrianople, which ushered in a twenty-four-year truce between the Holy Roman and Ottoman empires: 'We should like it even better if the present Holy Father were no longer with us, however great, inexpressible, unparalleled and extraordinary his holiness may be'.[11]

His Holiness was only with difficulty dissuaded from preaching a Crusade in support of the Duke of Alba's march from Genoa along the 'Spanish Road' to the Netherlands, to which he had contributed 'graces' including a Crusade levy that was another name for the sale of indulgences, in theory abolished by the Council of Trent. Philip prevailed on him to preach the crusade only against the Ottomans and refused his request for an assault on Geneva, viewed from Rome as the master coven of devil-worshipping Calvinists. Although Philip did see the Netherlands struggle as one in defence of the Roman church, he refused to treat it as such for the same reason his father had not invoked the Crusade against the German Lutherans – it would have united the opposition, increased the likelihood of outside intervention, and made it impossible to hire Protestant troops. For the same reason Philip opposed the bull of excommunication and deposition pronounced against Elizabeth of England in 1570, although later the geopolitical interests of Rome and Madrid came into closer coincidence and the only *formal* Counter-Reformation Crusades ever preached were by Gregory XIII and Sixtus V against England, which gave birth to the 1588 Spanish Armada and two subsequent attempts.[12]

Also in 1566, Suleiman the Magnificent embarked on his last campaign, dying of a seizure while besieging Szigetvar, a frontier fortress a mere 37 miles (60km) away from Mohacs, where he had destroyed the independent kingdom of Hungary in 1526 (*Map 4*). Unsurprisingly, with so much going on elsewhere historians have tended to overlook the significance of a simultaneous naval offensive carried out by Piali, which tidied up the Aegean for the Ottomans by taking possession of Chios in 1566, and Naxos, Andros and Sifanto in 1567, punishing the Genoese for their association with Spain. Sailing on to the Adriatic, Piali may have intended to employ the same technique against Ragusa, which had also sinned by leasing ships to the enemy, but the Ragusan oligarchy politely told him that although they would provide supplies for his fleet, if he attempted to enter port they would fire on him. Piali then sailed north, to the great alarm of the Venetians despite written assurances from Istanbul that his orders were to attack only Austrian Fiume and Trieste. The Senate summoned a draft of 6,000 soldiers to man defences along the islands sheltering the lagoon, the Arsenal began to spew forth galleys and Girolamo Zanne was appointed general of the fleet. The senators who rejected the Ottoman ultimatum of 1570 may have been influenced by a false belief that their show of strength in 1567 had turned Piali back.[13]

Selim did not possess the military prestige to make his accession a certainty. Only those who had led them in war enjoyed the respect of the timariot sipahis and, above all, the Janissaries who now began to play a role in Ottoman politics akin to the Praetorian Guard in imperial Rome. Not content with the traditional accession fee paid by Selim, they blocked his return to Istanbul and demanded more, sparking similar action by others. However, he was blessed to be the father-in-law of Mehmet Sokolli, Suleiman's last and greatest grand vizier, who as Beylerbey of Rumelia in 1551–56 had added Transylvania to the empire. Sokolli therefore possessed the authority Selim lacked, and restored order by appealing to the rebellious troops over the heads of the ringleaders, before executing the latter.

The heroic phase of Ottoman expansion was over, and like the later campaigns of Suleiman's reign, those carried out under Selim were aimed at consolidation. The spirit of religious live and let live that had served the Ottomans so well for two centuries had given way to a less tolerant attitude, embodied in Suleiman's codification of imperial laws to bring them into closer conformity with the teachings of an increasingly intransigent Ulema, while a new generation of Greek Orthodox clergy with no personal experience of Latin oppression became the leaders of popular resistance to Ottoman rule. Meanwhile the threat from dissident Islamic sects did not diminish, and in 1567 the provincial capital of Sana fell to highland devotees (since the ninth Christian century) of the alternative fifth imam Zayd ibn-Ali, requiring an expedition from Egypt to regain control of the Red Sea coast. The Zaydis withdrew to their mountain fastness, continuing a tradition of rabid resistance to imperial power that persists to this day.

Finally, Suleiman's policy of strengthening Muscovy – to weaken Lithuania and Poland in the competition for control over territories north of the Black Sea – boomeranged as the powerful, new kingdom of Russia took shape under Ivan the Terrible, and began to expand southwards into the territory bounded by the Don and Volga rivers, screened by free associations of steppe horsemen whose descendants still bear the Turkic designation of Cossack (*kozak*), a wild and daring spirit.

The period 1568–70 marked the apogee of Ottoman power. In 1568 an expedition sailed as far as Sumatra to support the Islamic ruler of Aceh against the Portuguese, whose successors the Dutch did not complete the conquest of the principality until 1913. Also in 1568, 10,000 Askeri and 6,000 labourers were sent to the new beylerbeyik of Caffa in the Crimea under Cherkes (Circassian) Kassim Pasha, and in 1569 a logistical base was established at Azov (*Map 5*) for an ambitious expedition to excavate a canal between the Don and the Volga not far from present-day Volgograd, ex-Stalingrad. This would have permitted the projection of Ottoman naval power into the Caspian Sea and control of the ancient Silk Road through Astrakhan, seized by Ivan the Terrible in 1557. However, it depended on the goodwill of Khan Devlet Giray of the Crimean Tatars, who had no desire to be absorbed by the Ottoman Empire and withdrew his cavalry screen in late 1570. This forced Kassim to retreat to Azov, abandoning the works and his artillery to the Cossacks, while Russian agents or homesick Janissaries then burned the stockpiled stores to ensure the expedition could not be renewed in 1571. Selim decreed that the cost of this reverse should be entirely borne by Mehmet Sokolli, whose ability to influence events may have been temporarily diminished thereby.[14]

If the Aceh expedition defined the eastern reach of Ottoman influence, the western limit was marked by the rebellion of the Moriscos, nominal Christian converts in what had been the Muslim kingdom al-Andalus, that erupted at the end of 1568. The forcible Christianization of the Iberian Muslims generated a 1501 revolt in the Alpujarras, the area south of the Sierra Nevada between Almería and Málaga, and another in Valencia in 1525. But since then and unlike the Jewish converts contemptuously known as *Marranos* (pigs), the Moriscos had not suffered serious discrimination before an edict in 1567 banned their songs and dances, while their women were forbidden to wear the veil and their public baths were to be destroyed because of the immoral acts that allegedly took place there. In addition their weddings were to be performed in public according to Christian rites, with their houses kept open on the day of the ceremony so that the local priests could ensure that no parallel rites were taking place. Philip cannot have been accurately informed about the hornets' nest he was stirring up by throwing this sop to priestly prurience and intrusiveness, for thanks to the revolt in the Netherlands he was without dependable troops in Spain itself.

The rebellion was supposed to break out across al-Andalus on New Year's Day, but Farax ben-Farax jumped the gun and tried to raise the Moriscos in the city of Granada on 26 December 1568. Early failures resulted in the rebellion only taking root in the Alpujarras, where it was easily supplied and reinforced from Algeria. It is not clear whether the Porte was actively involved from the first, or whether it was drawn in by the community of interest among the coastal Moriscos and the North African corsairs. Many of these were the children of Muslims who refused to convert and were expelled from Castile earlier in the century by none other than Cardinal Jiménez de Cisneros, sponsor of Pedro Navarro's expeditions and therefore with a double claim to being the catalyst of the Ottoman–corsair nexus. The following preamble from an imperial command of 16 April 1570 to Uluch Ali, Beylerbey of Algiers since 1568, suggests geographic confusion in Istanbul, and a notable failure to appreciate that the moment of greatest enemy weakness had passed:

> . . . the Lutheran sect [actually, Calvinist] has brought together a large body of troops and has pillaged and plundered the [Netherlands] provinces of the tyrannical and accursed Spanish, has taken their lands and defeated them. Also from this area [?] the Andalus, Islamic people, have revolted, the leaders of the accursed unbelievers have been roughly handled and they have been in a state of disorder . . . From this area [Algiers] troops and arms have been sent, assistance has been given, and the provinces of the tyrannical and accursed unbelievers are not free from being looted.[15]

Of course the Porte was delighted that heaven was punishing the evil-doer Philip, but one looks in vain for evidence of a co-ordinating role. Far from it – instead of devoting all his resources to supporting the Alpujarras insurgency, Uluch Ali seized the opportunity to march overland to Tunis and in January 1570 expelled the last of the Hafsids, Hapsburg puppets since 1535, although he failed to take the Spanish port-fortress of Goleta. Like the colonial rebels of the twentieth century the Moriscos were pawns in a great power rivalry. Had they seized and held a major port they might have drawn greater Ottoman support, perhaps causing the Porte to postpone its plans for consolidation at the other end of the Mediterranean, but given the distances involved it seems most unlikely. However this was not how it seemed to the Spanish, among whom the insurgency did indeed create a 'state of disorder' so great that Philip felt compelled to appoint his 20-year-old half-brother Juan to overall command of a dangerously mismanaged campaign in which the local landlords were at odds with crown officials, and both with the ecclesiastical authorities.

Unknown and perhaps incomprehensible to the Ottomans, who usually had to deal with the opposite problem, Philip had suffered a shattering loss in the death in July 1568 of his son Carlos, whose psychotic behaviour had finally obliged the king to incarcerate him six months earlier. This was followed in October by the death in childbirth of his beloved queen Elizabeth of Valois, which left him not only without a male heir but also bereft of an extremely valuable dynastic bargaining chip in his relations with the France of Catherine dei Medici and her last, sterile son Charles IX, by now beset with religious civil wars that offered prospects for a decisive Spanish intervention. The suddenly increased dynastic significance of Don Juan has not received as much attention as it deserves. It can be read between the lines of the long and detailed letter of instructions handwritten by the king himself and sent to Juan along with his letter of appointment as the successor to General of the Sea García de Toledo on 15 January 1568. Written when Philip had finally been forced to recognize his son's unfitness to rule, as well as again defining the duties of a military commander in constricting detail it contained a homily on princely virtue that echoed the didactic adornment the king not long afterwards commissioned for *La Real*, of which the following is representative:

> Truth in speaking and fulfilment of promises is the foundation of
> credit and esteem among men, and that upon which the confidence
> of society is supported and founded. This is more required, and is

much more necessary in men of very high rank, and who fill
great public posts; because upon their truth and good faith depend
the public faith and security.[16]

Juan had chafed in nominal command of a fleet run by grandees who
were in no doubt what the king's reaction would be should they permit a
hair on his brother's head to be harmed, but his entourage in the Alpujarras
could not exercise a similar degree of control. Philip was quite explicit in a
mild reproof he sent after learning that Juan was doing the rounds of
sentries incognito: 'You must keep yourself, and I must keep you, for greater
things, and it is from these that you must learn your professional
knowledge'. Although young and given to writing interminable sentences,
as to substance Juan was either naturally shrewd or very well coached, for
he was quick to point out that he was merely imitating a practice of their
father, Charles V:

... at my age, and in my position, I see that Your Majesty's interest
requires that when there is any call to arms or any enterprise, the
soldiers should find me in the front of them, or at least with them,
ready to encourage them to do their duty, and that they should know
that I desire to lead them in the name of Your Majesty.

Philip came back with detailed guidance on the duties of a field
commander in which the practices of Charles V were tightly defined as
well as extolled, removing the *ad patrem* argument from the young man's
rhetorical quiver. To no avail, for in an assault on the village of Serón on
17 February 1570 the Spanish soldiers panicked when counter-attacked,
and Juan rode forward to rally them. He was hit on the helmet by an
arquebus ball, while beside him his foster-father Luis Mendez Quijada was
mortally wounded by another that penetrated his armpit. Six hundred
Spanish soldiers were killed and the revolt revived, to endure through
much of 1570. The brothers were deeply pained by the death of Quijada,
but Philip was outraged that:

... you keep so ill your promise not to place yourself in jeopardy. ...
you ought not to vex me thus, and to lower the credit of my arms, and
add to that of our enemies, so greatly as would be the case if they were
to shed a drop of your blood. I therefore distinctly order you, and will

take it very ill if you disobey my order, not to do so any more, but to remain in the place which befits one who has the charge of this business and my brother . . . for everyone ought to do his own duty, and not the general the soldier's, nor the soldier the general's.[17]

When Philip sought a new role for his brother as the overall commander of the Holy League fleet in 1571, one consideration may have been that Juan was unlikely to get himself into trouble on board the finest galley in the Mediterranean, in the middle of an enormous fleet, surrounded by grandees sworn to protect him, and under the strictest instructions to heed the advice of the resolutely unheroic Gian'Andrea Doria. If Philip's reaction to news of Lepanto was muted, and his treatment of Juan colder thereafter, envy and the imminent confinement of his new niece–wife may have played a part – but a more likely explanation is abiding displeasure that his brother had not merely gambled the fleet but also his dynastically invaluable life on the roll of the dice that any battle must be. Furthermore he had taken this appalling risk after the end of the safe campaigning season, when it was impossible to follow up the victory to secure its fruits, an outcome Philip – fairly – attributed to his brother's appetite for glory.

The above were the broad brushstrokes overlaid on a canvas already covered with the pointillist activities of countless individuals and small communities. We naturally focus on issues of great power rivalry and ideological conflict, but the cumulative result of effectively self-governing groups of military–commercial entrepreneurs on land and sea across the whole theatre made them a collective great power in their own right.[18] If we consider the astonishing fact that in 1569, with the Alpujarras in flames, Philip offered the 'renegade' Uluch Ali not only Tunis – which he was soon to take by force anyway – but also a Spanish marquessate if he would *consent* to govern under Hapsburg rather than Ottoman auspices, and that Cervantes wrote of him as morally admirable (*Don Quixote* Part I, Ch. 11), the need for a more nuanced appreciation than the usual Muslim–Christian dichotomy becomes apparent. A study of the Ottoman-allied corsairs across the Mediterranean may well conclude, as Catherine Bracewell did in her valuable study of the Christian Croatian Uskoks of Senj: '. . . the epic songs of the border present [them] as heroes, affirming the possibility of freedom from authority [and] glorifying self-assertion . . . '[19]

CHAPTER SEVEN

PROLOGUE

THE 1570 CAMPAIGN

19 Jan.	Uluch Ali takes Tunis from Spanish puppet Hafsid ruler. Algiers corsairs raid Lanzarote, in the Canary Islands.
Early Feb.	Venetian ambassador reports accelerated galley-building in Istanbul. Venetian ships, merchants and goods seized across the Ottoman Empire.
4 March	Venice requests assistance of Pius V to achieve a Spanish alliance.
5 March	Pius V crowns Cosimo dei Medici Grand Duke of Tuscany.
6 March	Venice detains Ottoman envoy to France, imprisons Ottoman merchants.
10 March	Duce Pietro Loredan writes to Philip II expressing hope for an alliance.
25 March	Venetian senate rejects Ottoman demand for the cession of Cyprus.
30 March	Captain General Zanne leaves Venice with 30 galleys, 50 more to follow.
13 April	Zanne's fleet arrives Zara, immobilized by typhus epidemic for two months.
17 April	Piali departs Istanbul with 80 galleys, 30 galliots.
End April	Venice obtains grain at preferential rate from Pius V and Philip II.

Early May	Fortresses QMG Venier, from Corfu, takes Ottoman mainland fort of Sopoto.
Mid May	Piali lands 5,000 men on Tinos, assault on the fortress fails. Ali sails from Istanbul for Rhodes with 60 galleys and 170 transports.
22 May	Pius V agrees to grant Philip II additional 'graces'.
Early June	Piali joins Ali at Rhodes, combined fleet sails to Finike.
10 June	Pope authorizes bishop of Dalmatia to issue indulgences to volunteers.
11 June	Colonna appointed captain general of Papal fleet (12 galleys leased from Venice) and commander of the eventual combined Christian fleet.
12 June	Zanne's fleet leaves Zara, collects ships, galleasses at Hvar and Alessio.
Mid June	Delayed arrival of Ottoman army at Finike. Beylerbey of Karaman dismissed.
20 June	Colonna to Ancona, begins equipping 8 galleys, goes to Venice for the rest.
23 June	Zanne's fleet arrives at Corfu, orders Crete fleet to join him. Uluch Ali raids Tabarka, seizes a Lomellino galley.
30 June	Crete QM Quirini destroys Ottoman fort at Maina en route to Corfu.
3 July	Ottoman army lands at Salines. Quirini arrives at Corfu.
3–7 July	Failed attempt by Venier and land general Pallavicini to take Margariti.
15 July	Uluch Ali ambushes Malta squadron under Sant Climent off Licata.
22 July	Colonna to Ancona with 3 galleys plus Fausto's quinquereme.
23 July	Venetian fleet sails south from Corfu.
25 July	Lala Mustafa begins siege of Nicosia.
4 Aug.	Venetian fleet at Suda Bay, Crete.
8 Aug.	Pacification of Saint-Germain halts religious civil war in France.
9 Aug.	Colonna (12 galleys) arrives at Otranto.
12 Aug.	Doria (49 galleys) leaves Messina.
Mid Aug.	Quirini (20 galleys) raids Andros for rowers.
18 Aug.	Doria loads troops, supplies at Taranto.

20 Aug.	Doria arrives at Otranto.
22 Aug.	Papal–Spanish fleet (61 galleys) sails for Crete.
31 Aug.	Papal–Spanish fleet arrives at Suda Bay. Combined fleet approx. 200.
9 Sept.	Fall of Nicosia.
22 Sept.	Christian fleet at Castellorizo learns that Nicosia has fallen.
24 Sept.	Storm scatters returning fleet, 3 Papal and 14 Venetian galleys lost.
4–6 Oct.	Christian fleet reassembles at Candia. Riot forces them to leave.
6 Oct.	Doria parts company, reaches Corfu on 13th, Messina on 17th.
Mid-Oct.	Piali leaves 7 galleys at Famagusta, fleet returns to Rhodes, then Istanbul.
26 Oct.	Giustiniano arrives in Candia with 3 Maltese galleys.
November	30 active, 23 laid up galleys left in Crete under Quirini. Zanne, Colonna and Giustiniano sail to Corfu where most remaining Venetian galleys are laid up. Giustiniano returns to Malta, Colonna sets out for Ancona.
December	Storm drives Colonna into Cattaro, lightning destroys his flagship, wrecked again near Ragusa. Zanne dismissed, imprisoned on return to Venice.

The Ottoman decision to invade Cyprus in 1570 is usually ascribed to Selim's alcoholism (the island produces fine wines) and to the influence of his Jewish financiers, the two combined in the person of Selim's alleged drinking companion Joseph Nasi, scion of an immensely wealthy *Marrano* family forced out of Portugal earlier in the century. It is also alleged that exaggerated reports of the damage caused by an explosion and fire at the Venice Arsenal on 13–14 September 1569 encouraged Selim to strike, a claim which overlooks both that the 'Great Fire' of Istanbul occurred in the same month, and that Ottoman merchants in Venice would have accurately reported the relatively insignificant losses (four galleys and a ship) at the Arsenal. As to Nasi, while Sephardic hostility towards the Latin church and all its works is a given, Cyprus was a glaring anomaly within the Ottoman-dominated eastern Mediterranean and it cannot have taken much to persuade Selim to incorporate it within the empire. There does, however, seem to have been an element of historical taunting involved, for Cyprus was the last of the Crusader states still in Latin hands and Selim laid claim to it as King of Jerusalem. A more immediate grievance was the failure of the Venetians to police the coast of Cyprus, used by western corsairs as an advanced base to prey on Muslim pilgrim ships on their way to Egypt and Mecca.

After expelling the Genoese from the Cyclades islands Selim made Nasi the Duke of Naxos, Count of Andros and Paros, Lord of Milos and the Islands – Latin, not Ottoman titles. This may have been selective Ottoman punctiliousness regarding their treaties with the previous rulers of these islands, for if the titles persisted the treaties had not technically been broken, but it is also possible the intention was to create a semi-autonomous principality in order to attract Jewish settlers. It was certainly unusual to appoint a non-military governor to what were front-line islands, with the Venetian island of Tinos nestling among them, and Nasi does not appear to have made any effort to prepare them for Latin counter-attacks. He had his eyes set instead on the land of his forefathers, and prematurely commissioned a coat of arms for himself as King of Cyprus, reasoning that if the island was part of the kingdom of Jerusalem, the converse was also true. Hundreds of Jewish families were relocated to Cyprus after the Ottoman conquest, but whatever hopes for further advancement Nasi may have entertained were dashed after Lepanto, when Naxos (briefly) and Sifanto (until 1617) were regained by the Latins.[1]

The incandescent partisanship that swirled from the first around the war that followed still singes the historiography. Even Sir George Hill in his magisterial *History of Cyprus* flinched from underlining how greatly the lot of the inhabitants improved under Ottoman rule. With reference to Ottoman motives for embarking on the enterprise, the historiography has been unduly influenced by the reports of Marc'Antonio Barbaro, the Venetian ambassador (*Bailo*) to the Porte, who had a personal interest in concealing the embarrassing fact that Grand Vizier Mehmet Sokolli had played him like a violin. According to Barbaro, Sokolli was a friend of Venice but was overruled by Selim on the advice of a clique including Nasi and Third Vizier Piali, another imperial son-in-law, who harboured a grudge against Sokolli for demoting him from the post of kapudan and appointing Muezzinzâde Ali, also married to one of Selim's daughters, in his place.

In fact Piali was far from being a favourite and had been demoted for not pooling the bribes he took from the enemies of the Porte, long a source of general profit and amusement, and he was only granted a role in the Cyprus expedition because his wife prevailed upon her elder sister, Sokolli's chief wife, to lobby her husband to give him another chance.[2]

The land commander, Fifth Vizier Lala Mustafa, also owed his promotion (from Beylerbey of Damascus) to Sokolli, and an expedition in which all the senior officers were his placemen cannot have been other than planned and directed by the grand vizier himself. Western historians are perhaps too willing to project the instrumentality of corruption and disloyal competition prevailing in their own cultural catchment area onto an Ottoman court where bribes were perceived as tribute, and where – *at this time* – intrigue still counted for less than ability. Sokolli himself had been kapudan as well as one of Suleiman's most successful generals, but his need now was to cement Selim's hold on the throne with a successful military campaign performed in his name, and the only easy pickings were Venetian. The fact that the Venetians had paid 150,000 ducats to obtain a renewal of the treaty governing their tenure of Cyprus at the time of Selim's accession, and almost as much again every year in tribute and in (never disputed) compensation for the activities of corsairs that used the island as their base, was a sure indicator that there was very much more to be had. In addition the Porte received frequent embassies from Cypriots begging for liberation, and insistent demands from the Ulema for protection of pilgrims. Lastly the Venetians had embarked upon a belated programme of fortification on the island after Selim's accession. If Cyprus were to be taken, it was best done before they completed it.

In addition to the kapudan's remit (which included Gallipoli and Alexandria as well as the Aegean islands), the beylerbeyiks of Anatolia, Karaman, Dulkaldir, Aleppo and Damascus were mobilized for the Cyprus expedition (*Maps 5 & 7*). Even before the conquest of Cyprus was complete, the southernmost provinces of Anatolia (Teke) and Karaman (Alaye, Iüel), and the westernmost of Dulkaldir (Tarsus) were incorporated into the new beylerbeyik of Kibris, whose capital was Nicosia.[3] In the same year Tripoli was declared a beylerbeyik and, as we saw in the last chapter, Tunis was taken effortlessly from the Spanish puppet Hafsid ruler, together indicating a wide-ranging strategy for the full Ottomanization of the eastern Mediterranean. The Cyprus expedition fits into the pattern of Sokolli's desire to consolidate the empire, to win prestige for 'his' Sultan and to endow a new generation of officials and timariot sipahis who would owe their holdings to his patronage. To that end he encouraged the Venetians to continue wasting money on bribes, feeding wishful thinking that this was the cheap way to retain the remnant of their empire.

Sokolli's intent was plain to see in the treaties he concluded with Persia and Austria. To win Shah Tahmasp, conquered lands were given up and payment made for his betrayal of the Muslim law of asylum by allowing the elimination of Selim's brother Bayezid and his family, who had sought sanctuary at his court. No such concessions were necessary to achieve the Treaty of Edirne / Adrianople signed in February 1568, in which the Holy Roman Empire was granted an eight-year truce in exchange for an increased tribute for the sliver of Hungary it was permitted to retain. Lest there should be any doubt that the Ottoman Empire was freeing its hands to deal with the anomalous Venetian presence in the eastern Mediterranean, military stores were built up and the port works improved at Adalia and Finike in southern Anatolia, just as they had been in Caffa in the Crimea for the Don–Volga canal expedition. Finally, in February 1570 all Venetian ships, traders and their goods within the empire were seized, putting at least one noble Venetian banking family into debtors' prison. The Venetian ambassador begged Sokolli to send an envoy to Venice setting out the terms Istanbul would regard as acceptable for the resolution of its grievances, and on 25 March imperial courier Kubad duly delivered the following message:

> Selim, Ottoman Sultan, Emperor of the Turks, Lord of Lords, King of Kings, Shadow of God, Lord of the Earthly Paradise and of Jerusalem, to the Seigniory of Venice: We demand of you Cyprus, which you shall give Us willingly or by force; and do not arouse Our terrible sword, for We shall wage most cruel war against you everywhere; nor let you trust in your treasure, for We shall cause it suddenly to run away from you like a torrent; beware to irritate Us.[4]

Before it arrived the war party of Alvise Mocenigo in the Venetian senate had prevailed and Duce Pietro Loredan had written to Philip II expressing hope for an alliance. When the latter suddenly died and Mocenigo was elected in his place, it simply confirmed a decision already taken. Given the extreme vulnerability not merely of Cyprus but of the Venetian coastal holdings in the Balkans, it was a gamble turning on a calculation that Pius V would not only subsidize it, but also deliver support from Spain and Spanish Italy. Yet until the crisis in early 1570, in common with other Christian princes the Venetian oligarchy had regarded the new Pope as a loose cannon on the finely balanced deck of their relations with the Porte. This despite the fact that ever since the last Holy League in the late 1530s, the annual grant (*sussidio*) by the Papacy of a tenth from ecclesiastical revenues had underwritten Venice's defence of the Adriatic. On 27 February this was increased by an extra tenth or 100,000 ducats, but the Pope made any further assistance, financial or in kind, conditional upon Venice joining a new Holy League.

From the first Venetian policy was dedicated to obtaining the benefits of an alliance, in particular grain at preferential rates to compensate for crop failure on the Venetian mainland and the loss of supplies from Egypt, without conceding any constraint on diplomatic freedom. Further fatal ambiguity arose from the conflict between the need to take military action in defence of Cyprus while seeking to avoid upsetting the delicate balance in Dalmatia, where the Ottomans had established forward outposts to threaten Zara (Zadar), Sibenik, Trogir and Spalato (Split) in Dalmatia, or provoking them to strike against the tenuous string of poorly fortified Venetian ports along the Montenegrin–Albanian coast (*Map 4*). Venetian strategy throughout 1570 and well into 1571 is practically a textbook case of what happens when deterrence fails, for Sokolli's master plan discounted Christian solidarity. 'His magnificence the Pasha', reported Senate Secretary Jacopo Ragazzoni in late April 1571, 'said he was well aware to what degree [Venice] was esteemed by the princes of Christendom, and of what faith she might place in them'. Sokolli erred, but only just, the greater miscalculation being that of the Venetian war party, for they lost in Albania as well as Cyprus, their treasure did pour away in torrents, and despite Lepanto they were eventually obliged to make a grovelling peace.

The Pope could also exercise considerable leverage on Spain, whose maritime defences also depended on the sussidio. Pius V added the proceeds from the sale of indulgences (*cruzada*) and from the top contributor to the general ecclesiastical tithe (*excusado*) when Philip agreed in principle to join the Holy League in July 1570. This unlocked low interest loans from the Genoese entrepreneurs, which more than covered the cost of their own military contributions. While the finances of Sicily and Naples were strained by the cost of the war, the Spanish crown actually made a profit on it overall.[5] From his own words it seems Philip himself may not have fully appreciated this, but his ministers certainly did and a subtext to the Cyprus war is that Selim and Philip could continue it almost indefinitely without serious financial consequences to themselves. The period 1570–71 was the first (and only) time when Philip had the opportunity, sufficient means and, thanks to Ottoman complicity in the Moriscos revolt, a good reason to embark on a major war in the Mediterranean – *but he could not afford to become bogged down in it*. The slight smile he permitted himself when the cringing Venetian ambassador told him about the separate peace concluded on 7 March 1573 may well have been one of relief, for it meant that while he would continue to receive the Papal 'graces', he was free of his commitment to an annual offensive in the Mediterranean at a time when the renewed Netherlands revolt, now actively supported by England, required his full attention.[6]

The Horsemen of the Apocalypse ganged up on Venice in 1570. Months before the arrival of the Ottoman ultimatum, new taxes were levied on a population already beset by famine, new military and civil posts were sold to the highest bidder and, as in 1566, the Arsenal went into mass refitting and construction mode, while recruiters were sent to hire mercenaries as far away as Savoy and southern Germany. The Venetians paraded their large, well manned and equipped fleet for the benefit of Selim's courier before it departed under the command of Girolamo Zanne at the end of March, but whatever chance this belated display of readiness might have had of conjuring away the danger was undone by disease, for after the fleet arrived at Zara it was assaulted by typhus and lost so many rowers and soldiers that it ceased to be an effective fighting force. *This calamity defined the 1570 campaign*. Having, in a sense, finessed famine by invoking war, confident that they would thereby obtain grain from the Papal State, Naples and Sicily at a preferential rate, the Venetians needed to impose a significant check on the Ottoman offensive unaided in order to remain the arbiters of their own destiny. With Zanne's fleet immobilized by disease and mass desertion, it remained to be seen whether Cyprus could emulate the example of Malta and become an example and a reproach to Christendom.

Between 1567 and 1570 Nicosia, the Cypriot capital, had been given the full *trace italienne* treatment, with eleven well-designed bastions evenly distributed around its 3 mile (5km), perfectly circular circumference (*B&W Plate 6b*). Although it was militarily questionable to have made a city so far from the sea the principal fortified place on the island, there were compelling social and economic reasons to provide a haven large enough to contain all the Venetian landlords and local nobility, as well as a large number of Cypriot peasants. At the time of the siege of 56,500 souls in Nicosia only about 12,000 were fit for military duty, and the suspicion lingers that the rest were there mainly to ensure that friends and relatives outside the walls did not welcome the invader too enthusiastically. Its principal, known, defect was that it required a garrison of about 20,000, and clearly it was hoped that the enclosed peasants, having no alternative, would fight as hard for Nicosia as the Maltese had for Birgu and Senglea, and as other Cypriots later did for Famagusta. Given heroic leadership they might have done so, but the death or absence of better qualified candidates left the defence of Nicosia in the hands of Niccolò Dandolo, a man not only stupid but lacking both physical and moral courage. It is remarkable how often such individuals bob up in military history, drawn like moths to the flame of an activity for which they are totally unsuited, with invariably catastrophic results.

The Ottoman invasion really began with the dispatch of Murad Reis and twenty-five galleys from Istanbul to Rhodes in February, to provide flank cover for the invasion fleet. This followed in two stages, Piali departing Istanbul with a strike force of eighty galleys and thirty galliots on 17 April. In early May he landed 5,000 soldiers on Venetian Tinos, but re-embarked them after failing to take the fortress in several expensive assaults over ten days. He went on to Negroponte to scrape and tallow his hulls, and departed for Rhodes on the 28th. On 16 May Kapudan Ali and land commander Lala Mustafa sailed from Istanbul with the transports containing the artillery and other heavy stores, and collected other vessels as they sailed down the Anatolian coast and the Dodecannese. A combined fleet of 155 galleys and galliots, 70 fustas and fragatas, 8 galleasses, 20

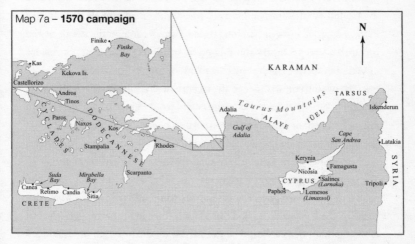

Map 7a – **1570 campaign**

Finike
Finike Bay
Kas
Kekova Is.
Castellorizo

KARAMAN

N

Andros
Tinos
Paros
Naxos
Kos
Stampalia
Rhodes

CYCLADES
DODECANNESE

Adalia
Taurus Mountains
ALAYE
İÜEL
TARSUS

Gulf of Adalia

Cape San Andrea

Kerynia
Nicosia
Famagusta
Salines (Larnaka)
CYPRUS
Lemesos (Limassol)
Paphos

Iskenderun

SYRIA

Latakia

Tripoli

Suda Bay
Canea
Retimo
Mirabella Bay
Candia
Sitia
CRETE

Scarpanto

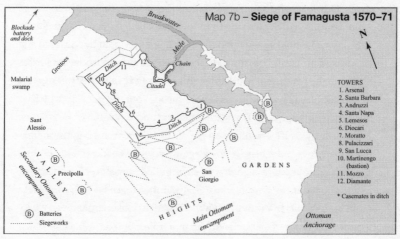

Map 7b – **Siege of Famagusta 1570–71**

Breakwater
Blockade battery and dock
Grottoes
Malarial swamp
Ditch
Mole
Chain
Citadel
Ditch
Ditch

Sant Alessio

N

TOWERS
1. Arsenal
2. Santa Barbara
3. Andruzzi
4. Santa Napa
5. Lemesos
6. Diocari
7. Moratto
8. Pulacizzari
9. San Lucca
10. Martinengo (bastion)
11. Mozzo
12. Diamante

* Casemates in ditch

VALLEY
Secondary Ottoman encampment
Precipolla

GARDENS

San Giorgio

HEIGHTS

Main Ottoman encampment

Ottoman Anchorage

Ⓑ Batteries
.... Siegeworks

horse-ferries, 5 large ships and 30 smaller merchant vessels assembled at Rhodes on 1 June. On 4 June this enormous armada sailed for Finike, arriving on the 17th, where it was supposed to be met by 34,000 men including 12,000 sipahis. These were not ready for a further ten days and, in marked contrast to the Christian norm, even this relatively brief delay cost the Beylerbey of Karaman his post. Meanwhile Piali sent six galliots on a reconnaissance mission, which landed a small force in the south of the island that was promptly annihilated by stradiots (Albanian light cavalry in Venetian service) under the command of Pietro Rondacchi.

The overall commander of the cavalry on Cyprus was Count Eugenio Sinclitico, who had returned to the island from Venice on 27 March with instructions not to attack any Ottoman beachhead, but rather to hole up in the fortresses, order those who could not be accommodated within the walls to disperse into the mountains, and await the arrival of the fleet. These instructions might have been overruled by Astorre Baglione, the robust new military governor of Cyprus who had arrived on 1 May with some of the 2,000 men he had raised for Venice in his native Perugia, but realizing that Nicosia would be doomed if all the ports on the island fell to the Ottomans, he had transferred to Famagusta, the only one where some attempt had been made to modernize the defences. Left in charge at Nicosia, Dandolo seized upon the instructions brought by Sinclitico and conducted an entirely static defence, even rebuking Rondacchi for his exploit in the south, and petulantly refused to send out infantry in support of the only cavalry sortie he permitted throughout the siege, to which he had grudgingly agreed in the face of the unanimous opinion of his officers. As a result the sortie – which had got among the Ottoman guns, slaughtered the crews and set fire to the siege works – was badly cut up. Feeling against Dandolo ran so high that he surrounded himself with halberdiers, and as the defences crumbled on 9 September these bought him a few more hours of life by cutting down the Venetian nobleman Andrea Pesaro, who sought him out, denounced him as a traitor and drew his sword.

The instructions from Venice for the defence of the island seem to have been based on a fundamentally false appreciation of the experience of Malta. In the struggle for Cyprus the Ottomans had much the shorter lines of supply and reinforcement, but even had they not the island was fertile and the invading force could maintain itself with cash, cultivating the goodwill of the islanders while greatly simplifying the logistics. Estimates of Ottoman numbers are always undependable, but when the vanguard of the invasion fleet arrived off Salines on 3 July, Lala Mustafa appears to have had with him only 6,000 Janissaries, 12,000 sipahis and an unknown number of volunteer cannon fodder. It took two weeks to land them all, along with the siege train, and no effort was made to attack the beachhead when it was at its most vulnerable. Lala Mustafa did not await the arrival of the rest of the army, coming from Adalia under Hussein Pasha, the new Beylerbey of Karaman, but marched inland with the troops to hand, sending 500 sipahis to make a demonstration in front of Famagusta. By 26 July, the investment of Nicosia was complete and over the following forty-six days the besieging force grew steadily, with new drafts arriving daily from Asia Minor and Syria, until for the final assault it was joined by 16,000–17,000 men (100 per galley) from the fleet. By that time the invading army, including labourers, may have exceeded 100,000 men, and no relief force the Christian powers could have assembled would have been able to retake the island.

Ottoman numbers soared after Nicosia fell to the fifteenth assault on 9 September, the wretched Dandolo having proved as stubbornly opposed to capitulation on terms as he had been to conducting a proper defence. All non-Cypriots were killed or enslaved during the three-day sack of the city, said to be the richest since the fall of Constantinople, and once word of this reached the mainland ships bound for Cyprus were nearly swamped by volunteers anxious to participate in the spoils. But the gain in numbers was accompanied by a sharp decline in quality, as the sipahis and many of the Janissaries returned home with their loot. This gave Baglione in Famagusta the necessary breathing space to turn the place into a much tougher nut to crack. Hassan Pasha believed Famagusta would follow the example of Kerynia, which prudently surrendered without a fight, and on 10 September sent Dandolo's head along with a demand to surrender to Marc'Antonio Bragadino, civil governor of Famagusta, who is said to have replied:

> I have seen your letter. I have also received the head of the lord
> lieutenant of Nicosia, and I tell you herewith that even if you have
> so easily taken the city of Nicosia, with your own blood you will

have to purchase this city, which with God's help will give you so
much to do that you will always regret having encamped here.[7]

If he wrote them these words were a brave front, for Famagusta was
desperately vulnerable (*Map 7*). The fortifications were inadequate, with the
only modern bastion built at great expense (500,000 ducats) to form an
acute angle whose flanks were not raked from adjacent towers, the rest of
the redoubts were round or polygonal pre-artillery towers, the old medieval
walls had been lowered but reinforced with terreplein only in places, the
ditch was too narrow and the glacis beyond inadequately covered by fire
(*Diagram 2* for an explanation of the terminology). Perhaps worst of all,
no attempt had been made to deny besiegers a reef providing a view of
the harbour from the east, or the headland to the west commanding the
narrow entrance to the port. Upon arrival, the appalled Baglione embarked
upon a whirlwind effort to repair these deficiencies. The glacis was extended
and a second covered way built, the ditch was widened and reinforced with
ravelins at the angles, with casemates built into the ditch for light guns to
fire along its length. He also built artillery platforms (cavaliers) within the
main towers, completed the terreplaining of the walls, levelled nearby
villages and poisoned their wells in the course of destroying everything
that might provide cover or be useful to a besieger, including the orchards
in the famous 'Gardens' to the south.

To defend a perimeter less than a third the length of Nicosia's Baglione
had a garrison of about 1,000 Italians, 3,000 Cypriots and 100 stradiots,
plus however many of the latter had escaped from Nicosia with Pietro
Rondacchi, whom Baglione immediately appointed to command them all.
During the course of the siege the defenders made twenty-six damaging
sorties, most led by Rondacchi but some by Baglione himself. On one occasion Baglione unhorsed and mortally wounded a richly dressed Ottoman
officer who had challenged him to single combat, and brought the dying
man back into Famagusta for all to see. One need look no further for an
explanation why the Cypriots in Famagusta fought so bravely under the
otherwise hated banner of Saint Mark. Baglione did not have a bodyguard
until near the end, and when one of his own captains was unwise enough
to be disrespectful, he killed him on the spot. Valette would have embraced
him as a brother, and the Knights of Malta could not have defended the

place better, but ultimately it would be for nothing unless a sizeable relief force arrived to lift the siege. None did, and let us now return to the Venetian fleet to see why.

We left the main body typhus-ridden in Zara, and there it remained for two months, while complaints by the Dalmatians about the brutal behaviour of the Venetian captains reached as far as Rome and provoked a Papal rebuke. It was not until the Pope instructed the bishop of Dalmatia to issue indulgences to any who volunteered and, even more remarkably, approval was received from the Venetian senate to increase the signing-on bonus, that enough men were recruited to permit the fleet to proceed. The lost soldiers proved irreplaceable because the epidemic was not confined to the fleet, and Zara had barely enough fighting men to defend its own walls. Indeed, heightened activity by marauding Ottoman irregulars on land and sea was another reason for the fleet to remain at Zara, and after it departed all the Venetian fustas were left behind under Almoro Tiepolo, to guard against the small-boat raiders operating out of the nearby Ottoman frontier outposts of Obrovac and Skradin. By the time it set sail for Corfu on 12 June Zanne's magnificent fleet, so proudly paraded before the eyes of Selim's courier in late March, was sadly reduced in number, in personnel, but above all in spirit.

Two weeks before Zanne departed Venice, Captain of the Gulf Marco Quirini with twenty-five galleys set sail for Crete, where twenty-two more were laid up and awaiting activation. Later he was appointed Quartermaster (QM) of Crete in replacement of Antonio da Canal, previously joint QM of the Sea along with Jacobo Celsi. Celsi was imprisoned along with Zanne after the 1570 campaign but Canal was reappointed, dividing command of the Cretan fleet. Likewise Sebastiano Venier was the Quartermaster General (QMG) of Fortresses based in Corfu until mid 1570, then QMG-designate of Cyprus, a post he made no serious effort to take up. Finally in December he was appointed to replace the hapless Zanne, news of which only reached him the following February, and Agostino Barbarigo was made QMG of the Sea. Thus the elders Venier and Barbarigo, judged 'extremely inexpert in matters of war and the sea' by their peers, were preferred to the experienced and competent Quirini and Canal even after the war had gone disastrously wrong for Venice.[8] Considerations of patrician hierarchy did not affect command of the soldiers intended for use on land, which reflected how many men an individual officer had recruited. The soldier of fortune Sforza Pallavicini, who had enjoyed Ottoman hospitality a few years previously after defeat and capture while under contract to the Viennese court, accompanied Zanne as overall commander of the 15,000-man land force because he had provided 5,000 of them himself.

To cut through the deferential smokescreen thrown up by the official Venetian historian, Marco Quirini was the only outstanding Venetian naval commander in this war.[9] Apart from the capture of the (abandoned) Ottoman fort at Sopoto, opposite Corfu, by Venier and Celsi on 7 June, and a failed attempt early in July by 5,000 men under Sforza Pallavicini, after the main fleet had arrived at Corfu, to take the small walled settlement of Margariti (*Map 9*), every effective action by any part of the Venetian fleet was the result of initiatives taken by Quirini. Absurdly ordered to join the rest of the fleet at Corfu, he left half of his command to guard Crete and on 30 June, while on his way north, he assaulted the strategically placed Ottoman fort on the headland of Maina, put the garrison to the sword and levelled the works. This in turn sparked the first of several doomed revolts among the Greeks of Morea, led by their priests, which were to complicate Ottoman calculations in the coming year. In late July Quirini led a brutal raid on Andros and press-ganged 500 rowers, and against the outrage this provoked among the Greeks on Crete must be set the fact that it caused Kapudan Ali to send Piali with 100 galleys from Salines to Rhodes in mid August, and thereby delayed the fall of Nicosia. Quirini probably calculated that the Venetians were so hated by the Cretans that it would make no difference, a view supported by the extremely accurate intelligence Cretans volunteered to Piali's scouts, enabling him to return to Cyprus for the final assault on Nicosia, confident that the Christian fleet was too weak and disorganized to intervene.

The Venetians had finally assembled in Crete, where they were joined by the Papal and Hapsburg fleets. Although the historiography of the whole war has been severely skewed by the projection back in time of Italian nationalism, the events leading up to this reunion and what happened thereafter have been the most distorted. As in science, in history a beautiful theory is often undone by an ugly fact. Here the theory, summarized by Setton in one of the most lengthily sourced observations in a densely foot-noted work, is that 'just as Philip had forbidden Don García de Toledo to make a direct attack upon the Turks during the siege of Malta . . . so now he gave Gian'Andrea secret instructions to preserve the royal fleet and during . . . 1570 to avoid encounter with the Turkish armada'.[10] There it might have remained had Rafael Vargas-Hidalgo not recently unearthed a cache of previously unexamined letters in the Doria archives, which present unimpeachable evidence that it was not that simple.[11]

The canonical account hinges on the inherently unlikely theory that the 1570 campaign failed because of a conflict between the interests of 'Spain', represented by Gian'Andrea Doria, and that of 'Italy' represented by Marc'Antonio Colonna, Duke of Paliano and Tagliacozzo, allegedly appointed both admiral of the small Papal flotilla and commander of the combined fleet over the objections of Philip II. In fact, both were *Hapsburg* vassals. While the Colonna were a Roman family, and both Paliano and Tagliacozzo were on the borders of the Papal State, Marc'Antonio was also Grand Constable of Naples, where both he and Doria held large estates. Furthermore Colonna was later appointed viceroy of Sicily, not a post Philip would have entrusted to anyone about whose loyalty he had ever entertained the slightest doubt. During the Cyprus war Colonna knew his every word and action would be subject to misrepresentation, so he documented every stage of the unfolding melodrama. His copious notes, plus an exchange of finger-pointing pamphlets with Doria during the winter of 1570–71, were edited and given an anti-Spanish spin by Guglielmotti, whose account has not hitherto been seriously questioned.[12]

Until the blow fell on Cyprus, Philip and Gian'Andrea were naturally more concerned that Ottoman war preparations were intended to complete Uluch Ali's conquest of Tunis by taking the Spanish fort at Goleta, and possibly to support the Alpujarras revolt. The Venetians also found it difficult to believe that their time had come after thirty years of peace, during which Ottoman naval efforts had been devoted to North Africa and the western Mediterranean, and were encouraged in this by Sokolli's deception of their ambassador. On 30 March Doria wrote to Philip suggesting that since it was by that time apparent that the Ottomans intended to invade Cyprus, it would be an opportune moment to recover Tunis. On 24 April Philip ordered Goleta reinforced and instructed Doria to take the Genoese galleys to join the Naples and Sicily squadrons under Santa Cruz and Juan de Cardona at Messina, and to assume command of the combined fleet. Philip seldom showed his hand, but in an address to the Toledo assembly in February he declared that the solution to the Alpujarras revolt was to challenge Ottoman power directly. The selection of Messina as the assembly point is significant, for had he seriously entertained Doria's proposal the obvious choice would have been Palermo, closer to Tunis and to Cagliari, where the Tercio of Sardinia under Sigismondo Gonzaga was awaiting embarkation.

The Pope's appointment of Colonna actually resolved the doubts that any exercise of temporal power by the Papacy were certain to arouse in the son of Charles V. No less than the Venetians, Philip also felt that the creation of a Papal fleet risked diverting ecclesiastical revenues that might otherwise have been included in the 'graces', and when Venice changed tack and provided twelve galleys to be manned and maintained by the Pope, he rightly perceived it to be a stratagem aimed at securing Venetian command of any eventual combined fleet. What the Doria archive reveals is that, far from being a reluctant participant in the Holy League, Philip quietly made it happen. On 25 March, fortuitously the day Kubad presented his master's insulting ultimatum to the Venetian senate, Philip wrote to his ambassador in Genoa:

> Now, with reference to [a previous letter referring to Venetian fears for Cyprus], I draw your attention to the fact that it would be well for the Republic to make a league with me against this enemy and require you to [communicate this] by letter or confidential messenger to the Duke of Urbino [Guidobaldo della Rovere, pro-Spanish ruler of a duchy strategically placed on the border of the Papal State and mainland Venice] so that he may find out if the time is right, given Venetian fear and suspicion of the Turk, to put into effect such an advantageous arrangement.[13]

Advantageous to whom, and in what measure, was of course open to debate, and it was the attempts of the Venetians to extract the maximum collateral advantage from their decision to resist Ottoman aggression, and Philip's refusal to let them off the hook they had devised for themselves, that delayed the formal declaration of the Holy League until May the following year. In sum, the League was not the result of Saint Pius bringing a reluctant Spain to the rescue of Venice, but of Philip using the Pope's good offices to force the Venetians to accept the logical consequences of their relative weakness. Before that, when he received confirmation that Colonna was to command the Papal squadron and the combined fleet, in a letter dated 15 July, Philip sent the following instructions to Doria in Messina (my italics):

> ... some of the early problems have been resolved now that His Holiness has appointed Marc'Antonio Colonna, who is of such confidence and devotion to my service, to be Captain-General of his galleys. ... I have resolved that you shall take the galleys I have ordered you to assemble in Sicily to join with those of His Holiness and the Venetians, taking with you the necessary [soldiers] from Sardinia and the rest that the Viceroys of Naples and Sicily shall make available, and that *you shall obey Marc'Antonio Colonna as General of the galleys of His Holiness and of the League and follow his standard, for as long as you shall be together*; all of which I order to be declared on my behalf, as it has been by [my representative] to the Papal Nuncio and to the ambassadors of Venice [negotiating the terms of the League in Rome].[14]

The letter then instructed Doria to find out if the Viceroy of Milan would release the Spanish troops of the Tercio of Lombardy, traditionally immovable because of the threat from France, or failing that to withdraw veteran troops from the Goleta garrison, which indicated either that Philip discounted the Uluch Ali threat – possibly from a misplaced faith that his offer of a marquessate was being taken seriously – or that he had decided attack was the best form of defence. Whatever the reasoning behind them, these instructions indicate a decisiveness not often associated with the prudent king. The sizeable fly in the ointment was that Colonna had no experience of naval operations, and the king added a final proviso that Doria was to interpret as overriding the obedience urged upon him:

> ... you should obey Marc'Antonio Colonna as stated above and, with the practical experience you possess, you should at all times draw the attention of [Colonna] to what you judge the correct course of action in all things, and you should look carefully where you put our galleys because of the great harm that any misfortune would bring upon Christendom, and advise me of all that you do and the reasons for having done it.

Unusually Philip himself signed the letter, and lest there should be any doubt what the above-cited paragraph meant, the king added a postscript in his own hand:

> While you are gathering your troops, you shall discover the condition and order of the galleys of His Holiness and the Venetians so that . . . you shall know how to proceed, for of course you realize how important the state of their galleys is to that decision.

This letter provides the key to understanding what followed, which was not a case of Doria preventing the relief of Cyprus for lack of willingness to fight, but of his accurate assessment that the Venetian forces were inadequate for the task. The opposite was the case with the superbly equipped and fully manned Hapsburg fleet of forty-nine galleys consisting of Doria's twelve, eight others from Genoa including four belonging to Ambrogio Negrone, second only to Doria among the Genoese creditors (*asientistas*) of the king, ten from Sicily under Cardona and nineteen from Naples under Santa Cruz. They were supposed to be joined by a squadron under the command of the Catalan Francisco de Sant Climent, captain-general of the Knights of Malta galleys, but on 15 July a flotilla of galliots commanded by Uluch Ali ambushed it off Licata and captured three of the four galleys, with eighty knights and as many postulants on board. Sant Climent escaped but on return to Malta was condemned, strangled, and his body put in a sack and dumped in the harbour. This can only have fed Doria's doubts about the wisdom of leaving Uluch Ali undisturbed to his rear, but when Santa Cruz returned from Sardinia on 8 August the fleet was ready to go, and zigzagged in a leisurely manner to Taranto, where more troops were boarded, finally joining Colonna at Otranto on 20 August. The winds were favourable and the journey could have been accomplished in four to five days, but Doria was buying time for his scouts to return with information concerning the parlous state of the Venetian fleet.

It would be tedious to do more than summarize the halting, squabbling progress of the combined fleet after it finally assembled on 31 August at Suda Bay, the great sheltered anchorage between Canea and Retimo on Crete. The tension between Colonna and Doria is easily understood in the light of the former's instructions to uphold the king's commitment to the yet-to-be-formalized League, and the latter's not to risk the king's fleet unless the Venetian contingent was up to scratch. Pallavicini gloomily concurred with the Hapsburg commanders that it was not, but Zanne's orders compelled him to make at least a show of sailing to the relief of Cyprus, and Colonna felt honour-bound to accompany him. The fleet sailed from Suda to Candia, where Zanne had to cannibalize two galleys in order to provide rowers for the rest, then to Sitia in eastern Crete where he cannibalized three more. Doria was so appalled by the indiscipline and poor ship-handling among the Venetians that he insisted on sailing apart from them during the crossing of 17–21 September from Sitia to Castellorizo (today Megisti, southernmost of the Greek Dodecannese islands), and when bad weather drove the rest into the Kas roadstead he rode the storm out at sea rather than risk sharing an anchorage with them.

Part of the fleet sailed on towards Finike Bay, but off Kekova scouts arrived with the news that Nicosia had fallen on 9 September. When they left Sitia the Papal and Hapsburg galleys had at least 100 soldiers each, but the Venetian contingent (122 galleys, 11 galleasses, 4 large and 10 smaller ships) carried only 12,000 soldiers, of whom a third were Corfiot and Cretan levies. Counting the rowers who might double as soldiers this translated into enough men to fight a sea battle, but not for any important amphibious operation. Nonetheless the Christian fleet now outnumbered the Ottoman, under the operational command of Piali at Salines or anchored off the Gardens of Famagusta. It is not clear where Kapudan Ali was at this time, but he may have already returned to Istanbul. On 23 September, the day a battery of basilisks emplaced on the Famagusta reef began to bombard the Arsenal tower and the Citadel spur, scouts brought Piali the unwelcome news that the enemy fleet he had believed incapable of advancing beyond Crete had reached Castellorizo. He scrambled to re-embark the men sent ashore for the last assault on Nicosia, and this imposed a delay on land operations that probably reprieved Famagusta for another ten months. Baglione, expecting Nicosia to hold out for much longer, had barely started his programme of improvements, and a massed assault by the army that had so recently stormed a far more formidable place might well have succeeded.

This was the only achievement the Christian fleet could claim. It was near the end of the safe campaigning season, and nobody disputed Doria's

argument that with Nicosia gone there was no reason to remain dangerously exposed off a hostile shore in an area notorious for sudden, violent
winds generated by the looming Taurus Mountains. The expedition
was cancelled and the fleet sailed to Scarpanto, reassembling there on 27
September, and in the words of Pallavicini, whose detailed report is another
source that must be read bearing in mind that it was a back-covering
exercise, 'the lord Gian'Andrea let it be known that he wished to return [to
Sicily], which gave rise to many strong words, especially between the most
excellent Colonna and himself'. Once again Doria pointedly put space
between his fleet and the rest, whose seamanship he regarded with poorly
disguised disdain. Rivalry also produced a uniquely instructive incident –
Santa Cruz proudly reported to Philip that three of the best Venetian
galleys challenged his to a race under oars, and that although the levantinas
were faster away from a standing start, the bigger ponentina soon over-
hauled them.[15]

Events amply confirmed Doria's judgement, for although he had his
fleet back at Candia on 30 September, the others were scattered by a storm
with the loss of three Venetian and two Papal galleys. Zanne and Colonna
reached Mirabella Bay on the 28th, and after a partial reassembly sailed to
Candia, where the leaders arrived on 5 October. They were unable to
remain, however, for a brawl between the townspeople and the soldiers
escalated into a bloody uprising and the fleet was compelled to move off-
shore, where a sudden squall wrecked one Papal and two Venetian galleys
whose captains had abandoned them. Doria did not linger and took his
intact fleet back to Sicily via Corfu, but when the rest sailed on to Suda
they were caught by another storm in which one more Papal and eleven
Venetian galleys were lost. At Suda they found three Maltese galleys under
the command of Pietro Giustiniano, prior of Messina, who had lost two
others en route to an ambush by eighteen galliots commanded by Uluch
Ali. On 4 November five Ottoman galliots caught Angelo Surian and
Vincenzo Maria Priuli, two of the best Venetian captains, en route from
Suda to Canea, and Priuli's galley was lost. Leaving Quirini at Crete with
fifty-three galleys (of which he laid up only twenty-three, keeping thirty
active), between 10 and 17 November the Venetian–Papal–Maltese fleet
sailed to Corfu where Giustiniano left to return to Malta, and much of the
remaining Venetian fleet was laid up for the winter. Zanne requested

permission to resign on the ground of ill-health, but instead he was dismissed and arrested upon return to Venice, where he was kept imprisoned without trial until his death in October 1572.[16]

Colonna's return to Rome was dogged by misfortune to an almost comical degree. First his reduced squadron was held up in northern Corfu for a month by adverse winds, then it was scattered and further diminished by a storm that drove Colonna's flagship, the Fausto quinquereme that had been previously been laid up for forty years, into Cattaro, where it was destroyed by lightning. Colonna, now reduced to travelling on a Venetian galley, was again shipwrecked on the coast of Ragusa, and after he finally reached Ancona he paused to give fervent thanks to the Madonna of Loreto and at the shrine of Saint Francis of Assisi before submitting his report of the debacle to the Pope in early February. Showing saintly forbearance, Pius V gave him 2,000 escudos to cover his personal losses and called upon Cosimo dei Medici, whom he had elevated to the rank of Grand Duke of Tuscany the year before in the teeth of Hapsburg disapproval, to provide the Papal fleet in 1571. For the further prosecution of the war he imposed six tithes on all Italian ecclesiastical revenues, appointing Venetian Cardinal Alvise Corner (who paid 68,000 escudos for the privilege) to collect it.

The Ottomans were not immune from disasters, and one of them sent out shock waves that were to have a significant impact on the events of 1571. The pick of the loot from Nicosia and the choicest Venetian youths spared for slavery were put aboard a large galleon belonging to Sokolli at Salines. After the fleet moved to the Famagusta Gardens anchorage, on 3 October a huge explosion, clearly heard and celebrated in the besieged city, destroyed this ship along with a nearby galliot and horse transport. The mythology has it that the explosion was engineered by a noble Venetian maiden who chose death before dishonour, but the only survivors were the scorched captain of the galliot and one or two of his crew, who were not in a position to corroborate this. On 6 October Piali left seven galleys with instructions to build a dock in the inlet under the guns of the battery covering the entrance to Famagusta harbour, and sailed with the rest to Rhodes where he unloaded his own loot. Leaving a guard force of twenty-five to thirty galleys at Rhodes and Chios, he returned to Istanbul with the remaining 130. Although the underlying offence was once again his unchecked avarice, particularly galling to Sokolli after the loss of his own share of the Cyprus loot, he was rebuked for not pursuing the Christian fleet back to Crete and permitted to resign, his life probably once again saved by the intercession of his wife.

Ottoman operations during 1570 correspond precisely to the tidal bore analogy made in Chapter One, and were to do so again in 1571, with the difference that the fleet sailed in two waves commanded by Kapudan Ali and Second Vizier Pertev, both land generals. Ali was now obliged to assume active command of a fleet accustomed to the direction of Piali, who had been a disciple of Barbarossa and was by far the most experienced naval commander in the Mediterranean. The contemporary Ottoman chronicler Hadji Khalfa stressed the enormous psychological importance of the mantle of Barbarossa, before whose mausoleum overlooking the Dardanelles all Ottoman vessels dipped their sails in salute for as long as the empire lasted.[17] Although there is no evidence that Ali or Pertev committed any egregious errors in their handling of the fleet, at the subconscious level where morale dwells the change must have had a negative impact on the captains and crews.

CHAPTER EIGHT

ACT I

THE OTTOMAN
OFFENSIVE OF 1571

26 Jan.	Quirini relief force from Crete arrives at Famagusta.
30 Jan.	Agostino Barbarigo appointed QMG of the Sea.
5 Feb.	Venetian QM in Dalmatia sent poison for wells.
16 Feb.	Quirini leaves Famagusta, Istanbul galleys sent to Rhodes.
21 March	Ali Pasha departs Istanbul, accumulates forces from Anatolia and the Aegean, arrives Cyprus early April.
Mid April	Quirini observes Uluch Ali's assault on the Strophades, retreats to Zante. Uluch Ali sails on to Modon.
25 April	Venier assaults Durazzo, reinforces Parga.
29 April	Army under Ahmed Pasha departs Edirne for Albania.
4 May	Pertev Pasha departs Dardanelles.
Mid May	Pertev at Kizil Hisar, joined by Uluch Ali and contingents from Morea. Canal joins Quirini in Crete.
19 May	Ottomans complete close investment of Famagusta.
25 May	Perpetual Holy League proclaimed in Rome.
Early June	Ali leaves 20 galleys at Famagusta, returns to Rhodes with the rest. Medici galleys for the Papal fleet arrive at Civitavecchia.
Mid June	Combined Ottoman fleet to Suda Bay, raids on Retimo and Sitia.

Late June	Ottomans raid Cerigo.
1 July	Ottomans unload loot at Modon and Navarino.
6 July	Ottomans raid Zante.
13 July	Venier and Barbarigo depart Corfu for Messina. Quirini and Canal ordered to follow with Cretan fleet.
15 July	Ottomans assault Butrinto, recover Sopoto.
17 July	Ottomans recover Durazzo.
18–23 July	Ottoman fleet takes Dulcigno, Antivari and Budua.
24 July	Part of Ahmed's army and the fleet besiege Cattaro.
25 July	Uluch Ali and Kara Khodja raid north.
26 July	Part of the army takes Alessio.
14 Aug.	Siege of Cattaro lifted. Ahmed marches to Ohrid.
10 Aug.	Ottoman fleet at Valona.
25 Aug.	Ottomans assault Corfu.
10 Sept.	Ottomans assault Parga.
14 Sept.	Ottomans depart Corfu.
20 Sept.	Ottomans arrive Lepanto.
24 Sept.	Uluch Ali escorts transports with sick, wounded and loot to Modon.

All Ottoman chroniclers agreed that the main reason for their defeat at Lepanto was that their fleet had been out for too long.[1] This gives Marco Quirini a strong claim to being the architect of the Christian victory, for it was his initiative in late January that caused the Porte to bring forward its plans for 1571. On 16 January he left Candia with twelve galleys and, to the eternal confusion of historians, four ships commanded by one Marc'Antonio Quirini, carrying supplies and about 1,200 Italian soldiers. Bearing in mind that this was the worst possible month to sail in the loom of the Taurus Mountains, the timing argues that Quirini intentionally exploited the Muslim holy month, for he arrived off Famagusta on 26 January, the first day of the Muslim sacred month of Ramadan. The galleys hugged the coast while the ships approached from the open sea to lure out the seven Ottoman sentry galleys, and when Quirini sprang his ambush three of them ran ashore, where he destroyed them with gunfire, while the others fled to bear an exaggerated report to the mainland. Quirini then destroyed the Ottoman battery and the dock that controlled the entrance, and towed the ships into Famagusta harbour. On the 27th he captured an Ottoman galleon carrying reinforcements, on the 29th a pilgrim ship, and later a French ship leased by the Porte as it departed the Gardens anchorage, which he learned to his great chagrin had slipped past him earlier when carrying the payroll for Lala Mustafa's army.

Quirini departed during the night of 16 February with his prizes and sailed directly back to Crete, arriving on the 21st, a remarkable display of seamanship and of the good fortune that favours the bold. He took the captured Ottoman soldiers with him as much-needed slaves for the galleys laid up in Crete, but left the Muslim pilgrims in the hands of Governor Bragadino, presumably for use as hostages to decent behaviour by the besiegers. To rub salt in the wound, during the night of Quirini's departure Baglione ordered his men down from the walls to give the impression the place had been evacuated. Anxious to be first among the spoils, the besiegers emerged from their trenches and rushed towards the city, mounted officers to the fore, at which the defenders sprang to their guns and opened fire, while Rondacchi led a mounted sortie from the Diamante sally-port that got among the batteries at Precipolla and slaughtered the gun crews.

The shock waves from this daring relief stirred the Porte into drastic action. The Bey of Chios, commander of the guard galleys at Rhodes, was held to be primarily responsible and beheaded, the Bey of Rhodes stripped of his seniority, and the Bey of Alexandria, known to the Christians (who had a high opinion of him) as Mehmet Scirocco, was appointed the new commander of the flank guard. Galleys from all Aegean ports were ordered to assemble at Rhodes and twenty more were immediately dispatched from Istanbul. Alexandria was part of the Kapudan's unique beylerbeyik, thus Scirocco was acting as Ali's deputy until he arrived in late March, having left Istanbul with thirty more galleys and assorted ships on the 21st. Thus with the exception of a second wave, which sailed under the command of second vizier Pertev Pasha from Istanbul directly to Negroponte on 4 May, the Ottoman fleet was mobilized from the end of Ramadan on

26 February, two months earlier than scheduled. This may indeed have made itself felt seven months later, but the immediate result was to flood Cyprus with men drawn by the prospect of another Nicosia, including tens of thousands of labourers from Dukaldir, giving Lala Mustafa the means to complete the investment of Famagusta and to begin the excavation of assault trenches (saps), deep enough for mounted men to use, that began to zigzag ominously towards the southern and weakest side of the city (*Map 7*).

Given the impossibility of recovering Cyprus, the defenders must have known that Famagusta had become at best a bargaining chip in negotiations between Venice and the Porte, which made its resolute defence over the next five months all the more remarkable, with Baglione and Bragadino keeping their people fighting despite an open offer of an honourable capitulation and free transport to a place of their choosing. When the 'useless mouths' (Cypriot non-combatants) were put outside the walls in mid April, Lala Mustafa could have left them to starve in no-man's-land, but instead had them escorted safely to their villages, and made sure those left behind saw how well they were treated. Traditionally a fortress was called upon to capitulate on terms when demonstrably cut off from outside aid, when the saps reached the ditch, and when a 'practicable breach' had been blasted in the walls. A garrison that resisted beyond the latter point was understood to have inflicted unnecessary casualties on the besiegers and could accordingly expect no mercy. It is important to appreciate these well-understood rules, for when the Famagusta commanders finally hoisted the white flag they were walking on the thin ice of forbearance by a general who had lost tens of thousands of men thanks to their obstinacy.

The saps reached the foot of the glacis on 1 May, and by 18 May the Ottomans had established themselves along the rim of the ditch. Considering the siege all but over, on 15 May Ali left a guard force of twenty galleys and took the rest back to Rhodes, from where they sailed on to join Pertev and Uluch Ali at the fortress of Kizil Hisar, in southern Negroponte. On 21 May a huge mine brought down the outer Arsenal tower, but the cavalier behind the tower still stood, and enabled the defenders to beat off a five-hour assault with heavy loss. By the end of June the besiegers had built an artillery redoubt overlooking the ruins of the Arsenal tower and as tall as the cavalier, but Baglione sealed off what had always been an exposed salient, and built further cavaliers behind the small Santa Barbara, Andruzzi and Santa Napa towers. The next mine went off under the ravelin in front of the Lemesos gate on 29 May, despite which the defenders hung on through another prolonged assault and even counter-attacked at the end. After further bombardment from three sides the wrecked ravelin fell on 9 July after a counter-mine was set off prematurely, killing more than 100 defenders as well as untold numbers of the attackers. This culminated in a day-long general assault across the whole of the southern front, which began when another mine demolished the wall between the Santa Barbara and Arsenal towers. Further assaults followed on the 14th, on the 15th when the attackers briefly broke in next to the Santa Napa tower, and on the 19th when they penetrated near the Andruzzi tower.[2]

On 20 July, with the Italian defenders whittled down to fewer than 500, all wounded, most of the dependable Cypriot soldiers also killed or wounded and supplies running short, the leading citizens of Famagusta petitioned Bragadino to seek terms, and on the 23rd Lala Mustafa, learning of this, summoned Baglione to surrender, saying there would be no mercy if he continued to resist. Bragadino had wisely left the direction of the defence to the professional Baglione, but now he refused to accept the inevitable and it took a further two general assaults to change his mind. When at last the white flag was raised on 1 August, Famagusta had withstood seventy-four days of bombardment by about 100 heavy guns, including four huge basilisks and powerful Venetian cannon brought from Nicosia, an impressive demonstration of the punishment even a second-rate fortress could absorb. Even now all might have been well, for Lala Mustafa conceded generous terms, but Bragadino ordered the remaining stocks of food and ammunition to be burnt, as well as large stocks of valuable cotton that had been used to protect the Lemesos tower cavalier. This was provocative, but paled beside the killing of the Muslim pilgrims, whose safe release was specified in the terms of capitulation.

Some of them escaped to inform Lala Mustafa, and there is little doubt that what followed was retaliation. On 5 August, after the rest of the garrison had boarded the Ottoman ships that were to transport them to Candia, Bragadino and his officers went to the Ottoman encampment to surrender the keys to the city. Bragadino was wearing a purple robe and walked under the scarlet parasol that denoted his rank, and crowned his folly by speaking haughtily to his conqueror. Lala Mustafa toyed with him, questioning him about the cotton and the prisoners, then showed rising anger as he demanded hostages against the safe return of the vessels he was sending to Crete. Feigned or real, he exploded in deadly rage when Bragadino refused, and with the exception of the Cypriot officers the rest were beheaded, although Hector and Nestor Martinengo were saved by Ottoman officials for ransom, and to leave accounts of the incident. Bragadino's ears and nose were cut off and after several days of humiliation he was skinned alive, his hide stuffed with straw and hung from the mast of a galley that paraded it along the coast of Asia Minor back to Istanbul. It was eventually bought and returned to Venice, where it occupies a sarcophagus in the church of Saints Giovanni e Paolo, set into a fresco depicting his final moments. An intriguing footnote to this ghastly episode is that among the Cypriot officers spared was one Captain Dardano, who had carried out the order to kill the pilgrims, and one has to wonder if, as personal insurance, he did not facilitate the escape of those who informed Lala Mustafa of Bragadino's bad faith.

News of the fall of Famagusta did not reach the western powers until two months later, testimony to how tightly the Ottomans now controlled the approaches to Cyprus. The siege became just an expensive mopping-up operation, and the focus of Ottoman attention moved westward for the rest of 1571. While the next stage of his strategy was in preparation, Sokolli continued to encourage the Venetians to believe he was their true friend, and that a major war was being conducted against the will of the most powerful grand vizier and kingmaker in Ottoman history. Despite rationing in Venice and near-famine in the islands, the senate clung to this slender thread of hope, and its representatives at the Holy League negotiations in Rome bought time for what they fondly believed were their secret peace negotiations by making ludicrous demands, among them one for 8,000 rowers to be provided by Spain.

The Venetian provincial authorities were not so passive, and the fusta fleet at Zara captured and burned Skradin in April, while in May the governor of Cattaro made a sortie with 200 men against an Ottoman fort on the headland commanding the approaches to Cattaro and nearby Perast, but was ambushed, lost half his men and was captured (*Map 4*). From Corfu Venier took advantage of the help offered by Albanians in revolt against Ottoman rule and captured isolated Durazzo. The Beys of Valona and Delvina had by this time sent urgent dispatches to Istanbul admitting they had lost control of their timars, but Venier did not know this and rejected Albanian appeals to assault Valona. Skirmishing took place throughout Dalmatia, particularly at Zara where a loose investment featured the occasional challenges to single combat with which the Ottomans customarily relieved the tedium of low intensity military oper-ations. But there was little locally generated activity because both sides were afflicted by epidemics and looming famine, while at this stage, after thirty years of peaceful coexistence, there was little enthusiasm for war among men who had grown up together, many of whom were blood brothers in hunting and jousting fraternities.[3]

In mid April the indefatigable Quirini was patrolling the Ionian coast of Morea with seven galleys when he encountered seven Algiers galleys and twelve galliots under the personal standard of Uluch Ali. Quirini retreated to Zante while Uluch Ali made a damaging raid on the Strophades before continuing to Modon for maintenance. Alarming though this news was to the Venetians, it greatly simplified the strategic picture for Philip, for if the Beylerbey of Algiers had sailed east with such a large proportion of his fleet, there would be no major Ottoman initiative in the west during 1571. That Philip, despite Doria's urging, chose not to take the opportu-nity to take back Tunis and instead pursued the Holy League option shows how determined he was to strike at the heart rather than the periphery of Ottoman power.

Whatever straws the Venetians were still clutching were snatched away when news reached them that a powerful invasion fleet under Second Vizier Pertev Pasha had left Istanbul heading for Greece, and that a land army under Fourth Vizier Ahmed Pasha (who was to succeed Sokolli as grand vizier in 1579), had set off along the Maritza river towards Sofia, collecting timariot sipahis along the way. Also a large contingent of the kapi-kulu with the heavy artillery and under the command of the Beylerbey of Rumelia had sailed to the mouth of the Vardar, near Salonika, intending to join Ahmed's army at Skopje (*Map 8*). This intelligence also simplified the strategic equation, for if the objective had been Dalmatia the highway would have been the Danube, and Crete was off the menu because even the Ottomans could not sustain three major invasions at the same time.

The senate immediately informed the QM of Dalmatia that he must make do from his own resources for the coming year, ordering him to poison wells and implement a scorched earth policy. Meanwhile the negotiators in Rome were authorized to accept two commitments they had previously resisted. The first was to provide reciprocal assistance in North Africa, a rigid Spanish precondition, the second was Pius V's no less adamant demand that the alliance should be a permanent crusading institution, from which none of the parties could withdraw without the consent of the others.

The Holy League agreement announced on 25 May had been solemnized five days earlier in the presence of Pius V in his capacity as Pope, and signed by representatives of himself as ruler of the Papal State, King Philip of Spain, the republics of Venice and Genoa, Grand Duke Cosimo of Tuscany, Duke Emanuele Filiberto of Savoy, Duke Francesco Maria (Della Rovere) of Urbino, Duke Ottavio (Farnese) of Parma, and the Knights of Malta. Its stated purpose was to wage war in perpetuity against the Ottomans and Muslims of Africa and the Middle East, its primary objective to recover Cyprus *and the Holy Land*, and to this end the parties would provide 200 galleys, 100 ships, 50,000 Italian, German and Spanish infantry, 4,500 light horse and an 'adequate' number of guns, ammunition and other necessities. Every year the fleet was to assemble by April at latest 'in eastern seas' to perform whatever the contracting parties had agreed at the end of the previous year's campaign. The Papal State undertook to provide twelve galleys, 3,000 infantry and 270 light horse and in addition to pay, from its own revenues, one sixth of the total cost of the League. Spain was to pay half the costs, Venice one third, and should the revenues from the Papal State prove insufficient, the shortfall would be covered by Spain and Venice in equal parts.

Food was to be supplied (in practice mainly by Sicily) at a preferential rate, and the Venetians made haste to make full payment, in advance, for long-term grain contracts that persisted beyond their abandonment of the Holy League in 1573. Any territory won in the eastern Mediterranean was to revert to its previous Christian owners, which would have created an interesting situation had the League recovered Cyprus, for the Duke of Savoy had an older and rather better claim than Venice, while Philip styled himself King of Jerusalem. Spain was to keep any conquests in North Africa, but otherwise the spoils of war were to be divided among the League members in proportion to their contribution. The latter stipulation explains why Pius insisted that his (genuine) nephew Michele Bonelli should have command of two galleys in the fleet supplied by Cosimo, and of four companies of Papal infantry, to ensure a return to his own family from the proceeds of the enterprise.

Place was reserved in the League for the Empire, France and Portugal, and the Pope undertook to continue his efforts to persuade the Empire to break its truce, and France its alliance, with the Ottomans. King Sebastian of Portugal, whose own Moroccan Crusade was to lead to the extinction of his line at Alcázarquivir in 1578, at this time was constrained by commitments in the Indian Ocean and the Red Sea, where his captains and the rebellions they encouraged were tying down sizeable Ottoman forces. Both sides in this conflict encouraged uprisings within each other's domains, and if the abandonment of the Moriscos to their fate was one example of a great-power heartlessness comparable to the colonial wars of the twentieth century, so too were the rebellions in Montenegro and Albania falsely promised decisive support by Venice. The Greeks wisely put no faith in Venetian assurances but looked to the coming of the Spanish, and the Patriarch of Morea, whose sedition had already provoked a recall to Edirne that he chose to defy, sent a plea by a trusted messenger that reached Philip in mid 1570:

> . . . not daring to put anything in writing, [the Patriarch says] that the inhabitants of Morea will rise up against the Turk if only they are given arms, and that it would be sufficient for these to be lances and swords, and a few breastplates, and that this could well be done throughout Greece now that the paid soldiers the Turk normally stations there have been drawn away [for the Cyprus invasion] . . . when asked how many weapons, he replied that he believed fifty thousand would suffice.[4]

Philip would have taken this estimate with a pinch of salt, but the prospect of repaying the favour for the Moriscos revolt must have been enticing, and when the Hapsburg fleet reached Genoa in June 1571 Juan wrote to complain that a large supply of swords and breastplates that was supposed to be awaiting him had not arrived from Milan. Since his own troops were already properly equipped, some of these may have been intended for the Greeks. However, as in the matter of the secret dealings with Uluch Ali and any other matter of extreme delicacy, Philip's reply to the Patriarch was either by deniable word of mouth, or else the documentary evidence was destroyed. It was no light matter for His Catholic Majesty to arm a struggle for Greek independence led by the schismatic Orthodox church, while simultaneously engaged in an alliance with the Latin Pope and the Venetians.

Having first put forward the candidacy of Doria, knowing it to be unacceptable to Venice, Philip then proposed his half-brother Juan for overall command, thereby resolving the problem of precedence among his own vassals and lifting the issue above intra-Italian vendettas. Now nominally second in command but still the conduit of indirect communications among the allies, Marc'Antonio Colonna remained between the proverbial rock and a hard place until Juan arrived to take up his command. Upon receipt of a letter from Philip reminding him of his allegiance and obligations as Grand Constable of Naples, he wrote to his close friend, General (since 1565) of the Jesuits and later Saint Francisco de Borja:

> I have heard that His Majesty had intended to write to me in terms more extraordinary. If it should come to that, I shall throw up the business, which will be a great relief to me. At the very time when I had thought my services would have been acknowledged, having scarcely been at Rome, and having given His Majesty no offence and, moreover, having last year saved the honour of his fleet, and this year helped to conclude the League, I find myself called upon to write a justification of my conduct.

Colonna was not only beset by the disloyalty of officers nominally under his command, but also from Roman families with a grudge against his for past wrongs. One with an axe to grind because of family lands given to the Colonna by Ferdinand of Aragon was Onorato Caetani, the commander of the Papal Guard and future lord of Sermonetta, and another rich source of self-serving letters concerning the doings of the League.[5] After Juan's arrival closed the door to further misrepresentation of his actions to the Spanish, Colonna dryly warned Duce Ludovico Mocenigo that 'my ill-wishers, wearying of portraying me so great a Venetian, are now saying that I neglect the service of Your Serenity'.

While the Spanish Hapsburg forces were mobilizing, once again the Venetians had to endure the consequences of believing that clever diplomacy could compensate for military weakness. The fact that the Austrian Hapsburg empire was not bound by the Holy League could only be a source of acute unease to men who had grown up in the shadow of the 1508–10 League of Cambrai formed against Venice by Pope Julius II, during which they had lost their ports in Apulia to the Spanish and, following shattering defeat by the French at Agnadello, had seen the forces of the Empire cross the Alps into their Italian mainland territory. The Venetian fleet was seriously undermanned in 1571 because the bulk of their mainland soldiers were retained to guard against Austrian opportunism, for they knew well there could be no overland threat from the Ottomans. At the same time the behaviour of the Venetian galley councillors (*comiti*, hence the captains were 'over-councillors' or *sopracomiti*) during 1570 had sparked a near-revolt in Crete, enthusiasm for Venetian service was at an all-time low in the Ionian islands, and even the usually dependable Dalmatians had been alienated. At Corfu, Venier took savage action to curb indiscipline among his officers, but Venice was compelled to empty her ever-bulging prisons to make up rower numbers.

Venier had sent Antonio da Canal south to Crete with sixteen galleys, thus dividing the fleet into equal parts of sixty galleys each, Venier also retaining six galleasses under the independently appointed Francesco Duodo. There had been eleven with Zanne's fleet, but five were now deployed elsewhere for harbour defence, the role for which they were best suited. These were the only fully manned units in the Venetian fleet, equipped with large numbers of the finest guns and the best professional soldiers. As such they raised the overall standard so greatly that when Venier departed Corfu for the Holy League rallying point of Messina on 13 July he took them with him, unhappily aware that otherwise the general shabbiness of his fleet would be in stark contrast with those of his allies. The galleasses thus became the depositories of Venetian prestige and pride, which explains their subsequent prominence in artistic representations of the battle. That they were powerful warships is unarguable, but they were a ball and chain for the agile galleys and only an unrepeatable chain of favourable circumstances was to permit these essentially defensive weapons systems to play an active combat role.

Map 8 – 1571 Campaign

Uluch Ali raids north

RAGUSA
MONTE NEGRO
Castelnuovo
Cattaro
Dukagin
July
Budua
Antivari
Dulcigno
Scutari
Alessio
Durazzo
Elbasan
Ohrid
September
Sofia
Kyustendil
Skopje
RUMELIA
Ahmed departs mid April
Edirne
Istanbul

Bari
ALBANIA
Janissaries and artillery
MACEDONIA
Salonika
THRACE

Taranto
Brindisi
Gallipoli
Otranto
Valona
Delvina
Sopoto
Butrinto
Mount Athos
Lemnos
Gallipoli
Ali to Cyprus late March

Venier and Barbarigo 13–23 July
Casoppo
Corfu
Yanya
EPIRUS
Pertev to Kizil Hisar early May
Skiros
Mytilene
ANATOLIA

Crotone
Parga
Preveza
Santa Maura
AETOLIA
Lepanto
Patras
Egriboz
NEGROPONTE
Kizil Hisar
Andros
Chios
Izmir

MESSINA
Cephalonia
Corinth
Athens
Ali returns from Cyprus joins Pertev early June
Samos

Zante
MOREA
Nauplia
Tinos
Naxos

Strophades
Navarino
Mizistra
Modon
Coron
Maina
Monemvasia
Rhodes

Uluch Ali mid April
Combined fleet to Suda Bay mid June

Quirino & Canal 13–31 August
Cerigo

Quirino & Canal 13–31 August

Canea
Retimo
Candia
Sitia
CRETE
CYPRUS

Venetian

- - - - ► Fleet

■ **Candia** Provincial capital

◎ **Cattaro** Outpost attacked

● **Budua** Outpost lost

● **Bari** Allied or neutral

Ottoman

– – – ► Fleet

– – – ► Land army

□ Patras Provincial (sanjak) capital

○ Coron Outpost

● Maina Outpost lost, recovered.

Revolts ① 1570–71 ② 1571–72

Venier never forgave himself for the devastation of the Adriatic settlements that followed his departure, but it was unquestionably correct to respect the principle of concentration, whatever the immediate cost. Once Ali's fleet joined Pertev and Uluch Ali at the fortress of Kizil Hisar in southern Negroponte, the Ottoman fleet numbered in excess of 250 galleys, all larger and better manned than their Venetian equivalents, plus forty to fifty corsair galliots and at least as many smaller oared fighting ships. In mid June, when this host arrived at Suda Bay in Crete, Quirini's and Canal's squadrons could only cower under the fortress guns at Canea and Candia. Enter Richard Knolles, second only to Busbeq in the 'must quote' category:

> The Turks being landed, and ranging up and down the Country, did what harm they possibly could, burning and spoiling all as they went; until that at last they were upon the suddain encountered by *Francesco Giustiniano*, who but a little before their landing, was come into the Island with a thousand souldiers; and now joyning with the Island people, notably charged them, being altogether dispersed and seeking after prey; and having slain many of them, enforced the rest to retire to their Gallies. The next day the Turks landing again in great number, burnt divers Towns and sacked *Sitia* and *Retimo*, where they took a rich prey, and carried away many Prisoners; but loaded with their Booty, dispersed and fearing nothing less than to be at that time set upon, they were assailed by *Lucca Michele* a valiant Captain, two thousand of them slain, and with the loss of their Booty and Prisoners, glad to retire unto their Gallies. Thus repulsed from *Crete*, they took their Course to *Cerigo*, *Zante* and *Cephalonia* . . . where beside other harms by them done, they carried away with them six thousand poor Christians into most miserable Captivity.[6]

Selim had promised 'most cruel war against you everywhere' if the Venetians refused to give up Cyprus peacefully, and this was a massive punitive *chevauchée*. Also, by shifting the centre of gravity to the west Sokolli prevented any further relief of Famagusta more certainly than Ali could have done by remaining on guard at Rhodes. But as well as demonstrating an enemy's inability to protect his subjects, a *chevauchée* also sought to draw him out of his defensive positions to do battle on unfavourable terms.

It was a mistake to use such a massive force simply to hit and run, leaving the Cretan galley squadrons intact, as it was to ravage the countryside with small raiding parties that were then defeated in detail, resolving the Greek Cretans' conflict of loyalties in favour of Venice. When Quirini and Canal sailed to Messina in August, their galleys were still undermanned by western Mediterranean standards, but the late-arriving volunteers they carried were animated by a ferocious desire for revenge.

But this is to exercise hindsight unfairly, for when Venier and Barbarigo fled from Corfu on 13 July, barely ahead of Uluch Ali and the Ottoman vanguard, they suffered crippling losses. In his report at the close of the 1571 season Venier admitted:

> I had [started with sixty] galleys, six galleasses and three ships
> [but] in the channel of Corfu two galleys and two ships laden with
> rations, munitions and soldiers had been captured by the enemy fleet,
> and one ship had also been taken at Cephalonia, and I had sent into
> the Gulf of Venice three galleys and I had lost seven by the accidents
> of the sea and fire, so that I remained with [the six galleasses and]
> forty-eight galleys not very well provided with soldiers on account of
> sickness, the capture of the ships, and the blockade of the vessels in
> the Gulf by the enemy fleet.

The already meagre Venetian contribution to the land force was thus eliminated, and with it the possibility that the troops on the transports might have been used to bring the galleys up to strength. Ali and Pertev kept Sokolli accurately informed about the state of the Venetian fleet, and after Quirini and Canal reluctantly obeyed Venier's order to join him in Messina, the Ottoman fleet had no enemies to the rear when it sailed on to rendezvous with Ahmed's overland advance, tasked to suppress widespread revolts in Epirus and Albania, where the Beys of Yanya, Delvina, Elbasan, Ohrid and Dukagin had lost control of the countryside. It was no coincidence that the low-level, permanent guerrilla war between Christian mountain bandits (*klepthes*) and lowland Muslim convert militias (*armatoles*) flared into major challenges to Ottoman authority in close proximity to Venetian outposts, and the coastal *chevauchée* by Ali and Pertev was intended to send a message to the Albanian and Epirot rebels to put not their faith in Venice. Venetian Parga and Butrinto were raided, Sopoto and Durazzo recovered, then the Venetian ports on the Albanian coast succumbed one after the other. Knolles described the rebels' situation as the pincers closed on them:

> . . . now deceived of their expectation, [they] bewailed their misery, and trusting to the promises of the Venetians, they had cast themselves and all theirs into most manifest danger. They of *Dulcigno* seeing themselves hardly beset both by Sea and Land, sent to *Pertev* Pasha, and covenanting with him, that they might in safety depart, delivered unto him the Town; and so *Sara Martinengo* Governor of the Town, which the Garrison Souldiers, were in four ships conveied in safety to *Ragusa*; as for the Citizens, promise was kept with them after the Turkish manner. In the same hurley the Turks took also the towns of *Antivari* and *Budua, Antivari* [being] both by situation and fortification strong, and furnished with good garrison: Nevertheless *Alessandro Donato* Governor thereof, a Man of no experience in Martial Affairs, overcome with the present fear, and despairing to be able to hold the Town, cowardly yielded the same unto the Enemy. Which his beastly Cowardice the Senate suffered not unpunished, but confiscating his goods, and removing him from the Senate, cast him into exile.

Ahmed arrived at Dukagin in July and divided his army, sending one part directly to Scutari and the other towards Cattaro, suppressing the foci of revolt around both places before taking Alessio and advancing south to deal with the Elbasan–Ohrid rebellion. With the end of the campaigning season approaching he could not linger at Cattaro, where his men joined forces with Pertev's for a three-week siege from 24 July to 14 August. When Ahmed's men disengaged to move on along the coast, the defenders made a sortie in which they killed 1,500.[7]

Ottoman plans for 1572 were set out in a detailed order dated 10 October, of course in ignorance of the battle fought three days earlier, sent to Ahmed in Ohrid acknowledging receipt of his dispatch of mid September in which he had reported drenching rains and severe morale problems. The land commander was assured that the sipahis from Valona, Delvina and Yanya who had been engaged in the conquest of Cyprus (and whose absence helps to explain the rebellions) were returning to take part in the 1572 campaign, and that:

I have ordered the sandjakbey of Kyustendil to march on Nova [Castelnuovo, at the mouth of Cattaro Bay]. When that order reaches you be vigilant to prevent the Muslim troops from dispersing. You must announce that the timars of those who are absent from their posts will be given to others such that they will be ready if – Allah forbid! – the enemy evildoers arrive to do harm. If there are places where the miserable infidels are vulnerable to attack, inform [the Beylerbey of Rumelia] so that he may winter nearby and, with the help of Allah, pursue [them] without delay next year.

We shall leave Sokolli's damp and dispirited land pincer here. Whatever else Lepanto may not have achieved, it aborted the Ottoman overland offensive of 1572 and saved Cattaro, and very probably the autonomy of Ragusa as well, which instead continued to profit so greatly from her rival's commercial paralysis that the Venetians tried to persuade their allies to assault it in 1572, in defiance of a specific prohibition inserted by Pius V in the Holy League covenant. It must have galled the Venetians particularly when the contract to supply twenty-five ships for the Spanish land force was won by the Ragusans, who sustained their pretence of neutrality by announcing that the transports had been commandeered. Just how close to the wind the Ragusans were sailing emerges from the letter from Sokolli received on 1 August by Kara Khodja, Agha of the Janissaries and Bey of Valona, in reply to his report that they had given refuge to a Venetian galley he had chased into Ragusa harbour:

> It is certain that those who have shown friendship and submission
> as well as those who have acted in a hostile or treacherous manner
> towards our Home of Happiness shall respectively, with the aid
> of Allah the all-powerful, be rewarded or suffer the consequences
> of their actions.

Kara Khodja and Uluch Ali together raided north from Cattaro, sending a wave of panic along the coasts of Dalmatia and Istria to Venice itself where, as in 1567, the sandbanks of the lagoon were hurriedly fortified and garrisoned. Further south, let us luxuriate one more time in Knolles's prose style:

Uluch Ali and *Kara Khodja*, both Men of great account and name
among the Turks, got leave for ten days of the Admiral, with sixty
Gallies to spoil the Islands near thereabouts subject to the Venetians.
Who coming to the island of *Korcula* . . . landed their Men, with
purpose to assault the Town . . . Which *Antonio Contarino* the
Governor thereof perceiving, in the dead time of night fled for fear . . .
into the Rocks and places of more safety . . . so that in the Town were
not left above twenty men, and about eighty Women, who with
Weapons in their hands, after the rest were fled, came to the Walls, as
wishing rather there to die, than to fall into the hands of the barbarous
Enemy. But at such time as the Turks began to approach the Town,
and the Women with Stones, Fire, and such Weapons as they had were
beating them off, and with greater courage defending the place than
was to have been in their Sex expected, by the goodness of God a great
Tempest arose suddainly out of the North, which so outragiously
tossed the Gallies that *Uluch Ali* and *Kara Khodja* were glad to give
over the assault, and to get them thence into a place of more safety.
Sailing along the Coast, they by the way spoiled *Hvar*, *Brac* and *Lissa* . . .
out of which they carried away with them fifteen hundred poor
Christians into captivity.

Once again we can see that this was to prove counterproductive when
the day of battle came, for the seven galleys from Dalmatia, four from
Corfu, two each from Zante and Cephalonia, and one from Istria distinguished themselves by their aggressiveness at Lepanto, losing five but
inflicting even greater damage in return. Among the less known of the
many Lepanto memorials are the pillar honouring Saint Justina in Kopar
(Istria), Adriatic port of today's Slovenia, erected by the captain of the local
galley *Il Leone*, a trophy in memory of Lujo Cipiko and his crew, lost in the
battle, at the Cipiko Palace in Trogir, and the figurehead of the Ottoman
galley captured by the local galley *San Jerolim* in the Hvar arsenal. In
addition the honour guard of the banner of Saint Mark on board Venier's
flagship was provided by the eldest sons of the fifteen leading families of
Perast, of whom seven were killed.[8]

Christian accounts attribute the retreat of the Ottoman fleet from the
Adriatic to fear that the Holy League fleet would move to Corfu and close

the Strait of Otranto, while contradictorily alleging that Kara Khodja, sent to scout the fleet at Messina, grossly underestimated the force there assembled. To the contrary, his all-black galley aroused no suspicion because Colonna had ordered his squadron dressed in mourning for the recent death of his beloved daughter, and Kara Khodja daringly rowed among the fleet as though passing in review. Ali, Pertev and Uluch Ali separately reported to Istanbul that he had counted 203 galleys, 6 galleasses, 70 fragatas and 28 ships, only five galleys fewer and five ships more than the roll-call reported to Philip at about the same time.[9] The reply from Selim/Sokolli was unequivocal:

> When news about the infidels' intention to attack became known by everybody here, the Ulema and all the Muslim community found it most proper and necessary to find and immediately attack the infidel fleet in order to save the honour of our religion and state, and to protect the Land of the Caliphate, and when the Muslims submitted their petition to the feet of My throne I found it good and incontestable. I remain unshakable in my determination.

As to the withdrawal of the Ottoman fleet from the Adriatic, this seems to have taken place during the time between dispatch and receipt of specific orders from Istanbul to winter in Cattaro Bay, where it was supposed to sustain itself by raids along the Dalmatian coast. The area was subject to vicious winter storms, as Colonna had discovered the year before, and with the end of the campaigning season approaching Ali and Pertev had good reasons other than the approach of the Holy League fleet to withdraw to the shelter of the Gulf of Patras. The fleet sailed to Valona for maintenance then to Corfu, arriving on 25 August and remaining until 14 September. Either discipline was fraying by this time, or else the Ottomans nurtured a special hatred for an island that had long been a thorn in their side, for the landing parties committed the sort of wanton atrocities and desecrations usually associated with irregulars. At the end, while withdrawing after setting fire to the town of Corfu, they were caught dispersed when about 1,000 cavalry sortied from the fortress, killing many and driving the rest back to their boats in disorder, although not before they had added 5,000 Corfiots to their bag. Some of the galley commanders also appear to have been heady with contempt for the Venetians and approached the fortress as though issuing a challenge, and three were sunk when the gage was gladly picked up by the expert gunners of the royal culverins on the walls.

The fleet that arrived at Lepanto on 20 September was depleted by men lost in action and many of the sipahis, never happy to serve on board galleys, who had transferred to Ahmed's army during the amphibious operations around Cattaro. The transports, heavily burdened with loot and about 8,000 valuable captives, were sent to Navarino escorted by sixty warships under Uluch Ali. Intelligence about this, but not of the escort's prompt return, reached the Holy League fleet at Guiscardo on 5 October, along with news of the fall of Famagusta and the cruel massacre of the Venetian garrison, together tipping the scales in favour of seeking battle. The Ottoman fleet had unloaded the spoils and captives from Crete at Modon on its way north, and after the battle a flood of dispatches to the local commanders and the Bey of Morea – along the lines of 'We know exactly the value of what was entrusted to you, so do not attempt to deceive Us' – reveal intense concern that the proceeds from the *chevauchée* should not be embezzled.

The fleet commanders may have decided they could not remain in Cattaro Bay not only because of the weather, but also because foraging in an area infamous for the ferocity of its Montenegrin and Albanian bandits / freedom fighters was likely to produce poor returns in exchange for constant attrition. But Sokolli, in a break with the Ottoman tradition of delegation to the men on the spot, sought to micro-manage the campaign, as we can see in his reply to a dispatch from Ali dated 9 September, in which he had reported that the Holy League fleet had reached Otranto and his intention to winter at Lepanto (my italics):

> All that you have reported was known to us. Moreover Mustafa, one
> of my imperial couriers, brought the news which he had heard from
> [the] Bey of Delvina, that the fleet of the Infidels had already reached
> Corfu. Pertev Pasha, my commander-in-chief, also reported to me the
> things that you reported. *Now I order that after getting reliable news about*
> *the enemy, you attack the fleet of the infidels fully trusting in Allah and his*
> *Prophet.* As soon as my order arrives you are to go to Pertev Pasha and
> hold a council together with the Beylerbey of Algeria, other beys,

commanders and sea captains acting all in perfect agreement and unity in accordance with what is found most suitable. If you think my imperial fleet should winter by God's will in those waters, as I had considered in my previous order, you may make up your mind about staying in the bay of Cattaro or in another port after consulting with Pertev Pasha, and submit to me the measures you will take *in order to be able to act in accordance with whatever my imperial command may be*.

On receipt of this Ali issued an order on 25 September that the fleet would winter in Cattaro, fully aware that the Holy League fleet stood in his way. He also summoned a council of war, and the interrogation of captives after the battle gives some hints of what was discussed, although the accounts are coloured by imaginative embellishments, whether by the captives or those recording their testimony it is impossible to say. Kara Khodja was away on another scouting expedition, but otherwise all the senior officers were present. Ali, Pertev, Scirocco of Alexandria and Uluch Ali of Algiers we have already met. The others were: Mahmud Reis, Grand Agha of the Janissaries; Kara Bive Pasha, Beylerbey of Syria; Djafer Agha Pasha, Bey of Tripoli; Dardagan Pasha, Bey of the Istanbul Arsenal; Mustafa Esdri Pasha, Fleet Treasurer; Hassan Pasha, previously Beylerbey of Algiers and son of the late Khair ed-Din 'Barbarossa'; Mehmet, Bey of Negroponte and son of the late Salih Reis, who had been Beylerbey of Algiers before Hassan; Hassan 'the Venetian', Bey of Rhodes; Previs Agha and Asiz Agha, like Kara Khodja captains of the Janissaries as well as Beys of Nauplia and Gallipoli respectively; Mahmud Haider, Bey of Mytilene; Djafer Chelebi, Bey of Gabès in Tunisia; and Kaya, Bey of Izmir, whom I have been unable to place in the order of battle at *Appendix C*.

Scirocco, the eldest, spoke first in representation of all who had campaigned with Ali since March, to complain of the dilapidation and exhaustion of the Egyptian, Syrian, Anatolian and Aegean contingents. This gave rise to an exchange between Hassan and Mehmet, the sons of Barbarossa and Salih Reis, after Mehmet supported Scirocco's cautious assessment. Hassan interjected that Salih, bravest of the brave, would have been ashamed to see his son shrink from battle, and Mehmet replied to the effect that it was a shame Hassan had not inherited his father's intelligence. The difference in battleworthiness between the fleets that had sailed under Ali and Pertev was sufficiently notorious for an Ottoman deserter to have informed the Holy League commanders about it on 23 August.[10] But the issue cannot have revolved around whether or not to offer battle, for Sokolli's order left no room for discussion. It is more likely that differences arose over Uluch Ali's recommendation of an open sea deployment, seeking to exploit their numbers to achieve a double envelopment of the Holy League fleet in the traditional scheme perfected by the Byzantine navy, with the fleet divided into four equal parts, three forward in a crescent formation of a head and two horns, and one back in reserve.

Ali and Pertev may have had experience of hooks being cut off at the elbow by Christian heavy cavalry, for they decided instead to concentrate their weakest galleys under Scirocco on the right, close to the shore, and to deploy their numerical advantage and the swift corsair galliots on the left, mainly in the seaward wing under Uluch Ali, to achieve a turning manoeuvre that would trap the entire Christian fleet against a hostile shore. In this scheme the Battle would fix the enemy line in place with a massive attack, freeing the Left Wing to swing around behind it. Both options envisaged a battle of annihilation, and while there is no reason to believe that Uluch Ali's plan would have produced a different result, it seems likely that many more Ottoman galleys would have survived had it been adopted.

Simultaneously, urgent requests for troops were sent out and every able-bodied male along the Gulf of Patras was rounded up and pressed into service. After the battle the tutor of Ali's sons, captured along with them, told Don Juan's secretary:

> That not only was everyone [from the areas around Lepanto] taken, but to such an extreme that only women were left to shut the doors of their houses. The Beylerbey of Greece, first cousin of the Grand Turk, boarded [the galleys] with as many as one thousand five hundred of the best soldiers in the province.

There was no Beylerbey of Greece, so this must have been the Bey of Morea. From orders issued to rush reinforcements from further north after news of the battle reached Istanbul, we know that he had called up sipahis and denuded fortresses across the entire peninsula, which makes the tutor's estimate of the numbers involved improbably small. Unknown to any of those feverishly making ready at Lepanto, another imperial order was on its way acceding to Ali's request to winter in the Gulf of Patras, and on 19 October, in ignorance of the havoc that communications delays had already caused, a further order was sent authorizing Ali to permit the Askeri to return to their homes for the winter. But by then he and many of his men had gone to a more permanent rest, and although they certainly under-estimated the fighting power of the Holy League fleet they confidently set out to destroy, there is no disputing that the prime responsibility for snatching defeat from the jaws of what had been a solidly victorious campaign lies at the door of its architect, Grand Vizier Mehmet Sokolli Pasha.

CHAPTER NINE

ACT II

THE HOLY LEAGUE RESPONSE

3 May	Santa Cruz arrives Barcelona with Naples fleet, sails on to Cartagena.
25 May	Holy League proclaimed in Rome, notification reaches Madrid 6 June.
5 June.	Don Juan departs Madrid.
15 June	Colonna departs Civitavecchia for Messina.
16 June	Don Juan arrives Barcelona.
26 June	King writes extremely restrictive instructions to Juan.
4 July	Santa Cruz returns to Barcelona.
11 July	Sancho de Leyva departs to clear the way for the rest.
20 July	Don Juan departs Barcelona.
23 July	Venier and Barbarigo arrive Messina.
24 July	Don Juan arrives Nice, collects Duke of Savoy's galleys.
26 July	Don Juan arrives Genoa. Sancho de Leyva's flotilla returns to Spain.
2 Aug.	Combined Spanish–Genoese fleet from Genoa to La Spezia.
4 Aug.	Doria and Cardona remain to board soldiers, Don Juan to Piombino.

1–5 Aug.	Famagusta capitulation and massacre.
7 Aug.	Don Juan at Civitavecchia, leaves galleys for Orsino's men to board.
8 Aug.	Don Juan arrives Naples.
13 Aug.	Quirini and Canal reluctantly depart Crete.
14 Aug.	Granvelle gives Don Juan the Papal banner of the Holy League.
15–19 Aug.	Don Juan held in Naples harbour by adverse winds. Sends order to Andrade in Messina to take four fast galleys and scout the Ottoman fleet.
22 Aug.	Don Juan arrives Messina, Santa Cruz remains in Naples.
31 Aug.	Quirini and Canal arrive Messina with Cretan fleet.
5 Sept.	Doria, Cardona and Santa Cruz arrive Messina.
10 Sept.	Kara Khodja scouts Holy League fleet.
16 Sept.	Holy League fleet departs Messina.
17 Sept.	Fleet off Capo Spartivento.
19–22 Sept.	Fleet held at Crotone by adverse winds.
22 Sept.	Fleet departs, Santa Cruz and Paolo Canal to Taranto and Gallipoli.
25 Sept.	Rest of fleet arrives Casoppo, northern coast of Corfu.
26 Sept.	Fleet arrives Corfu.
27 Sept.	Andrade scouts Ottoman fleet in Lepanto.
30 Sept.	Hapsburg fleet at Gomenizza. Santa Cruz rejoins.
1 Sept.	Colonna and Venier arrive Gomenizza. Ships remain in Corfu.
2 Oct.	Venier hangs Hapsburg Italian mutineers.
3–4 Oct.	Fleet to Guiscardo, northern Cephalonia, learns of the Famagusta massacre. Kara Khodja with two fustas scouts the fleet again.
5–6 Oct.	Fleet watering at Val d'Alessandria (Samo), Cephalonia.
6–7 Oct.	Fleet to Curzolari Islands.

The story of the Holy League response to the Ottoman offensive of 1571 is normally told around the assembly of forces, summarized above, which resulted in a fleet of about the same size as the preceding year, only now preponderantly Spanish Hapsburg as to fighting power. Chesterton summarized the drama of this assembly wonderfully:

> In that enormous silence, tiny and unafraid,
> Comes up along a winding road the noise of the Crusade.
> Strong gongs groaning as the guns boom far,
> Don John of Austria is going to the war,
> Stiff flags straining in the night-blasts cold
> In the gloom black-purple, in the glint old-gold,
> Torchlight crimson on the copper kettle-drums,
> Then the tuckets, then the trumpets, then the cannon, and he comes.
> Don John laughing in the brave beard curled,
> Spurning of his stirrups like the thrones of all the world,
> Holding his head up for a flag of all the free.

It is pleasant to confirm that, for once, myth and reality intersected in the handsome person of the 23-year-old Don Juan de Austria, who grew into the role of commander-in-chief under the direction of his half-brother's most trusted subordinates. In the principal documentary resource for study of the campaign, an appealing human story emerges from the extensive correspondence between retired Captain General of the Sea García de Toledo, who was seeking relief for crippling gout at medicinal baths near Pisa, and both Juan and the man appointed his lieutenant and mentor, Luis de Requeséns. It is apparent that Toledo and Requeséns conspired together to guide the young colt, building up Juan's self-confidence as well as his expertise to the point that he was able to win respect from the other veteran officers under his command, and to be seen to wield an executive authority which the king did not believe him mature enough to exercise, but which was essential for the enterprise to prosper.[1]

Luis de Requeséns y Zúñiga was a Catalan nobleman and Grand Commander of Castile (the senior rank under the king of the once-crusading Order of Santiago), who had been a close friend to Philip since childhood. When Luis's father Juan de Zúñiga, Charles V's chamberlain, married the

Requeséns heiress Estefanía (who was a ward of both the Emperor and the Pope), her mother insisted that their eldest son should bear the matronym first. The family connection with the Papacy ran deep and led to the appointment of Luis as ambassador to the Holy See in 1563, whence he promptly withdrew in protest over the precedence claimed by the French ambassador, returning upon the death of Pius IV to thwart the French candidate and to ensure the election of Pius V on 7 January 1566. When recalled to become Don Juan's mentor, he was replaced by his younger brother Juan de Zúñiga y Requeséns, the two constituting the axis around which Spanish involvement in the Holy League revolved. Their relative neglect in the accounts of this period may be attributable to a pride of birth extreme even by the standards of their prickly class, exacerbated by the fact that Catalans regarded (and still regard) the rest of Spain much as the northern Italians do their own southerners. As a result the letters of the Requeséns/Zúñiga brothers are less self-explanatory than those that men of humbler birth felt it necessary to write, although between the lines there is evidence of subtle intellects at work.[2]

Less than a year in age separated Luis from Philip, and they grew up together under the stern supervision of Luis's father. There were frictions, notably two occasions when Luis unhorsed Philip in tournaments under the eye of the Emperor, and a more serious one resulting from an incident in 1554 when Bernardino de Mendoza, then captain general of the galleys of Spain, avenged what he saw as disrespect by boarding the flagship of the Order of Santiago and casting its banner in the water. Juan de Zúñiga and a crowd of Catalan notables went to the port to kill him, compelling the viceroy to place them under arrest until Mendoza went on his way. When, in 1556, Philip did not punish Mendoza and affirmed the precedence of the flag of Spain, Luis resigned his command over the galleys of the Order and all other offices he held from the crown, a position from which he did not relent until 1563.

Nonetheless it was to Luis that Philip turned when he wished to appoint someone to fulfil the same role for Don Juan that Luis's father had for him. The formal appointment as Juan's lieutenant dated 22 March 1568 declared that Requeséns was plenipotentiary *whether Juan was absent or not*. On the same day Philip sent him a private letter granting him paternal authority over Juan, trusting to his discretion to do nothing in public that might diminish Juan's authority but to be with him on his flagship *at all times*:

> Your attendance upon Don Juan, as much in matters regarding his command as his person and everything else, is of very great importance and directed towards what is for us the main end, it being understood that upon it depends not only the good performance and proceeding of said command and office, but also for the good direction and progress of his life and actions that we so greatly desire.

Requeséns had no experience in naval matters, so his tutelage was clearly intended to provide the active component in Juan's education in matters of diplomacy and princely duties, a living supplement to the didactic ornamentation of the brand-new *La Real*. That Requeséns brought Toledo into play during the Lepanto campaign was perhaps not solely a matter of tact and discretion, but may also have reflected the fact that on the sole occasion Requeséns himself had command of a fleet, when bringing Naples Tercio troops to suppress the Moriscos revolt in mid March 1569, he was caught by a storm in the Gulf of Lions after departing Marseilles against the advice of his captains, losing eight of thirty-four, including the flagship of the Genoese Stefano di Mare, with the rest scattered across the western Mediterranean. It was known that he sailed into the storm because his pride was outraged when he saw a flotilla under Doria sail past, and this cannot have enhanced his credibility as a director of naval operations.[3]

At the time of his appointment Don Juan also received a long and friendly letter of practical advice from Sancho de Leyva, who but for the appointment of Juan would have succeeded García de Toledo, but whatever relationship might have developed between them was aborted when Juan went ashore to take command of the suppression of the Moriscos revolt, with the results we have seen. Requeséns was with him throughout the campaign, and although he may have been the source of the information about Juan's behaviour in the field that Philip complained about, he may also have been the guiding intelligence behind Juan's cunningly worded replies. Not everyone, indeed probably nobody except his half-brother would have expected the young man to be anything other than a fire-eater. After Juan called upon him on the eve of his departure from

Madrid to take up his new post as commander-in-chief of the Holy League, the Papal Nuncio approvingly reported:

> ... he spoke to me with such grace and so much courage that it has filled me with hope. Certain it is that he is a Prince so desirous of glory that if the opportunity arises he will not be restrained by the Council that is to advise him and will not look so much to save galleys as to gather glory and honour.

This being precisely Philip's opinion of his half-brother, he appointed an executive council consisting of Requeséns, Doria, Marquess Alvaro de Bazán of Santa Cruz (captain general of the Naples fleet, the largest Hapsburg contingent), Juan de Cardona (captain general of the Sicily fleet and a relative of Requeséns), Ascanio della Corgna (field master-general), the Count of Santa Fiora (field master of the Italian Hapsburg infantry), Gabrio Serbellone (field master of the artillery), Gil de Andrade and Juan Vázquez Coronado (Knights of Malta and Spanish commodores). Philip told Juan that he could give no order not previously agreed by Requeséns, in matters naval should heed Doria above all, *and that he should not risk battle without the unanimous consent of the first three.* To Juan's chagrin these written orders were also sent to his nominal subordinates, as he complained in a letter dated 12 July:

> ... with due humility and respect, I would venture to say that it would be to me an infinite favour and boon if Your Majesty would be pleased to communicate with me directly with your own mouth, which I here desire for two reasons, the chief that in affairs of this quality it is not for the good of Your Majesty's service that any one of your ministers should be enabled to argue with me as to what your pleasure is, none of them being under the same obligations to give effect to it as I am ... and because something is due to me inasmuch as God has made me Your Majesty's brother, and I cannot therefore avoid saying so, nor help feeling hurt, that I should have been so little considered that at the time when all think I have deserved something better at Your Majesty's hands and look to obtain it, I should behold a proof of the contrary in your order reducing me to an equality with many others of your servants, a thing certainly in my conscience

not deserved, having always held myself more ready for Your
Majesty's service than for vanities or any other things.

Meanwhile an 'other thing' in the form of his pregnant and frantic
mistress María de Mendoza was making his stay in Barcelona very trying.
The departure of the fleet was much delayed despite the fact that Philip
did not wait for confirmation that the Holy League had been concluded,
but ordered mobilization once he received notification from Zúñiga that
the Pope had agreed to release extraordinary 'graces' from ecclesiastical
revenues far exceeding any previously granted. As a result Santa Cruz and
the Naples fleet arrived in Barcelona in early May, and went on to Cartagena
to board troops from the Granada Tercio, formed from local levies to
combat the Moriscos rebellion, only to find them so depleted by desertion
that he had to organize another levy. The Barcelona fleet itself was not
ready, with two galleys still building and the rest lacking guns and other
vital equipment, while Andrade was held up in Mallorca trying to recruit
crews with promises. As men slowly gathered at the ports they ate into the
supplies assembled for provisioning the galleys, and so it might have gone
on indefinitely had not the senior commanders, as usual in the service of
Philip, resignedly reached into their own pockets. Thus it was that when
the viceroys of Naples and Sicily died in May and August respectively, in
the midst of trying to assemble troops and supplies for the Holy League
fleet, they were physically exhausted and heavily in debt after trying to
bring order to the chronic shambles that was the Hapsburg way of war.

To the Pope, fuming about the delay in Rome, the Nuncio in Madrid
wrote on 17 July that there was no ill-faith involved, rather that 'the doing
of things promptly is not something to be found in this country; better
said its normal condition is to do everything late'. Bearing in mind that
Requeséns was an expert practitioner of informal communications, the
letter he sent at this time to his brother in Rome was no doubt also intended
to be shown to the Pope:

> All the haste you have urged in your letters to the king, to Don Juan
> and to me has been entirely necessary and you have been most
> justified in doing so; but you wrong me if you think I have lacked
> diligence in this matter, for I have gone to the limit in saying the same
> to the king and his ministers, and in frustration and chagrin for the

lack of it; but the original sin of our court, which is never to complete or do anything in good time and opportunely, has grown worse since you were here and gets worse every day.

To get a little ahead of the narrative, it is not surprising to find that the constant presence of Requeséns became irksome to Juan, and after the fleet arrived in Genoa at the end of July he asked if his mentor might occasionally dine on his own galley. Possibly perceiving ingratitude in one to whom he had devoted the attention a father would normally reserve for his own son, and certainly with his pride mortally offended, on 1 August Requeséns wrote a long and to modern eyes overwrought letter to Philip, in which as the Spanish say he 'breathed through the wound'. The letter affirms that he had dined with Juan every night for three years (!), and that when they spoke Juan had agreed that the Italians might see a break in this practice to be a symbolic disavowal. However, he continued, the affront was unendurable and he would now only visit the flagship, concluding with words beneath the dignity he valued so highly:

> I well believe that there cannot fail to be adverse consequences, the greatest of them being that it will seem to those of the fleet and all of Italy that this change contains greater mysteries. And those who may wish to take advantage of it to involve Don Juan in other matters of greater importance that are not to the advantage of Your Majesty's service will be able to do so, but as Your Majesty can see the fault is not mine.[4]

This made the triangular correspondence with Toledo all the more significant, because although we lack the letters Requeséns sent, we can deduce that he prompted the exchange of letters between the other two. The first reply from Toledo to Requeséns is dated 1 August, the same day as the latter's personal letter to the king cited above, and states that most of the Holy League soldiers are raw recruits, and that unless he were assured of numerical superiority or specifically ordered to do so by the king, he would not seek battle:

> . . . were I in command I would be reluctant to come to sword-strokes without [the 8,000–9,000 veteran soldiers in Flanders], for I judge the harm that would come from any defeat . . . would be greater than the

benefit of any victory. Consider also that our fleet belongs to different owners, and that at times what will seem the correct course of action to some will not so seem to others, and that the enemy fleet is of one proprietor and obedience; those who were at Preveza [in 1538] know how significant this is. The Turks have won moral superiority over the Venetians, and even over us they have not much lost it, nor have our men much won it over them; and I also think that we know or believe that the Venetians are better at talking than fighting.

On the eve of the departure of the Holy League fleet from Messina in mid September, Toledo repeated his warning, which was also echoed in much-cited letters to Requeséns from his brother in Rome and Cardinal Granvelle, previously with Zúñiga one of the negotiators of the Holy League, and since June the viceroy of Naples, both of whom urged him to arrange things so that failure to do battle in 1571 should be blamed on the Venetians, although both also recognized that if the opportunity presented itself, it could not in honour be avoided. Toledo spoke for what was clearly an urgent consensus among the servants of the king ashore:

> For the love of God, consider well what a great affair this is, and the damage that may be caused by a mistake; but as it will be better for various good reasons that the Venetians should not know how much or why it is in His Majesty's interest that there should not be a battle, I pray you after having read this letter to Don Juan to destroy it, or at least do not let it get into other hands than those of the secretary [Juan de] Soto.

But as the Spanish say with reference to advice, it is another matter when you have to play the guitar. In a revealing letter dated 28 December to his future son-in-law Pedro Fajardo, which in a separate note he asked him to show to the king, Requeséns wrote (my italics):

> By a letter from the court I have learned it is said that Doria and I were of the opinion that the Turkish fleet should not be fought, and that others [i.e. Santa Cruz], whom I believe must be the ones who have spread this version, were of contrary opinion. Although I do not need to give explanations, for I have many witnesses to my performance of the duty with which I was born, I shall of my own free will inform

you, *as to my lord*, of what occurred in case you have heard or should hear otherwise. The first thing I have to say is that if I had been of that opinion, I could have based it on very good reasons, and spoken it clearly, and afterwards in the execution of it have done my duty as I was bound to do. But this is very far from being the truth, and the fact that we fought is sufficient proof of this; *for if I had voted against it, the battle would not have taken place*. In addition to Don Juan having been ordered by His Majesty to accept my opinion in these matters, he was not so influenced by other childish matters that had transpired [the dining episode] to have ceased showing me all the respect I could have desired, and to accept my judgement with very good will.[5]

Had Juan been a full prince of the blood there might be some reason to credit him with the final decision, for at this time and for centuries to come royalty was afforded an exaggerated deference. But he was not, and his brother pointedly did not grant him the right to the style of 'Royal Highness', making him merely one 'Excellency' among several in the fleet. However, the authority any commander-in-chief must possess was something only the Venetians begrudged, despite their dire experience of divided command in the 1570 debacle. Although Juan did not have the power to decide whether or not to do battle, he appears to have been responsible for *how* it was fought, and in this he was guided by the best. The advice given by Sancho de Leyva in 1568 included a recommendation that he should personally inspect every galley regularly, ensuring proper treatment of the rowers and that all weapons were well maintained, and this Juan did. In a ten-page letter dated 3 May 1571 from the great Duke of Alba in Flanders, he received invaluable practical advice about soldier psychology:

> Your Excellency should always show the soldiers a cheerful face, for as is well known they put much store in this; it is advisable that they should know that Your Excellency takes great care over their pay, that they should receive it when possible, and when it is not to ensure that they should receive rations of the proper quantity and quality when at sea, and that they should know that they owe this to your authority and diligence, and when [the rations are not as they should be], that you regret it and punish the lapse.[6]

This Juan also did, on 3 August personally quelling a near-mutiny among German and Italian soldiers who were refusing to board galleys at La Spezia by giving them his word that their arrears would be paid, an assurance they accepted from him but had rejected from Doria and Cardona. Later, at Taranto and Gallipoli in late September, Santa Cruz and Paolo Canal, commander of the Venetian ships, were also unable to persuade unpaid soldiers to board, but by then Juan had sailed on to Corfu and so these troops had to be left behind. The alchemy of command was at work and with the exception of Venier, who was by far the least experienced among them, Juan's subordinates behaved towards him as their commander-in-chief in fact as well as in theory, the objective professional necessity for which only those who have made war can readily understand. Thus Doria, the only one Juan came to regard as a friend, was able through him to get the ornate spurs on the larger ponentina galleys cut back to permit the bow armament to fire low, an order we may be sure their proud captains would have rejected out of hand had it come from anyone else.[7]

In the documentary record Doria's role in the 1571 campaign is curiously muted by comparison with his high profile in 1570, and again we have Vargas-Hidalgo to thank for the explanation. After Cosimo dei Medici did not renew the 1570 contract for his galleys with Madrid and found another client in the Pope, Doria tried to renegotiate his own contract from a position of strength. He declared that the 6,000 escudos per galley previously paid did not cover his costs, and offered to sell them to Spain. In poker parlance he raised and was called, because to his astonishment Philip, never a believer in maintaining a royal fleet if he could lease instead, agreed to the purchase. Doria's discomfiture was complete when he discovered that Madrid had negotiated to sell his galleys on to the Grimaldi, rival Genoese galley contractors and bankers. This would have undermined Doria's authority among his peers in Genoa, and in a grovelling letter from Messina dated 10 September he begged to be permitted to withdraw from the sale. On paper, therefore, his galleys were not his own and he did not enjoy the status of being the largest single proprietor in the fleet throughout the assembly period. This may also explain why Requeséns prompted Juan to seek naval guidance from Toledo, and why Doria felt it necessary to cultivate his young commander's friendship.[8]

Another reason for all the Italians to proceed with caution in their dealings with Don Juan was that the Spanish army in Lombardy pointedly flexed its muscles in May 1571, when it occupied Finale. This small marquessate was claimed by both Savoy and Genoa and lay within the confines of the latter, but the marquess, faced with popular disturbances provoked by his brutal misgovernment, was unwise enough to believe he could obtain Hapsburg support on his terms by threatening to appeal to the French. The Duke of Albuquerque, Governor of Lombardy, promptly disabused him and the Spanish remained in occupation until the last marquess sold his patrimony to them in 1598. The shock wave rippled through the other small northern Italian states and provided additional motivation for Parma, Urbino and the rest not to stint in their support of the Holy League. Cosimo dei Medici, with most of his galleys already at Messina under the command of Colonna, experienced a nervous few weeks until the Hapsburg fleet sailed past his coast-line, and when Juan paused at the presidio of Piombino on 4 August the governor informed him 'that the state of the Duke of Florence is in a great state of agitation, people believing that this fleet was coming to liberate them from, as they call it, the tyranny under which they live'. In sum, while the Holy League was drawn together by a common enemy, it was also bound together by a common fear.[9]

The exception that tested the rule, almost to breaking point, was Sebastiano Venier. Humiliated by his enforced retreat from the Adriatic, galled to find himself obliged to take Hapsburg troops aboard his galleys and, no doubt, further irritated by having to take orders from someone fifty-two years his junior, he was flagrantly disrespectful on at least one occasion prior to the incident at Gomenizza to which we shall return. The earlier episode was at Crotone on 20 September, when adverse winds held the fleet in port. According to Venier's own account Juan, who was very concerned about undermanning on the Venetian galleys, offered him the 600 soldiers awaiting embarkation at Crotone. Venier refused them and rebuked him for the delay, to which Juan replied that he could understand Venier's anxiety, and that he should go on ahead if he wished. Surely fully aware of the construction that would be put on his words, Venier retorted that it was Juan's duty to lead, at which the latter withdrew and later sent Colonna to advise the old man, as delicately as possible, that he 'must avoid breaking up the League'. It is most unlikely that there should have been any difference between Venetian and Spanish concepts of deference, authority and the language of honour, so when Venier later flagrantly ignored this warning it was meant as an insult, and so perceived.[10]

Toledo advised Juan to employ the Venetians in the front line, ahead of the Hapsburg fleet, as corresponding both to their own demand for the leading role and to his own low estimate of their dependability. Requeséns also had the gravest doubts about them, writing that it was an intolerable burden to sail with them because of their indiscipline, while Doria's contempt for their seamanship had been made patent in 1570. We can only, therefore, attribute to Juan the inspired decision to shuffle the contingents of the fleet, forcing them to sail from Messina in the order they would adopt in battle. At the operational level Juan followed Toledo's practical advice, conveyed in a letter to Requeséns:

> . . . we must not seek battle but rather have the enemy to come to us, seeking every occasion to force them to do so. If battle is given in enemy country it should be very close to their coast, in this way offering the soldiers in their galleys the temptation to abandon them; if in Christian country, it should be as far as possible from the coast to avoid the same danger for ourselves . . . Don Juan would be well advised not to have the whole fleet together, because the large numbers involved will certainly create confusion and severe inconvenience, as it did at Preveza. Instead it should be divided into three squadrons with the most trustworthy galleys at the wings of each, with space enough between them to permit [manoeuvres] without getting in each other's way, for this was the order employed by Barbarossa at Preveza.

Again in the absence of evidence that anybody else suggested it, the most likely credit for the decision to have the galleasses towed a quarter of a mile ahead of the battle line must lie with Don Juan, probably in consultation with their commander, Francesco Duodo. It was, however, a basic principle employed by successful generals throughout the sixteenth century to fight behind fieldworks or to create detached strongpoints ahead of their main line, to the point that of the thirty-two land battles named in the *Chronology*, omitting pyrrhic Moncontour and the battles of Garigliano, Novara, Pavia and Mühlberg, where the losing side was caught unprepared, only four were unequivocal victories for the side that attacked first.[11]

Toledo's tactical advice was contained in a letter to Juan himself, in response to very specific questions. Juan had also written that he was concerned lest he be judged by the number of galleys under his command, without reference to how weak the Venetians were. Amused, the old gentleman replied that Juan must resign himself to the fact that even if he took the entire enemy fleet there would be those who would demand why he did not take Constantinople:

> As to Your Excellency's query about whether the artillery in our fleet should fire first or whether to await the enemy's fire, I reply that since it is not possible to fire twice, as it is not without causing the greatest confusion, in my judgement the correct course is to do as the cavalry troopers say, and to fire the arquebus so close to the enemy that you are splashed by his blood; by way of confirming this I have always heard captains who know what they are talking about say that the noise of the bow spurs breaking and the thunder of the artillery should be as one or little apart, and this is my opinion also, and that no heed should be taken of whether the enemy fires first or later, but that [the gunners should] hold their fire until Your Excellency gives the order.

Unmentioned but surely burned into the collective subconscious of all the Holy League commanders was the annihilation of Hugo de Moncada's flotilla by Filippino Doria at the battle of Capo d'Orso or Amalfi, fought on 28 April 1528 during the French siege of Naples. Although it only involved eight galleys on the Franco-Genoese side and six galleys, two fustas, two brigantinas and several smaller craft on the Spanish, all were heavily armed and manned and it was a rare example of a 'set piece' galley battle in which both sides were fully prepared and desirous of battle. As a purely Christian affair, the valuable lesson it taught about fire control was not one the Ottomans had learned in their routs of the Venetian and Hapsburg fleets. Doria engaged Moncada frontally while his lieutenant Lomellino hooked around his flank, and when the galleys closed the Spanish fired first, and high. Doria fired his bow guns at point-blank range and killed fifty on the Spanish flagship, mortally wounding Moncada. Juan de Cardona's grandfather was also killed, and the brothers Ascanio and Camillo Colonna captured. For such a small-scale engagement the casualties were staggering, with 500 Franco-Genoese and 700 Spanish soldiers killed, many more wounded, and untold casualties among the rowers.[12]

With reference to the broad strategic question of whether to seek out the enemy in what was left of the 1571 campaigning season or to make an early start the following year, looming over the deliberations was the distinct possibility that the irascible Venier would unilaterally withdraw if operations were postponed. He had reason for his impatience, for as we have seen the Ottoman fleet withdrew from the Adriatic while the Holy League fleet was in Messina, and inflicted savage damage on Corfu in passing. However, the delay cannot be attributed solely or even mainly to reluctance and disorganization among the Hapsburg contingents, for the greatest problem Juan had to resolve was that the Venetian Adriatic fleet was not battleworthy, and Venier was too proud to admit it. Even the Cretan contingent under Quirini and Canal, judged by Venier to be the better manned and equipped half of the Venetian fleet, only arrived at Messina at the end of August, and was in urgent need of maintenance and resupply. Here Colonna played a crucial role, the goodwill he had earned during 1570 permitting him to persuade the Venetian commander to take 4,100 Spanish and Hapsburg Italian troops, although Venier adamantly refused the troops from Germany. The Venetian had left almost all his soldiers to garrison the fortress of Corfu and brought very few to Messina, as admitted in his report on the campaign, in which he recalled reporting the following to Don Juan on 23 August:

> Prospero Colonna was about to bring me two thousand foot, and I would have twelve hundred from Gaspar Toralbo, and four other captains were coming with eight hundred, which would [bring the number up to] five thousand two hundred, and that they would have been ready at this time had they not been hindered, as their rations still were, by the viceroy of Naples . . . [Don Juan] asked me how many soldiers I reckoned each galley should have, I replied usually from forty to fifty because our rowing crews all fought. He said that having a superabundance of soldiers he would supply the rest that were wanted [and] as to the rations an order would be given.

Thus before the arrival of Quirini and Canal with the sixty galleys from Crete, the Venetian fleet had a mere 1,200 soldiers, most of whom would have been on board the well-found galleasses. Again according to Venier, Juan reported eighty-four galleys with him or en route, including those of Savoy and Malta, 'and seven thousand Spaniards, and six thousand Italians, all good troops'. As to the comment about obstruction by the viceroy, we know from reports by Granvelle, Juan and Santa Cruz that the rowers and supplies assembled at Naples for the Hapsburg fleet were inadequate, and Granvelle either did not possess the personal wealth to make good the deficiencies or was wise enough not to spend it. As we saw in Chapter Three, the finances of Naples were in a chronically parlous state and although the greater part of the Sicilian fleet was held back (as, indeed, was the Spanish home fleet under Sancho de Leyva), the food in the stomachs of the men who fought at Lepanto, as well as such money as they had in their pockets, was mainly provided by Sicily.[13] That Spain and Sicily should have retained galleys to defend their coasts is not remarkable, but it was militarily illogical for the Venetians to have done the same, as if the combined fleet were defeated 'the Gulf of Venice' would have become an Ottoman lake. We should balance the uncertainty among the Hapsburg commanders with the fact that little of the large garrison at Corfu was embarked before the battle, and immediately after it ten Venetian ships, five galleasses and seven galleys, with enough infantry and cavalry to embark upon unilateral land operations, suddenly appeared to exploit the victory.

While still in Naples, Juan sent an order to Gil de Andrade in Messina to take the four fastest galleys in the fleet and scout the whereabouts and strength of the Ottoman fleet in the Adriatic, but no word had been received from him at the time the combined fleet set out. The only intelligence available was from the Ottoman deserter mentioned in Chapter Eight, referred to in the letter sent by Juan to Toledo on 16 September:

> According to the information I have received, although the enemy
> fleet is superior in numbers, it is not in the quality of men and vessels,
> and trusting in God our Lord, whose cause this is and who will there-
> fore assist us, the decision has been taken to seek it out, and so I depart
> tonight for Corfu, and from there will go wherever I may find it.

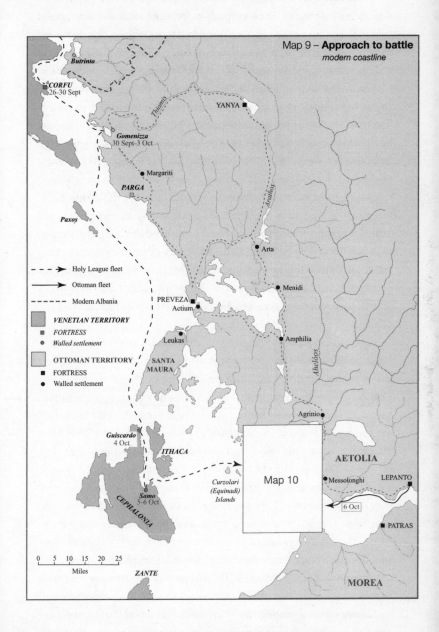

Map 9 – **Approach to battle**
modern coastline

Butrinto

CORFU
26–30 Sept

Thiamis

YANYA

Gomenizza
30 Sept–3 Oct

Margariti

PARGA

Paxos

Arachthos

Arta

Menidi

- - - → Holy League fleet
⟶ Ottoman fleet
- - - - - Modern Albania

VENETIAN TERRITORY
■ *FORTRESS*
● *Walled settlement*

OTTOMAN TERRITORY
■ FORTRESS
● Walled settlement

PREVEZA
Actium

Leukas

*SANTA
MAURA*

Amphilia

Acheloos

Agrinio

Guiscardo
4 Oct

ITHACA

AETOLIA

Map 10

Curzolari
(Equinadi)
Islands

Messolonghi

LEPANTO

Samo
5–6 Oct

CEPHALONIA

6 Oct

■ PATRAS

0 5 10 15 20 25
Miles

ZANTE

MOREA

Note the use of the passive voice with reference to the crucial decision, in contrast to an otherwise firmly active sentence. If not quite crossing the Rubicon, once the fleet left Messina it became progressively harder to avoid offering battle, although we may fairly speculate that Requeséns and Doria may have been confident that the Ottomans would not rise to the challenge. Attitudes hardened twelve days later, when they arrived at Corfu and saw the atrocities and desecrations perpetrated by the Ottomans less than two weeks earlier, but unfortunately it also filled Venier's cup of bitterness to overflowing. Far away in Madrid, with no inkling the fleet had sailed two weeks earlier, Philip wrote to Juan on 28 September instructing him to winter in Sicily and to make an early start in 1572, an order not received until he returned to Messina a month later. We should not make too much of this, for if the fleet had not set out by the time this order arrived it would have been because Juan's council had decided it was too late to do so. But it does highlight an impolitic lack of urgency in communications with the king, later compounded by Juan's failure to ensure that his own report of Lepanto reached Philip first, which was to provide ammunition for courtiers to feed the king's doubts about his half-brother's reliability.

Leaving Colonna with Venier in Corfu harbour, where the latter was supposed to (but did not) recover the soldiers he had left behind before departing for Messina, Juan sailed with the rest of the fleet to the bay of Gomenizza on the mainland. This settlement was in no-man's-land, garrisoned neither by the Venetians, who held Butrinto to the north and the fortress of Parga to the south, nor by the Ottomans, for whom the settlement of Margariti only a few miles inland marked the limit of the Bey of Yanya's authority (*Map 9*). No report of the campaign gives the reasons for the Holy League fleet to have assembled there, although one may have been fear of desertion if they remained in Corfu. But allied to this may have been a desire by Requeséns to overawe the Ottomans, and thereby reduce the possibility that they would emerge to do battle when the fleet sailed south. If such was the calculation it backfired completely, for Ottoman scouts captured some of the soldiers sent out to forage, and these unfortunates were sent to Ali and Pertev in Lepanto, who extracted extremely accurate intelligence from them not only about the numbers but also – and possibly tipping the scales in favour of battle – about the severe political divisions within the fleet, which had come close to undoing the League.

On 29 September a fragata from Andrade's scouting group arrived with the news that the Ottoman fleet had withdrawn to Lepanto, and that all the transports, escorted by sixty galleys commanded by Uluch Ali, had sailed to take the many sick and wounded to Modon. On receipt of this intelligence Juan sent an order to Corfu for Venier's and Colonna's galleys to rejoin the fleet and on 1 October a full-scale rehearsal of battle drills was carried out, with live firing that on several occasions came uncomfortably close to the fragata from which Juan and Requeséns were inspecting the action. In the evening a full council of war was held on board *La Real*, in which there was rare unanimity that the fleet should sail south to the Curzolari Islands and offer battle. Held in the bay by strong adverse winds, on 2 October there was another review in which the not very well hidden purpose was to reassess the battleworthiness of the Venetian galleys following the alleged boarding of soldiers in Corfu. Venier was furious to be caught in a lie about this, and pushed to the edge of his self-control by the fact that Juan sent the hated Gian'Andrea Doria to do the counting.

There are few certainties in history, but one is that in an explosive situation there never fails to be someone who provides the spark. Here it was Captain Muzio Alticozzi di Cortona, an officer of the Lombardy Tercio in command of the Hapsburg soldiers on board the *Armed Man*, a Retimo (Crete) galley whose battle station was on the Right Wing, under Doria. The galley commander of this and another galley on this wing was Andrea Calergi, whose authority may have been diminished by reason of being one of the very few Greek sopracomiti.[14] In addition Alticozzi was from Arezzo, an area with historic grievances against Venice, so there was little chance of sweet reason prevailing when friction between the Hapsburg troops and the Cretan crew flared into a brawl, according to Venier one of many such incidents that had so far gone unpunished. Venier sent his first mate and an ensign to calm things down, but Alticozzi and his men threw them overboard. Venier then sent his flagship captain and three ensigns, and in an exchange of fire Alticozzi was seriously wounded and two of the ensigns killed. The final fuel to the flames came when Paolo Sforza, a colonel in Alticozzi's Tercio, came alongside Venier's flagship and said that he would handle the problem. Alas, Sforza was on board one of Gian'Andrea's galleys and this was the final straw for the apoplectic Venier.

'By the blood of Christ,' the old gentleman shouted, 'take no such action unless you wish me to sink your galley and all on board. I will bring these dogs to heel.' The Venetian flagship then rowed over to the *Armed Man* and under the menace of her bow armament the mutineers surrendered. Not content with having defied the authority of Sforza and of Doria, whose wing it was, Venier now insulted his commander-in-chief by hanging Alticozzi and three others from the antenna of his flagship, and lifted them high for all to see. There followed a period of extreme tension during which some of the Hapsburg galleys took up position to assault the Venetians, while on board the latter the soldiers of the Lombardy Tercio menacingly formed up under their own officers in defiance of the galley captains. An outraged Don Juan summoned a meeting of his council, in which feeling against Venier ran strong. Requeséns felt that an example should be made of him, Doria said it was best to return to Messina and leave the Venetians to handle matters on their own, and Cardona was in favour of doing both. But Santa Cruz disagreed, saying they could not in honour now abandon the enterprise, and his view was supported by Andrade, Moncada and Vázquez Coronado, the Spanish Knights of Malta. Colonna, speaking after the others, first agreed that Venier was a loose cannon (*un uomo stravagantissimo*) whose disruptive presence could no longer be tolerated in the deliberations of the council, but then suggested that his place be taken by the Quartermaster General of the Sea, Agostino Barbarigo, while permitting the Venetian flagship to preserve her place on the left of *La Real*, pointedly flanked by the flagship of Genoa. Juan seized upon Colonna's compromise, and when Barbarigo was summoned he did not even confer with Venier before agreeing to it.[15]

This incident was crucial enough within the context of the Holy League, but the fact that Ali and Pertev learned of it from the captives hurried to them overland makes it of probably definitive significance. The Ottomans shared the views of García de Toledo about the dependability of the Venetians, and could reasonably assume that morale and unity of purpose alike were tenuous in the enemy fleet. After the battle, some told their interrogators that when they saw a gap open between the Holy League Battle and the Right Wing, they took it as confirmation of the Venetian defection their commanders had predicted. What they could not know was the effect that news of the capitulation of Famagusta and the massacre that followed was to have on the Holy League fleet. A dispatch from the governor of Crete reporting the gruesome details caught up with the fleet at Guiscardo, on the northern coast of Cephalonia, where it arrived in the afternoon of 4 October after sailing overnight from Gomenizza. That night, as the fleet rowed the 12 miles (19km) to the mouth of a stream at the site of ancient Samo where they were to fill their water casks, a cold rage silenced the bickering on board, even as a dense fog muffled the sound of the oars. Ambrogio and Antonio Bragadino, brother captains of the two galleasses on the Left Wing, would have been particularly affected by the news that the stuffed skin of their kinsman had been paraded along the coast of Anatolia. *Appendix B* seeks to establish credible parameters, but barring overwhelming asymmetry in numbers or technology, battle is an unquantifiable affair of the heart and the will. Objectively the fall of Famagusta rendered moot the founding purpose of the Holy League – but the flaring desire for vengeance it sparked briefly gave the alliance a unity of purpose it had not enjoyed before, and would not again.

The posturing of captains and the calculations of kings aside, we should not forget that the anonymous masses of soldiers, sailors and even the rowers of the fully indulgenced Holy League were animated by a common faith and purpose, a mood vividly captured by Chesterton:

> The Pope was in his chapel before day or battle broke,
> (Don John of Austria is hidden in the smoke.)
> The hidden room in man's house where God sits all the year,
> The secret window whence the world looks small and very dear.
> He sees as in a mirror on the monstrous twilight sea
> The crescent of his cruel ships whose name is mystery;
> They fling great shadows foe-wards, making Cross and Castle dark,
> They veil the plume graved lions on the galleys of St. Mark;
> And above the ships are palaces of brown, black-bearded chiefs,
> And below the ships are prisons, where with multitudinous griefs,
> Christian captives sick and sunless, all a labouring race repines
> Like a race in sunken cities, like a nation in the mines.
> They are lost like slaves that sweat, and in the skies of morning hung
> The stair-ways of the tallest gods when tyranny was young.

Nor should we underestimate the power of prayer in an age when it was unquestioned. In a letter of 26 September from Zúñiga to Philip in which he reported Juan's departure from Messina, he added, 'Pray God to grant him the victory that Christendom needs, as His Holiness is most diligent in doing: he fasts three times a week and spends many hours every day at prayer, and has sent to five or six churches in Rome to pray for [victory] ceaselessly'.

Bartolomeo Sereno, Onorato Caetani's lieutenant in the Papal Guard, perceptively described the attitude of Juan's Spanish councillors as they approached battle as being 'like snakes drawn by the power of a charm'. The military historian can usually assume that the Deity, being vigorously importuned by both sides, is likely to remain neutral when men decide to kill each other in large numbers, but there is a whiff of the supernatural about the palpable sense of inevitability that began to settle over the Holy League fleet after it departed Messina. Possibly Mehmet Sokolli, whose relations with the Ulema were not good, failed to ensure the intercession of the Imam of the Great Mosque, but the Ottoman commanders at Lepanto can be forgiven for believing that Allah had delivered their enemies into their hands when Kara Khodja returned on 5 October with a substantial undercount from a reconnaissance of the Holy League fleet at Samo during the night of 3–4 October, unaware that the Reserve under Santa Cruz was still en route from Guiscardo.

During the last council before the battle, the Holy League commanders agreed to persist in their plan to advance to the Curzolari Islands, whence they would control the mouth of the Gulf of Patras. Requeséns, Doria and Cardona were of the opinion that the fleet should remain in the shelter of the island of Petalas, but readily agreed to Santa Cruz's proposal that they should form for battle the following day, Sunday 7 October, and fire a salvo if the enemy did not appear. Whether they calculated that this would provoke or deter the enemy is a secret all involved took to their graves. In an extraordinary lapse neither fleet kept the other under observation at this crucial time, and so when Ali set sail on the 6th and stopped overnight to fill his water casks at a stream some 15 miles (24km) along the coast from Lepanto, he was as unaware that the Holy League galleys had sailed to the Curzolari Islands as they were of his movements.

Until the 1971–72 survey of the battle site (*Map 10*), it was very difficult

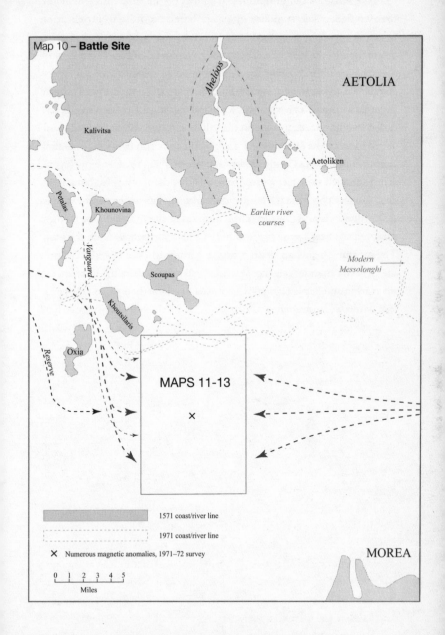

Map 10 – **Battle Site**

AETOLIA

Akelóos

Kalivitsa

Aetoliken

Petalas

Khounovina

Earlier river courses

Vanguard

Modern Messolonghi

Scoupas

Khoutsilaris

Oxia

MAPS 11-13

×

Reserve

MOREA

1571 coast/river line

1971 coast/river line

× Numerous magnetic anomalies, 1971–72 survey

0 1 2 3 4 5
Miles

to make sense of contemporary accounts of the final movements of the two fleets. The standard maps are based on those in Jurien de la Gravière's account published in 1888, but by that time silt deposited by the scouring Ahelóos, the largest river system in Greece (*Map 9*), had already altered the coastline to an unrecognizable degree. Once it is appreciated that there were several islands involved, the mystery of where Cardona's vanguard division was when the opposing fleets first spied each other, two hours after dawn on the 7th, is resolved – Juan had sent him ahead to scout the Petalas anchorage, while the main fleet made landfall further south. Santa Cruz was also well back, having rowed to investigate an unidentified sail which proved to be a Holy League straggler. No sooner had Juan sent observers to climb to the highest points on the nearby islands of Khoutsilaris and Oxia than the lookout at the masthead of *La Real* reported sighting a growing number of sails approaching from the east. The morning haze had cleared, and at a range of over 15 miles (24km) the rival commanders each ordered a signal gun fired, trumpets sounded the clarion and battle ensigns were raised to advise their respective fleets that battle was imminent.

CHAPTER TEN

ACT III

THE BATTLE

All the eyewitness accounts were written by men involved in the headbutting struggle at the centre, leaving the more fluid developments on the wings underreported. As to fact this is no great loss, because the tunnel vision of men in combat and the dense smoke of the black powder battlefield reduced the experience of all to a common denominator. They were also extremely reticent about what the authors themselves saw and did, probably because soldiers have always been loath to write about what happens at the sticking point, and Lepanto was a mind-numbing bloodbath fought mainly hand to hand. Even the diary of the rower Scetti does not describe the mechanics of battle among the rank and file, and although the epic poets Rufo and Ercilla provide some generic colour, Cervantes wrote little of his experiences at 'the sharp end'. Of the general accounts, with due allowance for the bias of the Venetian officers he interviewed at Corfu immediately after the battle, Diedo's is the only one written before 'the carapace of accepted fact hardened'.[1] Herrera and Contarini, both published in 1572, give the Spanish and Venetian canonical accounts. Paruta and Knolles wrote twenty to thirty years after the event, when the propaganda version was set in stone, and most of the later histories either had evident axes to grind, or were not sourced, or both. The honourable exception is Quarti who, despite writing at the height of the Fascist era, limited his nationalism to clearly signposted comment and permitted the wide range of sources available to him to speak for themselves.

For ease of reference the named actors are listed at *Appendix A*, and a pause at this point to peruse the estimate of forces at *Appendix B*, and the opposing orders of battle at *Appendix C* in conjunction with *Maps 11–12*, would be time well spent. One last word about the stage directions before the curtain comes up: the tactical analysis summarized in *Map 12* is based on the likely paths taken by the few galleys about whose movements there is reliable information, from their starting place to the location of the enemy galleys they fought. Some did not stop to take possession of the galleys they defeated, which were then claimed by others, and this may explain why Herrera and others attribute the defeat of Pertev's flagship at the centre to Cardona, which cannot be true for the latter arrived late and was engaged from the first in the gap that opened between the Holy League Battle and the Right Wing. Pertev was definitely engaged by Colonna, which sounds enough like Cardona to suggest another reason for this much-repeated error, but it is also possible that Cardona's severely damaged galley came upon Pertev's corpse-strewn and looted flagship after the fighting moved on. These reservations aside, the principal sources disagree over little save Doria's handling of the right flank, and only significant quotations or crucial points of interpretation are endnoted here.

The Holy League fleet emerged from the gap between Khoutsilaris and Oxia led by the Battle, followed by the right or seaward wing commanded by Doria, with the left or coastal wing under Barbarigo last. The reserve division under Santa Cruz had yet to reach the islands and probably passed to the west of Oxia, the marquess himself boarding a fragata to race forward to *La Real*, where he arrived 'dressed in richly gilded armour, very gallant with many plumes and overjoyed', to congratulate Don Juan on having found the enemy fleet. Meanwhile Doria was in no doubt that it was the other way around, and was far from overjoyed. Ordering the galleasses assigned to him cut loose, he led his division out to sea at full speed under oars, into the breeze filling the Ottoman sails. At some stage the wind turned to come from the west and the chaplains of the Christian fleet, mainly Jesuits on board the Hapsburg galleys and Franciscans on the Venetian, hailed this as a sign from God. In fact the wind shift was to limit the part played by the galleasses and made little difference to the Ottomans, who had already reduced to small foresails as they shook out into battle formation, for the Holy League fleet would have been a harder nut to crack amid the islands, and a pell-mell attack would not have produced the intended battle of annihilation. With the exception of Doria's division the two fleets formed up with ponderous deliberation, the Ottomans advancing slowly and the Holy League Battle marking time while the wings took their stations.

Contemporary illustrations either show the Ottoman formation as a traditional crescent, or else their Battle forming a line with the two horns curving outwards from a point slightly behind it. To those watching them approach it seemed they adjusted from a crescent to a line in response to the Holy League deployment, and nobody seems to have asked why they would do so when the crescent was manifestly the better formation for the more numerous fleet. The two Battles occupied the same frontage, the Holy League closed up and the Ottomans in a double line, with the galleys in the second covering the spaces between those of the first, thus permitting the line to expand or concentrate as the demands of combat dictated. Assuming constant speed through the water, when the Ottoman horns extended they would have done so progressively from the tips, and as each galley angled away this would have reduced her closing speed relative to the Battle. This would have had the effect of flattening the crescent as well as causing the innermost galleys of the horns to fall behind the steadily advancing centre. The Holy League fleet barely maintained way through the water and waited to receive the charge, as recommended by Toledo, with the strongest galleys at either end and the centre of each division, and the galleasses towed out far ahead of the line. They are usually credited with disordering the enemy formation, but it is likely the Ottomans always intended to attack in squadrons, aiming to overwhelm selected points, and the disruption caused by the galleasses may have been more apparent than real.[2]

Although the rest of the Holy League commanders failed to appreciate it at the time or fully admit it later, the two flanks faced radically different challenges. The coastal wing started with equal numbers and was still partially outflanked because the shallower draught of the Ottoman galleys permitted them to risk the sandbars (today barrier islands) lurking under the surface of the silt-laden waters off the islands of Scoupas and Khoutsilaris. However, in extending to perform this manoeuvre while avoiding the galleasses, the Ottoman attack became dispersed and was defeated in detail,

Map 11 – **Canonical Deployment**

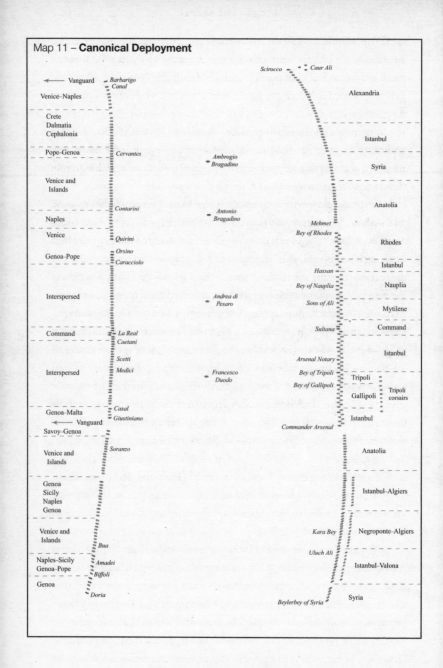

← Vanguard

Venice–Naples

Barbarigo
Canal

Scirocco
Caur Ali

Alexandria

Crete
Dalmatia
Cephalonia

Istanbul

Pope–Genoa

Cervantes

Ambrogio
Bragadino

Syria

Venice and
Islands

Contarini

Antonio
Bragadino

Anatolia

Naples

Mehmet
Bey of Rhodes

Venice

Quirini

Rhodes

Genoa–Pope

Orsino
Caracciolo

Hassan

Istanbul

Bey of Nauplia

Nauplia

Interspersed

Andrea di
Pesaro

Sons of Ali

Mytilene

Command

La Real
Caetani

Sultana

Command

Scetti

Arsenal Notary

Istanbul

Interspersed

Medici

Francesco
Duodo

Bey of Tripoli

Tripoli

Bey of Gallipoli

Gallipoli

Tripoli
corsairs

Genoa–Malta

Casal
Giustiniano

Istanbul

← Vanguard

Savoy–Genoa

Commander Arsenal

Venice and
Islands

Soranzo

Anatolia

Genoa
Sicily
Naples
Genoa

Istanbul–Algiers

Venice and
Islands

Kara Bey

Negroponte–Algiers

Bua

Uluch Ali

Naples–Sicily
Genoa–Pope

Amadei
Biffoli

Istanbul–Valona

Genoa

Doria

Beylerbey of Syria

Syria

230

while the opportune arrival of reinforcements from the Holy League Reserve helped turn it into a rout. In contrast the Holy League seaward flank was vastly outnumbered, the double rank of Ottoman galleys and galliots permitted the wing to extend like a set of sliding doors, there were no galleasses to obstruct them when they chose to charge, and Christian reinforcements were long in coming. As soon as he was close enough to count the masts Doria must have instantly understood the Ottoman battle plan and realized that he was in very deep trouble indeed, and with him the whole Christian fleet.

The Ottoman left is compressed in *Map 11* for presentational reasons, and the degree to which Doria's wing was outflanked from the start therefore understated. There was only one thing he could do in response, which was to shadow the leading element of the Ottoman horn while inclining away to prevent it going around him, technically 'refusing' the flank. Lack of confidence in his leadership among the Venetians under his command led to the fragmentation of his division and grievous losses, but the only surprise is that his entire wing was not destroyed. An extraordinary amount of piffle has been written about his reluctance to close with the enemy, even by Vice Admiral Jurien de la Gravière who really should have known better. Had Doria charged he might have been double-enveloped, or at best held by the Ottoman galleys in the front rank, freeing the nimble corsair galliots to fall on the rear of the Battle, and the anniversary of the battle would have become a red-letter day in the Muslim and not the Christian calendar.

Alba had warned Don Juan of the terrifying noise that preceded an Ottoman attack, capable on its own of breaking raw recruits, but with the contingents interspersed and packets of veteran troops scattered throughout the fleet there were few places where any substantial concentration of inexperienced soldiers stood alone, while of course fight or flight is not an individual decision in naval warfare. Several accounts refer to galleys that rowed back and forth without seeking to engage the enemy, but Herrera and Paruta both commented that there was no safety anywhere within the swirling free-for-all that developed, in which a galley fleeing one enemy could be attacked out of the smoke by another without warning. The sole outright shirker was an unnamed Venetian galley in the Reserve that fell out to pick up the stores and furniture dumped overboard from

Santa Cruz's flagship, a credible anecdote given what we know about the sopracomiti. Although twenty-one Holy League galleys were overrun, only Pietro Bua's isolated and surrounded Corfiot galley on the Right Wing is known to have surrendered.

This speaks volumes for the level of motivation across the fleet, and honours the mental preparation orchestrated by Don Juan. Splendidly arrayed he stood in the bow of a fragata, the Holy League banner held up amidships, and rowed in review across the front of the galleys to the left of *La Real*, exhorting the cheering men in their forecastles to avenge the atrocities they had observed at Corfu and the horrors of Famagusta, and not to let the infidels taunt them 'Where is thy God?' Displaying the crucifix that was later lashed to the forecastle of the all-Catalan flagship of Santiago (which can be seen today in the Lepanto chapel of Barcelona cathedral), Requeséns reviewed the galleys on the right, among them the Maltese *Saint Pierre* where 'brave Crillon' harangued the French Knights of Saint John: 'It is by the will of God that you are all come here, to punish the fury and wickedness of these barbarous dogs'.[3] Meanwhile the smaller vessels delivered the troops they carried to the line, and in return took on board the non-military impedimenta and the sick. One who refused to go was the fever-ridden Cervantes, who rose from his sickbed on board Doria's *La Marchesa*, in the middle of the Left Wing, and was given command of the soldiers on the skiff platform. On board the Papal–Tuscan *La Pisana* the chains on Aurelio Scetti and his fellows were removed, and he later recalled their enthusiasm:

> . . . the more so because they were so embittered against these enemies of God and were most desperate to fight, of which they gave very great proof on this day, the greater because they hoped thereby to win their so-desired freedom, which all were promised by their captains if victory was won. As a result much death was inflicted on the Turks by these rowers, who leapt upon the enemy galleys saying to themselves that either we die or win our liberty. While the battle lasted they showed their prowess, heeding neither the enemy's arms nor fears of any kind, although afterwards many made their way to other vessels so that they should not again be put in irons.[4]

Alas, poor Aurelio; anxious to return to Florence, there to resume the promising career as a musician cut short when he killed his young wife in a jealous rage, he took two prisoners back to *La Pisana*. He should perhaps have anticipated that his captain, Knight of Santo Stefano Ercole Balotta, would keep the valuable captives but not his cheaply given word, and Scetti remained at the oar for many more years. Beyond the anecdotal, his testimony confirms that although the Holy League was substantially outnumbered in hulls, once the non-slave rowers are factored in the Ottomans were outnumbered in fighting men as well as in artillery, and in close-quarter battle the former would have bestowed much the greater advantage.

This was a reversal of the norm, for as we have noted the signature of the Ottoman way of war was numerical superiority, with clouds of cannon fodder sent ahead of the sipahis and Janissaries to draw enemy fire. Although about equal in number to the soldiers, the usefulness of their unprotected and perfunctorily armed criminal rowers on board the Hapsburg and Papal galleys may have been marginal. But paid rowers were the majority on the otherwise undermanned Venetian galleys, and nearly trebled the number of potential fighting men while those from Crete, Dalmatia and the Ionian islands were in the main properly equipped men with bitter scores to settle.

On board the scarlet-hulled *Sultana*, no less splendidly adorned and almost as big as *La Real*, Ali spoke kindly to his own slave rowers: 'If today is yours, God grant it to you, but be assured that if I win this battle I shall set you free, and therefore perform your tasks as honestly as I have always dealt with you'. This may be poetic licence, but similar words were probably spoken by the commanders of all galleys with a significant number of condemned or slave rowers. In *La Austriada*, Rufo affirmed that the Ottomans were also reassured by:

Bombas de fuego, máquinas terribles de alquitrán, que en el agua mas se enciende;	Bombs of fire, filled with a fearful tar that in water hotter burns;
Astas y flechas, llenas de empecibles yerbas, cuyo veneno presto ofende;	Shafts and arrows tipped with lethal potions, quick to give death in turn;
Arcabuces, mosquetes insufribles,	Arquebuses, mosquetes dire,

cañones, de quien nada se defiende;	cannon from which none can shelter;
Y mucha confianza en la batalla,	And battle faith – for under fire
que es la mayor ventaja que se halla.	no advantage can be greater.

Kettledrums thundered from both sides, with the rattle of Ottoman castanets and the clash of cymbals answered by the rapid-fire of Holy League snare drums, while cornets, trumpets, horns and sackbuts (early trombones) added to the deafening crescendo. The men of the Tercios steadied themselves with their world-girding rallying call '*Santiago y cierra* [close ranks] *España*', but as the fleets came nearer the Ottoman war cries rose above all:

> The Turkish armada came forward so inflamed and proud that each
> moment seemed to them a thousand years, and upon spying us
> joyfully ordered fifes and tambourines to play, dancing and calling out
> to the Christians that they were wet hens, and promising themselves
> the triumph and victory over us.[5]

To set an example of carefree steadiness Don Juan and members of his suite danced a lively galliard on the upper deck of the forecastle, above the heavy guns and jutting out ahead of the line, and one wonders if he was able to induce the dignified Requeséns to join in. During the battle their impromptu dance floor was occupied by Gian'Andrea's deputy Pietro Francesco Doria with fifty men, the midships ramp was entrusted to flotilla commander Gil de Andrade with fifty more, and Tercio field masters Figueroa and Moncada commanded the men along the sides nearest the bow, where some of the benches had been decked over. Colonels Carillo and Zapata with fifty men each manned the skiff and oven platforms, and Castellanos (castle commanders) Salazar and Mesa commanded the arquebusiers on the side firing steps at the rear, standing above the five-man oars behind shield-walls. Juan's battle station was astern, behind a huge royal banner on its own flagpole, with Requeséns, the Duke of Sessa (grandson and namesake of the Great Captain), Marquess Bernardino de Cárdenas of Beteta, and flotilla commanders Juan Vázquez Coronado, Rodrigo de Mendoza and Juan de Guzmán, to name only a few of the notables who claimed places of honour next to the half-brother of their king.[6]

The significance of the bow, skiff and oven platforms was that with anti-personnel nets stretched over the rowing frames and backed by the pikes of the armed rowers and the midships detail, these were the only places from and to which boarding could be attempted, and where the fiercest fighting took place. Cervantes wrote that there were barely 2 feet (60cm) of deck space per man, 'bound and locked together' in the face of enemy guns 'not a pike's length away', and describes the scarcely believable courage required of men at these posts:

> ... and although conscious that the slightest false step will send him to Neptune's bottomless gulf, nonetheless driven by thoughts of glory he bravely attempts to force a passage ... hardly has one fallen whence he will not rise again than another takes his place, and should he [in turn] drop into the waiting jaws of death, another and another without pause ... [7]

One of military history's minor mysteries is why the greatly feared cannon-like siphons of 'Greek fire', the compound referred to by Rufo that ignited when mixed with water, vanished from Mediterranean warfare after the fall of Byzantium. But perhaps even more puzzling is why anyone on board the highly combustible galleys should ever have employed incendiary devices, given that once they were grappled together the flames that consumed one might easily envelop the other, or ignite a magazine with the devastating results we saw when Mehmet Sokolli's loot-laden galleon exploded off the Famagusta Gardens. Precisely this happened on the seaward flank, where someone on board Soranzo's *Christ over the World* fired the powder store when the galley was surrounded and overrun. A few galleys were sunk outright by gunfire, such as those hulled by the big centreline guns of the galleasses and Mehmet Scirocco's flagship on the coastal wing, shattered by the main armament of several Venetian galleys, but most of those lost were either scuttled after the battle or burnt during it. The most likely explanation for the concentration of magnetic anomalies detected by the 1971–72 survey precisely where the two Battles clashed is that flaming objects tend to draw together, and many of the defeated Ottoman galleys were burning too fiercely to permit the retrieval of their wrought iron guns before they sank. In *La Araucana*, Ercilla dwelled on the awful paradox of fire at sea:

Unos al mar se arrojan por salvarse	Some threw themselves into the sea
del crudo hierro y llamas perseguidos	in flight from merciless fire and steel,
otros que habían probado el ahogarse	others from drowning sought to flee
se abrazan a los leños encendidos:	by clinging to a burning keel:
así que, con la gana de escaparse	no matter how they tried to save
a cualquiera remedio vano asidos,	their lives, death found them just the same,
dentro del mar mueren abrasados	they burned to death amid the waves
y en medio de las llamas ahogados.	and drowned surrounded by the flames.

The last moment of silence before the guns began to speak was when the men of both fleets were called to prayer by signals from their flagships. On the *Sultana*, this was the hoisting of the sacred Muslim standard destroyed exactly a century later in a fire that consumed a wing of the Escorial palace. This banner, so heavily embroidered that it must have hung from a pole suspended at both ends, was Sufi in origin and had been captured when Suleiman the Magnificent took Baghdad. On one side it bore six circles of quotations from the Koran around the names of Muhammad and successors, with the founder of the house of Othman ahistorically included among the Caliphs. On the other, also bordered by quotations from The Book, blessings were asked for Sultan Selim amid 28,900 tiny squares each containing the name of God.[8]

On *La Real* a large crucifix was hoisted to the masthead above the banner sent to Don Juan by the Pope, with Christ over the arms of the Papacy, Spain and Venice. Trumpets summoned all to kneel for absolution on one side, and on the other to prostrate themselves in the confident assurance of a rapturous reception in paradise should they fall.

Like some prehistoric beast roaring defiance across a disputed pond, a blank charge from the main gun of the *Sultana* broke the silence to initiate the oddly formal ceremony of challenge and response with which battles of this period commonly began. *La Real* answered with a shotted gun, *Sultana* replied in kind and the Ottoman fleet surged forward at battle speed, opening to pass on either side of the galleasses. Either because in turning away they presented the Venetian gunners with a broadside shot, or else as a result of the same bravado that had doomed some of their fellows under the fortress guns of Corfu, at least two Ottoman galleys were shattered by the heavy 'forwardside' of the galleasses, several memoirists concurring that Duodo's flagship fired first and broke the back of one in full view of the cheering fleet.

Whatever further damage the galleasses did was hidden by smoke, but all could see that they parted the Ottoman wave like smouldering volcanic boulders on a seashore, and although this may have made little difference in the north, where the Ottoman line had already broken up into squadrons, at the centre it diluted the shock value of an unbroken line, nullifying the visual effect that might have been achieved by an orderly expansion as the front line opened and the second moved in to fill the spaces. Possibly no less important was that instead of all the guns firing together at a signal from the flagship, ragged and uneven salvos whistled over the mastheads of the Holy League. Throughout the age of black powder, participants unanimously commented how heartening it was to be shot at without effect, here celebrated by Rufo:

Del juego de la brava artillería	In the play of fierce artillery fire
A los turcos la pérdida tocaba,	The Turks were cast to lose this day,
Porque en las galeazas tanta habia,	Our galleasses deep with guns entire,
Que bien claro su efecto se mostraba,	Their vessels sent to greater depths away,
Y porque á nuestra armada en este dia	And while our own to great effect
El ser bajas las proas le importaba,	Had lowered bows to aim the cannon true,
Y también porque quiso el otomano	Theirs were the less alone in this respect,
Ganarnos, como dicen, por la mano.	As hand to hand they sought to make us rue.

While we may be sure not all the Holy League gun captains kept their nerve, enough of them fired together to leave an indelible impression, the noise unanimously likened to the crack of doom by the Spanish poets. Apart from the staggering effect this had on the Ottomans, the following breeze carried the billowing smokescreen over the enemy galleys and permitted Christian imaginations to conjure up visions of satisfactory carnage. Also, the host of Ottoman bowmen, trained to put an arrow in

Map 12 – **Opening Stages**

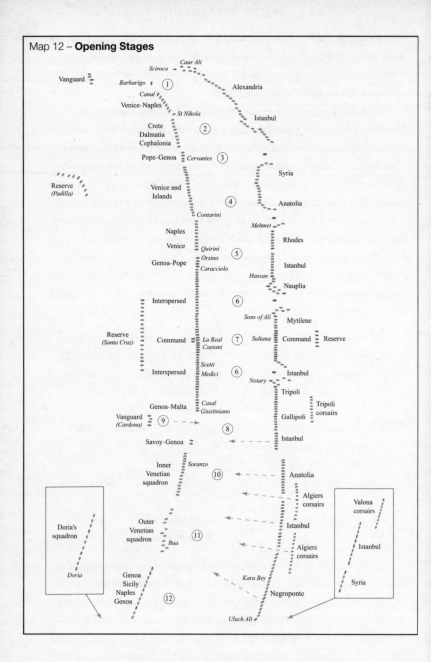

Vanguard

Caur Ali
Sciroco
Barbarigo ①
Alexandria
Canal
Venice–Naples
St Nikola
Istanbul
Crete
Dalmatia
Cephalonia ②
Pope–Genoa *Cervantes* ③

Reserve
(Padilla)

Syria

Venice and
Islands ④
Anatolia

Contarini
Mehmet

Naples
Rhodes
Venice *Quirini* ⑤
Orsino
Genoa–Pope *Caracciolo*
Istanbul
Hassan
Nauplia

Interspersed ⑥

Sons of Ali Mytilene

Reserve
(Santa Cruz)
Command *La Real* ⑦ *Sultana* Command Reserve
Caetani

Interspersed *Scetti* ⑥
Medici Istanbul
Notary
Tripoli

Genoa–Malta *Casal* Tripoli
Giustiniano corsairs
Vanguard ⑨ Gallipoli
(Cardona) ⑧
Savoy–Genoa Istanbul

Inner *Soranzo*
Venetian ⑩ Anatolia
squadron
Algiers
corsairs
Doria's
squadron Outer
Venetian ⑪ Istanbul Valona
squadron *Bua* corsairs
Algiers
corsairs
Doria Istanbul
Genoa *Kara Bey*
Sicily Syria
Naples Negroponte
Genoa ⑫
Uluch Ali

1. 'Love-light of Spain, hurrah!' – Don Juan de Austria
(*Museo Naval*, Madrid)

3

OPPOSITE PAGE
2. Sultan Selim II in an uncharacteristically vigorous pose (*Sonia Halliday Photographs*)

3. Hound of God Saint Pius V, Inquisitor-General and Pope (*Scala*)

4. King Philip II and new-born Crown Prince Ferdinand by Titian (*Art Archive*)

5. The hangman of Gomenizza – Sebastiano Venier by Tintoretto
(*Bridgeman Art Library/Kunsthistorisches Museum*, Vienna)

6a

6b

6a. Mannerism – Vasari's battle scene in the Vatican Sala Regia (*Scala*)

6b. School of Venice – Vicentino's battle scene in the Palazzo Ducale (*AKG*)

7. Baroque apotheosis – Veronese's battle scene (*Art Archive*)

8a

8b

8a. Rococo – Sebastian de Caster's stylized battle (*AKG*)

8b. Romantic – Luna's Don Juan in shining armour (*Bridgeman Art Library/Palacio del Senado*, Madrid)

KEY

1 Contingent led by Mehmet Scirocco and Caur Ali outflanks the Christian left. Barbarigo intercepts and fights alone until supported by the four galleys from the Vanguard, then by Canal's Naples–Venice group. Padilla's squadron of ten Naples galleys approaches.

2 The Crete–Dalmatia–Cephalonia group defeats the Istanbul galleys to its front.

3 Papal–Genoa group including Cervantes's *Marchesa* charges through the gap opened by Ambrogio Bragadino's galleass, hooks right to attack the Guard of Rhodes from the rear.

4 Giovanni Contarini's Venice–Islands group defeats Syria–Anatolia galleys disordered by Antonio Bragadino's galleass, wheels north.

5 Marco Quirini's Naples–Venice group and Orsino's Genoa–Papal group crush the Guard of Rhodes. Quirini's group wheels north, Orsino's group south.

6 Galleasses of Andrea di Pesaro and Francesco Duodo break up the Ottoman line.

7 Concentration of the strongest units on both sides around the fleet flagships.

8 Left of Ottoman Battle overlaps right of Holy League Battle held by Malta galleys, overwhelms isolated lantern galleys of Savoy (Moreto) and Niccolò Doria (Polidoro).

9 Cardona's late-arriving Vanguard group charges into the gap between the Holy League Battle and the Right Wing.

10 Inner Venetian squadron savaged by Anatolia galleys and Algiers galliots.

11 Outer Venetian squadron breaks ranks, returns in disorder and is almost annihilated by Istanbul–Negroponte galleys and Algiers galliots led by Uluch Ali and his son Kara Bey.

12 Inner non-Venetian squadron rows desperately to catch up with Doria's outer group, shadowing the leading element of the Ottoman Left Wing led by the Beylerbey of Syria.

a melon on a 50 foot (15m) pole from horseback, were unsighted during the crucial period when they could have fired accurately beyond practical handgun range.

Don Juan's highly experienced instructor–advisers would have concurred heartily with Napoleon when he declared that the moral is to the physical as three to one, and typically a force that has previously enjoyed easy success can be disproportionately dismayed when it encounters an unexpected check, whereas a more stubborn resolve will infuse those with defeats and humiliations to avenge. There is an irreducible element of uncertainty and luck in any military engagement, but when two sides more or less equal in numbers, equipment and training meet to put their preparations to the test, the issue comes down to countless individual adjustments to the plans made by admirals and generals, and these will be conditioned by mental predispositions as well as by circumstances. The schematic that follows seeks only to provide the conceptual clothes hanger – the blood-drenched garment of battle was stitched together in the unknowable hearts of men.

All accounts agree that the fighting lasted about four hours, that the coastal wings engaged well before the Battles crunched together, and that Uluch Ali and Doria manoeuvred for position for at least an hour after that, making the sequence in *Map 12* reasonably exact. If we estimate a ten-minute interval between each stage from the first contact at the top of the map at approximately 1200 hours, the leading Ottoman squadrons on the seaward flank would have attacked Doria's group at 1400, which is about right. Venier later grumbled that the wings never fully shook out into line and did not conform with the Battle, and some manoeuvres at the end of the battle can only have taken place if by that time *both* Holy League wings were sharply refused well to the west of the Battle. As we shall see in *Map 13*, the final positions would have been along the lines of an obtuse triangle, with the coastal wing bunched along the sandbars off the islands of Khoutsilaris and Scoupas, and the outer wings folding back upon the centre after extending far out to sea.

The coastal battle began when Scirocco and Caur Ali increased speed and led their groups around the enemy flank, such that Barbarigo's lantern was facing north-west when he finally intercepted them. He did so alone, for he had pulled well clear of the rest of his command and was sorely beset before the four Venetian galleys from the Vanguard led by Vincenzo Quirini and including Barbarigo's nephew Marino Contarini arrived to support him. These five greatly outnumbered galleys fought a desperate battle during which Barbarigo, who had raised his visor so that his voice should not be muffled, was hit in the eye by an arrow and was taken below to die. Despite repeated wounds Federico Nani, his captain, and Count Silvio di Porcia, embarked with his suite of gentlemen adventurers on the Venetian flagship, rallied their men and held out against the simultaneous attack of three or four Ottoman galleys in addition to Scirocco's. The men on Vincenzo Quirini's lantern fought on as bravely after he was nearly decapitated, probably by a shot from a swivel gun, while Marino Contarini had the satisfaction of seeing his guns disable the Alexandria flagship before he too was mortally wounded. They were nonetheless close to defeat when the group led by Antonio da Canal in his arrow-proof quilted suit came to their rescue, including two Naples ponentinas in addition to his lantern, and quickly subdued Caur Ali's galliots, while from the west ten Naples galleys sent by Santa Cruz from the Reserve and led by the Padilla brothers approached.

By seizing the tactical opportunity offered by the shallows Scirocco committed an operational blunder in addition to overextending his wing, for in the overall scheme of a general turning manoeuvre led by the over-loaded seaward flank he should have encouraged the enemy to advance into the trap. Instead the inner contingents of the Holy League Left Wing, led by Giovanni Contarini and Marco Quirini, themselves performed turning manoeuvres, reloading their bow armament as they went, while beyond them the two Bragadino galleasses also crawled north to cut off retreat to Lepanto. Giovanni completed his kinsman Marino's work and sank the enemy flagship, and after he plucked the mortally wounded Scirocco from the water, he judged it merciful to have him beheaded. Now Toledo's warning about the temptation of a friendly shore was proved correct as the surviving galleys of the Ottoman Right Wing broke and raced to beach themselves on the nearby islands. Some were prevented from doing so by rebellions among the slave rowers, others became stranded on sandbars well short of safety, and the waters were soon full of struggling Ottomans in panicked flight, as described in one of Ercilla's best octaves:

Cual con brazos, hombros, rostro y pecho,	One with powerful arms and chest
el gran reflujo de las olas hiende;	bends the surging waves to his will;
cual sin mirar al fondo y largo trecho,	another to deny the depths,
no sabiendo nadar allí lo aprende;	learns all at once the swimming skill;
no hay parentesco, no hay amigo estrecho,	no human bonds this test endure,
ni el mismo padre al caro hijo atiende:	not even fathers sons will mind:
que el miedo, de respetos enemigo,	for fear, the foe of all that's pure,
jamás en el peligro tuvo amigo.	in danger friend can never find.

The Alexandria galleys had formed part of Ali's fleet at Cyprus, and the attrition of their long campaigning season, plus their all-slave rowers, made them the weakest in the Ottoman fleet. But their collapse is also testimony to the ferocity of the Holy League counter-attacks led by Canal and Quirini, the most experienced senior officers in the Venetian fleet. No prisoners were taken here, and parties landed in small boats to hunt down the Ottomans who reached dry land. The relentless savagery of this mopping-up operation was remarked upon by all, without explaining it, but a detailed breakdown of the Holy League Left Wing reveals that it contained the majority of the galleys from Crete and other Venetian overseas dependencies. Three centuries later, Finlay estimated that although there were 30,000 Greeks serving in the two fleets, they 'exerted no more influence over the conduct of the warriors who decided the contest than the oars at which the greater part of the Greeks laboured'. Fernando de Herrera went even further and denounced the whole people:

¿Por qué, ingrata, tus hijas adonaste	Unworthy Greece, why gave you your daughters
en adulterio infame a una impía gente,	To shameful union with adulterers
que desea profanar tus frutos,	Who lust to violate your heritage?
y con ojos enjutos	Why shed you no tears before you engaged,
sus odiosos pasos imitaste,	Slavish their hateful footsteps to follow,
su aborrecida vida y mal presente?	Your past by villainous present swallowed?
Dios vengará sus iras en tu muerte,	God by your death will assuage his anger,

que llega a tu cerviz con diestra fuerte	His strong right hand your neck will sever
la aguda espada suya; ¿quién, cuitada,	With his keen sword. Wonder, as you cower,
reprimirá su mano desatada?	Who will now contain that unbound power?

Contradicting these sneers, most of the 9,000 Greeks, mainly from Crete, who served in the Holy League fleet were concentrated in the group that took on and overthrew the strong Istanbul squadron stationed south of the Alexandria galleys. Most accounts ignore this, but the official history prepared for the Venetian Senate praised Greek bravery and skill:

> The Italian foot won much commendations, nor did the Spaniards merit lesse praise; but of all the rest, the *Grecians*, shewing both courage and discipline; as those who were most accustomed to that kind of Militia, and knew all the advantages in wounding, and in escaping being wounded, behaved themselves with great praise and profit.[9]

Paruta made a distinction between Italians and Venetians so here, remarkably, he was valuing the Greek contribution above that of his own compatriots. He might also have said the same for the Dalmatians, the only Holy League galley lost on this wing being the *St Nikola* from Cres, which charged ahead of the rest and was overwhelmed. But we should not underestimate the stiffening effect of the Hapsburg infantry on board the Venetian galleys, and of the well-manned Naples ponentinas engaged on this wing. Canal's timely counter-attack was strengthened by two of them, while the sight of Padilla's approaching squadron cannot have failed to dishearten the Ottomans. At the junction between the Holy League Left Wing and Battle, the six Naples galleys that crunched in alongside his four enabled Marco Quirini to penetrate the Ottoman line and wheel north, sweeping quickly along the Ottoman line to achieve the final encirclement. This crucial breakthrough was facilitated by the Papal–Tuscan *La Elbigina* and three Genoese galleys stationed in the middle of the Left Wing, which charged through the gap opened by Ambrogio Bragadino's galleass and swung south to attack the side-by-side flagships of the Beys of Negroponte (Mehmet, son of Salih Reis) and of Rhodes. It was here that Cervantes received his crippling arquebus wounds, for although they too had been long at sea, these were some of the most experienced crews in the Ottoman fleet, and the troops on board included the all-firearms Janissaries and azaps of the élite Guard of Rhodes.

The northern shoulder of the Ottoman Battle consisted of the Rhodes contingent and a strong Istanbul squadron led by Hassan, Barbarossa's son. The left of the Holy League Battle, led by Paolo Giordano Orsino and including four Genoese lanterns as well as Caracciolo's Papal galley *La Toscana*, was opposite the junction of the two enemy squadrons and engaged Hassan's group, while Marco Quirini's Venice–Naples group took on the Guard of Rhodes. The latter collapsed after a fierce but relatively short engagement, the Venetian-born Bey of Rhodes prudently fleeing in a longboat before *La Elbigina* took his flagship. The group led by Hassan resisted longer, but when he was killed and his flagship taken the Ottomans lost heart, and Orsino's group was released to row behind the Ottoman line to the centre, where it delivered the finishing stroke to the command element. There Orsino took possession of the flagship of Mahmud Reis, Agha of the Janissaries, while Caracciolo captured the lantern galley of Fleet Treasurer Mustafa Esdri, once the ill-fated Papal flagship at Djerba. This was, after the *Sultana*, the richest prize of all, but we may doubt whether the Papal coffers were replenished with any of the treasure it contained, for it was a regrettable fact that the desperate storming parties – not for nothing known in English as 'forlorn hopes' – invariably ran amok once the objective was taken, and only a suicidally foolhardy officer would have attempted to deny them their traditional prerogative to kill and loot until their temporary madness passed.

By the time Orsino's group arrived on the scene, the outnumbered concentration of enemy lantern galleys at the centre had been over-whelmed in a desperate struggle against the most powerful units in the Holy League fleet and Santa Cruz's division. Despite artistic renderings showing the galleasses of Andrea di Pesaro and Francesco Duodo in the thick of the battle they did not get back into it until near the end, which suggests they may have been even further ahead of the Holy League line than shown in *Map 12*. This being the case, after the initial disruption their main contribution to the battle would have been to loom over the Ottoman line of retreat, like the Bragadino galleasses to the north. This in turn means the Ottoman line would have had time to re-form after passing on either side of them, as an infantry-minded army would have, but instead charged in squadrons like the cavalrymen most of them were. The result was that instead of the comprehensive double envelopment proposed by Uluch Ali at the council of war on 5 October, in the centre as in the north the Ottoman charges were contained and outflanked, and it was they who were encircled.

For envelopment to succeed the enemy must thrust his head into the noose by continuing to attack after his flanks have given way, and Ali Pasha had correctly anticipated that the Holy League fleet would not do him this favour. In his scheme the centre had only to hold until the Left Wing swung around behind the enemy Battle, and the fury of his attack drew in Santa Cruz and kept the attention of the Holy League commanders fixed to the front for about two hours, more than long enough for Uluch Ali's outflanking manoeuvre to succeed. As we shall see it did not, but in the light of the moral ascendancy won at Preveza and Djerba it was reasonable to expect the Holy League right to break, and we cannot fault Ali for not foreseeing that Uluch Ali would be held up until the centre was lost. On land much the same tactics had carried the Ottoman standards to victory after victory for over a century – but this was not a rapid battle of manoeuvre, rather a ponderous clash among what were in effect hundreds of mobile field fortifications, and it was their proven ability to storm these that argues so strongly in favour of the Tercio pikemen as the 'secret weapon' of the Holy League.

There was little room for tactical finesse once the crowded lantern galleys massed at the centre of both fleets came together. The *Sultana* slammed into the port bow of *La Real* and reared over the side at the level of the fourth rowing bench, but the advantage was lost because the Janissaries of the boarding party in the bow had been winnowed by artillery. Instead it was the Christians who gained the first lodgement and for an hour or more attacks and counter-attacks surged back and forth across the walnut planking and inlaid chequerboard deck of the Ottoman flagship, each of the great warships receiving a steady flow of reinforcements from supporting galleys through their stern companionways.

And so it was that battle was joined with the greatest vigour and fury, and with noise so great it seemed not only that the galleys must be tearing each other apart, but that the sea itself roared in protest at the appalling clamour, whipping its previously calm surface into foaming waves, and deafened men could no longer hear each other, and the sky vanished from their sight amid the darkening smoke from the flames.[10]

Ali Pasha was a renowned archer and used an exceptionally powerful bow, and possibly it was one of his arrows that Herrera records skewering a *La Real* soldier through both his breast and back plates. This would have been direct fire at very close range, for those further from the firing line, like Onorato Caetani in the stern of his galley a little to the south, were hit repeatedly by arrows without effect. However, even the fine armour worn by Cárdenas could not save his life when an Ottoman swivel gunner hit him squarely on the breastplate as he was leading troops forward after the first Christian surge was thrown back from the *Sultana*. The victim might as easily have been Don Juan, who cannot have carried a shield because he wielded the double-handed sword now in the Madrid Naval Museum, which was used to punch and parry like a quarterstaff, with one mailed hand on the blade and the other on the long hilt. Despite all Philip II's injunctions Juan became involved in hand-to-hand fighting, for he suffered a knife wound (*cuchillada*) in the ankle and did not recall receiving it, as he admitted with fatal candour in his post-battle letter to his half-brother. The king could have drawn two conclusions from this, the first that Juan was still a disobedient hothead, but the second and more telling that he was not wise enough to conceal his defiance of royal commands by attributing his wound to an arrow. Thus it could be that in the moment of triumphantly proving himself as a military commander, Juan failed to meet the more exacting standard set for him by Philip.

Two positions to the north of *La Real* on the flagship of Genoa, young Alessandro Farnese was even less constrained by princely dignity and prudence than his younger uncle Juan, and accompanied by only one soldier leaped aboard one of the lantern galleys from the Ottoman Reserve division, which attacked close behind the command group. In an extraordinary feat of arms he led the way along the length of the enemy vessel, hacking men down with a sword in either hand, until at the end his black armour was painted over with blood.

Venier, sandwiched between the Genoa and fleet flagships, should have benefited from their proximity but instead he was assaulted by two Ottoman lanterns and hard pressed until Giovanni Loredan and Catarino Malipiero from Santa Cruz's division came to his support. Caetani reported that Loredan also joined in his simultaneous battle with Kara Khodja and 'Dali' (presumably Delhi Bey from the Ottoman reserve), and that at the end, 'in one as in the other there were only six Turks left alive'. Loredan's galley was later overwhelmed, and it is an indicator of the relative fighting power of vessels involved that Venier's was the only Holy League lantern to get into difficulty in the wild mêlée at the centre, and that the only ones lost there were the three Venetian line galleys of Loredan, Malipiero and Gian'Battista Benedetti.

Not all the Venetian galleys in the Battle and the Reserve pulled their weight. When Caetani cast off his prizes and rowed to assist the Right Wing, he observed 'some Venetian galleys behind me closing in on the galleys I had taken. Their soldiers climbed aboard [and] must have found great booty, for those corsairs were very rich. Too bad, I did not give it another thought. I had not come to loot but to fight in the service of Our Lord'. Even allowing for the low esteem in which the Venetians were held by their allies, there are too many reports of this sort of opportunism to dismiss, and the fact that despite their relatively low fighting power they ended the battle with almost as many prizes as the more effective Hapsburg contingents argues strongly that it was generalized. Most of the Ottoman galleys on the northern flank ran ashore and were burnt in place, and the Venetian galleys on the southern flank were mauled, so whence could they have accumulated so many prizes if not from picking up the 'kills' of the Battle ponentinas after they rowed on to continue the fight elsewhere?

There is a rich tradition of female combatants in Hispanic military culture, from Isabella of Castile who rode in armour with her troops to the *soldaderas* of the Mexican Revolution. At Lepanto this was upheld by one María la Bailadora (Dancer) aboard one of the Spanish galleys, who is said to have disguised herself as a man to be with her soldier lover and to have fought with the best. It would be surprising if she were the only one, as sexual dimorphism was less pronounced at the time and women formed an integral part of the armies of the day, particularly in the Tercios where they functioned as the commissariat, if we can stretch the word to cover the haphazard manner in which the Hapsburg soldiers were fed and clothed.

The Spanish troops fought their way to the mainmast of the *Sultana* twice, and were pushed back both times, but during the third assault Ali was killed by a bullet in the forehead. Someone hacked off his head and brought it to Juan, who was bitterly offended by this lack of respect for a worthy adversary and ordered the head, and possibly the bearer, thrown overboard. But after the banner of Islam was lowered from the masthead and the cross hoisted in its place there ensued the same sudden collapse of Ottoman resistance that followed the deaths of Scirocco and Hassan. Christian chroniclers speculated on the reasons for the fragility of Ottoman morale, some claiming – heedless of the hollow laughter from the ghosts of St Elmo and Famagusta – that they normally broke if their first attack failed. Tending to confirm the alternative interpretation of a progressive collapse from the north, the galleys to the right of the Ottoman command element were from Nauplia and Mytilene and therefore would have had a high proportion of conscripted Greeks, whereas the two Istanbul and the Gallipoli contingents to the left would have been manned mainly by Islamic volunteers, the Tripoli Janissaries would have been concentrated in the galleys and all were backed by a strong contingent of Tripoli corsair galliots. This might not by itself have mattered so much, for opposite them the right of the Holy League Battle was actually stronger than the left, with a lower proportion of Venetian galleys and more lanterns. More significant was that the extremity of the extended Ottoman line could charge into the opening gap between the Holy League Battle and the Right Wing.

The blame for this must rest with Santa Cruz, who had his division much too closed up and rushed it prematurely to the battle in the centre, instead of using it to cover the gap on the right. Although there was no love lost between them, there is no disputing the feline assessment Requeséns made of his fellow grandee's performance in a private letter to the king:

. . . if there is any fault to be imputed to him it is that he charged too soon, because it seems the reserve division he was entrusted with should not be committed until the battle is going badly, and then to the place most in need of it, but instead he charged soon after we did, and better to err on this side than to hang back and after all the marquess and his galleys fought most honourably.[11]

Santa Cruz was a shrewd naval tactician, as he later proved in consecutive crushing victories over Franco-Portuguese fleets off the Azores in 1582–83. Had he lived to lead the Armada in 1588, who knows? Maybe, if we still spoke English, we would do so with a Spanish accent. It is not difficult to deduce that no less shrewd political tactics lay behind his actions at Lepanto – had he committed to the right and the centre been lost, and with it the king's half-brother, his career would have been over. If the right was lost the blame could be, and was, firmly fastened around the neck of his rival Doria. The soundness of this calculation was shown when he was appointed Juan's successor as Captain General of the Sea, and Gian'Andrea did not finally inherit his great-uncle's title until after Santa Cruz died.

Three lanterns were overwhelmed on the left of the Holy League Battle, the Papal *La Fiorenza* commanded by Tomasso dei Medici, Gian'Andrea's *La Doria* under Giacomo di Casal, and the Maltese flagship of Pietro Giustiniano, the prior of Messina. Caetani saw *La Fiorenza* overrun by one galley and six Tripoli galliots, suggesting the Christian galleys on this flank may have been less closed up than in our maps, and only Medici and sixteen others survived. Bearing in mind the intense blood feud between the Knights of Malta and the North African corsairs, and that the Venetian galleys on either side would have been disinclined to go to their assistance, the fate of the *Doria* was probably sealed by being stationed next to them. Alas for those who like their heroes to have the strength of ten because their hearts are pure, the heinous Order of Saint John covered itself with glory at Lepanto, handily defeating the first Ottoman wave although outflanked and outnumbered. Giustiniano's flagship – and, presumably, the *Doria* – only succumbed when Uluch Ali swung north to crumple the overextended Holy League Right Wing.

Sharing in the initial glory and likewise in the way of Uluch Ali's later onslaught, Juan de Cardona's Vanguard group of three Sicilian galleys and the flagship of the Genoese David Imperiale fought alongside the Maltese. Requeséns falsely reported to the king that his kinsman Cardona was in place when he conducted his pre-battle review, but here as in the north the Vanguard group arrived just in time to parry an Ottoman outflanking manoeuvre. Imperiale and every man with him died, and of the 500 soldiers of the Sicilian Tercio embarked on Cardona's galleys only fifty survived, he himself being wounded by an arrow, knocked down by an arquebus shot on the breastplate and finally badly burnt by an incendiary grenade. The fighting here was exceptionally fierce and prolonged, as epitomized by the fever-racked Sergeant Martín Muñoz of the Sicilian *San Juan*, who refused to be sent away with the sick and later fought his way to the mainmast of an Ottoman galley. Riddled with arrows and with one leg blown off he fell between two benches and raised himself to say 'Gentlemen, let each of you do as much', before lying down to die. Ercilla wrote of it:

Quien por saltar en el bajel contrario	One who leapt to board the rival ship,
era en medio del salto atravesado;	was speared in flight through the body;
quien por herir sin tiempo al adversario	another, desperate to come to grips,
caía en el mar de su furor llevado;	hurled by his passion into the sea;
quien con bestial designio temerario	another, made reckless by blood lust,
en su nadar y fuerzas confiado	and trusting to his strength and skill,
al odioso enemigo se abrazaba,	embraced that which he hated most,
y en las revueltas olas se arrojaba.	his foe in the rebellious waves to kill.

Requeséns also reported that no other royal galley (evidently excluding the Genoese) was more badly damaged than Cardona's, and that he had been very wise to stay with the Maltese galleys and not attempt to close the gap with the Right Wing, where he would have been isolated and over-whelmed. He no doubt had in mind the fate of the flagship of Savoy and the vice-flagship of Niccolò Doria, the innermost galleys of the Right Wing, which succumbed to the Istanbul group led by the Bey of the Arsenal and were found adrift after the battle, without a living soul on board to tell of the desperate battle they fought. Beyond them, the Right Wing consisted of a block of fourteen Venetian galleys, the majority from Crete, Dalmatia and Corfu, then a group of twelve ponentinas including three lantern galleys from Genoa and Naples, with one from Sicily, then a further group of eleven galleys mainly from the Venetian mainland, and finally two Papal, two Neapolitan, one Sicilian and six Genoese galleys, including five lanterns, led by Gian'Andrea. These became detached from one another and each in turn was pounced upon by a section of the Ottoman Left Wing.

Uluch Ali's command peeled off to attack in three phases, the first consisting of thirteen Anatolia galleys and eleven Algiers galliots, probably assisted by the Governor of the Arsenal's group after it had dealt with the isolated Savoy–Doria lanterns, which assaulted the inner Venetian group. Christian casualties here were severe, with no survivors from five of the galleys. But they cannot have been fewer among the Ottomans, especially after Soranzo's *Christ over the World* blew up, devastating the enemy galleys around it. Above all, the Venetians here contained an attack that would have tipped the scales in the struggle around the Malta galleys and Cardona, something for which no previous account has given them credit. It is less easy to be generous about the performance of the outer Venetian group, which defied Doria's authority and turned back. This not only opened a yawning gap between the two ponentina groups but also threw the Venetian galleys into disorder, and their indiscipline was savagely punished when Uluch Ali and his son Kara Bey descended on them with thirty-five Istanbul and Negroponte galleys, and a second group of twelve Algiers galliots.

Some ran, some stayed and fought, but the Venetians here imposed little delay on the development of the Ottoman battle plan. Pietro Bua, captain of the Corfiot *Gold and Black Eagle*, surrendered and his galley was towed to Lepanto, where he suffered the same ghastly fate as Marc'Antonio Bragadino at Famagusta. Possibly there was some history of vengeance for past wrongdoing involved, as no doubt there was for the formal execution of the Syrian captain Demir Bey after the battle, the only Ottoman captive to be put to death in this manner. More noteworthy is that a large group of Ottoman warships – Diedo states fifteen galleys and ten galliots – took themselves out of the battle at this stage to accompany this single prize back to port, which argues that their captains could see enough of developments further north to convince them there would not be any more. In the absence of all except the barest description from the participants, we must deduce what happened on this wing from the Holy League casualties and from such fragile deductive threads as these. The most straightforward written explanation (for most of the reporting was done by word of mouth) is contained in the letters from Requeséns to the king already cited, in which he damned with faint praise while pretending to smooth feathers ruffled by the less than fulsome report written by Juan's secretary immediately after the battle:[12]

> Gian'Andrea admits [literally 'confesses'] that *La Real* started fighting long before he did; but this was because the left wing of the enemy ... stretched out and did not wish at that time to attack, and that he did not charge Uluch Ali because he was fourteen or fifteen galleys inside the point of his horn, and Gian'Andrea's being the leader of ours all the enemy galleys outside [Uluch Ali's] attacked him frontally, and that it was his duty to fight their leader, which he did, and that when he could charge he charged and fought with many galleys and caused many to be taken or run aground.

The claws emerged from the velvet paw at the end of the letter, where Requeséns sweetly observed that no weight should be attached to the fact that Gian'Andrea's galley was one of the least damaged in the whole fleet, for after all as the great Duke of Alba had once said, 'one cannot die in despite of God's will ...' What Requeséns did not know was that Philip had given Doria a copy of the miraculous Virgin of Guadelupe, sent to him by the Archbishop of México, to which Gian'Andrea in his own report had the wit to ascribe his delivery from the ball that spattered him with the remains of his personal servant. However, it appears he did not close with the enemy sufficiently to suit Sigismondo Gonzaga, the field master of the Sardinia Tercio, who was likewise miraculously spared when a cannonball smashed the fragata to which he was descending from Doria's flagship in order to get more involved in the fighting.[13]

Marc'Antonio Colonna applied the stiletto in his report to the Pope, mentioning that before the battle Doria had taken down a fine crystal lamp from the stern of his flagship, and concluding like his namesake in *Julius Caesar* that of course this meant nothing, for Doria was an honourable man. The Pope concluded that Doria had behaved more like a corsair than a Christian general, in which opinion he was encouraged by the Venetians, anxious to draw attention away from the dismal showing of their own galleys on the Right Wing, who accused Gian'Andrea of rowing out to sea in order to avoid combat and to save his property from damage, although in fact his flagship was followed by only two others belonging to him, and the rest were distributed throughout the fleet. Doria's squadron was involved in desperate fighting when the Istanbul and Syria galleys at the point of the Ottoman horn finally attacked, one Papal and one Sicilian galley being wiped out and the Centurione lantern leased by the City of Genoa crippled before the inner Hapsburg squadron closed the gap created by the defecting Venetians. During this struggle artillery captain Federico Venusta of the Lombardy Tercio, on board one of Gian'Andrea's galleys (*La Damigella* – The Damsel), suffered the misfortune of having a grenade explode in his hand. He hacked off the remains, had a chicken carcass fastened over the stump (presumably to protect the exposed nerve ending) and fought on, saying his right hand remained to avenge the left.

The attack led by Uluch Ali and Kara Bey scattered the outer Venetian squadron but was halted by the inner one, Cardona's group and the Knights of Malta. All except three men on Giustiniano's lantern were killed, he himself badly wounded but saved by having a large sum of money to hand when the Algerines found him in his cabin. At this point a number of Christian galleys including *La Real*, which must first have paused to 're-bench' and bring up rowers from below deck, began to make their way towards the embattled Right Wing. As the smoke cleared Uluch Ali saw this, and realized that the battle at the centre was lost and that the galleys approaching from the north prevented him from sailing before the wind back to Lepanto. At the same time the group towing the Maltese flagship was forced to cut her loose when part of Doria's squadron swept back into the battle from the south, led by the Naples lantern *La Guzmana* whose captain was killed in the ensuing battle. The other Maltese galleys then recovered their shattered flagship, finding more than 500 corpses on board including those whom Giustiniano had bribed, joy at this double restoration of his fortune speeding his recovery from wounds that foe and friend alike had believed certainly mortal.

As indicated in *Map 13*, during the final phase of the Ottoman defeat the defining factor for those that managed to escape was the degree to which they were able to sail into the westerly breeze. Those galleys that carried

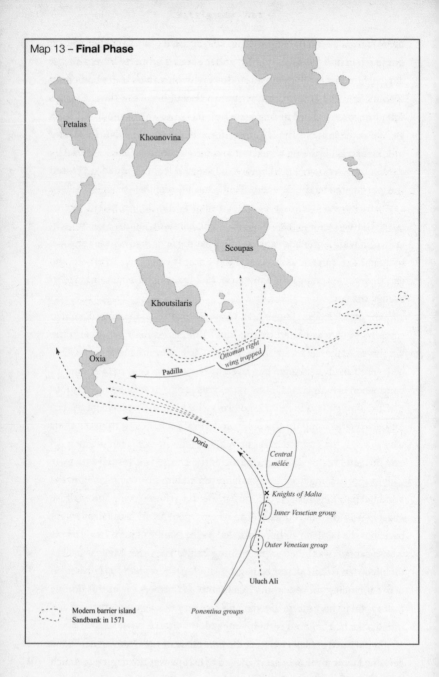

Map 13 – **Final Phase**

Petalas

Khounovina

Scoupas

Khoutsilaris

Oxia

Ottoman right wing trapped

Padilla

Doria

Central mélée

✗ Knights of Malta

Inner Venetian group

Outer Venetian group

Uluch Ali

Modern barrier island
Sandbank in 1571

Ponentina groups

spare rowers would have enjoyed an advantage, but nearly all would have been exhausted from hours of combat and the wind now became the arbiter of their fortunes. Uluch Ali led the way towards the gap between Khoutsilaris and Oxia islands, with the group led by Doria conducting a lateral pursuit and preventing him from tacking away to the south-west. Padilla's squadron of Naples galleys from the Reserve, which had remained aloof from the massacre of the Ottoman Right Wing, now rowed to close this gap, forcing Uluch Ali's group to point further into the wind. As we saw in Chapter Two, only a well-handled galley employing quarter rowing could match the performance of the galliot into the wind, and those that could not were trapped between Doria, Padilla and the island of Oxia. At the risk of sounding like counsel for the defence, it is a tribute to Doria's skill in husbanding the energy of his rowers that despite covering more distance than any other galleys in the fleet, they were able to remain on one flank of the fleeing Ottoman survivors while Padilla closed from the other. Of about thirty galleys and galliots following Uluch Ali, only eight were able to round the southern point of Oxia, and the rest were forced to surrender or run aground.

All commentators were no less forcibly struck by the vast wrack of battle left behind than they had been by the crack of doom with which it began. There were, of course, no contours to divide the horror into psychologically manageable portions, as would have been the case on land, and even veteran soldiers were stunned. Of the many attempts to describe it, the one by Guillén's anonymous memoirist is the most comprehensive:

> The greater fury of the battle lasted near to four hours and was so bloody and horrendous that the sea and the fire seemed as one, many Turkish galleys burning down to the water and the surface of the sea, red with blood, was covered with Moorish coats, turbans, quivers, arrows, bows, shields, oars, boxes, cases and other spoils of war, and above all many human bodies, Christian as well as Turkish, some dead, some wounded, some torn apart, and some not yet resigned to their fate struggling on the surface in their death agony, their strength ebbing away with the blood flowing from their wounds in such quantity that the sea was entirely coloured by it, but despite all this misery

our men were not moved to pity for the enemy . . . although they begged for mercy they received instead arquebus shots and pike thrusts.[14]

One might suspect hyperbole, but over 40,000 men were killed at Lepanto, and a further 10,000 survived their wounds (see *Appendix D*) – most of the 45–50,000 gallons of blood metaphorically spilled flowed with ghastly literalness into the calm waters of the gulf. It was the second highest body count of any single-day European battle after the almost unimaginable 58,000 killed in an area of less than a square mile at Cannae in 216BC.[15] Had it lasted any longer it would have ended, as many battles of the era did, with the complete physical exhaustion of both sides. This to emphasize that it was not just the scale but also the intensity of the struggle that makes it stand out from the many other battles of the period. As the fighting subsided, those not dying or attending to them, or busy finishing off the wounded and looting on the captured enemy galleys, would have cursed as brave men always have to note the involuntary shaking of their hands and the weakness of their knees as the adrenalin ebbed from their systems, and after the cheering was over some would have succumbed to nausea, while all would have suffered from post-battle melancholy.

CHAPTER ELEVEN

EPILOGUE

Heroic collective endeavours, of which there are few convincing examples in peacetime, provide the relatively rare occasions when the history of humankind is clearly distinguishable from the behaviour of anxiously expectant mice running around in a vast chamber pot. Lepanto was one such exalted moment and by all the rules of drama we should leave our story with the sun setting on the blood-red sea, as the battered Holy League fleet towed its prizes to the shelter of Petalas, a touch of bathos supplied by the brief reconciliation of Don Juan with Venier when the old man came on board *La Real* to pay his respects. Juan addressed him as 'father' and they embraced, weeping on each other's shoulders, and any playwright worthy of his trade would bring down the curtain at that point, to a cathartic ovation from an audience left breathless by the unremitting crescendo of Act III. Alas, I cannot, but should some latter-day Cecil B. De Mille (with the necessary FX resources) be interested, I would be delighted to write the screenplay.

The fleet was driven to shelter from a strong south wind that came up in the evening, which blew a number of unclaimed enemy galleys ashore. This was the happy time for the host of small craft that are never counted in the Holy League order of battle, whose shallower draught permitted them to row with confidence among the shallows around Khoutsilaris, Scoupas and Oxia, a venture not without peril with so many Ottoman survivors trapped on the islands. Dawn the next day brought armed competition from the captains of the fleet, Venetian sopracomiti to the fore, who scavenged the wrecks in fragatas and longboats. Mutual, founded, suspicions of bad faith over the distribution of the spoils promptly poisoned relations between the Venetian admiral and Don Juan (see *Appendix D*), and so it went down the chain of command. The first letter Venier received from the Senate in response to the news he sent of the victory, on which more below, anxiously instructed him to use all possible diligence to ensure that his captains did not take possession of the casks, artillery, goods and biscuit from the captured Ottoman galleys, because they would certainly sell them back to the enemy.[1]

Most of the beached galleys were burnt in place, either by their own crews or by the Christians because, after the liberated Greeks were put ashore, the Holy League lacked the resources to man them or even to take them in tow. It is evident that if every able-bodied male along the Gulf of Patras was swept up into the Ottoman fleet immediately before Lepanto, the return of the survivors with weapons in their hands and vengeance in their hearts explains the wave of revolts that came close to overwhelming the Ottoman authorities in the area. As news of the battle spread, the revolt in the Maina peninsula spread to neighbouring Monemvasia and threatened the provincial capital of Mizistra. Later revolts in Epirus were encouraged when the Venetian reinforcements took Margariti and retook Sopoto in late November, while the Greek Orthodox clergy roused their congregations to rebellion in Thessaly, Negroponte and even on the island of Lemnos and the sacred peninsula of Mount Athos.

Lesure considers this not *a* crisis, but *the* crisis of the Ottoman Empire, the turning point in its previously light-handed domination of what had once been the Greek Byzantine or eastern Roman Empire. Some have suggested that an historic opportunity to liberate Greece was lost, but as we have seen that would have required a unity of purpose conspicuously lacking in the Holy League. Don Juan was alert to the possibility and in December sent Requeséns, by then Governor of Lombardy, a letter requesting large amounts of weaponry from the Milan arsenal to arm the Greeks. However, the Ottoman authorities moved quickly to control the turbulent priests by ordering all Metropolitans to Istanbul, on pain of death and the loss of the immunity hitherto enjoyed by their churches and monasteries. There was not even an opportunity to exploit the victory by seizing Lepanto or another important Ottoman fortress immediately after the battle, for the ships carrying the land element were still at Corfu. In addition the

Ottoman devastation of the Venetian islands had been so comprehensive that even Venier's fleet had to send buyers to Messina for essential supplies. In his letter of 10 October Juan warned Philip that he foresaw no prospect of further gains because 'there is so much that must be done to refurbish this fleet, in which every day brings news of greater damage and of other matters without which it neither can nor should go forward'.

Chief among the 'other matters' was that relations with Venier had once more reached breaking point after he sent fast galleys to bear the news of the victory to Venice ahead of Don Juan's own dispatch. This was more than a flagrant breach of protocol, for it meant that news of Lepanto first reached the Pope and even King Philip via the Venetian courier network, claiming a prominence for their version of events that has dominated the historical record ever since. This said, it was presumptuously tactless of Juan not to write to his half-brother immediately after the battle. Instead, on 9 October (the day before he wrote to Philip), Juan sent old García de Toledo a lost letter in which, to judge from Toledo's reply of 5 November, he gave him fulsome credit for the victory. Nor did he have the wit to thank his king for the honour of commanding the fleet, something of which he was to be delicately reminded when Philip finally received his letter of 26 October a month later. Compounding Juan's casualness, this arrived just before the one sent on the 10th by hand of Lope de Figueroa, field master of the Granada Tercio, accompanied by the great banner of Islam. The king had received the news from the Venetians on 29 October and cannot have been pleased to be kept waiting for nearly a month before the arrival of Juan's dispatches. His reply of 29 November does not, of course, make reference to this, but in the following extract I have italicized indicators of frostiness:

> I have been pleased to a degree which it is impossible to exaggerate, and not less by the details I have learned [from others] of the great courage and conduct you showed in the battle, by planning and ordering it all in person, as was fitting for so important an affair, and by distinguishing yourself as well by directing others, which has without doubt been a chief cause and part of this victory. And so to you, after God, ought to be given, as I now give, the honour and thanks for it, *and some thanks are also due to me, because this great business has been*

accomplished by a person so near and dear to me, and so much honour and glory, in the sight of God and the world, gained for the good of Christendom and the detriment of its enemies. As regards your coming here this winter, you will already have been informed of the order sent to you [in late September] to winter at Messina, and the causes of it, and although it would delight me exceedingly to see you now, and exchange personal congratulations on occasion of this great victory, I postpone this pleasure because your presence [there] was never more important, in order that you may, with vigilance, see that no time is lost in the coming year, and to pursue the great achievements that may be hoped for from the recent success and your own eminent ability. *And touching the affairs of importance, which you say you must communicate with me, you may do so in writing or by means of persons to whom such matters may be confided.*

Juan's return to Madrid also risked overshadowing the imminent child-birth of Philip's niece–wife, who duly produced the heir we have seen receiving a palm frond from Titian's ineptly portrayed angel, the laurel wreath of victory in its other hand clearly intended for the bulbous head of the proud father. The Hapsburg fleet dispersed shortly after it arrived back at Messina on 31 October to a magnificent welcome, and there was nothing for Juan to do other than to take his pick of the ladies anxious to bed the victor of Lepanto. The inevitable result was that quite large numbers of people today can legitimately (*sic*) claim descent from him. Among his more serious liaisons was one with Diana di Falangola, whose daughter Juana de Austria, born on 11 September 1573, lived in Naples all her life and was to build the memorial plaza in honour of her father still to be seen on Capri.[2] But what would have been ample fulfilment for any normal young man was scant consolation for a frustrated prince, and on 24 November 1571 Juan wrote a sad little letter to Gian'Andrea Doria that captures the moment:

Every day I feel more alone; and when I am not, I wish I were alone again. I wish for, but expect no comfort from these times. I am con-sumed with envy for those [times] spent by others, happier but no more in love than I am. I spend my time building castles in the air, but in the end all of them, and I, blow away in the wind . . .[3]

Human interest aside, the main story in the aftermath of Lepanto was the speed of the Ottoman recovery. On receipt of the first news of the disaster, sent from Santa Maura by Uluch Ali on 8 October and received by Mehmet Sokolli in Istanbul on the 24th, salvoes of dispatches went out, among them a reply instructing Uluch Ali to 'gather together the dispersed vessels and stay in whatever place you judge appropriate'. Another dispatch to the Bey of Delvina ordered him to abandon Sopoto, removing the guns and razing the walls, another still to the Bey of Yanya clamoured for information:

> How many soldiers have you available for your defence? Are the
> fortress garrisons complete and what is their state? What information
> do you have of the vile infidels? Where exactly are they? What are
> their plans and preparations? Where do they intend to attack? What
> well-known persons among them were killed in the battle and how
> many of their ships were sunk? Has anyone from Our imperial fleet
> arrived in your territory? In what state are they? How many ships
> have arrived? Which ones? [4]

From this in conjunction with the summary of the first report, which stated simply that 'the Imperial fleet encountered the fleet of the wretched infidels and the will of God turned another way', we may conclude that Uluch Ali, logically enough, had been unable to report the full extent of the catastrophe and that Sokolli entertained hope that the fleet might merely have been dispersed. Selim, in Edirne at the time, received a fuller account a day earlier in a report sent by Pertev dated 12 October, which reported the death of Ali and the total destruction of the Ottoman Battle. Instead of the termination order he no doubt expected, Pertev received a reply from Selim reassuring him that 'a battle may be won or lost. It was destined to happen this way according to God's will'. Also on the 28th, Sokolli wrote to Pertev in the same vein:

> The outcome in war is uncertain. It must have been the will of God
> that matters should have developed in this manner, as it appeared in
> the mirror of Destiny. It is the verdict of God, the High, the Great, the
> Master and Benefactor. We hope that God the all-powerful will soon
> make possible all kinds of humiliations and the crushing of the
> enemies of the Religion and the Empire.

Lesure concludes that the immediate effect of Lepanto was to concentrate all power in the hands of Sokolli, who undertook the immediate defence of the Empire and reconstruction of its armed forces with an astonishing attention to detail, down to telling the frontier commanders how and where to post lookouts. But there was no shift of power in the Porte, proof of which is that the Grand Vizier acted immediately and decisively; that Selim did not reply to Pertev until he had consulted with Sokolli; and that it was the Sultan who returned to Istanbul rather than Sokolli to Edirne. Much of what followed was the feet paddling frantically underwater while the imperial swan sailed serenely on the surface, as Sokolli conveyed in an interview with the Venetian ambassador Barbaro in which he compared their loss of Cyprus to an amputation of an arm, the loss of the fleet to a shave after which the beard would grow back stronger than ever. He even tried to order counter-attacks against Corfu and overland against Dalmatia, using Tatar mercenaries, but whether these plans were ever realistic is impossible to establish – what matters is that they were taken very seriously by Venice, which could consequently make only limited attempts to exploit the victory (including the pointless recovery of abandoned Sopoto), and by the court of Vienna, which saw no reason to abandon its dearly bought neutrality.

On the same day as the replies to Pertev, an imperial firman appointed Uluch Ali to be the new Kapudan and Beylerbey of the Isles, while Hassan, the 21-year-old grandson of Barbarossa, replaced him as Beylerbey of Algiers. Sokolli ordered Uluch Ali to gather up Pertev and his survivors, see to the general defence of the Aegean archipelago, and patrol a line between Negroponte and Chios. As the situation deteriorated in southern Greece the tone of Sokolli's dispatches became more menacing, with blame finally fastened on the Beys of Lepanto, Morea and Mizistra, who were all transferred to Asia Minor. On 10 November Sokolli wrote to Ahmed Pasha at Ohrid demanding a list of all those who had left the standards, who were to be deprived of their timars. The result of Sokolli's micro-management was that wary passivity became the norm among the beys, none prepared to take any initiative without authority from the Porte – for example the Bey of Lemnos, who was harshly rebuked for refusing to oppose a Venetian raid without orders. Officials acting in a vengeful manner towards Christians in their areas also had to be rebuked and reparations paid. Finally, after the Beys of Scutari, Prizren and Dukagin let the Venetians occupy the ruined fort of Budua without resistance, they were warned that they deserved dismissal and 'all sorts of punishments'.

To add to the chaos, plague broke out all along the Adriatic coast to Morea, and most of the settlements at risk had become ghost towns. The thousands of Greeks freed from Ottoman slavery also posed a problem, both sides expecting a general uprising. Although Selim initially wanted to massacre all Christians within the empire, Sokolli's argument that they were too valuable as a labour force prevailed. But draconian reprisals were taken against the rebellion in Patras, including the execution of the Metropolitan. The Metropolitan of Salonika was only saved from a similar fate by the payment of 2,000 ducats to Sokolli by Patriarch Michael Cantacuzène, and his fellow priests from Mount Athos were shipped to Istanbul in chains.

The vital effort was the reconstruction of the fleet, directed by Uluch Ali, who was renamed Kilich Ali (Ali the Sabre) by Selim himself after he sailed into Istanbul harbour at the head of eighty-seven vessels, flaunting the captured banner of the Knights of Saint John. Sokolli expansively told him that 'if necessary we shall make anchors of silver, rigging of silk and sails of satin. If you lack anything for the equipment of a vessel, you have only to ask it of me'. In a private letter to Selim, Kilich Ali revealed that he was not comfortable in Sokolli's embrace: 'I beg my blessed Padichah not to require me to address myself to him through other persons; I will speak further on this matter when I am next to you'. Whatever his reservations, he worked closely with the Grand Vizier to rebuild a larger fleet than the one lost at Lepanto, including eight *maonas* modelled on the Venetian galleasses. Every galley had at least one heavy gun on the centreline, the galleasses had twenty, and from this time forward the majority of Ottoman troops on land and sea were equipped with handguns. In May 1572, the French ambassador reported that although the new crews and soldiers were inexperienced, the timber used to build the fleet unseasoned, the cannon of suspect quality and Kilich more feared than trusted, nonetheless:

> . . . in five months they have built 150 vessels with all the artillery and
> equipment needed and, yes, they have resolved to continue this pace
> for an entire year. . . . Already their general is prepared to set out to

sea at the end of this month with two hundred galleys and one
hundred galliots, of corsairs and others, without the Grand Seigneur
having used a single écu in his treasury for this huge expense. In short,
I should never have believed the greatness of this monarchy, had
I not seen it with my own eyes.[5]

We have seen how this ambassador's fine diplomatic work was undone
by the Saint Bartholomew's Day massacre, and this was only one of the
reasons Philip II had to celebrate the gruesome event. The Ottoman court
was also in contact with the Protestant rebels in the Netherlands and sent
them financial assistance, although as the following letter of solidarity
reveals, the Porte was a bit vague about precisely who they were fighting:

... the faithless one they call Papa does not recognize his Creator as
One, ascribing divinity to Holy Jesus (upon Him be peace!) and
worshipping idols and pictures he has made with his own hands, thus
casting doubt upon the Oneness of God and instigating many servants
of God to that path of error.... Since you have raised your swords
against the papists and since you have regularly killed them, Our
imperial compassion and royal attention have been devoted in
every way to your region.[6]

Whatever contribution the Ottomans made was simply fuel to a fire
well stoked by others, for the situation of the Spanish authorities in the
Netherlands deteriorated sharply as the 1572 campaigning season
approached. When Elizabeth of England closed her ports to the Dutch
corsairs known as 'Sea Beggars', as much to eliminate non-tribute paying
competitors to her own sea dogs as to oblige the Duke of Alba, who had
been fulminating about them for years, they promptly seized Brielle in
Zeeland and reopened the land war in the Low Countries. The Treaty of
Blois between France and England of 22 April 1572 was the culmination
of Alba's worst fears and a triumph for Sir Francis Walsingham (c. 1530–90),
Elizabeth's ambassador in Paris and founder of the tradition of covert operations that, along with the fortitude of her soldiers, has so often redeemed
Britain from the dithering incompetence of her ruling élite. Elizabeth was
unfazed by the Saint Bartholomew's Day massacre, and employed the
leverage of the French alliance to obtain from Alba the Treaty of Nijmegen,

by which English troops were withdrawn from the Netherlands and those who rebelled against either of the two sovereigns were not to be granted sanctuary in the territory of the other. Philip II was incensed by an agreement that lifted the threat of Spanish subversion from the Protestant succession in England in exchange for measures Elizabeth intended to implement anyway, and coupled with the exhaustion of Alba's personal fortune it heralded the end of his stern administration.[7]

On 4 December the preceding year there had been a pale shadow of a traditional Roman Triumph for Marc'Antonio Colonna, Onorato Caetani, two Papal nephews and the Chevalier Romegas, whom last we saw seizing the rich prize that precipitated the siege of Malta, and who had fought on the Papal flagship at Lepanto rather than with his brother knights on the *Saint Pierre*. Sneered at by the French and Spanish ambassadors, and boycotted by the Orsini and other prominent Roman nobility, about 5,000 men (including a mere 170 prisoners) paraded through the city to a reception by the Pope in Saint Peter's Square, after which everybody fired their guns and went home. Spanish disapproval led to the event being underplayed to the point of becoming an embarrassment to those involved, the absence of any Hapsburg representatives explicitly intended to underline that the days of Papal temporal power were over.[8]

Moral authority was another matter. Whatever those in high places may have thought privately about the probable political consequences of a resonant Hapsburg–Roman Catholic victory over the infidels, publicly the battle of Lepanto was celebrated across Europe, even among diehard Huguenots and the Protestant fundamentalists of Scandinavia and the British Isles. Montaigne probably spoke for many when he commented that Don Juan had won a handsome victory, but that it was to be seen whether this represented any permanent change in God's intentions for humanity. The fact that he should even have mentioned the possibility, however sardonically, indicates that many across Europe construed Lepanto as the harbinger of a new dawn. Irritating though it doubtless was to both the Venetian Senate and the court in Madrid, the prestige of the victory accrued correctly and overwhelmingly to Saint Pius V, the overt organizer, paymaster and propagandist of the Holy League, and the one participant who had put all his cards on the table from the first.

Hagiography has it that upon the hour of battle Pius was at prayer in his private chapel and felt it in his heart, and that several hours later he rose from his knees to inform his attendants that he had seen the Virgin Mary guiding Her soldiers to victory. When the Venetian courier arrived to confirm the news he lapsed into near-blasphemous hyperbole by comparing Don Juan to John the Baptist. If the prematurely elderly pontiff truly expected the Messiah to appear on the heels of the victory, he should perhaps have relaxed a regime of austerity bordering on masochism in order to live long enough to see it. As it was, although he did not survive to celebrate the Saint Bartholomew's Day massacre, he was also spared the chagrin of witnessing his beloved Holy League accomplish almost nothing during 1572, as Philip kept his fleet in Messina through most of the campaigning season while his attention was riveted on France and the Netherlands. The Pope died on 1 May 1572, his prescient last words said to be:

> You will not easily find one who has a stronger desire to root out the enemies of Christ's faith and the cross . . . but by the blood of Christ I entreat you to elect as speedily as possible a zealous man in my place, and not to choose him on mere worldly considerations. The year is already far advanced. What has to be done must be done soon, and if this year passes without some memorable action, men's spirits will fail them and our labour and the great victory will be fruitless.

So it proved. Venetian enthusiasm was almost unbounded and they committed resources to the 1572 campaign they had withheld the previous year, yielding without demur to the Spanish request that Venier should be removed. Although retaining his title, he was informed that Giacomo Foscarini had been appointed to replace him as fleet commander in a letter dated 9 February 1572. Colonna and Foscarini dared do little against the new Ottoman fleet and the tactical skill of Kilich Ali, and even when joined by Don Juan and an even larger Hapsburg contingent than he had commanded in 1572, the only trophy to be taken during the 1573 campaign was a large lantern galley captured off Modon thanks to the rashness of its young commander on the anniversary of Lepanto. This was Hassan, Barbarossa's grandson and Beylerbey of Algeria, who was killed by his Christian slave rowers.[9]

Those who have generally given the Venetians more credit than they deserve for Lepanto have also harshly judged their decision to cut their losses and make peace on whatever terms they could get following this debacle. Since we have not subscribed to the first, the second requires less explanation. Cyprus was beyond recovery; the war was strengthening Ragusa at the direct expense of Venetian trade; plague-decimated Dalmatia, Cattaro and the Ionian islands were hostages to fortune; and there was no reason to expect that Philip would permit Don Juan to act any more promptly and decisively in 1573 than he had in 1572. Accordingly the terms of the capitulation were signed by Marc'Antonio Barbaro in Istanbul on 7 March 1573, which included the payment of a 300,000-ducat indemnity, and although the annual tribute of 8,000 for Cyprus was cancelled, payment for Zante was increased from 500 to 1,500. The *status quo ante bellum* was restored in Dalmatia and Albania, but to rub salt in the wound the ruins of Sopoto had to be formally surrendered. The news was not well received in Rome, Pope Gregory XIII ordering the Venetian emissaries from his presence lest he do violence to them, and immediately annulling the annual *sussidio* of 500,000 ducats and the donation by the clergy of 100,000. To the palpable relief of the Venetian ambassador to Madrid, Philip took it calmly:

> He showed no emotion except that, when towards the end he learned that the conditions of peace had been accepted, there was a slight ironical twist of the lips. It seemed as though his Majesty wanted to say, without interrupting us, 'O-ho, you've done it, just as they all told me you would'.

During the winter of 1571–72, Philip retained hope that Uluch Ali might still be won over by bribery, and in a coded letter to Juan dated 20 February 1572 urged him 'to do all possible to attract the said Aluchali to what is desired'.[10] Perhaps under instruction from Sokolli, still spinning his web of lies around the credulous Barbaro in Istanbul, evidently Kilich Ali somehow managed to keep the Spanish king on the hook despite his recent elevation to the inner circle of Ottoman power. Disabused by the new kapudan's flawless performance of his duty during 1572, Philip at last became receptive to the urging of Gian'Andrea Doria to act against Tunisia while Ottoman naval power was concentrated in the eastern Mediterranean. Doria had received the news of the Venetian capitulation with poorly concealed glee, and his advocacy coupled with his close personal influence over Juan brought about the occupation of Tunis on 11 October 1573, beyond the end of the normal campaigning season to give time to consolidate the conquest.

This proved to be a disastrous dispersion of effort, for in late August 1574 the Ottoman fleet commanded by Kilich Ali himself and a land force under the young convert Cicalazâde Sinan Pasha struck not at Tunis but at La Goleta, which had always been the key to Tunisia. Pagano Doria, Gian'Andrea's brother, was killed when the fortress fell on 25 August and the newly built fortifications of Tunis were surrendered by Gabriele 'Gran Gabrio' Serbellone on 13 September. As one last reminder of the deep family ties that have held Italian society together through centuries of political fragmentation, he was ransomed not by his parsimonious Hapsburg employer but by relatives including his cousin Carlo Borromeo, the Cardinal Archbishop of Milan. In return he was among the foremost of Borromeo's deputies during his outstandingly brave relief efforts during the plague and famine that assaulted Milan in 1576, for which even had he not also been so instrumental in the Reformation of his church, Borromeo deserved the canonization pronounced in 1610, a mere twenty-six years after his death.

Although few would have predicted it at the time, the wars for the Mediterranean were essentially over until French and British imperialism came to redraw the map in the nineteenth century. Selim died in 1574, and uneasy relations between his successor Murad III and Grand Vizier Mehmet Sokolli, coupled with menacing noises off from the resurgent Persians, put a stop to any further major military adventures in the Mediterranean. The Spanish monarchy again defaulted on its debts in 1575, followed by an attempt to subvert its Genoese creditors and the interruption of payment to the Tercios in the Netherlands, which led to the sack of Antwerp in 1576. Sir Francis Drake's circumnavigation of the world, raiding Spanish possessions as he went, and renewed war between the Ottoman and Persian empires, led to informal truces between Madrid and Istanbul in 1577–78, and finally a regularly renewed formal truce in 1580. There was one last twitch of rivalry at the margins of both when an Ottoman-backed pretender seized the throne of Morocco in 1576, but after he, the monarch he had overthrown and King Sebastian of Portugal were all killed when the last anti-Islamic Crusade was destroyed at Alcázarquivir in 1578, it became, as it has remained, an independent kingdom, while Philip added Portugal to his compendium of kingdoms.

The last years of Requeséns were made miserable trying to contain the revolt in the Netherlands, and after he died in 1576 from a recurrent tumour on the spine, his body was taken back to Barcelona by a fleet of twenty galleys commanded by Alexandre Torrelles, captain of the flagship of Santiago at Lepanto. He was succeeded by Juan de Austria, who had a no less frustrating experience in the service of his opaque and indecisive half-brother until he died of typhus in 1578, having earlier detected in time an assassin sent by Walsingham. Clearly many dishonourable things were contained in the correspondence between the court and both Requeséns and Juan, for Philip ordered it all burnt along with Juan's personal documents, and the historiographic void has been filled by much colourful speculation. The suspicion that Philip may have ordered his half-brother's assassination is an extrapolation from the murder of Juan's secretary, which the king undoubtedly sanctioned on the basis of poisoned advice from his own private secretary. The no less popular myth that there was some deep plot afoot for Juan to marry Mary Queen of Scots (against whom Walsingham's designs were successful), was largely an invention of the desperate English Roman Catholics, clutching at straws.[11]

Thus the grim, unromantic reality of the sequel. Let us close instead with an episode that illustrates a lost commonality of manliness and generosity across the religious divide, and which explains why Chesterton wrote the following in Don Juan's memory and honour:

> Dim drums throbbing, in the hills half heard,
> Where only on a nameless throne a crownless prince has stirred,
> Where, risen from a doubtful seat and half attainted stall,
> The last knight of Europe takes weapons from the wall,
> The last and lingering troubadour to whom the bird has sung,
> That once went singing southward when all the world was young.

At Lepanto, the flagship of Santiago captured the lantern containing Ali Pasha's two young sons as it rowed in a last-ditch effort to assist their father. After they were transferred to *La Real*, Juan gave up his personal chambers to the boys, and two days later they encountered the son of

Bernardino de Cárdenas, in tears for the death of his father. The elder of the two rebuked him: 'Is that all? I, too have lost my father, and also my fortune, country and liberty, yet I shed no tears.' He died in Rome a few months later, but the younger one was freed by Juan upon receipt of an imploring letter from his sister, Selim's niece, in May 1573. Ever the gallant, Juan returned her gifts along with her brother and several other captives, his reply closing with the words: 'You may also be assured that, if in any other battle he or any other of those belonging to you should become my prisoner, I will with equal cheerfulness as now give them their liberty, and do whatever may be agreeable to you'.[12]

Not to be outdone, the Sultan sent Juan a browbeatingly munificent cargo including costly fur robes, silk and gold bedcovers, tapestries, tableware, inlaid saddles and stirrups, stands of scimitars, bows and arrows, along with an even more generous message:

> From Selim, son of the most high, most invincible and most glorious Suleiman II, Emperor of the Turks, King of Kings, Conqueror of Provinces, Extinguisher of Armies, terrible over lands and seas, to Juan de Austria, captain of unique virtue. I do not disdain to give you a place amid my high considerations and to bestow upon you my golden seal, which brings happiness to those who look upon it. Your virtue, most generous Juan, has been destined to be the sole cause, after a very long time, of greater harm than the sovereign and ever-felicitous House of Othman has previously received from Christians. Rather than offence, this gives me the opportunity to send you gifts. You should consider and esteem them as more valuable than anyone else has had the fortune to receive because they come from one who, being the greatest among men, makes himself almost your equal by his present generosity. . . . Pray God to guard you from our anger.

Whatever his failings in correspondence with the king his half-brother, Juan knew how to rise to the occasion of an immensely flattering tribute from the son of the emperor who alone had matched the stature and ambition of his own father Charles V:

> By hand of Acomatz of Anatolia, eunuch, I have had the good fortune to receive your letter and gift. The one honours your generosity, the

other bears witness to the virtue it has pleased God to grant me for the defence of his faithful and the offence of the House of Othman. I, a boy of little experience as you then styled me, initiated the harms your armies may have suffered. Consider how far this may develop, now that you admit me to be a Captain of unique virtue. For all I thank you and in return I return to you the Greek spy you sent among us to discover our preparations. I could have had him killed, [instead] I have not only spared his life but have also permitted him to view at his leisure my provisions and intentions, which are to make perpetual war upon you. Consequently you will not disdain to count as of sovereign degree among your so great grandeurs that Juan de Austria, the Christian, has accepted the gifts of Selim, Turkish Emperor, and has replied to his letters.[13]

Selim was dead within the year, Juan followed him four years later, and Sokolli was assassinated the year after that. I may not have been able to bring down my curtain on the moment when the destinies of all three crossed so spectacularly, but I can close with the memory that illuminated the last dark hours of the victor of Lepanto, the moment when under a clear blue sky, in the sight of the Christian host and in the face of an enemy fleet that stretched from horizon to horizon, he danced a carefree galliard on the forecastle of the mighty *La Real* with God's following breeze ruffling his hair.

PRINCIPAL ACTORS

Alba, Duke of (Fernando Alvarez de Toledo), field master-general of the Spanish army in the Netherlands, sent practical advice on soldier psychology to Don Juan.

Ali Pasha – see Müezzinzâde.

Andrade, Gil de, Knight of Malta, Spanish commodore, fought on *La Real*.

Appiano, Jacobo, commander (under Colonna) of Tuscan galleys leased by Pope.

Arcos, Count Vinci Guerra di, Italian colonel of German infantry.

Asiz Agha, Bey of Gallipoli, killed.

Austria, Juan de, Knight of the Golden Fleece, Holy League commander-in-chief.

Avalos, César de, commander of the troops on ships that remained behind at Corfu.

Barbarigo, Agostino, Venetian QMG of the Sea, commander of Left Wing, killed.

Bazán Alvaro de – see Santa Cruz.

Bazán, Alonso de, brother of Santa Cruz, Spanish commodore.

Beteta, Marquess of (Bernardino de Cárdenas), Knight of Malta, Spanish commodore, killed on *La Real*.

Biccari, Count of (Ferrante Caracciolo), chronicler who fought on the Papal–Tuscan *La Toscana* at the right of the Holy League Battle.

Bonelli, Michele, nephew of Pius V, nominal commander of two galleys.

Bracciano, Duke of (Paolo Giordano Orsino), commander of the fleet infantry.

Caetani – see Sermonetta.

Canal, Antonio da, aka 'Canaletto', QM and co-commander of Crete fleet.

Cárdenas – see Beteta.

Cardona, Juan de, Knight of Malta, captain general of the Sicily fleet and commander of the Vanguard.

Caracciolo – see Biccari.

Carrillo – see Priego.

Carrillo, Luis, son of the Count of Priego, commanded skiff platform on *La Real*.

Centurione, Julio, commander–proprietor of a galley leased by Genoa.

Cervantes, Miguel de, soldier on *La Marchesa*.

Colonna – see Paliano.

Colonna, Pompeo, brother of the Duke of Paliano.

Colonna, Prospero, field master of the Venetian infantry.

Contarini, Giovanni, leader of a mixed Venice and Islands group on the Left Wing.

Contarini, Gian'Battista, chronicler.

Contarini, Marino, nephew of Barbarigo and member of the Vanguard group that came to his support, killed.

Córdoba – see Sessa.

Corgna, Ascanio della, nephew of Pope Julius III, Holy League field master-major.

Crillon, Louis des Balbes de Berton de, French Knight of Malta, fought on the *Saint Pierre*.

Dardagan Pasha, Bey of the Arsenal, killed.

Diedo, Gerolamo, chronicler who interviewed Venetian captains shortly after the battle.

Djafer Agha Pasha, Bey of Tripoli (Libya), escaped.

Doria – see Melfi, Torriglia.

Doria, Niccolò, commander–proprietor of two galleys leased by Spain.

Farnese – see Parma.

Figueroa, Lope de, field master of the Granada Tercio.

Florence, Duke of – see Tuscany.

Giustinian, Pietro, Knight of Malta, prior of Messina and commander of Malta galleys.

Gonzaga – see Mantua.

Gonzaga, Ottavio, colonel of the Lombardy Tercio.

Gonzaga, Sigismondo, field master of the Sardinia Tercio.

Grimaldi, Giorgio, commander–proprietor of two galleys leased by Spain.

Guzmán, Juan de, Spanish commodore, fought on *La Real*.

Hassan 'the Venetian', Bey of Rhodes, escaped.

Hassan Pasha, son of Barbarossa, killed.

Herrera, Fernando de, aka 'The Divine', poet and chronicler.

Imperiale, David, commander–proprietor of two galleys leased by Spain.

Kara Bive (?) Pasha, Beylerbey of Syria, killed.

Kara Khodja, Agha and Bey of Valona, killed.

Caur Ali, famous Alexandrian (?) corsair, killed.

Legni, Andrea di, commander of Savoy galleys.

Leyva, Sancho Martínez de, commander of the fleet that remained in Spanish waters.

Lodron, Count Alberico di, Italian colonel of German infantry, killed.

Lomellino, Piero Battista, commander–proprietor of five galleys leased by Spain.

Mahmud Haider, Bey of Mytilene, killed.

Mahmud Reis, Agha of the Janissaries, captured.

Mantua, Duke of (Guglielmo Gonzaga), became duke in 1550, sent troops.

Mare, Stefano di, commander–proprietor of two galleys leased by Spain.

Medici – see Tuscany.

Mehmet, Bey of Negroponte, son of Salih Reis, killed.

Mehmet Scirocco, Bey of Alexandria, commander of the Right Wing, killed.

Mehmet Sokolli Pasha, Ottoman Grand Vizier 1565–79.

Melfi, Duke of (Gian'Andrea Doria), proprietor of ten galleys (counted as twelve for payment) leased by Spain and commander of the Right Wing.

Mendoza, Rodrigo de, Spanish commodore.

Mon(t)cada, Miguel de, Knight of Santiago, field master of the Naples Tercio.

Montefieltro – see Urbino.

Müezzinzâde Ali, Kapudan Pasha 1569–71, killed.

Mustafa Esdri Pasha, Ottoman fleet treasurer, captured.

Negrone, Gian'Ambrogio, proprietor of four galleys leased by Spain.

Orsino – see Bracciano.

Padilla, Martín de, Spanish commodore, led Reserve squadron to assist the Left Wing.

Padilla, Pedro de, Knight Commander of Santiago, colonel of the Naples Tercio.

Paliano and Tagliacozzo, Duke of (Marc'Antonio Colonna), Grand Constable of Naples, commander of Papal fleet, Holy League deputy commander.

Pallavicini, Sforza, *condottiere* in the service of the Empire and Venice.

Parma, Prince of (Alessandro Farnese), son of Ottavio, nephew of Juan.

Parma, Duke of (Ottavio Farnese), became duke 1547, married Margaret de Austria, Juan's half-sister; signatory of the Holy League, sent troops under son Alessandro.

Pertev Pasha, co-commander Ottoman fleet, escaped.

Paruta, Paolo/Paulo, wrote history of the Cyprus war and Lepanto in the 1590s.

Porcia, Count Silvio di, Venetian infantry commander.

Priego, Count of (Fernando Carrillo), Juan de Austria's ADC, with him on *La Real*.

Quirini, Marco, aka 'Stenta', QM and co-commander of the Crete fleet.

Quirini, Vincenzo, leader of Vanguard group that came to the support of Barbarigo, killed.

Requeséns y Zúñiga, Luis de, Grand Commander of Castile (order of Santiago), locum for the king and deputy to Juan de Austria.

Romegas, Mathurin d'Aux Lescout de, French Knight of Malta, on Colonna's flagship.

Rovere – see Urbino.

Santa Cruz, Marquess of (Alvaro de Bazán), captain general of Naples fleet and commander of the Reserve.

Santa Fiora, Count of (Mario Sforza), field master-general of the Italian Hapsburg infantry.

Sarna, Count of (Vicenzo Tutavila), colonel of the Lombardy Tercio.

Sauli, Bendinelli, commander–proprietor of a galley leased by Savoy.

Savoy, Duke of (Emanuele Filiberto), duke from 1553, Hapsburg commander under Philip II at Saint Quentin 1559, signatory of the Holy League, sent three galleys under Legnì.

Savoy, Francesco di, deputy commander Savoy galleys, killed.

Scetti, Aurelio, condemned rower and chronicler who fought on the Papal–Tuscan galley *La Pisana* at the right of the Holy League Battle.

Serbellone, Gabriele aka 'Gran Gabrio', Knight of Malta, Prior of Hungary, Inspector of Fortresses in Naples and Sicily 1566, Governor of Tunis 1573–74.

Sereno, Bartolomeo, chronicler who fought on Caetani's flagship at the right of the Holy League Battle, later a Benedictine monk.

Sermonetta, Prince of (Onorato Caetani), captain of the Papal Guard.

Servia, Fr Miguel, Juan's confessor, chronicler who served on *La Real*.

Sessa, Duke of (Gonzalo Fernández de Córdoba), grandson of the Great Captain.

Sforza, Paolo, colonel of the Lombardy Tercio.

Spinola, Ettore, commander of the Republic of Genoa galleys.

Toledo – see Alba; Villafranca.

Torrelles, Alexandre, captain of the Requeséns (Order of Santiago) flagship.

Torriglia, Marquess of (Pagano Doria), brother of Gian'Andrea, killed at Goleta 1574.

Tuscany, Grand Duke of (Cosimo dei Medici), Duke of Florence 1537, Grand Duke from 1569, leased twelve galleys under Appiano to the Pope.

Tutavila – see Sarna.

Uluch/Kilich Ali, Beylerbey of Algiers, escaped, appointed Kapudan Pasha.

Urbino, Prince of (Francesco Maria della Rovere), in representation of his father.

Urbino, Duke of (Guidobaldo della Rovere), duke from 1538, signatory of the Holy League, sent troops under son Francesco Maria.

Vázquez Coronado, Juan, Knight of Malta, Spanish commodore, captain of *La Real*.

Venier, Sebastiano, commander Venetian fleet, duce 1577–78.

Villafranca, Marquess of (García de Toledo), Captain General of the Sea 1563–68, mentor of Don Juan.

ESTIMATE OF FORCES

HOLY LEAGUE

	Contingent	Galleass	Super-flag	Lantern	Galley	Total
VENICE	Mainland	6	–	6	56	68
	Crete	–	–		29	29
	Dalmatia	–	–	–	8	8
	Ionian Is.	–	–	–	8	8
	SUBTOTAL	6	–	6	101	113
HAPSBURG	Naples	–	1	5	23	29
	Genoese	–	3	13	11	27
	Spain	–	1	6	5	12
	Sicily	–	1	1	4	6
	SUBTOTAL	–	6	25	43	74
OTHER	Pope	–	2	2	8	12
	Malta	–	–	1	2	3
	Genoa City	–	1	2	–	3
	Savoy	–	1	2	–	3
	SUBTOTAL	–	4	7	10	21
	TOTAL	6	10	38	154	208

OTTOMAN

	Contingent	Lantern	Galley	Flag	Galliot	Total
MAINLAND	Istanbul	21	51	–	–	72
	Anatolia	2	25	2	–	29
	Gallipoli	1	10	–	–	11
	SUBTOTAL	24	86	2	–	112
GREECE	Negroponte	4	15	–	–	19
and	Nauplia	1	10	–	–	11
AEGEAN	Rhodes	1	9	–	-	10
	Mytilene	1	9	–	–	10
	SUBTOTAL	7	43	–		50
EGYPT	Alexandria	1	21	–	–	22
and SYRIA	Syria	2	11	–	–	13
	SUBTOTAL	3	32	–	–	35
CORSAIRS	Algiers	2	–	3	20	25
	Tripoli	2	5	3	8	18
	Valona	1	1	2	7	11
	SUBTOTAL	5	6	8	35	54
	TOTAL	39	167	10	35	251

DISTRIBUTION BY BATTLE STATION

Holy League

Contingent		Left	Main	Vanguard	Right	Reserve
VENICE	Mainland	17	23	4	11 *	11
	Crete	18	3	–	8	–
	Dalmatia	3	1	–	3	1
	Ionian Is.	4	1	–	3	–
	SUBTOTAL	*42*	*28*	*4*	*25* *	*12*
HAPSBURG	Naples	8	3	–	6	12
	Genoese	3	10	1	13	–
	Spain	–	10	–	–	2
	Sicily	–	1	3	2	–
	SUBTOTAL	*11*	*24*	*4*	*21*	*14*
OTHER	Pope	1	7	–	2	2
	Malta	–	3	–	–	–
	Genoa City	–	2	–	1	–
	Savoy	–	2	–	1	–
	SUBTOTAL	*1*	*14*	*–*	*4*	*2*
	TOTAL	**54**	**66**	**8**	**50**	**28**

* two galleasses not engaged, not counted.

Ottoman

Contingent		Right	Main	Left	Reserve
MAINLAND	Istanbul	11	37	20	4
	Anatolia	13	–	13	1 (Chios)
	Gallipoli	–	11	–	–
	SUBTOTAL	*24*	*48*	*33*	*5*
GREECE	Negroponte	1	–	18	–
and	Nauplia	–	11	–	–
AEGEAN	Rhodes	–	10	–	–
	Mytilene	–	10	–	–
	SUBTOTAL	*1*	*31*	*18*	*–*
EGYPT	Alexandria	25	–	–	–
and *SYRIA*	Syria	8	–	5	–
	SUBTOTAL	*33*	*–*	*5*	*–*
CORSAIRS	Algiers	–	–	25	–
	Tripoli	–	7	11	–
	Valona	–	1	9	–
	SUBTOTAL	*–*	*8*	*45*	*–*
	TOTAL	**58**	**87**	**101**	**5**

Don Juan sailed from Messina with 208 galleys, six galleasses and twenty-two ships, a count broadly confirmed by Kara Khodja, Bey of Valona, who conducted a daring daylight inspection of the Holy League fleet in mid September. Contrary winds kept the ships, with about 3,500 troops (mainly German) on board, in Corfu, along with four galleys 'cannibalized' by the rest of the Venetian fleet, which still remained undermanned by comparison with the larger western (*ponentina*) galleys of the allied fleets. On the day of battle there were also two unidentified Venetian stragglers. For the Ottomans we must depend on the list in Contarini, purged of duplications. This was compiled from prisoner interrogations and therefore may exaggerate their numbers, for the captives would have been alert to leading questions, and motivated to say what their questioners wanted to hear.

Most estimates give the Holy League about 26,000 soldiers, although this figure includes the Germans left behind at Corfu, but for a useful breakdown we must allocate them (and the seldom mentioned rowers and crew) according to a nominal schedule, trusting that averaging will smooth out anomalies. One such was the 300-plus fighting men on board Don Juan's flagship, made possible because she was pushed by two other galleys and was able to 'de-bench' by laying boards across vacated rowing benches. A comparison of the dimensions of *La Real* with those of the main Venetian types gives an idea of how little deck space was available, bearing in mind that the bow spur accounted for about a tenth of overall length, and that soldiers could stand only in the forecastle, the stern, on the midships gangway, on narrow firing steps along the sides, and on the small platform on either side normally occupied by the oven and the skiff (see *Diagram 1*). Ottoman line galleys were more flimsily built but generally longer (50m) and wider (6m) than even the largest Venetian galleys, while some of the Hapsburg galleys captured at Djerba in 1560 fought at Lepanto as lantern galleys under the banner of Islam. The distinguishing characteristic of the galliot was that it had a proportionally longer waterline and deeper keel, hence a narrower beam and less deck space.

Dimensions	*La Real*	*Galleass*	*Lantern*	*Galley*
Weight empty (tonnes)	236	600	180	140
Length overall	60.0m	54.0m	46.3m	41.7m
Beam	6.2m	8.6m	5.5m	5.1m
Width rowing frame	8.4m	10.8m	7.3m	6.7m
Draught	2.1m	3.0m	1.8m	1.7m

Contracts between the Spanish crown and the Genoese entrepreneurs confirm that the defining difference between a line galley and a lantern was the number of soldiers they were capable of carrying, normally fifty on the former and seventy-five on the latter. However, at Lepanto the *ponentinas* carried far more, the extra soldiers boarding immediately before the battle from the smaller vessels that accompanied the fleet. The 'super-flagship' category is a statistical convenience to allow for the flagships packed with the personal suites of noble-men and senior officers. All were listed as lanterns, for which Spain paid one and a half times the line galley rate, which explains the discrepancies between administrative documents and actual hull counts. With the caveat that armies of this period were not organized in such a manner as to simplify life for histori-ans, Hapsburg soldiers (commanders in parentheses) were from the Tercio of Granada (Lope de Figueroa), Tercio of Naples (Miguel de Moncada and Pedro de Padilla), Tercio of Sardinia (Sigismondo Gonzaga), Tercio of Sicily (Diego Enriquez), Tercio of Lombardy (Counts Paolo Sforza of Santa Fiora and Vicenzo Tutavila of Sarna), and troops from Germany (Italian Counts Vinci Guerra di Arcos and Alberico di Lodron). Also on the Spanish payroll were 1,200–15,000 mercenaries, half recruited by Paolo Giordano Orsino and the rest by a host of other captains. Princes Alessandro Farnese of Parma and Francesco Maria della Rovere of Urbino brought contingents of about 300–400 men each in repre-sentation of their fathers, who were signatories of the Holy League in their own right. Knights of the crusading orders from as far afield as Burgundy and Germany, and others listed as 'captains of adventure', about 2,500 in all, served at their own expense, against the hope of participation in the fruits of victory.

Figueroa's Tercio boarded the Spanish galleys, Enriquez's Tercio the Sicilian, Farnese and his men took ship on the City of Genoa galleys, Rovere and his on those of Savoy. About 900 Germans were on the Imperiale, Mare and Negrone galleys, Orsino's men were on the Grimaldi galleys and two of Lomellino's, and the Venetian galleys took about 4,100 men from the Tercios of Naples and Lom-bardy. Enriquez himself was on Juan de Cardona's flagship, Padilla with his brother Martín on the Naples galleys in the Reserve, Figueroa and Moncada had side commands (*arrumbadas*) of about fifty men each on *La Real*, Tutavila was with the Naples galleys, Sforza was with Gian'Andrea, and Gonzaga with Lomellino. Oddly, the Venetian nobleman Niccolò Suriano and his suite were on a Spanish galley, while Ascanio della Corgna, field marshal major of the Holy League, was on the Sauli galley leased by Savoy.

Ottoman galleys mounted fewer guns and would normally have carried even more men than the ponentinas, but their manpower at Lepanto was dimin-ished by disease and desertion, to the point that they were obliged to cannibal-ize some thirty to forty galleys, which remained behind in Lepanto harbour. Christian accounts usually inflate Ottoman numbers by including thirty to forty fustas (small galleys with twelve to fifteen two-man benches per side) in what was otherwise a vestigial reserve squadron, while omitting to mention some twenty to thirty private venture fustas and brigantinas on the Holy League side, as well as fifty-seven large barges (*fragatas*) that accompanied the larger galleys. In the following count the sub-galliot vessels have been excluded from both sides, because after giving up the troops they carried they would have been used mainly for communications, although – like the galley skiffs – some may have been used to send boarding parties to the disengaged sides of enemy galleys. Once the Ottoman fleet was broken the smaller vessels would have joined in the looting on one side and acted as rescue ships on the other.

MANPOWER SCHEDULE

Venetian

Vessel Type	Personnel			Ordnance	
	Crew	Soldiers	Rowers	Heavy	Medium
Galleass	100	150	270	5	8
Lantern	40	100	156	1	6
Line galley	30	80	144	1	4

Ottoman

Vessel Type	Personnel			Ordnance	
	Crew	Soldiers	Rowers	Heavy	Medium
Lantern	40	150	156	1	4
Line galley	30	120	144	1	2
Flag galliot	30	100	126	1	0
Galliot	25	80	108	–	1

Ponentinas

Vessel Type	Personnel			Ordnance	
	Crew	Soldiers	Rowers	Heavy	Medium
Super-flag	75	200	260	3	6
Lantern	40	150	208	1	6
Line galley	30	120	144	1	4

Galleasses and the larger ponentina galleys had ports for two medium guns low astern, but with the exception of these and the swivel guns, which could be mounted anywhere, the rest of the ordnance on all the vessels at Lepanto was fixed and forward-firing. Heavy guns are 12-pounders or greater weighing 3,000 pounds or more and include bombards/basilisks, the larger culverins and all except the smallest (quarto) cannon. Medium guns are 3, 6 and 9-pounders, mostly culverins, weighing 800 to 2,500 pounds.

The estimate of rowers is conservative and excludes the spare rowers most galleys carried, although where they could have gone when off duty is a mystery. Benches are usually given per side, from which we have to deduct one bench per side for the skiff and oven platforms on all except the galleasses, but to avoid confusion I give the total number of working benches instead. Bearing in mind that these are *averages* and that no two vessels even within the same category were exactly alike, galleasses and super-flagships have been allotted fifty-four and fifty-two five-man benches respectively and lesser Hapsburg–Papal Lanterns fifty-two four-man benches. The rest had three-man benches, the Venetian and Ottoman Lanterns with fifty-two, ordinary galleys with forty-eight, flagship galliots (Flag) with forty-two and ordinary galliots with thirty-six.

Muslim and Catholic conscripts and condemned criminal rowers knew they would be permanently enslaved if their side lost and are therefore counted as auxiliary combatants (A), as are the volunteer Greek sailors serving in both fleets. Greek *rowers* pressed into service by the Ottomans are listed as non-combatant (B), but not in the Venetian fleet for reasons explained in the text. It is unlikely that the Ottomans would have risked arming men of such uncertain loyalty, while shackling them literally linked their hopes for survival to the fate of their galley and freed soldiers from guard duty. The fortunes of war having generally gone against the Christians in the decade before Lepanto, the Knights of Malta contingent was the only one in the Holy League rowed entirely by Muslim slaves. The Sicily and Naples contingents had 16 and 12 per cent slaves respectively, and 10 per cent across the rest of the Hapsburg–Papal fleet is a reasonable assumption.

In the Ottoman fleet, slaves powered about a quarter of the Mainland fleet, the Egypt–Syria contingent was mainly if not entirely rowed by them following the conquest of Cyprus, while some corsairs employed them in an 'engine room', a practice extended to all of them in the following calculations and estimated to have been one third of their rowers. If allowance is made for casualties and those on the vessels that escaped, we are left with the canonical figure of 12,000–15,000 Christians who might be said to have been liberated, although a high proportion would have been the constrained but not strictly speaking enslaved Greeks.

DETAILED BREAKDOWN OF ESTIMATED FORCES

Holy League

Contingent		Vessel		Combatants		Rowers		Guns	
		Type	No.	Crew	Soldiers	A	B	Heavy	Medium
VENICE	Main	Galleass	6	600	900	1,620	–	30	48
		Lantern	6	240	600	936	–	6	36
		Galley	56	1,680	4,480	8,064	–	56	224
	Crete	Galley	29	870	2,320	4,176	–	29	116
	Ionian Is.	Galley	8	240	640	1,152	–	15	90
	Dalmatia	Galley	8	240	640	1,152	–	15	90
		Subtotal	*113*	*3,870*	*9,580 **	*17,100*	*–*	*151*	*604*
HAPSBURG	Genoese	Super-flag	3	225	600	702	78	9	18
		Lantern	13	520	1,950	2,434	270	13	78
		Galley	11	330	1,320	1,426	158	11	44
	Naples	Super-flag	1	75	200	234	26	3	6
		Lantern	5	200	750	915	125	5	30
		Galley	23	690	2,760	2,915	397	23	92
	Spain	*La Real*	1	100	300	270	30	3	6
		Lantern	6	240	900	1,123	125	6	36
		Galley	5	150	600	648	72	5	20
	Sicily	Super-flag	1	75	200	218	42	3	6
		Lantern	1	40	150	175	33	1	6
		Galley	4	120	480	484	92	4	16
		Subtotal	*74*	*2,765*	*10,210*	*11,544*	*1,448*	*86*	*358*
OTHER	Pope	Super-flag	2	150	400	468	52	6	12
		Lantern	2	80	300	374	42	2	12
		Galley	8	240	960	1,037	115	8	32
	Genoa	Super-flag	1	75	200	234	26	3	6
	City	Lantern	2	80	300	374	42	2	12
	Savoy	Super-flag	1	75	200	234	26	3	6
		Lantern	2	80	300	374	42	2	12
	Malta	Lantern	1	40	150	–	208	1	6
		Galley	2	60	240	–	288	2	8
		Subtotal	*21*	*880*	*3,050*	*3,095*	*841*	*29*	*106*
		TOTAL	**208**	**7,515**	**22,840**	**31,739**	**2,289**	**266**	**1,068**

* Of which 4,100 were Hapsburg infantry.

Ottoman

Contingent Area	City	Vessel Type	No.	Combatants Crew	Combatants Soldiers	Rowers A	Rowers B	Guns Heavy	Guns Medium
MAIN	Istanbul	Lantern	21	840	3,150	2,457	819	21	84
		Galley	51	1,530	6,120	5,508	1,836	51	102
	Anatolia	Lantern	2	80	300	216	72	2	8
		Galley	25	750	3,000	2,700	900	25	50
	Gallipoli	Lantern	1	40	150	117	39	1	4
		Galley	10	750	3,000	2,700	900	10	20
		Flag galliot	2	60	200	189	63	2	–
		Subtotal	*112*	*4,050*	*15,920*	*13,887*	*4,629*	*112*	*268*
GREECE and GREEK ISLANDS	Negro ponte	Lantern	4	160	600	–	624	4	16
		Galley	15	450	1,800	–	2,160	15	30
	Nauplia	Lantern	1	40	150	–	156	1	4
		Galley	10	300	1,200	–	1,440	10	20
	Rhodes	Lantern	1	40	150	–	156	1	4
		Galley	9	270	1,080	–	1,296	9	18
	Mytilene	Lantern	1	40	150	–	156	1	4
		Galley	9	270	1,080	–	1,296	9	18
		Subtotal	*50*	*1,570*	*6,210*	*–*	*7,284*	*50*	*114*
EGYPT–SYRIA	Alexandria	Lantern	1	40	150	–	156	1	4
		Galley	21	630	2,520	–	3,024	21	42
	Tripoli	Lantern	2	80	300	–	312	2	8
		Galley	11	330	1,320	–	1,584	11	22
		Subtotal	*35*	*1,080*	*4,290*	*–*	*5,076*	*35*	*76*
CORSAIR	Algiers	Lantern	2	80	300	104	52	2	8
		Flag galliot	3	90	300	252	126	3	–
		Galliot	20	500	1,600	1,440	720	–	20
	Tripoli	Lantern	2	80	300	104	52	2	8
		Galley	5	150	600	480	240	5	10
		Flag galliot	3	90	300	252	126	3	–
		Galliot	8	200	640	576	288	–	8
	Valona	Lantern	1	40	150	208	104	1	4
		Galley	1	30	120	96	48	1	2
		Flag galliot	2	30	200	168	84	2	–
		Galliot	7	175	560	504	252	–	7
		Subtotal	*54*	*1,465*	*5,070*	*4,184*	*2,092*	*19*	*67*
		TOTAL	**251**	**8,165**	**31,490**	**18,071**	**19,081**	**216**	**525**

SUMMARY

Hardware

Category	Holy League	Ottoman
Galleasses	6	–
Super-flagships	10	–
Lanterns	38	39
Galleys	154	167
Flagship galliots	–	10
Galliots	–	35
Total line of battle	**208**	**251**
Heavy guns	266	216
Medium guns	1,068	525
Total major ordnance	**1,334**	**741**

Personnel

		Holy League	Ottoman
Crew	Fixed gun crews	4,268	2,500
	Swivel/hook gunners	1,247	2,500 [1]
	Other duties/weapons	2,000	3,165
	Total crew	**7,515**	**8,165**
Soldiers	Officers and gentry	4,000 [2]	2,500
	Sub-officers	2,000	5,000
	Drums, horns, etc.	1,125	2,250
	Sipahi bowmen	–	17,740
	Janissary handgunners	–	3,000 / 1,000 [4]
	Venetian crossbowmen	2,740 [3]	–
	Venetian handgunners	2,055 / 685 [4]	–
	Hapsburg–Papal handgunners	1,920 / 640 [4]	–
	Hapsburg–Papal pikemen	7,675 [4]	–
	Total soldiers	**22,840**	**31,490**
	Total professional military	**30,355**	**39,655**
Auxiliaries (rowers who may have fought)		31,739	18,071
	Total possible combatants	**62,094**	**57,726**
Non-combatant rowers (slaves and Greeks)		2,289	19,081
	TOTAL personnel	**64,383**	**76,807**

Notes

1. The Ottomans stripped Aetolia and Morea of azaps, fortress troops who also supplied the marines to the fleet, who were specialists in the use of hook and swivel guns.

2. Includes 2,500 noblemen, captains of adventure and their suites.

3. The Venetians still employed crossbowmen in large numbers, here estimated to be half of their own as opposed to borrowed Hapsburg troops.

4. The proportion of arquebuses to mosquetes in a Tercio was 3:1, and this proportion has been applied to the Venetian handgunners and to the Janissaries, an all-firearms corps, with the figures split accordingly.

ORDERS OF BATTLE

Key

(C) – known captured

(E) – known escaped

(K) – known killed

Sources:

Mainly Contarini and *Documentos Inéditos*,

commentaries from Caetani, Caracciolo, Diedo, Scetti, etc.

Holy League Left Wing (54)

Origin	Type	Name / Flag	VIP / Notes	Captain
Venice	Lantern	Fleet QMG	Agostino Barbarigo (K)	Federico Nani
Venice	Lantern	Fleet co-QM		Antonio da Canal
Venice		*Fortune*	Severe casualties	Andrea Barbarigo (K)
Naples		*La Sagittaria*		Martín Pirola
Naples		*La Victoria*		Ochoa de Ricalde
Venice		*Three Hands*	Severe casualties	Giorgio Barbarigo (K)
Candia (Crete)		*Two Dolphins*		Francesco Zen
Canea (Crete)		*Winged Lion*		Francesco Mengano
Cres (Dalmatia)		*St Nikola*	All killed, scuttled	Kolan Drazic (K)
Canea (Crete)		*Our Lady of Canea*		Filippo Polani
Candia (Crete)		*Sea-Horse*		Antonio dei Cavalli
Candia (Crete)		*Two Lions*		Niccolò Fradello
Kopar (Istria)		*Lion*		Dominico del Tacco
Cephalonia		*Crucifix and Two Trees*		Marco Cimera
Cephalonia		*St Virginia*		Cristoforo Crissa
Candia (Crete)		*Lion with Sword*		Francesco Bonvecchio
Candia (Crete)		*Christ*		Andrea Cornaro
Candia (Crete)		*Angel of Candia*		Giovanni Angelo
Candia (Crete)		*Pyramid*	Severe casualties	Francesco Bon (K)
Candia (Crete)		*Woman on Horse*		Antonio Eudomeniani
*Pope		*La Elbigina*	Took Rhodes flagship	Fabio Galerati
*Lomellino		*La Lomellina*		Agostin Caneval
*Gian'Andrea		*La Marchesa*	Cervantes	Francesco Sancto Pietro
*Gian'Andrea		*La Fortuna*		Gian'Luigi Belui
GALLEASS – Ambrogio Bragadino				
Venice		*Christ over the World*		Simon Guoro
Venice		*Risen Christ*		Federico Venier
Corfu		*Christ*		Cristoforo Condocolli
Venice		*Christ with banner*		Bartolomeo Donato
Krk (Dalmatia)		*Christ with Banner*		Ludovik Cikuta
Canea (Crete)		*Christ Resurrected*		Giorgio Calergi
Canea (Crete)		*Christ resurrected*		Giorgio Calergi
Retimo (Crete)		*St Theodore*		Niccolò Avonal
Candia (Crete)		*Christ Blessing*		Giovanni Corner (K)
Canea (Crete)		*Risen Christ*		Francesco Zancaruol
Canea (Crete)		*The Wheel*		Francesco da Molin Jr
Brescia		*St Euphemia*		Horacio Fisogna
Canea (Crete)		*Two Arms*		Michele Vizzamanno
Canea (Crete)		*Christ and Lion*		Daniele Calefati
Venice		*Gold Falcon on Arm*		Niccolò Lippomano
Zante		*Panaghia*		Nicola Mondino
Venice		*Our Lady with Palm*		Marc'Antonio Pisani
Venice		*The Trinity*	Captured Scirocco	Giovanni Contarini
GALLEASS – Antonio Bragadino				
*Naples		*La Fama*		Juan de la Cueva
*Naples		*San Juan*		Juan García de Vergara
*Naples		*La Envidia*		Toribio de Acevedo
*Naples		*La Brava*		Miguel de Quevedo
*Naples		*Santiago*		Alonso de Guardiola (K)
*Naples		*San Nicolás*		Cristóbal de Monguía
Venice		*Risen Christ*		Gian'Battista Quirini
Venice		*Angel with Lilies*		Onofre Giustiniani
Venice		*St Dorothy*		Paolo Nani
Venice	Lantern	Fleet co-QM		Marco Quirini

* Non-Venetian elements in an otherwise entirely Venetian wing.

Ottoman Right Wing (58)

Commander	Fate/Notes	Type	Origin
Mehmet Scirocco (K)	*Sunk by gunfire*	Lantern	Bey of Alexandria
Kara Cubatt			Alexandria
Bagli Saraf			
Djafer Kiaia			
Caur Ali (K)		Flag galliot	
Ali the Genoese (E)		Flag galliot	
Megil Reis		Flag galliot	
Previs Reis			
Osman Chelebi			
Bive Casapoli			
Dervis Agha			
Osman Orkhan			
Bayezid Siman			
Pervis Reis (K)			
Osman Ali			
Mustafa the Genoese (E)			
Delhi Agha (K)			
Dardagan Bardabeli			
Kasli Kiaia			
Yussuf Agha			
Yussuf Magar			
Calafat Ceder			
Ceder Agha			
Dermigi Pari			
Mat Hassan			
Soliman Bey (K)			Istanbul
Ibrahim			
Saban			
Kiaia Chelebi			
Son of Kara Mustafa (K)		Lantern	
Ceder Siman			
Jaran Saba			
David Yussuf			
Arnaut Ferrat			
Salak Reis			
Izel Memi			Tripoli (Syria)
Schender Selim			
Lumaghi Yussuf			
Bardach Chelebi			
Bagdad Hassan			
Guzel Ayubi			
Bru-Ali Piri			
Rodlu Ali			
Agha Pasha (K)		Lantern	Istanbul
Sinan Mustafa			Anatolia
Giegior Ali			
Calipei Memi			
Merul Mustafa			
Heder Lumet			
Sinan Dervis			
Murat Reis (K)			
Memi Durmis			
Al-Gagia Sinan			
Aghadi Rustam			
Cingeve Mustafa			
Yussuf Chelebi (K)			
Djafer Mustafa			
Mehmet Bey (K)	*Son of Salih Reis*	Lantern	Bey of Negroponte

Left of Holy League Battle (30)

Origin	Type	Name/Flag	VIP/Notes	Captain
Lomellino	Super-flag	Flagship	Paolo Giordano Orsino	Piero Battista Lomellino
Lomellino	Lantern	Vice-Flagship		Unknown
Savoy (Sauli)	Lantern	Vice-Flagship	Ascanio della Corgna	Bendinelli Sauli
Genoa	Lantern	Vice-Flagship	Count of Santa Fiora	Pellerano
Pope		*La Toscana*	Ferrante Caracciolo	Metello Caracciolo
Venice		*Merman*		Giacomo Trissino (K)
Venice		*Our Lady and Crucifix*		Giovanni Zen
Hvar (Dalmatia)		*St Jerolim*		Ivan Balcic
Venice		*St Giovanni*		Pietro Badoer
Bergamo		*St Alexander*		Gian'Antonio Colleone
Sicily		*La Vigilancia*		Silvestre Marquito
Mare	Lantern	Flagship		Gregorio di Aste
Venice		*Tree trunk*		Hieronimo da Canal
Venice		*Mongibello*		Bertucci Contarini
Candia (Crete)		*Fortune on a Dolphin*		Francesco Dandolo
Gian'Andrea		*La Constanza*		Ciprian di Mare
Naples		*La Ventura*		Vicente Pascalo
		GALLEASS – Andrea di Pesaro		
Spain (Rocafull)	Lantern	*La Rocafulla*	Juan de Rocafull	Diego Ortuño
Pope		*La Victoria*		Baccio Guirte di Pisa
Venice		*Pyramid*		Marc'A. Santuliana
Venice		*Christ*		Hieronimo Contarini (K)
Spain (Vázquez)		*San Francisco*		Cristóbal Vázquez
Pope		*La Pace*		Jacobo Perpignano
Gian'Andrea		*La Perla*		Gian'Battista Spinola
Venice		*Wheel and Serpent*		Gabriele da Canal
Venice		*Pyramid*		Francesco Bon (K)
Venice		*Palm Leaf*		Hieronimo Venier (K)
Spain (Andrade)	Lantern	*La Andrada*	Juan Ponce de León (K)	Bernardo Ça Noguera
Spain (Andrade)		*La Granada*		Pablo Batín

Holy League command element (7)

Origin	Type	Flag	VIP/notes	Captain
Genoa	Super-flag	Flagship of Genoa	Prince of Parma	Ettore Spinola
Venice	Lantern	Flagship of Venice	Sebastiano Venier	Francesco Dandolo
Spain	Lantern	Flagship of Santiago	*Astern*	Alexandre Torrelles
Spain	Super-flag	Holy League	Juan de Austria	Juan Vázquez Coronado
			Luis de Requeséns	Juan Ça Noguera
Spain	Lantern	Vice-flagship of Spain	*Astern*	Luis de Acosta
Pope	Super-flag	Flagship of the Pope	Marc'Antonio Colonna	Orazio Orsini (K)
			Michele Bonelli	Mathurin de Romegas
Savoy	Super-flag	Flagship of Savoy	Prince of Urbino	Andrea di Legni

Right of Ottoman Battle (39)

Commander	Fate/Notes	Type	Origin
Hassan the Venetian (E)	*Taken by La Elbigina*	Lantern	Bey of Rhodes
Delhi Djafer			Rhodes
Occi Reis			
Prostunagi Oglu			
Gazizi Reis			
Calafat Oglu (K)			
Dromus Reis (K)		Lantern	Istanbul
Har Betei			
Orkhan Reis			Rhodes
Delhi Piri			
Djafer Agha			
Bacla Reis			Istanbul
Coz Ali			
Calac Reis			
Oluz Reis			
Hassan Pasha (K)	Son of Barbarossa	Lantern	
Saraf Reis			Nauplia
Alman Reis			
Gurucli Oglu			
Arnaut Chelebi			
Magar Ali			
Djafer Chelebi Bey (K)		Lantern	Bey of Chabala (?)
Delhi Chelebi			Nauplia
Kara Piri Agha (K)			
Sinan Reis			
Kara Mustafa			
Sali Arnaut			
Previs Agha (K)		Lantern	Bey of Nauplia
Baluci Oglu			Mytiline
Barzarzi Mustafa			
Sinan Bali			
Aghadi Reis (K)			
Sons of Ali Pasha (C)	*Taken by Santiago flagship*	Lantern	Istanbul
Osman Reis			Istanbul
Delhi Yussuf			Mytiline
Ferat Bali			
Kiaia Chelebi			
Bagdar Reis			
Haluaghi Mustafa			

OTTOMAN COMMAND ELEMENT (6)

Commander	Fate	Type	Origin
Mahmud Bey (K)	Taken by Orsino	Lantern	Agha of Janissaries
Mustafa Esdri Pasha (C)	Taken by Caracciolo	Lantern	Fleet Treasurer
Mahmud Haider Bey (K)	Taken by Venier	Lantern	Bey of Mytiline
Ali Pasha (K)	Taken by *La Real*	Lantern	Kapudan
Pertev Pasha (E)	Taken by Colonna *	Lantern	Land General
Kara Khodja (K)	Taken by Caetani	Lantern	Bey of Valona

* Possession taken by Cardona – see text.

Right of Holy League Battle (29)

Origin	Type	Name/Flag	VIP/Notes	Captain
Pope	Lantern	*La Grifona*	Onorato Caetani *	Alessandro Negrone
Venice	Lantern	*St Theodore*		Theodoro Balbi
Niccolò Doria	Lantern	Flagship		Niccolò Doria
Spain (Mendoza)	Lantern	*La Mendoza*		Pedro Ortíz
Canea (Crete)		*Mountain and Sun*		Alessandro Vizzamano
Venice		*John the Baptist*		Giovanni Mocenigo
Gian'Andrea	Lantern	*La Victoria*		Filippo Doria
Pope		*La Pisana*	Aurelio Scetti	Ercole Balotta
Spain (Andrade?)		*La Higuera*		Diego López de Llanos
Venice		*Christ and a Cross*		Giorgio Pisani
GALLEASS – Francesco Duodo				
Venice		*St John*		Daniel Moro
Pope	Lantern	*La Fiorenza*	*Severe casualties*	Tomasso dei Medici
Naples		*San José*		Eugenio de Vargas
Naples	Lantern	*Benavides*	Commodore	Francisco de Benavides
Spain (Mendoza?)		*La Luna*		Manuel de Aguilar
Venice		*Bird on a Branch*		Luigi Pasqualigo
Venice		*Lion with a Cross*		Piero Pisani
Venice		*St Jeronimo*		Gaspar Malipiero
Grimaldi	Lantern	Flagship	Giorgio Grimaldi	Giacomo di Lorenzo
Imperiale	Lantern	Vice-flagship		Niccolò delio Genovese
Venice		*St Christopher*		Alessandro Contarini
Zante		*Judith*		Marino Sigouros
Candia (Crete)		*Ermine*		Pietro Gradenigo
Venice		*Half Moon*		Valerio Valleresso
Gian'Andrea	Lantern	*La Doria*	*Most killed, scuttled*	Giacomo di Casal (K)
Malta		*Saint Pierre*		Pierre Saint Aubin
Malta		*San Juan*		Alonso de Tejada
Malta	Lantern	Flagship of Malta	*Most killed, scuttled*	Pietro Giustiniano

* Also memoirist Bartolomeo Sereno

VANGUARD (8)

To support of Barbarigo on extreme Left Wing

Origin	Type	Name / Flag	VIP / Notes	Captain
Venice	Lantern	*The Sun*	*Severe casualties*	Vincenzo Quirini (K)
Venice		*Madonna*	*Severe casualties*	Piero Malipiero
Venice		*St Catherine*	*Severe casualties*	Marco Cicogna
Venice		*St Magdalene*	*Most killed, scuttled*	Marino Contarini (K)

To gap between Battle and Right Wing

Origin	Type	Name / Flag	VIP / Notes	Captain
Sicily	Super-flag	Flagship	*Severe casualties*	Juan de Cardona
Sicily	Lantern	Vice-Flagship	*Severe casualties*	Juan Nuñez de Palencia
Sicily		*San Juan*	Martín Muñoz	Scipión Vasallo
Imperiale	Lantern	Flagship	*All killed, scuttled*	David Imperiale (K)

Left of Ottoman Battle (42)

Commander	Fate/Notes	Type	Origin
Alci Oglu			
Karam Delhi			
Brus Ali			
Salak Fakir			
Ferat Karadja			
Tramuntana Reis (K)		Lantern	Istanbul
Soliman Chelebi			
Delhi Ibrahim			
Murat Khorosan			
Demir Bali			
Kabil Heit			
Murat Trasil Agha (E)		Lantern	Arsenal Notary
Pervis Sinam			
Dardagan Ali			
Djafer Karan			Istanbul
Dervis Sach			
Kurd Ali			
Djafer Agha Pasha (E)	*Taken by Negrone flagship*	Lantern	Bey of Tripoli (Libya)
Kara Ahmed			
Rustan Chalmaghi			
Durmis Oglu			Tripoli (Libya)*
Schender Dernigi			
Mohammad Ali			
Asiz Agha (K)		Lantern	Bey of Gallipoli
Selim Siak			
Heder Baci			
Sinam Mustafa			Gallipoli*
Sali Reis			
Delhi Iskander			
Dum Maiva		Lantern	Istanbul
Pervis Lumaghi			
Yussuf Bali			
Sinam Bardaghi			Gallipoli*
Yussuf Finigi			
Delhi Osman			
Piri Bey (K)		Lantern	
Delhi Suliman			
Piri Sisnam			Istanbul
Hadji Oglu			
Kiaia Saraf			
Dervis Chelebi			
Dardagan Pasha (K)		Lantern	Commander Arsenal

* The Tripoli corsairs listed with the left wing were actually behind the Tripoli–Gallipoli galleys here.

Holy League Right Wing (50)

Origin	Type	Name/Flag	VIP/Notes	Captain
Savoy	Super-flag	Flagship	*All killed*	Ottaviano Moreto (K)
Niccolò Doria	Lantern	Vice-Flagship	*All killed*	Pandolfo Polidoro (K)
*Venice		*Hercules and Lion*		Renier Zen
*Candia (Crete)		*Queen with Chain*		Giovanni Barbarigo
*Venice		*Child in Chains*		Paulo Polani
*Venice		*Christ over the World*	*Blown up*	Benedetto Soranzo (K)
*Retimo (Crete)		*Armed Man*	*Gomenizza mutiny*	Andrea Calergi
*Retimo (Crete)		*Golden Eagle*		Andrea Calergi
*Canea (Crete)		*Palm Tree*	*All killed, scuttled*	Giacomo di Mecco (K)
*Corfu		*Angel with Sword*		Stelio Carciopulo
*Rab (Dalmatia)		*St Ivan*	*All killed, burned*	Ivan de Dominis (K)
*Trogir (Dalmatia)		*Woman and Snake*	*All killed, scuttled*	Lujo Cipik (K)
*Venice		*Crucifix*	*All killed, scuttled*	Antonio Pasqualigo (K)
*Candia (Crete)		*Our Lady*		Marco Foscarini
*Corfu		*Risen Christ*		Francesco Corner
*Venice		*San Victoriano*		Vangelista Zuria
Grimaldi	Lantern	Vice-Flagship	↑	Lorenzo Treccia
Mare	Lantern	Vice-Flagship	*The inner Venetian*	Antonio Corniglia
Sicily		*La Margarita*	*squadron (above) did*	Battaglino
Gian'Andrea		*La Diana*	*not follow Doria's lead*	Gian'Giorgio Lasagna
Naples		*La Gitana*		Gabriel de Medina
Naples		*La Luna*		Giulio Rubio
Naples		*La Fortuna*		Diego de Medrano
Naples		*La Esperanza*	*The outer Venetian*	Pedro del Vasto
Lomellino		*Fury with Serpent*	*squadron (below)*	Giacomo Ciappé
Lomellino	Lantern	*Lomellino*	*later turned back in*	Giorgio Greco
Negrone		*La Negrona*	*disorder*	Niccolò da Costa
Negrone	Bastarda		↓	Lorenzo da Torre
*Candia (Crete)		*Heart in Flames*		Antonio Bon
*Candia (Crete)		*Golden Eagle*		Girolamo Zorzi
*Venice		*San Cristoforo*		Andrea Tron
*Venice		*Christ*	*All killed, scuttled*	Marc'Antonio Lando (K)
*Venice		*A Wheel*		Francesco da Molin Sr
*Candia (Crete)		*Hope*	*All killed, burned*	Giacomo Cornaro (K)
*Padua		*King Attila*		Pataro Buzzacarin
*Venice		*St Joseph*		Niccolò Donato
*Corfu		*Gold and Black Eagle*	*Taken to Lepanto*	Pietro Bua (C, K)
*Cattaro (Dalmatia)		*St Trifun*	*All killed, scuttled*	Girolamo Bisanti (K)
*Vicenza		*Tower with woman*		Ludovico da Porto
Naples	Lantern	*La Guzmana*		Francisco de Ojeda (K)
Naples		*La Determinada*		Juan de Carasa
Sicily		*La Sicilia*	*All killed, scuttled*	Francesco Amadei (K)
Genoa (Centurione)	Lantern	*Genoa*	*Severe casualties*	Giulio Centurione
Pope		*Santa Maria*		Pandolfo Strozzi
Pope		*San Giovanni*	*All killed, scuttled*	Angelo Biffoli (K)
Negrone	Lantern	Vice-Flagship		Luigi Gamba
Negrone	Lantern	Flagship		Gian'Ambrogio Negrone
Gian'Andrea		*La Monarcha*		Niccolò Grimaldi
Gian'Andrea		*La Damigella*	*Federico Venusta*	Niccolò Garibaldo
Gian'Andrea	Lantern	Flagship	*Sigismondo Gonzaga*	Gian'Andrea Doria

Galleasses of Piero Pisani and Jacobo Guoro left behind, not engaged.

* Venetian elements in a preponderantly non-Venetian right wing.

Ottoman Left Wing (101)

Front Line – 58 galleys

Galley	Squadron
Cingal Sinam	
Cior Mehmed	
Hassan Sinan	
Higna Mustafa	
Cadelmi Memi	
Usciuffi Memi	
Pisma Reis Lantern	Anatolia
Kara Murat	
Cumi Memi	
Passa Dervis	
Tagli Osman	
Tacci Sisman	
Jesil Oglu	
Ram Hassan	
Kader Sidir	
Giuzel Djafer	
Osman Reis (K) Lantern	
Calam Memi	
Giesman Ferat	
Zumbul Murat	
Icupris Hassan	Istanbul
Tumis Soliman	
Galcepi Yussuf	
Cecedel Hassan	
Sarmusac Reis Lantern	
Osman Bagli (K)	
Nasut Fakir	
Kaiatchi Memi	
Sitina Reis Lantern	
Gimigi Mustafa	
Rustam Cinigi	
Bal Ali	Negroponte
David Ali	
Karam Hidir	
Magar Ferrat	
Kara Bey (K) Lantern	
Arnaut Ali	
Curmur Rodh	
Koz Cluagin	
Kuzli Memi	
Bal Agha	
Nafis Reis Lantern	Negroponte
Piri Reis (K) Lantern	
Calam Bastaghi	
Djafer Hidi	
Ferat	
Memi Bey Oglu (K)	
Uluch Ali Pasha (E) Lantern	
Talitaghi Reis	
Osman Piri	
Rus Chelebi	Istanbul
Tatar Ali	
Kazan Reis Lantern	
Demir Bey (*) Lantern	
Yussuf Ali	Tripoli (Syria)
Kara Alman	
Murat Brassan	
Kara Bive Pasha (K) Lantern	

Second Line – 43 galliots

Galliot	Corsairs
Haserghi Reis Flag	
Demir Chelebi	
Dervis Hyder	
Kalat Ali	
Abdallah Reis	Tripoli (Libya) corsairs
Kara Chelebi (E) Flag	*(behind left of Battle)*
Piali Murad	
Osman Sebet	
Sinam Mustafa	
Aghadi Ahmed	
Djafer Reis Flag	
Magli Reis (C) Flag	
Sirizi Memi	
Occi Hassan	
Cumgi Yussuf	
Gul Pervis	
Kara Piri (K) Flag	Algiers corsairs
Jaculi Amat	
Calabodan Soliman	
Sair Djafer	
Cior Memi	
Kara Djaly (E) Flag	
Karaman Ali	
Alman	
Sinam Chelebi	
Aghadi Mustafa	Algiers corsairs
Dagli Ali	
Algier Seyth	
Son of Uluch Ali	
Piri Selim	
Murat Dervis (K)	
Hesus Oglu	Algiers corsairs
Muhuczur Ali	
Jaia Osman	
Salih Delhi	
Abbazzar Reis (K) Flag	
Delhi Murat	Valona corsairs
Scin Sciander	
Alman Bali	
Beylerbey of Algiers	
Hassan Sciamban	
Hassan Sinam	
Cumi Falaga	Valona corsairs
Osman Ginder	
Seit Agha Flag	

*Demir Bey was the only Ottoman captain formally put to death after surrender

Beylerbey of Syria

Holy League Reserve (28)

To support Left Wing (10)

Origin	Type	Name / Flag	VIP / Notes	Captain
Naples		*La Bacana*		Juan Pérez de Murillo
Naples		*La Florida*		Rodrigo de Zugasti
Naples		*La Constancia*		Juan Pérez de Loaisa
Naples		*La Marquesa*		Juan de Maqueda
Naples		*La Tirana*		Juan de Rivadeneyra
Naples	Lantern	*Santa Barbara*	Pedro de Padilla	Martín de Padilla
Naples	Lantern	*San Andrés*		Bernardino de Velasco
Naples		*Santa Catarina*		Juan Ruiz de Velasco
Naples		*Santo Angel*		Unknown
Naples		*San Bartolomeo*		Pedro de Velasco

To support Battle (18)

Origin	Type	Name / Flag	VIP / Notes	Captain
Venice	Lantern	*Christ*		Marco Molin
Venice		*Truth*		Giovanni Bembo
Venice		*Hands, Sword*	*All killed, scuttled*	Giovanni Loredan (K)
Venice		*Faith*	*Severe casualties*	Gian'Battista Contarini
Venice		*Column*	*All killed, scuttled*	Catarino Malipiero (K)
Venice		*The World*		Filippo Leone
Naples	Lantern	*Vice-Flagship*	Alonso de Bazán	Monserrate Guardiola
Venice		*Magdalene*		Luigi Balbi
Venice		*Hope*	*All killed, scuttled*	Gian'Battista Benedetti
Venice		*St Peter*		Pietro Badoer
Naples	Super-flag	*Flagship*	Alvaro de Bazán	Manuel de Benavides
Sibenik		*St George*		Cristoforo Lucic
Venice		*St Michael, Lion*		Giorgio Cochin
Venice		*Sibyll*		Daniel Tron
Pope		*La Soberana*		Ercole Carafa
Pope	Lantern	*La Serena*		Alfonso Appiano
Spain (Andrade)	Lantern	*La Ocasión*	Count Niccolò Suriano	Pedro de los Ríos
Spain (Vázquez)	Lantern	*Flagship of Vázquez*		Antonio Vázquez C.

Ottoman Reserve

To support Command Element

Commander	Fate	Type	Origin
Murat Dragut Reis (E)		Lantern	Istanbul
Delhi Bey (K)	Taken by Caetani	Lantern	Istanbul
Kaidar Memi Bey (K)		Lantern	Bey of Chios
Djafer Bey (K)		Lantern	Istanbul
Murat Reis (K)		Lantern	Istanbul

CASUALTIES

Most accounts agree that 8,000 were killed outright in the Holy League fleet, of whom 5,200 were Venetian, 2,000 Hapsburg and 800 Papal. A further 4,000 died and 10,000 recovered from their wounds. The majority of the fatal casualties were on the twenty-one galleys with a nominal complement of 5,708 (246 crew, 2,130 soldiers, 3,332 rowers) overwhelmed with the loss of all or almost all on board. The Venetians lost fourteen line galleys, seven from the mainland, four from Dalmatia, two from Crete, and one from Corfu. Of the ponentinas, Gian'Andrea Doria, Sicily and the Papal–Tuscan contingent each lost one line galley, and the Knights of Malta, David Imperiale, Niccolò Doria, and Savoy each a lantern, the last a 'super-flagship'. Twelve more galleys with a nominal complement of 3,669 (365 crew, 1,320 soldiers, 1,984 rowers) reported disabling casualties. Of these Barbarigo's lantern and five line galleys were mainland Venetian, and one line galley was from Crete. Three of the five ponentinas were from the small Sicily contingent (Cardona's super-flagship, his vice-flagship and one line galley), the other two being the lantern leased from Centurione by the City of Genoa, and one Papal–Tuscan line galley.

Although also the most numerous contingent, the losses among the Venetian levantinas (20 lost or disabled out of 107 engaged, excluding the galleasses) points to their lower fighting power relative to the ponentinas (13 of 95), especially considering that most of the losses among the latter were incurred in the struggle against many times their number at the gap between the Battle and the Right Wing. Location helps to explain why four of the six Sicily galleys were lost or disabled, but the loss of four of the eight all-volunteer galleys from the Dalmatian ports suggests some other factor, the known fate of the *St Nikola* pointing to fury and blind courage getting the better of such little formation-keeping discipline as prevailed in the Venetian fleet.

Contarini itemized only 4,873 Venetian dead, including Agostino Barbarigo, 17 galley captains, 8 nobles, 5 chaplains, 6 councillors, 5 directors, 6 scribes, 7 pilots, 32 skilled workers, 124 mates, 132 gunners, 925 seamen, 1,333 soldiers and 2,274 rowers, to which we can confidently add most of the 800-odd Hapsburg soldiers embarked on the lost and disabled Venetian ships. Fernández Duro reports fifteen Hapsburg galley captains killed, as well as sixty Knights of Malta and 'almost all' the Knights of Santo Stefano on the Papal galleys. Wounded notables included Don Juan, Venier, Santa Cruz, Cardona, the Prince of Urbino, Count Silvio di Porcia, the Count of Santa Fiora and Paolo Giordano Orsino. The Hapsburg and Papal casualty figures seemingly do not include their rowers, denied even statistical recognition of their humanity, but it is reasonable to assume that losses among them would have been substantially less than on the lower freeboard Venetian galleys. If we add a nominal 700 Hapsburg and 300 Papal rowers to the total we will not be far wrong, for a total of about 13,000 killed and mortally wounded, 20 per cent of all those embarked on the Holy League galleys.

Only about forty Ottoman galleys and galliots escaped. The ability to sail into the wind that enabled Uluch Ali's group to get away points to most of them being galliots, as were ten of the group of twenty-five that returned to Lepanto with Bua's galley, leaving only seven escapees from the Right Wing and the Battle. Ten galliots and 117 galleys were captured (also three fustas), which means about eighty-four galleys and galliots were destroyed. Contarini estimated thirty-four captains of flagships, 120 galley commanders, 25,000 crew, soldiers and rowers killed. Thirty-nine horsetail standards and 3,486 men were declared captured and about 12,000 Christian slaves liberated, for a total of 41,000 or 53 per cent of those embarked in the Ottoman fleet. The vessels that got away might have carried another 10,000, and as many may have escaped in small boats or found safety ashore after successfully beaching their galleys. The discrepancy between these figures and our estimated total is easily explained – a mere 3,486 prisoners could not have depressed the price for slaves across the Mediterranean in 1571–72, making it reasonable to assume that several times this number were hidden below decks and not declared when the time came to divide the spoils.

Don Juan's calculation of the division of spoils (D.I. 227–234) is fascinating, not least because his attempt to levy a commander-in-chief's double tithe on the spoils was explicitly intended to claw back some of the loot he and his advisers were confident the Venetian and Papal captains were holding back. When the fleet reassembled at Petalas, the Hapsburg galleys declared possession of 58 galleys, 8 galliots, 63 heavy guns, 11 pedreros, 119 smaller guns and 1,685 slaves. The Venetian and Papal galleys declared 59 galleys, 2 galliots, 3 fustas, 54 heavy guns, 6 pedreros, 137 smaller guns and 1,801 slaves. This was then apportioned as follows:

Spain	58 galleys	8 galliots	1,743 slaves
Venice	39 galleys	2 galliots	1,162 slaves
Pope	20 galleys	3 fustas	581 slaves

Venier insultingly disputed Juan's claim for a personal share on the grounds that he was not really the commander-in-chief but merely the executor of the individual fleet commanders' decisions, to which Juan replied by taking six galleys and 164 slaves from the Venetian share without further ado. His proposal for the redistribution of the artillery was also disputed, and it was agreed that along with the matter of the galleys and the slaves it should be referred to the Pope for arbitration. If it was, nothing came of it. Juan gave about 350 slaves to his Hapsburg subordinates, which is almost exactly 20 per cent of the Venetian and Papal shares, so evidently he laid no claim to the share corresponding to his half-brother. He gave Requeséns a galley, surely can have done no less for Santa Cruz and Cardona, and may also have made good the losses suffered by Sicily, Savoy, Genoa, Imperiale, Gian'Andrea and Niccolò Doria with the prizes he claimed from the allies. This would have been done discreetly, however, for at the same time he was denying a Venetian request that their losses should be taken into consideration in the distribution of prizes.

ENDNOTES

(see Bibliography for full references)

PART I   ICONIC BATTLE

Introduction

1 There is no evidence that either Khair ed-Din or his elder brother Aruj had a red beard. The *nom de guerre* may have been carried forward from Emperor Frederick 'Barbarossa' Hohenstaufen, who in his time also posed a major threat to all of Italy.

2 This is, broadly speaking, the view of the *mentalités* school that took over after the symbolic parricide that marks these changes of intellectual orthodoxy in France, although its tenets were prefigured – as one of many themes – by *père* Braudel.

3 Braudel (2) 109.

4 Regarding the Renaissance and its aftermath this difference is more of overall emphasis than of historiographic consensus, as can be appreciated from the excellent essays in Rogers.

5 See Ventura.

6 There is a magnificent full-scale replica of Don Juan's galley *La Real* in the Museu Marítim, Barcelona (B&W Plate 1b).

7 These are in D.I. and Contarini. The sole exception are the Greeks Andrea and Giorgio Calergi, each named as the captains of two separate galleys that fought together on the Right and Left Wings respectively.

CHAPTER ONE   The Stage

1 Pryor is the original source of the upper part of **Map 3** and, in conjunction with Braudel, essential for a full understanding of Mediterranean geopolitics.

2 Ottoman logistics were the wonder of the world. Busbeq reported that they commonly employed 40,000 camels and as many mules in support of their armies, but of course these could not handle the big guns necessary for siege warfare.

3 It took the conquistadors almost a century to subdue the island of La Gomera, a process barely complete when Columbus made a last stop there before sailing to America in 1492. The racial differences are pronounced and the locals refer to mainland Spanish as 'Goths', recalling the invasion of Spain in 456AD by light-skinned Visigoths.

4 Hourani gives just enough detail to make sense of the bewildering succession of dynasties in north Africa and Spain. As they affect our story the Marinids and Saadis who held Morocco against both Iberian and Ottoman attempts to conquer it are the most significant, while the Nasrids in Granada, Hafsids from Tripoli to Bougie and Zirids around Algiers were either brushed aside or became the puppets of the new imperialists. Hess (1) argues persuasively that events in the area cannot be reduced simply to factors of great power rivalry, but the generalization is valid enough for our focus.

5 Zinsser remains the most entertaining and generally informative book on this subject.

CHAPTER TWO   Props

1 Illustrations in Gardiner show rigging attached to the spur in two-masted galleys, but not on the standard single-masted galley.

2 Holmes 236.

3 Coniglio 363–370. A note on the back in Philip II's handwriting says these were inflated prices and, ominously for his half-brother's entourage, that responsibility lay not with him but with 'those supposed to obtain good value for the crown'.

4 Anderson (1) *passim*.

5 Tenenti (1) Part 1, Chapter III, 'La Galère Idéale', from which the earlier 'perfect galley' quotation.

6 Mallett is an exhaustive examination of the cost-effective Venetian system, but Tenenti makes it clear that not enough was spent to make it as effective as it might have been.

7 Quoted in Lesure.

8 Payne-Gallwey contains a valuable appendix on the composite bow originally (1903) published separately. See also Bradbury.

9 Guilmartin (1) Appendix 6.

10 Adapted from Arnold 31.

11 Hale (1) gives examples of equipment orders received by the Arsenale in 1570–71, which indicate an enormous ordnance inventory.

12 Hall (1) combines scientific analysis and a balanced view of its social and political impact.

13 Colliado cited in Cipolla.

14 Oakeshott considers the armourer's art to have reached its apogee in the mid sixteenth century, with fifty to sixty alternative pieces to adapt a suit to different tournament requirements. In the field most only wore upper body armour.

15 Furttenbach 10, small reproduction Gardiner 154 (the Genoese galley is on 172).

16 An argument heavily supported in the documentary appendices of Gárate.

CHAPTER THREE **The Players**

1 The most dependable general narrative is Inalcik (1), while (2) is the standard analysis. Facts and quotations concerning the Ottomans are from these sources unless otherwise attributed.

2 Despite defeats in 1387, 1390, 1397, 1417, 1423, 1451 and 1468, the Karamanids counter-attacked in 1413, 1422, 1427, 1443 (with Christian collaboration) and 1500, supported Chem against his brother Bayezid II in 1481–82 and joined the Shi'ite rebellion sponsored by Shah Ismail of Persia in 1511–12. No other people put up comparable organized resistance.

3 Fisher 136.

4 Hanlon 30–35. This is the only work in English to address the issue of the continuing role of the Italian military class in European history after the age of the *condottieri*.

5 See Shaw, Ch. 5 for the Ottoman war machine.

6 Goodwin 56.

7 Busbeq 76.

8 *Ibid*. 137–138.

9 Coles 87.

10 There is no equivalent to Mallett for the other Mediterranean powers. Olesa's title promises more than it delivers, although galley construction details and costs are useful.

11 For the Spanish empire Elliott (1) and (2) still stand out. Koenigsberger details the failure to create adequate imperial institutions. See also Pierson and Kamen.

12 Davis 42–56.

13 See Parker (1) and (2).

14 Hanlon 59.

15 Koenigsberger 48.

16 Davis 75.

17 *Leviathan* IV, Ch. 47.

CHAPTER FOUR **The Plot**

1 Hale (3) 251–252, argues that Jan Cornelisz Vermeyen, who accompanied Charles to Tunis and drew the preliminary sketches for these tapestries, was the first true war artist.

2 Cook 3.

3 See Draz and Haleem.

4 Gibbon, Edward, *The Decline and Fall of the Roman Empire*, Ch. L.

5 Hanson 269 – alas, for I consider his *The Western Way of War* to be one of the two or three best books ever written on the subject of why and how men make war.

6 Setton III, 364–365. His title is misleadingly modest. Facts and quotations concerning the Papacy are drawn from this source unless otherwise attributed.

7 One might speculate on the apparent continuity between this and the manner in which the rest of the western world is regularly called upon to rescue Italian cultural treasures.

8 Braudel (1) II, 830.

9 Housley (1) XVIII, 263.

10 Warner might have got there, had she not

been intent on another agenda. The next big step in the adaptation of classical goddess worship came in 1854, when the Blessed Pius IX (1846–78), another beleaguered pope, resolved the knotty problem of how the Mother of God could have carried the Christ child in a womb tainted by original sin by pronouncing the doctrine of the Immaculate Conception (not to be confused with the Virgin Birth).

11 See Kelsay.

12 Although Frazer (1) is an awesome totem in its own right, happily for contemporary attention spans Frazer (2) has recently been reprinted.

13 See Riley-Smith (2), from which the immediately following ideas and quotations.

14 Elliott (2) 90–91.

15 See March and Serrano.

16 Housley (1) I. 20.

CHAPTER FIVE Billboard

1 See Coutauld and Shearman. Hale (3) and Paret answer many questions, but not the ones that concern me.

2 See Newton.

3 See Gombrich and Fenlon.

4 See Checa.

5 Zapperi is excellent on the Farnese connection, and a reminder that the word 'nepotism' comes from the Italian for the nephew-ism/grandson-ism of the Popes.

6 Hall (2) for the links among architecture, art and power in the work done by Vasari for Cosimo dei Medici. See also Wittkover.

7 Michelangelo's preparatory sketches are at the Ashmolean and Leonardo's plan was copied by Rubens, in a sketch now at the Louvre.

8 The sources and didactic purpose of the decorations are meticulously detailed in Carande, from which also **Diagram 3**.

9 See Paulson, from which this and the Nostradamus citations. My translations.

10 Note the play on 'lantern' as both a source of light and a symbol of naval rank.

11 Murrin also identifies many interesting themes that are not germane to mine.

12 A reference to Velázquez's famous portrait *Las Meninas*.

13 Note the suggestion that Philip poisoned his half-brother.

PART II MILITARY BATTLE

CHAPTER SIX Scene Setters

1 For Zonchio and Preveza see Guilmartin (2).

2 Appositely, the Spanish ¡Ay! ¡Ay! translates as 'Ow! Ow!', or 'Woe is me!'

3 Hugo de Moncada was killed in 1528 in the battle of Capo d'Orso (see Chapter Nine) during the Franco-Genoese siege of Spanish Naples. Directing the siege works was Pedro Navarro, who had taken service with the French after King Ferdinand refused to ransom him following defeat and capture at Ravenna in 1512. Later in 1528 Andrea Doria took Genoa out of the French alliance and became the Hapsburgs' captain general of the sea, while cholera devastated the besieging French army. Navarro was captured and hanged.

4 The Genoese may have drawn false reassurance from the fact that in 1558 they had successfully bribed Piali not to assist the French in an assault on Corsica.

5 For Djerba see Fernández Duro (1). For Cosimo's services to the Papacy and a fuller explanation of the Santo Stefano subterfuge see Hanlon.

6 Busbeq 217.

7 Anderson (2) and Manfroni for the basic narrative, aiming off for the chauvinism of most historical works written in Italian from the latter nineteenth to mid twentieth centuries.

8 This and following narrative from Bradford.

9 Setton III, 400.

10 Davis 22.

11 Braudel (1) II, 1029.

12 Housley (2) 319.

13 Setton IV, 898–903

14 Allen 22–28. For the wider perspective see Kortepeter.

15 Hess (2) 14.

16 D. I. The letter of appointment is six pages long (304–309), the letter of instructions twenty-seven (311–337).

17 The translations of the quotations illustrating the relationship between Philip and Juan, although not the interpretation, are from Petrie.

18 Tenenti (2) details how they expanded to fill the great power vacuum in the Mediterranean after Lepanto. As well as Fisher, Bono and Earle provide a useful balance.

19 Bracewell 303.

CHAPTER SEVEN

Prologue –The 1570 Campaign

1 See Roth.

2 The narrative in this chapter is drawn from Hill as revised in Setton IV.

3 Inalcik (2) 192.

4 Hill 888.

5 See Parker (3).

6 Bilateral relations between Madrid and Rome are thoroughly covered in Serrano (1). Half of the first volume of his follow-up (2), all of its documentation, and the whole of the second volume deal with the prolonged anticlimax following the battle.

7 Cited by most sources but dismissed as fiction by Hill.

8 Setton IV, 990. The phrase is *'inespertissimi da guerra e di mare'*.

9 Paruta is the single most influential source for all accounts of the Cyprus war.

10 Setton IV, 973.

11 See Vargas-Hidalgo.

12 Guglielmotti (1) incorporated into the sixth volume of Guglielmotti (2).

13 Vargas-Hidalgo 111–112.

14 *Ibid.* 132–136.

15 *Ibid.* 141.

16 See Tucci.

17 See Chelebi.

CHAPTER EIGHT

Act I –The Ottoman Offensive of 1571

1 See Inalcik (3).

2 Count Nestor Martinengo, a survivor of the final massacre, was in command of the section from the Andruzzi tower and the cavalier built in the cemetery (Campo Santo) behind it, to the Santa Napa tower. His brief account was first published in Ventura.

3 Wilkinson, 301 *et seq.*

4 See Carinci.

5 Vargas-Hidalgo 126–127.

6 This and following quotations are from Rycaut.

7 The Ottoman documentation for this campaign is cross-checked by Inalcik (2) and Lesure, from which all comments and quotations illustrating the Ottoman point of view.

8 From the English summaries in Novak.

9 D.I. 203–215.

10 D.I. 192.

CHAPTER NINE

Act II –The Holy League Response

1 D.I. is the default source for all quotations not otherwise attributed.

2 See March, and for the Requeséns/Zúñiga genealogy see Clopas.

3 Fernández Duro (2) 112–113. Doria was sailing in the opposite direction, away from the storm.

4 Vargas-Hidalgo 251–254.

5 March 19–20.

6 D.I. 273–283.

7 The Venetian galleys were set up to fire low as a matter of routine, and it is most improbable that veteran Sicilian and Neapolitan galleys would have had spurs that got in the way. Possibly their amputation was something that needed to be done only by those few ponentina lantern galleys built, like *La Real*, to perform representational/ceremonial functions.

8 Vargas-Hidalgo 265.

9 Note that Juan did not style Cosimo 'Grand Duke of Tuscany', the title with which he had been formally invested by Pius V, which neither branch of the Hapsburg dynasty recognized until Cosimo's successor, humbly employing the style of Duke of Florence, formally petitioned the emperor for elevation to the higher rank.

10 Guglielmotti (2) 306.

11 Hall (1) 214.

12 Manfroni 277–278.

13 See Arenaprimo for a proud overstatement of the Sicilian contribution.

14 Other Greek sopracomiti were Giorgio Calergi with two Canea galleys, the Zante galleys of Marino Sigouros and Nicola Mondinos, the Candia galley of Antonio Eudomeniani, and the Corfu galley of Cristoforo Condocolli. Manoussacas gives several more names, but they do not cross-check with Contarini or D.I.

15 Fernández Duro (2) 149–150; Setton IV, 1051.

CHAPTER TEN Act III –The Battle

1 Holmes 155.

2 Quarti (1) 54.

3 Crillon acquired the sobriquet by which history remembers him when King Henri IV sent him the following jovial message in 1598: 'Hang yourself, brave Crillon! We fought at Arques and you were not there. Farewell. I love you regardless.'

4 Garnier 206–207.

5 Guillén 18.

6 Rufo enlisted with the Duke of Sessa but was on another, unspecified Spanish galley near the centre, not with him on *La Real*.

7 *Don Quixote*, Part I, Ch. 38.

8 Martínez-Hidalgo 105–107.

9 Paruta 142.

10 Herrera 152.

11 March 52–53.

12 March 48–54 and 54–59 for the Requeséns letters; D.I. 239 and 259 for Soto's report.

13 D.I. 36.

14 Guillén 18–19.

15 See Goldsworthy for numbers killed at Cannae; no figure is available for surviving wounded.

CHAPTER ELEVEN Epilogue

1 Setton IV, 1065.

2 Her daughter was to marry Federico, grandson of Marc'Antonio Colonna.

3 Cited in Borino.

4 Lesure, Inalcik (3) and Mantran concur in their analysis of the Ottoman documents, which, alas, do not include dispatches from the field but only the replies from the Porte.

5 Setton IV, 1075.

6 Lewis 177.

7 Törne 124, 154.

8 See Borino – it was an excruciating experience for Colonna, torn between his loyalty to the Pope and his obligations to Philip. Whatever passed between him and Madrid was by word of mouth but evidently he handled the episode well, for his career did not suffer.

9 Setton IV, 1085.

10 Fernández Duro (2) 184.

11 Törne 63.

12 Petrie 192.

13 Garnier Annexe II.

BIBLIOGRAPHY

Adamson, John (ed.), *The Princely Courts of Europe 1500–1750* (London 2000).

Allen, W.E.D., *Problems of Turkish Power in the Sixteenth Century* (London 1963).

(1) Anderson, R.C., *Oared Fighting Ships* (London 1976).

(2) Anderson, R.C., *Naval Wars in the Levant* (Liverpool 1952).

Aparici y García, Col. José, *Colección de documentos inéditos relativo a la célebre batalla de Lepanto* (Madrid 1847).

Arenaprimo di Montechiaro, Giuseppe, *La Sicilia nella battaglia di Lepanto* (Pisa 1886).

Arnold, Thomas, *The Renaissance at War* (London 2001).

Aymard, Maurice, 'Chiourmes et galères dans la seconde moitié du XVIe siècle', in Benzoni.

Balistreri, Gianni, *Sebastiano Veniero* (Rome 1971).

Benzoni, Gino (ed.), *Il Mediterraneo nella seconda metà del '500 . . .* (Florence 1974).

Berenson, Bernhard, *Venetian Painters of the Renaissance* (New York 1984).

Bono, Salvatore, *I corsari barbareschi* (Turin 1964).

Bordoy Cerda, Miguel, *Mallorca, Lepanto y Cervantes* (Palma 1971).

Borino, G.B., et al., 'Il trionfo di Marc'Antonio Colonna', *Miscellanea della Società Romana di Storia Patria*, 1938 (XVI).

Bracewell, Catherine, *The Uskoks of Senj* (Cornell 1992).

Bradbury, Jim, *The Medieval Archer* (Woodbridge 1985).

Bradford, Ernle, *The Great Siege: Malta 1565* (London 1961).

(1) Braudel, Fernand, *The Mediterranean and the Mediterranean World in the Age of Philip II*, Vols I and II (London 1973).

(2) Braudel, Fernand, 'Bilan d'une Bataille', in Benzoni.

Busbeq, A.G., *Travels into Turkey* (first translation into English, London 1744).

Caracciolo, Ferrante, *Commentari alle guerre fatti coi Turchi da don Giovanni d'Austria dopo che venne in Italia* (Florence 1581).

Carande Herrero, Rocío, *Mar-Lara y Lepanto* (Seville 1990).

Carinci, G.B., *Lettere di Onorato Caetani* (Rome 1870).

Carrero Blanco, Luis, *La Victoria del Cristo de Lepanto* (Madrid 1948).

Cerezo Martínez, Ricardo, *Años cruciales en la historia del Mediterráneo 1570–1574* (Madrid 1971).

Chambers, David, *War, Culture and Society in Renaissance Venice* (London 1993).

Checa Cremades, Fernando, *Tiziano y la monarquía hispánica* (Madrid 1994).

Chelebi, Katib (trans. J. Mitchell), *History of the Maritime Wars of the Turks* (London 1831).

Cipolla, Carlo, *Guns and Sails in the Early Phase of European Expansion* (London 1965).

Clopas Battle, Isidro, *Luis de Requeséns, el gran olvidado de Lepanto* (Barcelona 1971).

Coles, P., *The Ottoman Impact on Europe* (London 1968).

Colliado, L., *Plática manual de artillería* (Milan 1592).

Conforti, Luigi, *I Napoletani a Lepanto* (Naples 1886).

Coniglio, Giuseppe, *Il viceregno di Napoli e la lotta tra spagnoli e turchi nel Mediterraneo*, Vol. II (Naples 1987).

Contarini, Gianbattista, *Historia delle cose successe dal principio della guerra . . .* (Venice 1572).

Cook, M.A. (ed.), *A History of the Ottoman Empire to 1730* (Cambridge 1976).

Costiol, Hierónimo de, *Primera parte de la crónica del muy alto y poderoso príncipe Don Juan . . .* (Barcelona 1572).

Coutauld, Jeanne (ed.), *Studies in Renaissance and Baroque Art* (London 1967).

Cunningham, Andrew and Grell, Ole Peter, *The Four Horsemen of the Apocalypse* (Cambridge 2000).

Davis, James (ed. and trans.), *Pursuit of Power: Venetian Ambassadors' Reports on Spain, Turkey and France in the Age of Philip II 1560–1600* (New York 1970).

Dennistoun, James, *Memoirs of the Dukes of Urbino*, Vol. III (London 1909).

Diedo, Gerolamo, *La battaglia di Lepanto* (Venice 1572/Milan 1863).

D.I.: see Fernández Navarrete.

Draz, M.A., *Introduction to the Qur'an* (London 2000).

Duffy, Christopher, *Fire and Stone* (London 1975).

Earle, Peter, *The Corsairs of Malta and Barbary* (London 1970).

(1) Elliott, J.H., *Imperial Spain 1469–1716* (London 1963).

(2) Elliott, J.H., *Europe Divided* (London 1968).

Fenlon, Iain, 'Lepanto and the Arts of Celebration', *History Today*, September 1995.

(1) Fernández Duro, Cesáreo, 'El Desastre de Los Gelves' in *Estudios históricos del reinado de Felipe II* (Madrid 1890).

(2) Fernández Duro, Cesáreo, *Armada Española desde la unión de los reinos de Castilla y Aragón*, Vol. II (Madrid 1896).

Fernández Navarrete, Martín et al., *Colección de documentos inéditos para la historia de España*, Vol. III (Madrid 1843).

Finlay, George, *The History of Greece under Othoman and Venetian domination* (Edinburgh 1856), Vol. VII of his *History of Greece*.

Fisher, Sir Godfrey, *Barbary Legend* (Oxford 1957).

Fossati, Claudio, *La Riviera e la battaglia di Lepanto* (Salò 1890).

(1) Frazer, Sir James, *The Golden Bough*, 15 vols. (Cambridge 1907–15).

(2) Frazer, Sir James (ed. Robert Fraser), *The Golden Bough* (Oxford 1994).

Furttenbach, Joseph, *Architectura Navalis* (Ulm 1629).

Gárate Córdoba, José María, *Los Tercios de España en la ocasión de Lepanto* (Madrid 1971).

Gardiner, Robert (ed.), *The Age of the Galley* (London 1995).

Garnier, François, *Le journal de la bataille de Lépante* (Paris 1956).

Goldsworthy, Adrian, *Cannae* (London 2001).

Gombrich, E.H., 'Celebrations in Venice of the Holy League and the Victory of Lepanto', in Coutauld.

Goodwin, Jason, *Lords of the Horizons* (London 1999).

(1) Guglielmotti, Alberto, *Marcantonio Colonna alla battaglia di Lepanto* (Florence 1862).

(2) Guglielmotti, Alberto, *Storia della Marina Pontificia*, Vol. VI (Rome 1887).

Guillén Tato, Julio, *Hallazgo de la crónica inédita de un soldado en la batalla de Lepanto* (Madrid 1971).

(1) Guilmartin, John F. Jr, *Gunpowder and Galleys* (Cambridge 1974).

(2) Guilmartin, John F. Jr, *Galleons and Galleys* (London 2002).

(1) Hale, J.R., 'The fighting potential of sixteenth century Venetian galleys' in Hale (2).

(2) Hale, J.R. (ed.), *Renaissance War Studies* (London 1983).

(3) Hale, J.R., *Artists and Warfare in the Renaissance* (New Haven 1990).

(4) Hale, J.R., *Renaissance Venice* (London 1973).

(5) Hale, J.R., 'From peacetime establishment to fighting machine: the Venetian army and the war of Cyprus and Lepanto', in Benzoni.

Haleem, Muhammad Abdel, *Understanding the Qu'ran* (London 2001).

(1) Hall, Bert S., *Weapons and Warfare in Renaissance Europe* (Baltimore 1997).

(2) Hall, Marcia, *Renovation and Counter-Reformation* (Oxford 1979).

Hanlon, Gregory, *The Twilight of a Military Tradition* (London 1998).

Hanson, Victor Davis, *Why the West Has Won* (London 2000).

Herrera, Fernando de, *Relacion de la guerra de Cipre y suceso de la batalla naval de Lepanto* (1572 / Mallorca 1971 including ode '*Por la Vitoria del Señor Don Juan*').

(1) Hess, Andrew C., *The Forgotten Frontier* (Chicago 1978).

(2) Hess, Andrew C., 'The Moriscos: An Ottoman Fifth Column in Sixteenth-Century Spain', *The American Historical Review*, LXXIV: 1, October 1968.

(3) Hess, Andrew C., 'The Battle of Lepanto and its place in Mediterranean History', *Past and Present* 57 (November 1972).

Hill, Sir George, *History of Cyprus*, Vol. III (Cambridge 1948).

Holmes, Richard, *Firing Line* (London 1985).

Hourani, Albert, *A History of the Arab Peoples* (Harvard 1991).

(1) Housley, Norman, *Crusading and Warfare in Medieval and Renaissance Europe* (Aldershot 2001).

(2) Housley, Norman, *The Later Crusades 1274–1571* (Oxford 1992).

(1) Inalcik, Halil, *The Ottoman Empire: the Classical Age 1300–1600* (London 1973).

(2) Inalcik, Halil, *The Ottoman Empire: Conquest, Organization and Economy* (London 1978).

(3) Inalcik, Halil, 'Lepanto in the Ottoman Documents', in Benzoni.

Irwin, Robert, 'Islam and the Crusades 1096–1699' in Riley-Smith (1).

Jurien de la Gravière, Vice Admiral J.B., *La guerre de Chypre et la bataille de Lépante*, Vol. II, (Paris 1888).

Kamen, Henry, *Philip of Spain* (London 1997).

Kelsay, J. and Johnson, J.T. (eds.), *Just War and Jihad* (New York 1991).

Khalfa, Hadji: see Chelebi.

Kinross, Lord, *The Ottoman Centuries* (New York 1977).

Knolles, Richard, *The General Historie of the Turkes* (London 1603): see Rycaut.

Koenigsberger, Helmut, *The Government of Sicily under Philip II of Spain* (London 1951).

Kortepeter, C.M., *Ottoman Imperialism during the Reformation* (London 1972).

(1) Lane, F.C., *Venice: A Maritime Republic* (London 1973).

(2) Lane, F.C., 'Venetian Naval Architecture about 1530', *Mariner's Mirror*, January 1934.

(3) Lane, F.C., *Venetian Ships and Shipbuilders of the Renaissance* (Baltimore 1992).

Lesure, Michel, *Lépante: la crise de l'empire Ottoman* (Paris 1972).

Lewis, Bernard, *The Muslim Discovery of Europe* (Oxford 1993).

López de Toro, José, *Los Poetas de Lepanto* (Madrid 1950).

Lorenzo, Antonio Maria de, *La Calabrie e la battaglia di Lepanto* (Bologna 1881).

Mallett, M.E. and Hale, J.R., *The Military Organization of a Renaissance State* (Cambridge 1984).

Manfroni, Camillo, *Storia della Marina Italiana dalla caduta di Constantinopli alla battaglia di Lepanto* (Rome 1897).

Manoussacas, Manoussos, 'Lepanto e I Greci' in Benzoni.

Mantran, Robert, 'L'écho de la bataille de Lépante à Constantinople' in Benzoni.

March, José María, *La batalla de Lepanto y Don Luis de Requeséns* (Madrid 1944).

Martínez-Hidalgo, José María (ed.), *Catálogo de la Exposición Conmemorativa del IV Centenario de la batalla de Lepanto* (Barcelona 1971).

Ministerio de la Marina, *La batalla naval de don Juan de Austria* (Madrid 1971).

Molmenti, Pompeo, *Sebastiano Veniero e la battaglia di Lepanto* (Florence 1899).

Mulon, G.I., *I Sardi a Lepanto* (Cagliari 1887).

Murrin, Michael, *History and Warfare in Renaissance Epic* (Chicago 1994).

Museo Naval, *Conferencias sobre Lepanto*, 4 vols. (Madrid 1948).

NACE: New Advent Catholic Encyclopedia at www.newadvent.org

Newton, Eric, *Tintoretto* (London 1952).

Novak, G. (ed.), *Lepanstka bitka* (Zadar 1974).

Oakeshott, E., *European Arms and Armour* (London 1980).

Olesa Muñido, Francisco-Felipe, *La Organización Naval de los Estados Mediterráneos y en especial de España . . .*, Vol. I (Madrid 1968).

Paret, Peter, *Imagined Battles* (Chapel Hill 1997).

(1) Parker, Geoffrey, *The Army of Flanders and the Spanish Road* (Cambridge 1972).

(2) Parker, Geoffrey, *The Dutch Revolt* (London 1977).

(3) Parker, Geoffrey, 'Lepanto: the Costs of Victory', in Parker (4).

(4) Parker, Geoffrey, *Spain and the Netherlands* (London 1979).

Paruta, Paulo (trans. Duke George of Monmouth), *The History of Venice* (London 1658).

Paulson, M. and Alvarez-Detrell, T., *Lepanto: Fact, Fiction and Fantasy* (University Press of America 1986).

Payne-Gallwey, Ralph, *The Book of the Crossbow* (London 1995).

Petrie, Sir Charles, *Don John of Austria* (London 1967).

Pierson, Peter, *Philip II of Spain* (London 1975).

Pomponi, F., *La participation des Corses à la bataille de Lépante* (Bastia 1972).

Pryor, John, *Geography, Technology and War* (Cambridge 1988).

(1) Quarti, Guido, *La battaglia di Lepanto nei canti popolari dell'epoca* (Milan 1930).

(2) Quarti, Guido, *La guerra contro il Turco in Cipro e a Lepanto* (Venice 1935).

(1) Riley-Smith, Jonathan (ed.), *The Oxford Illustrated History of the Crusades* (Oxford 1995).

(2) Riley-Smith, Jonathan, 'The State of Mind of the Crusaders' in Riley-Smith (1).

Rogers, Clifford (ed.), *The Military Revolution Debate* (Boulder 1995).

Rosell, Cayetano, *Historia del combate naval de Lepanto* (Madrid 1853/1971).

Roth, Cecil, *The House of Nasi: The Duke of Naxos* (Philadelphia 1948).

Rycaut, Sir Paul, *The Turkish History* (London 1687).

Scetti, Aurelio, *Memoirs*: see Garnier.

Schwoebel, Robert, *The Shadow of the Crescent* (Nieuwkoop 1967).

Sereno, Bartolomeo, *Commentari della guerra di Cipro e della lega . . .* (Cassino 1845).

(1) Serrano, Luciano, *Correspondencia diplomática entre España y la Santa Sede durante el pontificado de San Pío V*, Vols. I–IV (Madrid 1914).

(2) Serrano, Luciano, *La Liga de Lepanto*, Vol. I (Madrid 1918–20).

(3) Serrano, Luciano, *España en Lepanto* (Barcelona 1935).

Serviá, Miguel, *Relación del suceso de la Armada de la Liga . . .* (1572/Mallorca 1971).

Setton, Kenneth M., *The Papacy and the Levant 1204–1571*, Vols. III and IV (Philadelphia 1984).

Shaw, Stanford, *History of the Ottoman Empire and Modern Turkey*, Vol. I (Cambridge 1976).

Shearman, John, *Mannerism* (London 1967).

Sola, Victor María de, *Lepanto y Don Juan de Austria* (Cádiz n.d.).

Stirling-Maxwell, Sir William, *Don John of Austria*, Vols. I and II (London 1883).

(1) Tenenti, Alberto, *Cristoforo Da Canal: La Marine Vénitienne avant Lépante* (Paris 1962).

(2) Tenenti, Alberto (trans. J. and B. Pullan), *Piracy and the Decline of Venice* (Berkeley 1967).

Throckmorton, P., Edgerton, H. and Yalouris, E., 'The Battle of Lepanto Search and Survey Mission 1971–72', *The International Journal of Nautical Archaeology and Underwater Exploration*, II.1 (March 1973).

Törne, P.O. de, *Don Juan d'Autriche et les projets de conquête de l'Angleterre*, Vol. I (Helsingfors 1915).

Tucci, Ugo, 'Il processo a Girolamo Zane, mancato difensore di Cipro', in Benzoni.

Vale, M.A., *War and Chivalry* (London 1981).

Vargas-Hidalgo, Rafael, *La batalla de Lepanto según cartas inéditas de Felipe II, Don Juan de Austria y Juan Andrea Doria . . .* (Santiago 1998).

Ventura, Sebastiano, *Raccolta Di Varii Poemi Latini, Greci, e Volgari* (Venice 1572).

Warner, Marina, *Alone of All Her Sex* (London 1976).

Wilkinson, J. Gardner, *Dalmatia and Montenegro*, Vol. II (New York 1971).

Wittkover, R. and Jaffe, I. (eds.), *Baroque Art: the Jesuit Contribution* (New York 1972).

Zapperi, Roberto, *Tiziano, Paolo III e I suoi nipoti* (Turin 1990).

Zinsser, Hans, *Rats, Lice and History* (Boston 1935/London 1985).

INDEX